D0443875

Publications by the Ripon Society

The Ripon Society publishes a bimonthly magazine and newsletter, *The Ripon Forum,* and numerous research papers and policy statements from time to time.

The society's national headquarters is located at 509 C Street, N.E., Washington, D.C. 20002, and has chapters in the following locations: Boston-Cambridge, Chicago, Detroit, Hartford, Los Angeles, Memphis, Minneapolis, Nashville, New Haven, New Jersey, New York, Philadelphia, Pittsburgh, Seattle, and Washington, D.C.

JAWS OF VICTORY

JAWS
OF VICTORY

The Game-Plan Politics of 1972,
the Crisis of the Republican
Party, and the Future of the
Constitution

The Ripon Society and
Clifford W. Brown, Jr.

LITTLE, BROWN AND COMPANY——BOSTON—TORONTO

FIRST EDITION

T 06/74

Portions of this book first appeared in *Harper's Magazine* and *The Ripon Forum*.

Library of Congress Cataloging in Publication Data

Ripon Society.
    Jaws of victory; the election of 1972, the future
of the Republican Party, and the crisis of the Constitution.

    Bibliography: p.
    1. Republican Party. 2. Presidents--United States
--Election--1972. 3. Watergate Affair, 1972-
I. Brown, Clifford Waters, 1942-   II. Title.
JK2357 1974.R56   329.6'023   74-6203
ISBN 0-316-11201-1

Published simultaneously in Canada by Little, Brown & Company (Canada) Limited

PRINTED IN THE UNITED STATES OF AMERICA

*This book is dedicated
to the memory
of my Aunt Amey.*

If you once forfeit the confidence of your fellow citizens, you can never regain their respect and esteem. It is true that you may fool all the people some of the time; you can even fool some of the people all the time; but you can't fool all of the people all the time.

— ABRAHAM LINCOLN

Contents

APPENDICES

Foreword

The Ripon Society has published an analysis of each presidential election since it was founded in 1962. In our first two books, *From Disaster to Distinction* (1964) and *The Lessons of Victory* (1968), we focused largely upon the election results and tried to interpret what the statistics implied for the future of both the Republican party and the country as a whole. We looked at the trends revealed by each election and drew conclusions about how the party could recover from the Goldwater debacle in the first case and how it could expand its paper thin mandate in the second.

After the election of 1972, however, we felt that a new approach was necessary. To be sure, we did not ignore the statistics: we gathered and processed more voting statistics, survey research data, and financial disclosure material than ever before — including a computer analysis of 40,000 disclosed contributions of $100 or more made to presidential candidates between the April 7 filing deadline and the November election (see Appendix I). But we felt that the 1972 election demanded an analysis far beyond any that an interpretation of its statistics could provide. It was, after all, an unusual year. There was the McGovern phenomenon. There was the Eagleton affair. There was the historic landslide that became irrelevant in a few months. There was unprecedented ticket-splitting. And there was Watergate in all its dimensions. These "unusual" events, however, became less and less surprising to us the closer we looked at them. Somehow they all began to fit into a larger pattern of political action and response. We therefore felt that the best contribution we could make to the potentially vast literature on the 1972 election would be an analysis of the new patterns of political behavior that are now emerging. People are simply *thinking* about politics today a lot differently than they were a decade ago, and as our thoughts and perceptions change, so do our practices.

But the purpose of this book is not simply to set forth a thesis on the election; it is to stimulate a debate. We think that we may have found some of the principal causes of our current discontents — and the solutions for some of our problems. We hope that we have put our diagnoses and prescriptions in such a way that those who disagree with us will feel the need to present alternatives. In any case, we are certain that in the openness of free and spirited controversy a lot of light will be shed upon the subject — and the subject needs a lot of light these days.

The Ripon Society is a group of progressive Republicans — mainly businessmen, professionals, and academicians — who are dedicated to the principle of making the Republican party a more enlightened institution. The society, founded in the early 1960s, is named after Ripon, Wisconsin, the birthplace of the Republican party. Although it has no official connection to the party, all its members are Republicans. Its activities include research, writing, and political involvement. It is not a mass organization, since its members are all expected to make contributions of time and effort, but it does claim to be influential. Many of its members have been elected to public office and many others have been appointed to high government positions. A number of Nixon administration policy proposals were first seen in a Republican context on the pages of the *Ripon Forum,* the society's bimonthly magazine and newsletter. These include revenue sharing, welfare reform, government reorganization, the volunteer army, expansion of East-West trade, the abolition of farm supports, and a new China policy.

The society has also been responsible for a suit against the Republican National Committee that attempts to achieve a more equitable distribution of delegates to the 1976 presidential nominating convention. Above all, the society considers its greatest contribution to the Republican party to be the stimulation of controversy and excitement in a party that might otherwise appear stodgy and dull. It is in this spirit that we offer our 1972 election analysis.

RON K. SPEED
PRESIDENT OF THE RIPON SOCIETY

Minneapolis, Minnesota
October 1973

Preface

This book represents an enormous amount of work by a large number of people. It is the product of a massive study of the 1972 election, its results, and its aftermath conducted by the Ripon Society and lasting for more than a solid year. Dozens of people made direct contributions; dozens more obtained and processed the information on which our conclusions are based. Scores of people were interviewed. Questionnaires were sent out. Newspapers from every state in the Union were read and diligently clipped. A huge file of polling data from both nationwide and local survey research firms was compiled. A vast number of maps, charts, and graphs were designed to interpret the data. Official and unofficial election returns were obtained and processed into cognizable forms. Task forces were set up to collect information on a number of areas. We even had our own almost full-time Watergate investigator. One of the largest projects we undertook was to obtain the *complete* financial disclosure reports from the General Accounting Office and to punch selected information from them onto 40,000 computer cards. This information was used to analyze the patterns of contributions made between April and November of 1972. We assembled an incredible amount of information — enough to fill several books this size. We could not begin to use it all here, but some of it will see the light of day elsewhere.

The writing of this book took place during the unfolding drama of Watergate. We all kept wondering (along with everyone else) just what was going to happen next. Fortunately for us — and unfortunately for this country — the avalanche of surprises tended to confirm our major thesis: that the 1972 election marked an undesirable turning point in the direction of an excessive use of strategic thinking and war-gaming techniques in American politics, and that the electorate was understandably reacting very negatively to this phenomenon. As we go to press in the fall of 1973 with more revelations expected, we are understandably anxious about the future. We are certain, however, that the major conclusions of this book will withstand the surprises of the coming months.

There are so many people who should be thanked that it is difficult to know where to begin. I have arranged them by categories: first, those who made special efforts beyond the writing of chapters or parts of chapters; second, authors of chapters and parts of chapters; third, general consultants; fourth, those involved with the computer project; fifth, those involved with gathering election data; sixth, those who wrote state reports; seventh, our manuscript readers; and eighth, those involved with production and mechanics.

Special Thanks

First of all, I would like to acknowledge the large amount of help I received from Josiah Lee Auspitz, past president of Ripon and doctoral candidate at Harvard University. In addition to co-authoring the first chapter with me, he has been helpful in dozens of ways, always ready with an excellent suggestion or an expressive phrase that captures the essence of an argument. He has helped me with many conceptual problems and has been a constant source of intellectual inspiration.

I would also like to thank Howard Gillette, another past president of Ripon. Throughout the entire enterprise he constantly made helpful suggestions about the scope and direction of the book, he recruited people to work on projects, he wrote Chapter 2, and he read the entire first draft of the manuscript, making many useful suggestions.

I would like to thank Rick Creighton, a graduate student at the State University of New York at Albany, who wrote the programs for the computer analysis of the GAO financial disclosure project. He spent countless hours dealing with countless problems on this enormous project. He is a tireless worker and the success of the project was in large measure the result of his tenacity and skill.

I would also like to thank Marc Aaronson, a young genius who was in charge of putting the financial disclosure data on tape so that it could be processed, and Jack Eiferman, a tireless and intelligent worker who supervised the computer analysis of the occupations of campaign contributors.

Richard and Robert Behn deserve many thanks for their respective contributions, advice, hard work, and irreverent criticisms. Dick read the entire manuscript through *twice* (an unusual punishment), and Bob contributed extensively to the next to last chapter.

Tanya Melich deserves special thanks for her long and detailed comments on every chapter in the book, and especially for her suggestions on Chapter 14.

Thanks go to Al deAprix, my research assistant at SUNY Albany, who assembled all our polling information, who read and commented on many parts of the manuscript, and who did numerous odd jobs on the project.

I would also like to thank Mike Natchures, Mike Lieberman, and Rich Aiken, three students at SUNY Albany, who spent many long hours of their spare time working on election statistics and gathering data for the project. Also, I wish to thank Frank Ouellette of Albany, New York, for many arduous hours spent making charts and graphs and doing numerous other tasks. Thanks go to Ted Earl for doing many helpful things and assisting in critical situations.

Thanks go to my colleague Jonathan Knight, who worked extensively on the financial disclosure data and who read and commented on large portions of the manuscript.

I should also like to thank Albert Hyde of SUNY Albany for making most of the charts and graphs that appear in the book, and his wife who typed part of the manuscript.

Special thanks go to my father, Clifford W. Brown, for doing an incredible job in preparing the newspaper material on which so much of the analysis is based, and for doing an enormous amount of the cartographic work that was so useful in analyzing election results.

Special thanks also go to the Graduate School of Public Affairs at the State University of New York at Albany for its support on several projects whose results appear in this book. We trust these efforts will make a contribution to research and scholarship and will provide data for serious students of politics of all political persuasions.

Special thanks also go to Assistant Dean Sandro Barone of the Graduate School of Public Affairs, State University of New York at Albany. He was most helpful in many ways too numerous to mention.

Thanks also to George Gilder for getting me into this project to begin with and to Ralph Loomis for sustaining it during its early months.

Most of all, I would like to thank Rosa Ruckner and Sheila Silver, who provided me with tremendous help and assistance throughout this entire project. Rosa served as a research assistant, project manager, general supervisor, and friendly critic. Without her help and loyalty this book could never have been written. Sheila typed the entire manuscript and served as a general assistant throughout the spring of 1973. My debt to both is enormous.

Chapter Authors and Contributors

Chapter 1 was written jointly by Josiah Lee Auspitz and me.

Chapter 2 was written by Howard Gillette, assistant professor of American Studies at George Washington University.

Chapter 3 was written by "John Q. Publius," who was in a position to know, and therefore must remain anonymous.

Chapter 4 was written in three parts. The section on Hispanic voters was written by "Publius," the section on the Business and Industry Division of the Committee to Re-elect the President was written by the authors of Chapter 13, and the section on youth was written by George Van Riper and Mark Yavornitzki, two young men very active in the New York State Republican party.

Chapter 5 was researched by Gregg Rushford and written jointly by him and me. An enormous amount of credit must go to Mr. Rushford for performing a very difficult task well.

Chapters 6 and 7 were written jointly by Wesley Pippert of Washington, D.C., and myself. Wes Pippert is a former aide to Senator Percy and is now a reporter for UPI. He comes from South Dakota and has been covering George McGovern since his first campaign in 1956, longer than any other reporter. He was assigned to the campaign of 1972 by UPI. The statistical information that appears at the end of the chapter was verified by an extensive study done by Peter Natchez of Brandeis University. Mike Halliwell consulted on the chapter. The information on the Eagleton affair comes from highly placed sources in the McGovern campaign.

Chapter 8 was written by Steve Haft, program officer at the Fund for the City of New York. Consulting on this chapter was Jim Westman, a student at SUNY Albany.

Chapter 9 was written by Peter Natchez and myself. Special thanks go to all those who participated in the information-gathering projects that provided the state-by-state data for this chapter (they are listed below), and especially to David Ellbogen, who gathered the precinct material for Chicago and provided much of the analysis concerning its extensive ticket-splitting.

Chapter 10 is my complete responsibility.

Chapter 11 was written by me on the basis of material collected by Pam Curtis of Washington, D.C., Bill Oliver of Congressman Mosher's staff, and Daniel J. Swillinger, former political director of Ripon and currently assistant dean, School of Law, Ohio State University. Thanks also go to Tina Harrower for useful suggestions.

Chapter 12 was assembled on the basis of the GAO financial disclosure project acknowledged in detail below.

Chapter 13 was written by a task force of several members including Richard Dykeman, Martin Gold, and two very important anonymous members, all of Washington, D.C. Larry Finklestein, also of Washington, served as a consultant.

Chapter 14 was written jointly by Professor John Ellwood of the State University of New York at Fredonia, John Brotchel, a graduate student at Rutgers, and myself. Tanya Melich consulted extensively on the chapter.

Chapter 15 is my responsibility. Special thanks go to Elly Peterson for the description of the traditional Republican woman.

Chapters 16 and 17 were written by me in conjunction with Dr. Robert Behn of Duke University — a Ripon official of longstanding — and Lee Auspitz, who made many useful suggestions about parties and professionals.

The first appendix was assembled from the GAO material compiled by people acknowledged below.

Thanks also go to Dr. Landis Jones of the University of Kentucky at Louisville who wrote an excellent chapter on Spiro Agnew that we had to delete at the last minute. His thesis was so sound, his predictions so accurate, and his conclusions so dramatically vindicated that it was no longer necessary to make the point he made: that if Spiro Agnew got into trouble or suffered a reverse no one would come to his aid.

General Consultants

The following served as general consultants and gave us excellent ideas and friendly criticisms at many points along the way: Dr. Richard S. Alben, Dr. Al Balutis, Terry Barnett, Mark Bloomfield, Mike Brewer, Daron Butler, Howard Cohen, Betsy Deardourff, Al Felzenberg, David B. Goldberg, Pat Goldman, Walter Goldstein, Alice Heyman, Ralph Loomis, Robert Marcus, Howard Reiter, Frederick W. Schwartz, Jr., Roy Speckhard, Lee Stelzer, and Sol Zalcgendler. Gus Southworth spent many hours preparing material on the nominating process that will be published elsewhere. His advice and counsel were appreciated. Dr. Thomas Baylis made many useful suggestions about the title.

Computer Projects

Many thanks go to all those who participated in the analysis of the GAO financial disclosure material.

I want to thank the General Accounting Office for being most helpful in making the data available and letting us invade its premises for several weeks. Thanks go to Rick Baker, Debba Curtis, Ronnie Kohen, and Betty Podell, who diligently searched out the occupations of our random sample.

Thanks also go to all those who helped us process this data into usable form by graphing it and "Motting" it (see Appendix I). These included Richard Aiken, Carol Anderson, Patrick Corcione, Al deAprix, Ted Earl, Mike Natchures, Frank Ouellette, and Rosa Ruckner. Thanks also go to my cousin, Randall Steere, for making a number of preliminary graphs. Four final graphs were drawn by Al deAprix and the rest by Al Hyde of SUNY Albany.

Thanks go to those who punched the data on cards. These included Jeff Markman and Anita Russman.

I would also like to thank those who consulted on the general project. These include Robert Pfeiffer and John Watson of the Computer Center at SUNY Albany and Herbert Gerjuoy, Lynda Watts, and Lee Stelzer of the Graduate School of Public Affairs.

Jonathan Knight spent much time and effort on this project and many thanks go to him for his suggestions and assistance.

Most of all I would like to thank Rick Creighton, Marc Aaronson, and Jack Eiferman, whom we mentioned above. Their tireless work was truly appreciated.

Election Information

Many thanks go to all those who helped to gather information on election results and survey research data.

I would like to thank ABC, CBS, and NBC for making available a number of postelection surveys. I would like to thank John Becker of Becker Research, Irwin Harrison of Decision Research, and Patrick Caddell of Cambridge Research for making polling data available to us. I would also like to acknowledge the Sindlinger Company of Philadelphia for our use of information and graphs, and Yankelovitch Inc. for survey data used by Peter Natchez.

I would like to thank all those volunteers who helped me process data on the election. They include Al Champociero, Al deAprix, Mike Lieberman, Dick Loomis, Mike Natchures, Ted Salem, and Robert Weinberger.

State-by-State Information

A lot of material contributed to this project never saw the light of day or appears in greatly condensed form. Many people sent us excellent state analyses that had to be cut because the book became altogether too long. Nevertheless they, too, should be thanked. In addition to many other Ripon correspondents all over the country the following persons should be noted: Jonathan Brown, Donato D'Andrea, Murray Dickman, David Ellbogen, Bill Emerson, Al Felzenberg, Mike Halliwell, Jim Harrington, John Holcombe, Jim Manahan, John Ogden, Ronald Powelson, Field Reichart, and Rick Taft.

Manuscript Readers

I would like to thank the following people for spending much time poring over the many versions of the manuscript and rendering helpful advice and criticism: Lee Auspitz, Peter Baugher, Dick Behn, Herbert Gerjuoy, George Gilder, Howard Gillette, David Goldberg, Walter Goldstein, Berna Gorenstein, Jonathan Knight, Tanya Melich, Peter Natchez, Richard Rahn, Robert Stewart, and Peter Wallison. I would also like to thank William Phillips of Little, Brown and Company for his helpful comments on the manuscript and his great patience and perseverance, and Luise Erdmann, who did such a fine job copyediting a taxing manuscript.

Production and Mechanics

I want to give special thanks to the Graduate School of Public Affairs at the State University of New York at Albany for its help and assistance with the production and mechanics of this book. Ann Wright and Donna Parker were most helpful indeed, as were Ada Bradley, Edith Connelly, Helen Ecker, Betty Jones, Betty MacIntosh, and Diane Remmers. I want to thank them all for reading my handwriting and typing the manuscript.

I would like to thank other typists who helped at critical junctures in the course of this project: Barbara Hale, Mrs. Patricia Shea, and Mrs. Marge Weich. I also want to thank Howard Brumbaugh of SUNY Albany for carrying endless sacks of newspapers and mail to my second-floor office in Draper Hall.

I also want to thank Deborah Bowen, M. Victoria Golden, Sue Stafford, and the other members of the Ripon staff for helping with the production of this book in many, many ways. Their endless efforts are one of the major factors that keeps the whole society operating.

Finally, I want to thank my mother, Mrs. Clifford W. Brown, for typing several chapters. She has typed some part of almost everything I have written.

Other Praise

Our thanks must also be extended to E. Howard Hunt, G. Gordon Liddy, James McCord, and company. Their incompetence delayed the publication of this book and led to many editorial nightmares, but it also gave us the opportunity to find out more about what Richard Nixon was saying in his office than anyone ever found out about what Larry O'Brien was saying in his. Our thanks also go to the U.S. Postal Service for delivering letters to the *Manchester Union Leader* — and for losing one manuscript, 300 file cards, and several pieces of our mail. Finally, our sympathy must be extended to the Manhattan mugger who snatched the handbag of one of our members and made off with a large amount of our New York election material. It was done in the true spirit of politics circa 1972.

CLIFFORD W. BROWN, JR.
STATE UNIVERSITY OF NEW YORK

Albany, New York
October 1, 1973

I

THE CAMPAIGN OF 1972

1

Strategic Politics

For five years the Nixon White House strove continually to increase its power, yet by the end of five years it had succeeded only in destroying its power. What happened? Why did an administration that prided itself so much on the soundness of its political strategies and the cleverness of its game plans fail so miserably?

It is easy to conclude that the Nixon administration's problems came from its illegal activities, but to say that the President and those around him were scoundrels and thugs is to miss the point badly. After all, Mr. Nixon's White House associates in their personal lives were no less upright than their predecessors. They were good family men, religious, abstemious, understated, dedicated, hard-working, and very rarely tinged by the venality that has been associated with many similar men in past administrations. In fact, the President's closest confidants, Haldeman and Ehrlichman, seemed to lack even the conventional aspiration of men in their position to join the ranks of the capital's millionaire lawyers and lobbyists. Why, then, did these men behave as they did, and why did their actions serve only to destroy them?

The answer to their difficulties lies in the use they made of political strategy. To use their own phrases, they suffered from a game plan mentality that led them to believe that the essence of politics was outpointing antagonists and adversaries; they had such an undue fascination with strategy and tactics that they soon began to feel that government and politics were chiefly a matter of playing and winning games. And they took their signals from the President himself. As one of the GOP campaign strategists expressed it, "Very early on we tried to set up a positioning

3

statement for the President. The President likes football analogies, and relationships of field position and ball control were really the essential elements of what the campaign organization tried to do." But it was often unclear whether they thought they were playing on a football field or a battlefield. As they marched resolutely to their goal, they employed all the logic of military strategy: deterrence, contingency planning, escalation, diversionary tactics, counterintelligence, and sabotage. It seemed at times that the White House had decided to reverse Clausewitz's famous maxim: politics for these game players was the continuation of warfare by other means.

This war-gaming attitude may have seemed promising to the Nixon managers — to many it was the essence of modern practice — but overall it proved disastrous because it began to destroy the moral basis of their authority. The crises of 1973 were not simply the result of a few criminal actions or a number of misguided policies; instead, they were the result of a deep-seated attitude on the part of the administration, an attitude of manipulation that was seriously at odds with the whole concept of the rule of law on which the authority structure of our society is based. Although the reckoning was postponed, they began from the very beginning to load the dice against themselves.

Strategy and Authority

When the Nixon managers came to power in January 1969, they recognized that their position was strategically insecure. The President was a minority President, his power base was relatively small, his party had been divided deeply in the past along ideological lines, and the nation as a whole seemed to be splitting itself into competing factions that felt they could gain their objectives only at the expense of other groups. Such a situation was potentially dangerous and seemed to require a special emphasis on political strategy to cope with it.

The Nixon managers, therefore, began to formulate a number of plans to improve the President's power position. They launched an extensive program to bolster his image — and they tailored many White House practices to that end. They tried to take charge of the Republican party and to create powerful political instruments outside the party to further their chances of electoral success. They took full advantage of their position in the White House and began to deal severely with their presumed adversaries in the press, the Congress, the universities, and the foundations. And they placed the maintenance of the President's power position at the center of their calculations. Each of their strategies seemed quite logical, but as each began to increase the *power* of the President it simultaneously undercut his *authority*. In a society such as ours, governmental authority comes from two sources: the Constitution and the actions

4

of the government itself. To maintain their legitimate authority, public officials must perform tolerably well, maintain their credibility, show loyalty to their supporters, behave civilly toward the opposition, and lead the country with a firm sense of purpose and direction. When they do their authority and power will increase. But the Nixon managers proceeded to undercut, in turn, each of these props to their authority.

Words vs. Deeds

The traditional approach to creating a presidential power base is very straightforward. Devise a set of programs that will appeal to a large constituency and then carry them out. Put together a legislative program, fight for it, hopefully get it enacted, and then set up the means of administering it. If you are clever — and lucky — in a year or two you will have some concrete results to show for your efforts and a grateful constituency that will support you in the future. If you do enough of this for a long enough time you will presumably build a solid political coalition.

This approach seems very simple in theory, but there are clearly a number of problems with it. Often it is difficult to get legislation through a balky Congress. There are long time lags before results appear — and credit realized. Someone is likely to be affected adversely by almost any program, and that can be politically costly. Most of all, a policy-oriented approach to government requires long-range commitments in a fluid political situation, and such commitments can reduce political flexibility. You can get tied down to something that your opponent might exploit later. "Keep your options open" is the first rule of political strategy, but keeping your options open is the very antithesis of making the kind of commitments that lead to policy objectives.

Impressed with these difficulties, the Nixon managers began to look for an alternative method of building their power base (after a few frustrating months of attempts at policymaking). Public relations seemed to offer a short-cut to power. If the President could demonstrate a high degree of popularity, the argument ran, then his Gallup poll ratings would enable him to deal with his antagonists and to achieve his policy objectives. It seemed like good strategy to concentrate on image-building — and then to use the improved image to help implement the policies.

Therefore the administration began to focus more on symbolic issues than on policy objectives, on words more than deeds. The public relations experts began to replace the policymakers in the power positions of the White House. Promising administration programs, such as the Family Assistance Plan, the Philadelphia Plan, the New American Revolution, and many others were brought forth for their symbolic significance and then quietly shelved when their public relations value declined. The great

5

"controversies" of the administration, meanwhile, became public relations spectaculars fought over manageable pseudo-issues such as demonstrators, Lieutenant Calley, and busing. (The latter is itself a real issue, but the administration's use of it was largely symbolic because it never really intended to do anything concrete about the problem.)

The administration, then, sought to increase its power position by concentrating on image-building. The problem was that whenever the time came to *use* some of the power for a policy commitment, the argument usually prevailed that to do so would sacrifice support that might be used later. The one exception to this practice was in foreign policy, where the President showed a willingness to follow through on his words and run political risks at home, but in domestic affairs very few commitments were ever kept for long. This did not mean that there were no domestic objectives achieved: the enactment of revenue sharing and the volunteer army and the creation of the OMB and the EPA were all sound accomplishments, but the overall focus of the administration was increasingly in the direction of symbol. (We discuss this tragedy in Chapter 2.)

The strategy of concentrating on the President's image seemed to be sound — and it led to some initial successes. However, as the administration soon found out, a power base built on images, symbols, and personal popularity is fragile. It can be wide, but it will be thin. It can be easily created, but it is easily destroyed. If a reverse occurs, the whole edifice can collapse very quickly, as the events of 1973 showed. The problem is that a focus on image tends to soften, not harden, the loyalty of normally solid constituencies — and they are then less willing to sustain a politician when he gets into trouble. Image-orientation can also create contempt for the image-builders among the permanent bureaucracy, whose job, after all, is to respond to policy leadership. Thus the Nixon managers, in their successful attempt to increase the President's popularity, tended to soften his basic support and create some potentially powerful antagonists in the process.

Utility vs. Veracity

This focus on image and public relations encouraged another self-defeating strategy that was embraced with passionate zeal: formulating public statements on the basis of their utility, not their veracity. To the Nixon White House the sole purpose of public statements was to influence, not to inform.

When a statement is issued as part of a game plan, the truth of that statement becomes only strategically relevant — relevant, that is, if the assertion might be contested or the statement might sound implausible. The assertion that a statement is either "operative" or "inoperative" betrays a strategic mentality that regards statements as *instruments*. In the short run, his approach to politics provides many benefits, and it can be used

6

extensively as part of maintaining an image. With prudence such a stratagem can work for a long time. But if used extensively, not selectively, someone is bound to be caught and all the strategic advantages dissipate very rapidly. Credibility is one of the most important components of authority. It cannot be manufactured, it must be earned, and it can only be earned by telling the truth consistently.

Management vs. Politics

The Nixon managers also decided upon a third strategy to increase their power position. It seemed to make sense to put politics on a "sound managerial basis" and to re-create the Republican party along modern management lines. Having used the Office of Management and the Budget to introduce sound management techniques into governmental programs, they tried to imitate this success in party politics. This modernization would help them immeasurably, they reasoned, because they could create an effective political instrument, control it, and wield it to their advantage. During the first years of the administration they made a number of steps in this direction, but their major effort to rationalize politics was the Committee to Re-elect the President (affectionately called CREEP by its admirers and detractors alike). This massive and mighty political machine was the basis of their 1972 election triumph and they were justly proud of its achievements (discussed in Chapters 3 and 4). However, its extensive successes were purchased at a price.

CREEP was created apart from the Republican party. The Nixon strategists viewed the proficiency of the party professional with a great deal of contempt — and with some justification. They felt that the party was archaic in most regions of the country and that modern political problems demanded modern political institutions to cope with them. This was certainly sound analysis, but the creation of an organization apart from the party began to undercut the loyalty of the party to the President.

CREEP was an organization unto itself, its loyalties were to Nixon, not to the party. It was created to engineer a presidential, not party, victory, and its tactics were designed to increase the long-run power position of the President, not the growth or prosperity of the party. Its fund-raisers interfered with party fund-raisers. Some of its personnel were pirated from party responsibilities. It encouraged Democrats to vote for Nixon — but not for other Republicans. Its leaders even supported the reelection attempts of Democrats who were friendly to White House interests. After the election, it began to talk about retooling the Republican party into a New Majority party.

All of these practices were instrumental in achieving the massive victory of 1972 — and in augmenting the power of the White House. Yet it was a relatively cool Republican party that greeted victory in 1972 and it was a very cold party that greeted the events of 1973. Had the President run more as a Republican, had he showed more loyalty to the *party* during the election, had he employed more party officials, had he made his election a party, not personal, triumph, then the Republican party would have stuck by him with more loyalty and tenacity during the disasters of 1973. But he created a distance from the party that the party never expected from Richard Nixon — and that distance persisted. Watergate was a bitter pill for the party to accept because it was not responsible for it but still had to take the blame for it.

Deterrence vs. Accommodation

Depersonalizing politics provided the psychological climate for the administration to engage in another strategy: deterring its domestic opponents from attacking it. It seemed plausible that one of the easiest ways of maintaining a power position would be to reduce the power of opponents and potential opponents, to deter them from taking harmful action, and to keep them from becoming a danger. Therefore the Nixon managers set out to let everyone know who was boss. To achieve this objective they made extensive use of threats. Individual congressmen, members of the press, officials of the bureaucracy, and potential opponents in the public at large were blacklisted and badgered by the administration.

The problem was that the logical response to deterrence, in the absence of authority, is always defiance — sometimes immediate, sometimes postponed, but defiance nevertheless. Thus, the more the Nixon managers threatened, the more they created the incentive to retaliate. Those whom they attacked waited for the opportune moment to strike back, and that moment came. The whole policy of trying to threaten "enemies" simply created more resolute antagonists. Many threats were successful because those threatened respected the authority of the White House to make and carry out such threats. But the more the practice continued, the less authoritative the threats appeared, and the greater the willingness to make counterthreats.

Power vs. Purpose

When a person or a government exercises power for the sake of a legitimate purpose — and acquires power in pursuit of that purpose — then the quest for power has the consent and support of those who accept the purpose as legitimate. But when no clear purpose can be set forth, then the pursuit of power appears illegitimate and dangerous. During its first four years the overriding domestic purpose of the Nixon administration appeared to be the narrow pursuit of power: its focus on image-building, party control, and deterrence certainly indicated this strategy, and there were many episodes to confirm the assumptions of those who would not give them the benefit of the doubt: the attempt to purge dissenters from the party and the cabinet, the repeated attempts to quiet the press, the exploitation of crime and student unrest for short-term electoral advantage, the attempt to smear moderate Democrats and liberal Republicans as "radiclibs," the dropping of reform programs the moment their public relations value declined — all these painted the public picture of an administration bent on power rather than purpose.

Of course the Nixon inner circle steadfastly maintained that it did have purposes: the preservation of order, the strength of our national defense, the vigor of the economy, the efficiency of the government, and the cultural war against permissiveness and weakness. But it did very little to achieve these goals. Insecure in its power position, it decided to postpone a major commitment to most of these objectives until it could get an electoral victory in 1972. If Nixon could win — and win big, the argument ran — it would finally have the necessary momentum.

After the spectacular election victory, everybody watched the administration very closely. Would it exercise its mandate for the sake of its own power or would it finally get around to achieving its purposes? With a fatal hubris, it allowed itself to seek both at the same time.

Just after the election the Nixon managers put forth a series of legitimate goals: paring down excessive spending, reorganizing the government, phasing out Great Society failures, introducing much-needed management techniques and decentralized approaches to old bureaucratic programs. But the quiet climate of civility in which such innovations might be appreciated was shattered by the White House itself: with its gleeful and vindictive dismissals of Father Theodore Hesburgh, the chairman of the Civil Rights Commission; its conscious attempt to make the spinning-off of OEO programs into a humiliation for blacks, liberals, and lawyers; its renewed attack on the press — bolstered this time with new proposals for regulation and criminal prosecution; its plan to phase out the existing Republican organization and replace it with its own New Majority apparatus; the President's uncompromising rage toward Vietnam dissenters; and its many attacks both verbal and procedural on the prerogatives of Congress. As if to summarize the administration's contempt for the national legislature, Attorney General Richard Kleindienst told a congressional committee that if it didn't like what the President was doing, it could always impeach him.

With these actions, and with a four-year history of power seeking, the administration suddenly appeared to be a major threat to all these people. By the logic of deterrence theory, those who were threatened had to assume that these actions were part of a gigantic power play. Anticipating the worst, their only logical response seemed to be retaliation. And retaliate they did.

Thus the Nixon strategists proceeded in a way that systematically undermined the authority and power of the presidency. By concentrating on image-building, they generated contempt in the bureaucracy and skepticism in their constituencies. By focusing on the utility, not the veracity, of their pronouncements, they destroyed their credibility. By exploiting the loyalty of the party, while depersonalizing politics, they weakened an institution that might have supported them strongly and also reduced its incentive to do so. By employing deterrence policies extensively, they created enemies who rapidly ceased to respect their authority and who impatiently waited for the moment to strike back. By formulating objectives in terms of their own power position, they destroyed their sense of purpose and thereby undercut their legitimate rationale for being in office. They could not have done a more complete and self-destructive job.

And as if all these attacks on the informal basis of their authority were not enough, they turned to attack the formal source of their authority — the Constitution. They claimed privileges and prerogatives that they had no right to assert. They viewed the law itself as an object of strategic manipulation: instead of instinctively obeying it, they began to calculate the payoffs of disobeying it. They adopted a strategic, rather than constitutional, view of the other organs of government; they tried to bluff and blackmail Congress and to employ the great agencies of the executive branch for partisan political objectives. They broke the rules of the electoral process. They attempted to subvert the judicial process by destroying legal evidence, committing perjury, and dismissing prosecutors. Above all, they treated the Constitution as a football to be maneuvered, positioned, and manipulated as part of their game plans. All of these moves were made in pursuit of what they regarded as sound strategic objectives, but it is not surprising that all of these moves tended to undercut the moral basis of their power.

The Nixon strategists, who were not blind or stupid, began to sense this loss of authority, but they tried to rescue the situation by employing the *symbols* of authority. When they could find no other justification for their actions, they exploited the reputation of the office. They continually put the President's prestige on the line — and thereby squandered that prestige. They began to use small symbols of authority: staged spectaculars, flags in lapels, and White House pomp.

Such strategies might succeed in some societies, but not in the United States. Americans are intelligent, generally decent, practical, and strong. They don't like to be deceived and they don't like to be manipulated, especially by narrow game players in pursuit of sterile strategic objectives. The Nixon strategists forgot that in America authority comes from substance, not from symbol. It is earned. It comes from a sense of purpose and performance, from honesty, credibility, and genuineness. It comes from working within the constitutional structure of the Republic. It comes from democratic behavior in accord with democratic principles. It cannot be replaced by symbol, pomp, and manipulation. The necessity to exploit all the trappings of office was simply a confession of weakness.

These props were the devices of insecure individuals who feared for their authority. They would have been unnecessary for people who knew how to exercise power resolutely within the framework of the Constitution.

If the President of the United States wants to maintain and augment his power, then he must have — and communicate — a sense of purpose and commitment. He must inspire his subordinates and associates, not threaten and manipulate them. When he employs coercive tactics — as he must — he should do so in the context of easily understood constitutional goals. He must work toward serving his legitimate constituencies. Above all, he must behave as Americans expect their President to behave. When he does, his power will be vast, his prestige solid, and his mistakes forgiven. But should he revert to narrow game plans, he will bring down upon his position the full force and fury of all those who have an interest in the established order and the prevailing structure of authority.

The Nixon managers took on a large part of the authority structure of the society. (That they got so far is a tribute to the prestige of the office Richard Nixon was elected to.) Were these managers just bad strategists, or was something more subtle at work here? What larger perspectives led to their fascination with building images, preserving options, and increasing their power? What drove these men to behave in such a fashion? Why did their strategies, which seemed so sophisticated, realistic, and hardnosed, turn out to be so incredibly naïve? Strategic thinking is complex, and it is important to examine more closely this style of thought that is becoming so prevalent in our society.

Strategy, Tradition, and Morality

The Nixon staffers can certainly be excused for having an interest in games and strategies. Americans have always been fascinated by the logic of conflict, and in recent years they have become even more so. During the past two decades our leading defense intellectuals, corporate executives, economists, lawyers, and the large majority of our professionals became captivated by the new doctrines of strategic thinking, which include game theory, decision theory, deterrence theory, policy analysis, balance of power analysis, simulation, operations research, contingency planning, and many other useful specialties. In military policy the dominance of these doctrines has become almost total. Decision theory and strategic thinking are now core subjects in the curricula of many graduate schools of public policy. They are purveyed to the government by the Rand Corporation and the Hudson Institute. In early 1973 the conservative *National Review*, long the bastion of more traditional thinking, ran a lead article urging that strategic thinking — called "Consciousness Alpha" by these brave new conservatives — be made a subject of instruction in our high schools.

11

With such unanimous canonization, it is little wonder that the politician has followed suit. John Kennedy, leading the way, was imitated in rapid succession by the strategists of the New Left movement, the strategists of the political consulting firms, the strategists of the Right, and finally by the strategists of Nixon's New Majority. It is their shared devotion to high strategy that enables all of these people to say with justification that they are practitioners of the "new politics." Richard Nixon may have popularized the term "game plan," but in its sophisticated form the logic employed by his team bears the stamp "Made in Massachusetts." It was perfected by some of the best and brightest minds of a whole generation, in part reacting against excessive moralism in American thought, in part to counter similar strategic thinking by disciples of Lenin, Hitler, and Mao Tse-tung, and in part because they found that the exercise liberated them from the restraints of traditional moral values.

There is nothing wrong with this way of thinking as long as strategy is kept in its proper place. We could not do without it. Our modern complex society requires intelligent decisionmaking in every sector of the national community. Business and industry have found means of employing the new strategic sciences to increase our national efficiency. In government, education, medicine, law, and other professions, our society performs better than it would otherwise because it has adopted intelligent strategic practices. In its proper employment, the science of strategic decisionmaking is the benefactor of modernity.

In this proper role, strategy is employed to attain objectives. It is used to prescribe how to go from here to there, how to overcome obstacles in order to reach a desired end, how to get what you want by the most efficient means possible. As such it is subject to abuses — we are all familiar with the problem of the ends justifying the means — but these limitations are well known and an honest decisionmaker will be aware of them.

But strategy by itself is not enough. It can be used profitably to attain goals, but cannot be allowed to set its own objectives. It can operate intelligently only within a framework where goals are set by nonstrategic considerations.

The reason for this is clear: strategy is concerned only with procedure and process: how to go from where you are to where you want to be. Since it is concerned exclusively with procedure, procedural goals are the only goals it can prescribe — and all procedural goals boil down to one: proceed well; that is, succeed, win, and prosper. This is why the *concept* of success, continual prospering, is the only goal that strategy can really formulate. The *meaning* of success — that is, the nature or value of one's actual achievement — is beyond the scope of strategic definition. Strategy, then, can only operate productively within a framework where goals are defined by other means. When it does not, success for the sake of success, winning for the sake of winning, and power for the sake of power are the only remaining rational objectives and these are both sterile and ultimately self-defeating.

Despite this fact, however, many modern decisionmakers seem to focus more on process than on goals. Once they accept the premise that they must preserve their overall strategic position, they tend to give precedence to instrumental goals, not intrinsic goals, since instrumental goals help them maintain their power.

Modern strategic thinkers have developed certain rules for keeping the process going well. (These are not always stated explicitly, and when they are they can be stated in various ways, but they might include "keep your options open," "preserve a winning image," "anticipate the worst possible contingency," and "maximize your power position.") These rules, of course, could be useful in attaining a given objective; the danger is that they may become ends in themselves. They may come to take precedence over any given goal or objective if the preservation of the process is seen as fundamentally more important than any intrinsic goals that could be attained through the process.

Now in business and other professions this tendency is controlled and regulated by the clear set of objectives that the situation imposes. A businessman has goals: produce a product according to certain specifications, solve a labor dispute, improve morale in the office, increase sales, make a profit for the company, and so forth. But a politician does not have these kinds of constraints. It is his role to formulate goals and gain a consensus on them.

What happens, however, when a politician decides to use strategy to define, rather than to attain, his goals? He begins to behave like the White House managers during Nixon's first term. He focuses on process. He commits himself to a winning streak based (he hopes) on a series of well-chosen instrumental goals. He focuses on maintaining his image and his public relations position. He perpetually looks to the next election. He focuses more on the utility than the veracity of his statements. He obligates himself to as little as possible, forever postponing the use of his power in an open-ended attempt to preserve it. His focus shifts from performance to power, from service to winning.

As this happens, his success is judged not by his accomplishments but by his position relative to others: is he ahead of or behind them, are they stronger than he is or weaker, is he winning the game or are they? As his relative position becomes increasingly important to him, he begins to concentrate on undermining his fellow politicians; he feels that he is in a zero-sum relationship, where every gain for them is a loss for him. And because he has begun to think of himself in these terms, he reasons that his opponents must be thinking this way too. Therefore, especially in an adversary process like an election, he feels that he must anticipate all the possible stratagems of an opponent and move to forestall them. Hence his maxims are those of escalation and deterrence. "You must get him before he gets you." "You are justified in doing to him what he might do to you." "You must take all sorts of precautionary measures against the slim chance that he might do something to you. Otherwise you might just lose."

As the logic of this kind of strategic thinking becomes clear, it is easy to understand some of the activities of the professional strategists employed by the Nixon administration and the sources of their game plan mentality. Their commitment to winning at all costs, their willingness to employ every means legal and illegal to attain that end, their perpetual focus on the next election at the expense of the ordinary governing procedures of the Republic, their lack of commitment to any lasting domestic policy, their focus on public relations at the expense of substance, their attempts to augment the power and mystique of the executive — and to isolate it — their assumption that a pronouncement of the government should be based on its utility not its veracity, their willingness to use deception extensively as an instrument of policy, their hypersensitivity to matters of security, their perception of opponents as enemies to be targeted, their buggings, burglaries, and other actions of a paramilitary nature, their extensive use of deterrence and other strategic methods of political intercourse when dealing with the press, the Congress, the courts, the public, the bureaucracy, and each other, and their willingness to use saboteurs, agents provocateurs, and pseudo-events to manipulate public opinion — all these are examples of a strategic mentality run riot.

It is easy to see how these practices led to an erosion of their authority, and how such practices, by destroying a sense of genuine purpose, will always destroy the moral basis of any government and thereby reduce its power. After all, elected officials are sent to Washington to run the government, to make policies, and to carry out programs. They are not elected to play games and to acquire power simply for the sake of perpetuating their ability to maintain options. They are supposed to make commitments. They are supposed to exercise power positively and constructively. They are supposed to accomplish something. And the government that they serve is supposed to operate for the benefit of the people, not for itself. But the new political thinking tends to erode these purposes in a dramatic way.

The strategic mentality, then, has some very disturbing dimensions to it. Unless it can be kept to its proper employment of helping decision-makers attain concrete objectives that are defined by other values, it will become an open-minded affair that forces its adherents to behave increasingly like men in combat, fighting perpetually to attain objectives that are increasingly defined by the dynamics of the conflict, not by their own will and choice. This phenomenon, so dangerous to our democratic principles and to the orderly functioning of our government, we call *strategic*

14

politics, and its practitioners we call hyperstrategists, to distinguish them from those who employ strategy to attain objectives in the normal way.

Strategic thinking in all its forms has become so widely accepted in our society that any reservations about it seem either stupid or naïve. After all, we are a nation of strategists and game players, winning is a national pastime, and outwitting an opponent can be a great deal of fun. Our very language has changed to accommodate the new concepts: points in time, options, phaseouts, contingencies, missions, and feedbacks have joined the game plan as important political concepts. Making decisions on the basis of cost-benefit analyses or projected outcomes is now a universally accepted practice — as it should be when legitimate goals are clearly defined.

But outcome analysis is not the only way of defining objectives. Objectives can be derived from moral principles, from respect for people and institutions, from a sense of fairness and duty, from a commitment to service, or from a commitment to some concrete principle. Politicians can view themselves as representing a constituency rather than maximizing power. A truly sophisticated politician will recognize that objectives formulated on the basis of such principles will increase the sources of his authority and make him both politically and psychologically much more secure. He will employ strategy in the pursuit of his objectives, but he will seldom let it define them.

For example, if you went to Senator Clifford Case of New Jersey and offered him a bribe, he would turn you down, not because he would calculate the possible advantages and disadvantages of accepting or refusing a bribe, but because Senator Case does not accept bribes at all. It is not even a matter of policy for Senator Case to refuse bribes, it is a matter of principle. Cost-benefit analysis does not enter the picture at all.

If you went to Senator William Saxbe of Ohio and suggested to him that he should weigh his words for their strategic effect, he would tell you with a chuckle or two that you had taken leave of your senses. He would tell you that his honesty was the source of his popularity and respect among the press and the public. It was also the reason that the White House turned to him in desperation after Attorney General Elliot Richardson resigned.

If you went to the offices of Minority Leader Hugh Scott, offered him your services as an expert deterrence strategist, and suggested that he might adopt your methods in dealing with his colleagues, he would tell you that you were hopelessly naïve. The senator from Pennsylvania, a shrewd political strategist, would say that deterrence policies, rational coercion, and strategic deception would simply not be effective for long in the political medium of the United States Senate.

If you went to Senator Charles ("Mac") Mathias of Maryland and said

15

that you had a game plan whereby he could maintain and augment his reputation for honesty, integrity, and decency, he would look at you in astonishment. This successful politician knows that decency is not the product of calculation or of narrow strategy but of fundamental values.

If you went to Senator Jacob Javits of New York and told him that his emphasis on legislative performance was out of date, and that image-building should be more important to him, he would quickly set you straight. He would tell you that performance generates support of a far more lasting and secure variety than the dexterous appearance of performance.

If you went to Senator Robert Dole of Kansas, and told him that you had a scheme for exploiting party loyalty, the former Republican national chairman would tell you that political loyalty is a commodity that cannot be exploited — not for long, at any rate. He would proceed to explain that loyalty is not the product of narrow strategy and that people distinguish very quickly between those who are genuinely loyal and those who are "loyal" simply for the benefits that might accrue from appearing to be loyal. Although a narrow game player may reason that loyalty has its advantages, the senator from Kansas would tell you that genuine loyalty is exhibited most clearly when it runs against a short-run advantage.

But if you went to see the new strategists in the Nixon White House, you might get a different set of responses. When you told them that they could build a constituency on public relations, they would readily concur. When you told them that they should exploit party loyalty and augment their own position at the expense of the party's position, they would say that to do otherwise would be naïve. When you suggested that they should focus less on policies and performance, more on appearances and political strategies, they would agree. When you told them that they could create the appearance of decency when it was lacking, they would say Amen. When you recommended to them that they make extensive use of deterrence and war-gaming while dealing with other politicians, they would say that they had been doing it for years. When you suggested that they could solve all their problems by retooling their image, they would reply "How else?" And if you offered them some conspiratorial cash, they would probably subject your offer to a cost-benefit analysis.

The contrasts between the senators and the Nixon managers illustrate the difference between strategic politics and the more traditional varieties of politics that operate within legislatures and political parties. The traditional politician's medium is a personal one. His route to advancement is through a party or legislative channel. His rewards come from services that require a vast amount of face-to-face contact. His perception of politics is much more in human terms, and his attitude toward the electorate remains highly personalized: he relies for his information more on mail, word-of-mouth, and direct contacts than on opinion surveys and public relations experts. In bargaining and log-rolling he uses manipulation and coercion, but the kinds of coercion he uses are severely defined by the rules of that diffuse but real political club of which he is a member. His instruments of bargaining are much more personal — more often positive than negative — and his relationship to those with whom he deals is much more intuitive than logical. By face-to-face dealings he soon learns the value of his own credibility, and the value of subtlety in dealing with people. He learns that threats and bribes that appear to be neither are more effective than those that appear to be what they really are. He learns the value of being civil to an opponent. He appreciates the advantages of reciprocity. Making friends, not enemies, is the key to his influence. And he engages in a lot of humbug that often earns him the contempt — but seldom the fear — of a public that is prepared to forgive him for the practices of his inferior profession.

Furthermore, the traditional politician is constituency- and party-oriented. Sometimes he construes his sense of *constituency* very narrowly by representing a faction within his district or a powerful interest that dominates his region. Sometimes he construes his sense of *interest* very narrowly by changing his views and adopting his policies to the wiles and whims of the electorate. But representation is the focus of his activities. The flexibility and options that the traditional politician works to preserve are in the service of promises to constituent interests.

In a politics of representation, after all, the ordering principle is loyalty. The representative is loyal to his constituency: he delivers. The constituency is loyal to the representative: it delivers by reelecting him. In this atmosphere of loyalty it is easy for party organizations to grow and flourish; they can come to represent a constituency, they can continue to deliver to that constituency, and loyalty can become a powerful requirement for their internal organization. Representative politics is a politics of commitment; and, within the limits imposed by the exigencies of human nature, it is a politics of trust. This does not mean that such politics is necessarily peaceful since there can be great conflicts between the representatives of different constituencies. Nor does this mean that loyalty is always a virtue. What it does mean is that the relationship between the traditional politician and his constituency is personal, clearly defined, and reasonably stable.

These relationships still exist at the lower levels of our politics and in many cases at the level of the House of Representatives in Washington. Some senators, especially from the smaller states, have been able to maintain the personal relationships of the old politician. But those politicians who represent a large state or who hope to have a national constituency have come to rely increasingly on impersonal media. They too tend to find their procedures "objectified" and their practices strategized.

17

The traditional politician is not the only person whose practices are being eroded by the new techniques of strategic thinking. The moralist is suffering a similar fate. He, too, is moving in the direction of high strategy and his practices are becoming more and more subject to its dictates. As this happens *morality* tends to become *ideology* and his long-range goals tend to become undermined by the narrow expediencies of the moment. As he adopts a strategic approach to moral questions, his larger values become postponed for the sake of more immediate tactical achievements. Instead of providing a lasting code of procedure, morality tends increasingly to provide an ultimate justification for very expedient practices. The McGovern campaign, as we shall see, provides a wealth of examples of this tendency.

Both the moralist and the traditionalist are thus being subverted by the strategist; and this is unfortunate, for we really need a proper mixture of all three in the society. The moralist is supposed to give our system a concern for transcendent values. He turns our attention to justice, peace, freedom, and equality. The politician provides the necessary concern for procedural values to prevent excessive friction between competing groups. His concerns are moderation, due process, compromise, persuasion, consensus, and accommodation. The strategist gives us a concern for performance. He is interested in efficiency, effectiveness and the management of complex systems. The voices of these three are present in all of us: The moral voice sets our values and beliefs; the political voice enables us to formulate our goals so that the interests, beliefs, rights, and energies of others are taken into account; and the strategic voice enables us to execute these goals. Previously one could argue that our political process, whatever its faults, would suffice to check the excesses of both strategic and moralistic thinking. But this argument is now hard to sustain.

What has changed is not the mere presence of hyperstrategic thinking but the absorption of politics and morals into strategy: both the traditional politician and the moralist over the past decade have become high strategists. As a result, the moralist has begun to ask not whether an action is just, but what kinds of justice have a strategic payoff. He has thus moved from an operating moral code to an abstract moralism designed to give him the rhetorical upper hand over his opponent. The politician has begun to ask not how he can reconcile conflicting interests, but how he can project a winning image. He has thus moved from personal contact with his constituents to remote manipulation of them. And the strategist, now in demand by both the "boss" and the "reformer," tells the one how to manipulate the media and the other how to manipulate his movement. As a result of the demand for his skills he has become less furtive, and his art is almost universally acclaimed for the first time in our intellectual history. Lest we forget, our native intellectual tradition was once marked by fulminations against the "calculation" and the "Machiavellianisms" that were seen as the corrupt legacies of discredited European politics.

The Nixon managers are not the only people who created difficulties for themselves by employing political strategy in an unsophisticated way. Many of George McGovern's problems during the summer and fall of 1972 can be traced back to his use of highly *tactical* methods to confront *political* difficulties with his party, with organized labor, and with the general public. McGovern won the nomination because his managers were tactically proficient at turning out a constituency that was ready-made for them. They were not, however, proficient at creating a constituency. By trying to do so with highly tactical methods, they ended up in a worse position than they would have been in had they not tried at all. Politics is not the same as strategy, and when a narrow strategist enters a highly personalized and political atmosphere — such as the Democratic party or the labor movement — the result may well be a disaster. When a moralist tries to do so, the result may be equally disastrous. McGovern paid heavily for the political inexperience of strategic managers who could not understand the basis of the political loyalties that defined the relationships among the power centers of the Democratic party. (We examine his campaign in Chapters 6 and 7, and the convolutions of his relationship to the labor movement in Chapter 8.)

It may seem surprising to refer to the McGovern campaign as a strategic exercise, but it certainly was one. Many people have suggested that his campaign was "ideological" while the campaign of the President was "pragmatic," that the nature of their campaign organizations differed vastly and that the American voter was presented not only with a choice between personalities but between basic approaches to politics. This simply was not the case. Although the two candidates were different and the ideas of their followers were different, both organizations were run by high strategists. And, as is inherent in the nature of high strategy, its own rules predominated and its practitioners came more and more to resemble each other.

If the McGovern campaign was founded on principle or purpose or ideology, these values soon were replaced by the imperatives of strategy. The campaign taken as a whole presents an excellent series of examples of high strategy: the long-range attempts to manipulate the rules to the advantage of certain elements of the party, the extensive exploitation of these rules in caucus after caucus, the supercession of winning for equity in the conduct of the campaign, the exploitation of a few primary victories to manipulate the media's interpretation of events, the preconvention threats to bolt the party in order to pressure the regulars into accepting McGovern on McGovern's own terms, the convention strategy to scuttle the women on the crucial first roll call and the subsequent tactic

19

to seat the Daley delegation instead of the Illinois reformers (a tactic abandoned in mid-ballot only because it became too obvious to succeed), the shifting of positions on issues after the nomination, the design of an electoral college strategy that wrote off most of the country and sought a victory based on a minority of popular votes, McGovern's table-hopping among the national press corps to undercut Eagleton the very day after he had vowed full support of him in public, and the calculated decision by the McGovern staff (vetoed by the candidate himself) to destroy Eagleton in September by leaking additional damaging information they had — all these are examples of strategists at work. Frank Mankiewicz and Gary Hart in their professional life styles were indistinguishable from Charles Colson, Fred Malek, and the other Nixon managers in theirs, as Mankiewicz himself lamented to his friend Tom Braden.

The Larger Context: A Permanent Strategic Politics?

So far we have looked at strategic politics in terms of 1972. We have seen how it tends to subvert policy, how it can lead to Watergates, and how both the politician and the moralist have a tendency to succumb to its dictates. There are, however, some specific side effects to strategic politics that have equally lasting implications. The most important of these is that the practices of the "new politicians" are helping to destroy the two-party system: they are undercutting political parties and are creating a condition of nonalignment among the voters. How does the use of strategy per se destroy the political party and its loyalties? Consider the following sound rules of the new political strategists, which are simply codifications of principles we have discussed already.

STRATEGIC RULE #1: *Focus on fluidity, wherever you find it.*

The target of a campaign is logically the unstable voter, the ticket-splitter, the "swing voter." After all, a campaign is presumably designed to move voters, to change their minds. It makes little sense to pay much attention to those who are solidly with you or against you. In the election, therefore, this means that you should ignore party loyalists up to the point where they are willing to leave you and spend your major effort prying loose potential swing voters. To the fluid, not the committed, belong the spoils. In the McGovern campaign before the convention, for example, his strategists took the antiwar liberal for granted as they tried to reach out for the Wallace voter. After the convention they ignored the blacks, Chicanos, and other minority groups in their efforts to focus on the presumably more fluid suburbanite. Alternatively, the Nixon camp made massive efforts to attract "Democrats for Nixon" and in many regions of the country exploited the loyalties of its Republican supporters by ignoring them. "Ignore anybody who has no place else to go" is a good strategic maxim.

These practices are relatively new. In traditional politics the focus was more on turning out the faithful and the loyal than influencing the fluid.

STRATEGIC RULE #2: *If you cannot find fluidity, use pseudo-issues to create it.*

The minority candidate or party may not be able to win simply by attracting the fluid voter, and so it becomes strategically necessary to *create* some fluidity in the opposition camp, to entice previously committed voters into a condition of weakening commitment or no commitment at all. Since the starting point of political calculation remains the party designation, the major focus of strategic politics has been the employment of vast amounts of resources by both parties for the almost exclusive purpose of destroying the loyalties in the other party.

There are always issues that will pry loose voters from the opposing camp. Some of these involve real changes in policy, others are pseudo-issues that involve the appearance, rather than the reality, of change. President Nixon's use of the busing issue after the Florida primary in 1972 was such a pseudo-issue. He had no intention of changing the Supreme Court guidelines on this question, as a close reading of his speech revealed and as his subsequent dropping of the issue also showed. Kennedy's 1960 alarums about a missile gap were a pseudo-issue designed to win anticommunists and defense-oriented interests in the South and Southwest from Nixon. The gap was forgotten after the election.

STRATEGIC RULE #3: *Keep your options open.*

One never knows what pseudo-issue may be useful a year or even six months in advance of an election. Hence the best strategic counsel to a candidate is to keep his options open so that he can move in any direction. This means making as few commitments as possible and keeping the opposition guessing about the direction in which you may move. Jack Kennedy in 1960 campaigned both to the left and the right of Nixon, preserving all the time the option to be more "conservative" in defense matters and more "liberal" on domestic problems. In 1972, Nixon preserved his option of replacing Agnew until the Democratic nominating convention (contrast this with Eisenhower's approach to the same problem) and McGovern left open the option of bolting his party. At the same time a *reputation* for making and keeping commitments is useful, and this can often be kept by manipulating appearances, which involves fewer commitments than dealing with reality. Public relations, therefore, take precedence over political performance under the new rules.

21

STRATEGIC RULE #4: *Ignore your own party selectively.*

In 1972 both Nixon and McGovern set up campaign organizations entirely separate from the party structure. These were organizations of experts: in media strategy, direct mail strategy, special groups strategy, fund-raising strategies, turnout strategies, and so forth. These new agglomerations of strategists are replacing the traditional party in a national campaign.

Parties are based on loyalty historically. But, as we have seen, the purpose of strategic politics is to exploit the loyalty of the faithful in the search for the support of the nonfaithful. Hence a tension arises between a strategic politician and his party organization in two basic ways. First, since the strategist is reaching out beyond the doctrines of the party for issues to expand his base of support, the party loyalists may have increasing reservations about how extensively the strategic politician is representing *them*. Second, the strategic requirements of victory require a high premium upon professionalism and expertise in the management level of a modern campaign. Since tenure and promotion within a party structure depend more upon loyalty and personal qualifications than upon competence in gamesmanship, a candidate bent upon victory tends to recruit his staff from outside the party hierarchy. There are three strategic advantages to this. His own organization is more flexible in extending its appeal to voters whom the party cannot in good conscience attract; his organization can assemble without excessive political difficulty a much higher level of expertise than the party can; and, since the experts are hired hands, the candidate doesn't have to hear from them after the election, so long as he pays their bills. In the confrontation between the loyalist and the strategist, the strategist wins. His skills are more in demand; he is a much more valuable commodity. Power gravitates toward him and away from the party regular. By employing him the candidate keeps his options open for the task of governing.

STRATEGIC RULE #5: *Govern as if you were still campaigning.*

Government by Gallup poll is a logical result of game plan thinking. Having made few commitments to attain victory, the strategic politician has generated support that is broad but not deep. He has won the marginal preference of the fluid voter and weakened the devotion of the loyal party voter. Hence he has no solid base of support to tide him over short-term reverses in public opinion. His aim, then, will logically be to avoid such reverses, and he can do this most efficiently by the same manipulation of appearances and verbal formulas that served him so well in his campaign. He logically should concentrate not on performance, but on taking credit for the things that go well and shifting blame for those that don't. Media exposure makes governing by Gallup poll possible and strategic politics makes it seem necessary.

Even though these rules may have disastrous consequences for our politics as a whole, politicians are following them with increasing diligence. They are becoming standard operating procedures for the new professionals and they have a self-fulfilling logic to them; to neglect them, it would seem, is to court political disaster. The problem is, however, that the voter, too, can become a strategic politician. He also can begin to bargain and to focus on the fluid. He, too, can keep his options open and withhold his loyalties. If the politician does not deliver to him there is no need for him to remain loyal to the politician. This reaction has already begun.

The Public Reacts

First of all, the electorate has begun to perceive that the uncommitted are in the best bargaining position with respect to the politicians. If the fluid get the spoils then it makes sense to be fluid. Large blocs of previously loyal voters are beginning to assert that they can no longer be taken for granted by either party. Black and Chicano leaders have publicly adopted this line in many regions of the country. George Wallace has used it extensively in the South. But other voters are behaving this way as well. The suburbanite, the working-class Democrat, the moderate Republican, and the Jewish voter are all beginning to behave much more independently. They are shopping around between parties and candidates, no longer satisfied with what the politicians or the old organizations are trying to deliver to them. The point is that strategic politics makes traditional political alignments irrational, counterproductive, and ultimately impossible.

There is no single statistic that can demonstrate this change; every single kind of indicator — from precinct analyses to opinion surveys, to election returns, to candidate pair-offs in Gallup polls — has its well-known methodological deficiencies. But the combined evidence is overwhelming.

Ticket-splitting, once the exception in American politics, is now the norm. A postelection Gallup poll showed that 60 percent of the electorate split its ticket in 1972. In 1968 — a three-party situation — this figure was 54 percent, of which 14 percent were Wallace voters. This national figure suggests a significant increase that is borne out in statewide results, where ticket-splitting has also increased dramatically over the last two decades according to several reliable indicators.

The trend seems to outstrip even the most avant-garde analyses of it. Walter DeVries and Lance Tarrance, in their important 1971 book, *The*

Ticket-Splitter, saw this phenomenon as confined largely to better informed, higher-income suburban voters. The Ripon Society's own early analyses prepared by Christopher W. Beal in 1968 stressed that both "frontlash" and "backlash" ticket-splitters were a small and identifiable portion of the electorate among whom there were fairly predictable trade-offs. This is no longer the case. In part because of television, in part because of social mobility, and in part because of state electoral law changes (so that one does not have to be an electrical engineer to split a ticket on voting machines), ticket-splitting is now open to everybody. The evidence now seems to indicate that no group in the population is significantly less prone to split its ticket than any other. Suburbanites have been joined around the country by blacks, Chicanos, blue-collar ethnics, farmers, and Southerners. Party regularity is simply disappearing.

Second, the ticket-splitting phenomenon is accompanied by extreme volatility in "trial heat" polls of the electorate. Ticket-splitting voters typically change their expressed voting intentions during the campaign, so that polls matching one candidate against another are increasingly unreliable as early measures of likely outcomes. Formerly this phenomenon was confined only to party primaries and partisan elections where party loyalty was not a stabilizing factor. Now the same fickleness has moved to the state and national levels. As this trend continues, American presidential and state politics come to reflect the instabilities of a non-partisan mayorality contest. Under such conditions the whole idea of a lasting coalition or an electoral mandate begins to fade, especially when the same shifts in approval occur after the election as well. One need only recall the way in which the Eagleton issue, the "social issue," and the "Watergate issue" have affected the fortunes of Richard Nixon. Such volatility is, as we have suggested, a perfectly reasonable response by the electorate to the strategic attitudes of the politician.

If one has a tidy mind, or a preoccupation with historical precedent, one may be tempted to conclude that the current fluidity is merely a sign of transition. Surely, one thinks, there will soon be a realignment along neat ideological lines. But the evidence does not now support this hope and will not support it without concerted action to change the voters' perceptions of the political elite. The voter is, after all, only responding in a reasonable manner to the actions of the candidates themselves. He often sees that the candidate is manipulating the electorate; why should he not react in kind, adopt his own game plan, and manipulate the party system?

The result of this strategic interaction is a growth in cynicism by voters and politicians alike, since the game plan mentality generates an attitude of mutual contempt. The political strategists view the voters cynically because, from the viewpoint of decision theory, they are depersonalized objects to be manipulated. The electorate also views the politician cynically since he is not doing his job of governing the country. He is not delivering to the electorate; he is not representing it; he is simply playing games with the voters and with other politicians. The two attitudes feed upon each other.

Against their better judgment, elected officials are caught in a system that increasingly forces them to become poseurs, manipulators, and maneuverers in a drift toward game plan politics. Moreover, because this is now done in full public view, it undermines the moral coherence of society to all who look to politics for leadership. As the voter looks on the politician with contempt, his voting behavior will become more erratic. As this happens, the politician will become more strategic, thus incurring more contempt. Both responses are understandable, yet taken together they lead to demise of parties and a degeneration of representative politics.

The rest of this book addresses itself to these problems. Part I describes the impact of strategic thinking upon the political practices of 1972. Part II examines the impact of the new politics on the power structure of the Republican party. Part III provides some suggestions for restoring the constitutional balance of our institutions and revitalizing our parties.

2

Strategic Government: Nixon's First Term

President Nixon's first term in office provides a classic example of strategic politics at work: in many ways the entire four years can be viewed as an unending struggle to devise a winning electoral strategy. Certainly considerations of narrow strategy were not the administration's only concern, but after the first six months in office political tactics and election strategy rapidly replaced policy considerations as the dominant focus of White House calculations. The details of this tragedy bear examining.

The Positive Opening

COHERENCE AT HOME

The Nixon administration started out, at any rate, on a positive policy-oriented basis in domestic affairs. To begin with, the President moved quickly to structure his administration for intelligent decisionmaking. He established, by executive order, a new cabinet-level Council for Urban Affairs to enable the administration to exercise greater control over domestic policy. This council was necessary, he declared, because "the American national government has responded to urban concerns in a haphazard, fragmented and often woefully shortsighted manner . . . what we never had is a policy; coherent, consistent positions as to what national government would hope to see happen, what it will encourage, what it will discourage." The President also established an Office of

26

Intergovernmental Relations under the chairmanship of Vice President Agnew, with a mandate to coordinate federal policies with local and state officials. The basic rationale or philosophy for these moves was that the American people, fed up with governmental inefficiency and waste, demanded major structural reforms in the federal bureaucracy. In a speech to the National Governors Association, Nixon quoted a section of Peter Drucker's *The Age of Discontinuity,* which had been publicly recommended to him by both the *National Review* and the *Ripon Forum:* "There is mounting evidence that government is big rather than strong; that it is fat and flabby rather than powerful; that it costs a great deal but does not achieve much. . . . Indeed, government is sick — and just at a time when we need a strong, healthy and vigorous government." Stated simply, Drucker's answer to the sickness of government lay in government reorganization and the devolution of power out of Washington so that the federal government would "do less to achieve more." The President's objectives, which he was to reemphasize in 1971, were to organize around "purposes" not programs, in line with Drucker's recommendations. For the first time, they indicated governmental acceptance of management by objectives, incentives, and results, a policy long since adopted by corporations. In time these proposals envisioned a new role for government as manager for society rather than as solver of problems by direct bureaucratic means. The point was that government should set national priorities for society when possible and encourage other sectors to do the job in accordance with local circumstances. Success would be judged by results, not by the size of an agency's budget.

The Urban Affairs Council's new executive secretary, Daniel Patrick Moynihan, though identified as a liberal Democrat, carried the Drucker thesis in the early months of the Nixon term. He liked to point out, in exercising his power to review domestic policy, that since 1960 the number of domestic programs, each with its own separate budget and bureaucracy, had gone from 46 to about 400. Clearly the federal government in Washington had become top-heavy and unequal to public expectations of performance. Nonetheless he cautioned the President against dismantling too hastily the liberal welfare programs of previous administrations. As a result much of the Johnson program lived on in amended form.

The first result of Moynihan's influence was the President's decision merely to modify, rather than eliminate, the Office of Economic Opportunity, the keystone of the Johnson antipoverty program. To the surprise of many Republicans he recommended the retention and current-level funding of the community action programs that so many conservatives opposed. In doing this he indicated that he would not turn back the clock on social progress but would attempt to make government programs more efficient. In announcing his decision to transfer the Head Start program to HEW and the Job Corps to the Department of Labor, he emphasized the need to coordinate existing programs, not to destroy

27

them: "The public generally and the poor especially have a right to demand effective and efficient management. I intend to provide it."

The President furthermore proposed a special contribution of his own to the war on poverty: a program for minority enterprise. This was not just another Great Society program. Rather, it was a plan sketched out in his "Bridges to Human Dignity" campaign address of May 2, 1968, to provide poor people with a stake in their society by "giving them a piece of the action." A number of black leaders, including Georgia legislator Julian Bond, scoffed at "black capitalism" as "no better than white capitalism." But the language and the intent of the Nixon plans reflected a growing desire in the black community to establish black pride through economic self-determination, a desire communicated directly to Mr. Nixon during the campaign by Roy Innis of CORE. In the May 2 speech, candidate Nixon claimed that "the old approach was custodial" while "the new approach is remedial: to involve the poor in the rebuilding of their own communities, and in the fostering of self-reliance and self-respect." This approach was aimed at all minority groups, but had its greatest appeal in the black community.

For critics who dismissed black capitalism as mere window dressing and an inadequate solution to the problems of the working poor, the President offered another measure, known as the Philadelphia Plan, to get minority workers into exclusionary construction unions. Promoted by Secretary of Labor George Shultz, the plan was designed to pressure unions working on federal contracts to admit minority workers to membership and to train them, a measure that the Democratic party, with its close ties to labor, had never been enthusiastic about.

Many other initiatives were instituted during the spring months of the administration. The President took the first step toward the establishment of an all-volunteer army, he moved to eliminate political patronage from the Post Office, and he created a cabinet-level Council on Environmental Quality. Over Easter weekend 1969 he presided over a historic session for domestic policy that adopted an outline for a thorough overhaul of the nation's antiquated welfare system and instituted a far-reaching program to revitalize all government by sharing federal revenues with states and localities.

The President's progressive initiatives were not the result of any great shift in his thinking, but were the logical fulfillment of a set of proposals he made in a series of thoughtful radio addresses during his primary campaign in the spring of 1968. In these speeches he had advocated what he called "a new alignment for American unity," which would include not just traditional Republicans and the "silent center" but "new liberals," the new South, and black militants as well. "Let's not oversimplify," he warned. "The[se] voices are not joined in any harmonious chorus — far from it. The ideas of the new alignment differ in emphasis. But they do not conflict in the way the old alliance of power bases used to conflict. . . . Now the new alignment's greatest need is to communicate with all its elements, rather than along in parallel lines that never converge."

As the Republican nominee, Nixon had abandoned the rhetoric of the "new alignment" as a concession to southern support, but after his election he began the process of communicating at least "with all its elements." His appointment of Moynihan and Henry Kissinger furnished a bridge to "new liberals" who had already broken step with orthodox liberal tradition. The appointment of civil rights leader James Farmer as undersecretary of HEW pointed the way to reconciliation with the one group that had most uniformly opposed his election. Within three weeks of his inauguration he met with a number of black leaders, including Roy Wilkins, the influential chairman of the NAACP, who publicly predicted that Nixon intended to "rectify" the problem of Negro dissatisfaction with him. Two top-ranking officers of the Ripon Society, Lee Huebner and John Price, joined the administration as presidential speechwriter and counsel to the Urban Affairs Council, respectively, and a *Ripon Forum* editorial said: "In domestic policy, despite limited financial room for maneuver, the President has pledged new programs and new priorities. . . . If followed through, these Nixon initiations will far surpass in their impact the contributions of the War on Poverty, with its grandiose claims and meager achievements."

In domestic policy, then, the President began to act on the series of proposals he had made during the campaign. His "new alignment" philosophy had coherence and substance. It was a responsible problem-solving approach to domestic policy and it started off with much promise.

COHERENCE ABROAD

Foreign policy also saw some promising starts. During his campaign Nixon had kept a low profile on the war, saying that it would be inappropriate to reveal details of his plan for peace. Nevertheless, in public and private, he had reiterated his commitment to wind down the war without sacrificing any pro-Western government in Saigon. In the months after his election he followed the basic policy he had submitted to the 1968 Republican Convention, that "rather than further escalation on the military front, what [the war] requires now is a dramatic escalation of our efforts on the economic, political, diplomatic and psychological fronts. It requires a new strategy, which recognizes that this is a new and different kind of war. And it requires a fuller enlistment of our Vietnamese allies in their own defense."

On May 14, 1969, the President made public an eight-point plan for mutual reduction of forces in Vietnam, proposals that he said represented his desire to "take some risks for peace." For the first time, an American President indicated a willingness to withdraw troops on a set timetable of one year and to recognize the National Liberation Front as a potential element in a new South Vietnamese government. Concerned with the rise of public restiveness over the continued fighting in Vietnam, the President took a conciliatory position, saying: "I do not criticize those who disagree with me on the conduct of our peace negotiations. And I do not ask unlimited patience from a people whose hopes have too often been raised and then cruelly dashed over the past four years." He was apparently so confident that his offer would finally break the deadlock in Paris that he reminded the public of his campaign promise to end the war. "I am determined to keep that pledge. If I fail to do so, I expect the American people to hold me accountable for that failure."

A month later, at Midway Island in the Pacific, the President gained not only an endorsement from President Thieu for his eight-point plan but also a promise of new elections under international supervision. Nixon added for the first time a pledge for the gradual withdrawal of American troops. This new initiative, he said, was made possible by the improved ability of the South Vietnamese to defend their own country. It also responded to the public demand for signs of progress in Vietnam and the failure to gain the help of the Soviet Union in securing an early settlement.

By June, then, President Nixon had embarked on a new two-track strategy in Vietnam, one aimed at satisfying American public opinion, the other aimed at convincing the opposition it was worth negotiating early, despite a clear commitment for ultimate American withdrawal. In order to encourage Hanoi, Nixon reversed the earlier American policy that had ruled out any Communist participation in South Vietnamese politics. He also signaled his sincerity about deescalation by deciding to withdraw not just support troops, as the Joint Chiefs of Staff had urged, but combat troops as well.

COHERENCE OVERALL

The President had every reason to be elated in August when he returned from a round-the-world trip that included a visit to Vietnam. He had wrung important concessions from Thieu and had placed the war in a new international framework through the "Nixon doctrine." Just after his return he presented to the Congress his domestic program, with its dramatic new plans for welfare reform and revenue sharing. Days later he revealed his sense of jubilation as he received the Apollo astronauts at the summer White House.

Behind the President's high spirits lay the fact that he now had a working framework of reform for his foreign and domestic policies. Both his revenue sharing and welfare programs offered major alternatives to tired-out New Deal approaches. The former represented the first dispersal of power out of Washington in over thirty years back to localities closest to the problems at hand. The latter combined a policy of national minimum payments to welfare clients in all federally supported programs with sizable monetary incentives to encourage welfare recipients to improve their skills and enter the work force.

On September 1 the President wove together his reform program in a speech to the National Governors Association. First, he said, the challenge lay in making government governable again:

- overhauling its structure;
- pruning out those programs that have failed or that have outlived their time;
- ensuring that its delivery systems actually deliver the intended services to the intended beneficiaries;
- gearing its programs to the concept of social investment;
- focusing its activities not only on tomorrow, but on the day after tomorrow.

Such a strategy for reform at home, he continued, depended on the success of a strategy for peace abroad, a strategy that "means maintaining defense forces strong enough to keep the peace, but not allowing wasteful expenditures to drain away resources for progress." It was an upbeat speech, full of idealism and vision, based on traditional Republican values: efficient and responsible government delivering to its constituency in a quiet but effective manner. It was a set of coherent projected accomplishments that might well have characterized the first Nixon term. But strategic politics intervened.

Strategies and Symbols

By staking out a moderate course of action, the President was confronted by two problems, the conservatives and the South. Both had supported his nomination and election. Both expected to receive something in return. Both had elsewhere to go. The conservatives (especially the South) presented a series of risks and opportunities: minimally, the risk that they would desert to a third-party movement; maximally, the opportunity that they might be tied into a Republican nationwide majority. Their very flexibility therefore made them the central focus of the Nixon strategists.

31

The Republican party had had some form of southern strategy for a number of years. President Eisenhower had carried a number of southern states and he had fostered the growth of a moderate party in the South based on the leadership of the business community. In 1960, Vice President Nixon had actively sought southern support with a policy of moderation and limited government. He had been almost as successful as Eisenhower. In 1964 a revolution occurred with the Goldwater movement when the Arizona senator carried five Deep South states with large majorities, although it should be remembered that his performance in the region varied immensely compared to those of Eisenhower and Nixon — he did the best where they did the worst and vice versa. Goldwater's opposition to civil rights legislation, his policy of states' rights conservatism, and his personal style made these consolation prizes possible. The consolation at the moment, however, seemed small indeed since the cost of carrying these states seemed to be the loss of practically everything else, but one point had been demonstrated: a conservative Republican could carry the region or do well there against a middle-of-the-road southern Democrat.

In 1968 the Republicans lost the Deep South decisively to George Wallace while holding onto precarious leads in most of the Outer South states. Had the Wallace factor not been there, it seemed plausible to argue that Nixon would have swept the region from Humphrey. Hence the South became a very important possibility for Republican presidential prospects. The region, however, had not moved decisively to the Republicans, as local and statewide races continued to demonstrate. From the standpoint of parties it had simply become unbelievably flexible, going with overwhelming majorities to the more conservative candidate. And when a region is flexible, its bargaining power is very great. To be sure, in a two-way race with a "normal" Republican moderate running against a "normal" Democratic liberal, the South could almost be taken for granted by the Republican. But to avoid such a situation, to avoid being "taken for granted" by anyone, as the line ran, the South embraced George Wallace, who consciously exploited the South's flexibility between the parties to increase its bargaining position. This was the argument used time and again by the Alabama governor, a classic example of strategic politics at work, where a constituency is brought into a bargaining relationship of major proportions with the two parties. In the absence of the Wallace factor, the administration might well have ignored the South but expected its support. With the Wallace factor, the administration felt that it had to bargain for the South, and to do so it began to ignore or take for granted many of its other constituencies, some of which also became disillusioned and therefore flexible. A third-party movement (or an nth-party movement) is an eminently logical occurrence when the two major parties either neglect a constituency or take it for granted. Dealing with a very fluid situation, however, is not always easy because of the strategic relationships involved. To deliver to the South on the terms that George Wallace might extract in a pure bargaining situation might well put the party back into its Goldwater position. But to ignore the Wallace situation might be also quite counterproductive. The administration tried at first to deal with this problem on the level of policy. Frustrated, it then shifted to the realm of symbols.

THE FAILURE OF POLICY

The issue of school segregation was the first crucial policy area that tested administration intentions with respect to the South. At the Republican convention and during the campaign Nixon had repeated his belief that school desegregation had been too vigorously pressed under the Johnson administration. He had stressed "cooperation, not coercion," and his southern allies, particularly South Carolina's Strom Thurmond, told political audiences to expect Nixon to establish a return to the freedom-of-choice concept destroyed in HEW decisions to cut off federal funds to schools that failed to desegregate according to guidelines laid down by the Johnson administration. Nixon himself had endorsed the freedom-of-choice concept at a campaign appearance in Charlotte during the fall of 1968. When asked by WFMY news director Charles Whitehurst whether he thought withholding funds under HEW guidelines was a valid approach, Nixon replied, "I think that the use of that power on the part of the federal government to force the local community to carry out what a federal administrator or bureaucrat may, what he may think is best for that local community, I think that is a doctrine that is a very dangerous one. It is one that I generally would not approve." The appointment of former South Carolina state chairman Harry Dent as the chief White House political aide gave white Southerners every reason to believe their interests would be well protected there. In addition, they found an ally in Attorney General John Mitchell, whose young political adviser Kevin Phillips was polishing off a book, *The Emerging Republican Majority*, that vigorously endorsed a southern strategy. Evans and Novak reported that President Nixon, shortly after he took office, would certainly withdraw the federal desegregation ultimata to southern school districts dispatched in the last days of the Johnson administration: "Although details are vague, it is likely that Nixon will give the South just about what it wants: token integration resulting from a minority of Negroes volunteering for white schools under 'freedom-of-choice' plans," they wrote. "Nixon's southern backers are serenely confident he will not disappoint them."

But the administration started out instead with positive policies in the field of civil rights as it had in other areas. At HEW, secretary Robert Finch and his liberal Republican director for civil rights, Leon Panetta, proceeded to follow guidelines laid down by the previous administration and prepared to cut off funds for recalcitrant school districts. They felt, as apparently a campaigning presidential candidate did not, that they were constrained by a May 1968 Supreme Court ruling in *Green* v. *County School Board of New Kent County, Virginia* that ineffective "freedom-of-choice" desegregation plans would no longer suffice, and that school boards were obliged to devise plans "that promise realistically to work, and promise realistically to work *now*." Having resisted tremendous pressure from Mitchell and Thurmond, on January 29 Finch announced a cutoff of funds to five southern districts (including two in South Carolina) with the minor sop that they could retrieve the funds if they submitted satisfactory desegregation plans within sixty days. In making the announcement, however, Finch adopted language dictated by the White House that still left the controversy open, saying it would be his intent "to reassess all of the department's procedures to develop policies which will encourage negotiations, provide flexibility and fairness, and assure enforcement of the law consistent with the interpretation the President repeatedly expressed in the campaign."

The fact that Harry Dent had not been able to turn back HEW in a decision affecting his own state did not go unnoticed by southern Republicans, who rallied behind Mississippi state chairman Clarke Reed in an effort to force the administration to reverse its position. For the next four months HEW and Justice Department officials worked under intense political pressures to find a compromise that would meet Finch's desire to satisfy the law and Mitchell's desire to make good the President's campaign promises. Apparently looking to the South for a sign of good faith, Mitchell announced on June 26 that the administration would oppose extension of the landmark 1965 voting rights act when it came before Congress later in the year. The administration offered a number of reforms, including elimination of voting tests in all states, but the key provision lay in Mitchell's proposal to delete the requirement that all changes in state voting statutes be cleared with the Department of Justice prior to enactment. The proposal immediately drew intense opposition from civil rights activists in and out of Congress, including Senate Republican whip Hugh Scott, who called it "a step backward" that would "take the heat off states which discriminate by giving the federal government a much heavier burden of proof."

Whatever intentions Mitchell might have had, he exacerbated the heightened suspicions that the Nixon administration would compromise basic civil rights for the sake of partisan political advantage. Thus, when Mitchell and Finch finally announced their "revised guidelines" on July 3, liberals read the worst possible interpretation into the event. Despite the fact that the administration refused to extend the 1969–70 deadlines for school desegregation that Southerners had expected — saying only "there may be sound reasons for some limited delay" — the reaction in the civil rights community was generally hostile. Apparently embarrassed by his earlier favorable prediction about the Nixon administration, Roy Wilkins told the NAACP convention at Jackson, Mississippi, that the administration was guilty of "breaking the law." Southerners, on the other hand, quickly realized that Nixon had failed to meet their demands, which led ultimately to repeated charges during his first term that Nixon gave conservatives all the rhetoric and none of the policies they demanded.

In an unrelated tactical maneuver to keep John Stennis happy as leader of the ABM floor fight, the administration managed to heat up the desegregation issue again by intervening on behalf of thirty-three Mississippi school districts that faced the loss of federal funding in a case pending before a court of appeals. This unprecedented action — pitting the federal government against integration — coincided with the announcement of Clement Haynsworth as the President's choice to replace Abe Fortas on the Supreme Court and with the publication of Kevin Phillips's book.

These three events stirred up a reaction among liberal and moderate Republicans. Senate Republican leader Hugh Scott joined other moderate party officials to denounce publicly the southern strategy in no uncertain terms. Though publicly uncommitted on the Haynsworth nomination, he refused to work for the administration position and ultimately cast a vote with the majority against the President's choice.

By the fall of 1969, the administration's attempts to make a policy gesture toward the South — which looked like a southern strategy in the making — and the continuation of the war in Vietnam brought about a split between the President and the Republican moderates, especially in Congress. The conservatives moved quickly to exploit this situation. Since the moderates held most of the policy positions and the conservatives many of the public relations positions, the contest within the administration between moderates and conservatives took the form of a contest between substance and rhetoric. Rhetoric won. The President was easily persuaded to mount a counterattack upon his critics, and the conservative rhetoricians became the focus of administration attention as they supplied the ammunition. The policy approach to government was replaced by a rhetorical approach, and, one by one, the positive positions that had been advocated during the opening months of the administration were quietly shelved. After all, the positive policies of the domestic council had angered the conservatives. The conservative policies of the southern strategy had angered the moderates. It seemed logical to shift to public relations as a way out of such difficulties.

In this fashion the conservatives established their ascendancy within the White House and began to implement a strategy to destroy the Democratic coalition, not with policies (which they could not implement because their power within the administration was not in the policy realm) but with public relations efforts. Agnew became both the vehicle and the symbol of this attempt, which, characteristically, turned into an attack not so much on the policies but on the personalities and political life style of the opposition (or on what the opposition symbolized).

From this point on it was downhill for the Moynihans, the Romneys, the Hickels, the Volpes, and other policy-oriented members of the administration. Moynihan's departure did not actually take place until after the 1970 election, but his eclipse began much earlier. His replacement by John Ehrlichman as chief of the Domestic Affairs Council in the fall of 1969 was highly symbolic of this entire process of splitting rhetoric from substance — a policy that the President's closest political adviser, John Mitchell, dramatized by saying, "Watch what we do, not what we say."

THE ATTACK

During the first nine months of the new administration, Agnew had fit in well with the positive Nixon approach to government. As he toured the country speaking on behalf of the Nixon program, he reiterated the belief he had stressed upon receiving his party's nomination, "that there is a better way to balance the complex relationship between federal, state and local government than is presently being exercised. I know that federal government must work more constructively, creatively, and above all more simply in meeting the problems of prejudice and poverty in our cities." As late as October 11, 1969, at a Republican fund-raiser in Montpelier, Vermont, he had stressed reform, closing his speech with a commitment to liberal principles: "We must make our cities livable, our environment pure, focus the power of our brilliant technology on the problems of hunger, health and housing in America and throughout the world." Eight days later, however, he completely shifted his approach.

Speaking in New Orleans, Agnew lashed out at the liberal leadership of the Vietnam Moratorium as "an effete corps of impudent snobs who characterize themselves as liberal intellectuals." Then, moving on to a Republican dinner in Jackson, Mississippi, on October 20, he set the pattern that would be repeated continuously in campaign speeches through the 1970 elections. While denying the administration was pursuing a southern strategy, he claimed that "for too long the South has been the punching bag for those who characterize themselves as liberal intellectuals." Through guilt by association, he linked these unnamed critics with radicalism: "This group may consider itself liberal, but it is undeniable that it is more comfortable with radicals." Furthermore, he stated flatly, "These are the ideas of the men who are taking control of the Democratic party." Then, surpassing Kevin Phillips himself, Agnew

36

made his final partisan pitch: "In my judgment, the principles of most of the people of Mississippi are the principles of the Republican party. . . . I believe that most of the people of Mississippi now belong in the Republican party."

The effect of the Agnew barrage was dramatic and predictable. The hard-line conservative ideologues who had hammered away at the Nixon reform program loved the new administration style, while administration critics were naturally thrown on the defensive. The war issue became mixed up with the issue of demonstrations as Agnew turned away from defending the President's actions in Vietnam to attacking his critics. In Harrisburg on October 30, he articulated a policy of "positive polarization" and concluded, "America cannot afford to write off a whole generation for the decadent thinking of a few. America cannot afford to divide over their demagoguery . . . or to be deceived by their duplicity . . . or to let their exercise destroy liberty. We can, however, afford to separate them from our society — with no more regret than we should feel over discarding rotten apples from a barrel."

The White House kept its public distance from Agnew until word came pouring in that his rhetoric was having its intended effect by firing up party loyalists and putting the administration's critics on the defensive. On October 30, the very day of the Harrisburg attack, the President publicly backed Agnew as "doing a great job for the administration." Such an admission was tantamount to abandonment of any "new alignment for American unity" in favor of a strategy of polarization.

The Agnew rhetoric was not a defensive reaction to events of the moment. Instead, it was a calculated effort to revive a specifically conservative realignment in American politics. Both the language and the object of the Agnew attack were well known to Goldwater ideologues, who believed they had carried out a holy crusade against the eastern liberal establishment and their allies in the press. The words themselves were provided clandestinely by presidential speechwriter Patrick J. Buchanan, a long-term conservative activist. Like the Goldwater campaign, the administration seemed to advance on the premise that there was a conservative majority waiting to be mobilized. All that needed to be added was the strategy, worked out by Agnew's staff over the summer, to impale the Democrats on the stake of upper-middle-class privilege. The southern strategy was, in fact, a national strategy to align middle-class whites against the Northeast in particular and "kids" and blacks in general.

The President's Vietnam speech of November 3, 1969, designed in large degree to counter demonstrations, appeared to be an abandonment of the conciliatory approach he used in May and a hard line against his critics: "North Vietnam cannot defeat or humiliate the U.S. Only Americans can do that." Advocates of the Agnew approach attributed increased support for Nixon's Vietnam policy to the administration's hard line, while ignoring that the same speech detailed extensively all the positive things he had done to achieve peace by negotiation. Whatever the immediate effect on the public, the administration had embraced seriously a strategy that divorced its rhetoric from its own policies. Once Agnew had politicized the Vietnam issue and the President had accepted the politicization, every subsequent action gained the aura, to some degree, of political manipulation. If the policies had followed the rhetoric, those for whom the rhetoric was intended might have responded positively, but in the end, the administration boxed itself in with rhetoric that alienated those who tended to take it seriously while not reaching those who were more inclined to await policy implementation beyond the rhetoric. This phenomenon reached its culmination during the campaign of 1970.

The First Disaster

The spring of 1970 was certainly an eventful one. The desegregation controversy flared up again, with the President making statements supporting the southern position but pursuing the more moderate policies directed by the Supreme Court. He directed symbolic acts toward the South with the firing of Leon Panetta and the proposed appointment of G. Harrold Carswell. Conservative ascendancy in this policy area became increasingly clear, yet the Nixon actions had to remain more symbolic than real because of bureaucratic pressures and court decisions.

The Cambodian invasion produced further shock waves and created additional alienation between the President and the moderates. By this time it was clear that, despite Nixon's sagging opinion polls, the policy of polarization would continue because he had turned his political apparatus over to the conservative strategists.

Nineteen seventy also saw the rise to power of Murray Chotiner, Nixon's 1950 and 1952 campaign manager. Originally slated for a post at the Republican National Committee that Rogers Morton refused to approve, Chotiner had been shelved for a year in the office of the Special Representative for Trade Negotiations before moving to the White House in January. Though he kept a low profile during his first few months on the job, by June he was reported "as the single most reliable and influential political channel to the President inside the White House" by columnist Marianne Means. In the absence of any overall planning for the fall campaign, Chotiner moved in, assuming responsibility for thirty-one states, while Harry Dent covered the other nineteen. Most important, Chotiner brought to the campaign the aggressive style he had made famous in California. Garry Wills quotes Chotiner as once remarking, "There are many people who say we want to conduct a constructive campaign and point out the merits of our own candidate. I say to you in all sincerity that, if you do not deflate the opposition candidate before

38

your own candidate gets started, the odds are that you are going to be doomed to defeat."

Not one to dwell on administration difficulties, Chotiner decided that the Republicans should put their opponents on the defensive, to deflate them before they could exploit administration problems, particularly in the economy where unemployment had risen from 3.9 percent in January to 5.1 percent in August. Thus the key to the campaign would lie in diverting public attention away from bread-and-butter issues to more intangible and symbolic issues such as crime, drugs, pornography, and permissiveness (these issues in themselves are not necessarily symbolic, but the use made of them was). Barry Goldwater had already tested such an approach in 1964 by appealing to people's status concerns over their economic self-interest. Kevin Phillips's book was full of examples of how cultural changes affecting the white middle class could be exploited by the GOP. A companion book directed at the Democratic party by Richard Scammon and Ben Wattenberg, *The Real Majority*, isolated the "social issue" of crime and the related issue of permissiveness as potential campaign material. All that remained was the implementation of the Agnew strategy of "deflating" opponents through guilt by association.

The GOP opportunity appeared especially great in the Senate, where 24 Democrats and only 11 Republicans were up for reelection. As beneficiaries of the 1964 Johnson landslide and the 1958 Eisenhower recession, most of the Democrats had gained office by relative good fortune and could be considered vulnerable. To avenge his defeats on Supreme Court nominations in the Senate, the President gathered an impressive array of talent to fight the fall campaign. But it was clearly Spiro Agnew who was given the spotlight in the campaign to pick up the seven new Senate seats needed for a Republican majority.

The vice president opened his campaign on September 10 in Springfield, Illinois, by exploiting the "social issue." Taking as his target what he called radical liberals in the Senate, he hammered away at Democrats who were "guilty" of "a whimpering isolationism in foreign policy, a mulish obstructionism in domestic policy, and a pusillanimous pussyfooting on the critical issues of law and order." Agnew took the offensive in blaming Democratic spending for the country's economic ills, but the emphasis in his speech was on Democratic softness on crime, drugs, and pornography: "How do you fathom the thinking of these 'radical-liberals' who work themselves to a lather over an alleged shortage of nutriments in a child's box of Wheaties — but who cannot get exercised at all over that same child's constant exposure to a flood of hard-core pornography that could warp his moral outlook for a lifetime."

These were themes Agnew repeated endlessly throughout the fall campaign. In his travels through thirty states he conjured up all the evils imagined by the Far Right and blamed the Democrats for encouraging such problems. By October he had added Republican Senate candidate

39

Charles Goodell to his list of "radiclibs" scheduled for defeat, saying in Minot, North Dakota: "When a man continually takes positions contrary to his own party's official views, his party label does not shield his apostasy." When Republican chairman Rogers Morton came to Goodell's defense, Agnew responded by dismissing his fellow Marylander as a "mere party functionary."

The President himself maintained his relative political distance from the Agnew campaign, but with four special assistants (Safire, Buchanan, Anderson, and Harlow) assigned to the Agnew entourage, his office clearly maintained control. He told a House luncheon group in September he was not going to take a major role in the forthcoming campaign. But as reports came in that the public was tiring of the Agnew style (the October Harris survey found that Agnew had declined four points in the ratings since he started the campaign) and as the economy continued to worsen, the President committed himself to a major campaign schedule through November. He consulted with neither party chairman Morton nor John Mitchell about the extent or the nature of his activity. He decided in virtual isolation to campaign not just in critical states with good Republican prospects as he had in 1969, but to intervene wherever he felt he could make a difference. Furthermore, he decided not to take his reform program to the American people, but rather to engage in an Agnewesque attack on student demonstrators. Though he usually mentioned briefly his proposal for welfare reform, other proposals for revenue sharing, minority enterprise, and his grand scheme of foreign policy were forgotten. From the moment of his first speech in Burlington, Vermont, where security officials were ordered to allow a small portion of a student demonstration to enter the area where the President spoke, Nixon used the students as an excuse to rally his audience to stand with "the great Silent Majority."

The Nixon-heckler duel culminated in San Jose on October 29, when demonstrators responded to Nixon's provocative victory gesture by throwing rocks at the presidential party. It was a shocking event, one that might well have rallied public support to the office and the man who held it. But the decision to use the event politically by rebroadcasting the President's hard-line response in Phoenix the next day made it seem almost as if the administration were relishing it. On election eve voters were treated to a Republican-sponsored fifteen-minute black-and-white tape with an imperfect sound recording that GOP National Finance Chairman Jeremiah Milbank said "made the President sound like Donald Duck," followed by a sober and technically perfect response from Senator Edmund Muskie asking for a repudiation of the Republican "politics of fear."

The final result of the 1970 campaign was anything but the kind of GOP triumph many Republicans expected as a by-product of their return to national power. They picked up a net gain of only two Senate seats while losing eleven gubernatorial seats and a number of legislatures. Even in the South, where the hard-line approach might have been expected to work, Republicans lost four out of five Senate races and six of seven contested governors' seats.

The President chose to present a brave front, claiming in public and private that "the election, ideologically, was enormously successful" and that "you can give your friends in the press odds on the presidential success in 1972." Yet his reelection prospects never seemed dimmer. His standing continued to slip in the polls so that in December, following his political exposure in twenty-three states during the election campaign, his approval rating fell to a new low of 52 percent. A Gallup poll for October showed a dramatic waning of traditional Republican strength as it reported, for the first time in its history, that a larger percentage of professionals and businessmen called themselves Democrats than Republicans. Even Kevin Phillips, who had left the administration to write a syndicated newspaper column, sought to disassociate himself from the 1970 brand of Nixon politics. Accurately assessing what had happened, he wrote: "You can't build an administration on slogans. Slogans come back at you after a while. . . . The administration didn't enter the campaign with much of a record, so they had to indulge in name calling."

Policy Once More

Brave assertions to the contrary, President Nixon regarded the 1970 performance as a debacle. Strategic politics had failed; the rhetoric had not worked. As a result, he reverted to a policy-oriented approach to government. In effect he returned to the themes of governmental reorganization and efficiency that he had stressed two years before and had abandoned during the campaign year of 1970. The problem was that these themes that had held so much promise before, and that might have pulled the country together had they been carried through, no longer appealed to a party and to an electorate becoming increasingly strategized. The southern strategy, the war rhetoric, and the symbolism of the "social issue" had taken their toll with both party and public.

By stressing positive programs, however, the President once again appealed to a centrist coalition. He announced plans to consolidate volunteer programs into one "action" agency that would publicly embrace the idealism and even the ferment of youth. He also sought to erase his image as the architect of exclusionary politics, and proposed a Republican party of the open door, "open to all people, all parties, all faiths, all races." Then, in his second State of the Union address, he returned to the grand themes of his 1969 message to the nation's governors and wove together all the elements of his domestic reforms into a proposal for a "new American revolution." To his past appeals for welfare reform,

41

revenue sharing, and environmental protection he added the goals of improved health care, full employment through an expansionary budget, and an extensive program of governmental reorganization. "Tonight," he said, "I shall ask not simply for more new programs in the old framework. I shall ask to change the framework of government itself — to reform the entire structure of American government so we can make it fully responsive to the ends and wishes of the American people."

Despite its rather overblown rhetoric, the Nixon approach promised a major breakthrough in policy formation for long-range goals — a stark contrast to the short-run strategic considerations of the 1970 campaign. The central theme was that the American people's disillusionment with governmental inefficiency and waste demanded major structural reforms. This was a restatement of the Drucker thesis, which had served as a model for his earlier reform proposals and was the central thesis in the recommendations of an Advisory Council on Executive Organization, appointed by the President under the chairmanship of Roy L. Ash, president of Litton Industries.

The most appealing aspect of these reforms was the prospect of replacing the divisive targets of the fall campaign (crime, race, drugs, pornography, students) with less polarizing targets for unity (bureaucracy, rising taxes, decline in services, unresponsiveness). As Ripon president J. Lee Auspitz wrote in the *Washington Post* on January 24, 1971, "Most Americans, indeed, want participation, responsive government and managerial efficiency; most chafe at taxes and red tape. So there is no need to argue that Mr. Nixon has hit on a real issue. To be successful, however, he must make it a good government issue. He must actively seek the independent, largely middle-class constituency that has fallen away from him in the past year."

Good government issues, however, had a way of being lost in the more dramatic events surrounding the Nixon presidency, and, despite an initial flurry of publicity for the governmental reorganization proposals, little was done in the White House to sell either the Congress or the public on the reforms. And because little was done, the proposals themselves began to look more and more like public relations gimmicks.

Back to Public Relations and Election Strategy

The policy phase of 1971 was in fact short-lived as the administration quickly turned its energies in other directions. The Pentagon papers case and the President's intervention on behalf of Lieutenant William Calley provided diverting possibilities, and the desegregation issue surfaced again as the courts continued to apply the dictates of the 1968 Green decision. The pattern of the past repeated itself. The moderate and progressive proposals remained the administration's policy line; the conservative rhetoric remained its public relations posture. Neither group was satisfied. The moderates were annoyed because their policy proposals, while endorsed, were seldom enacted. The conservatives were annoyed because their rhetoric had no basis in policy. The public was also annoyed. In the spring of 1971 the President dropped below 50 percent approval rating in the Gallup index. The result of this dissatisfaction was a revolt within his party.

The southern strategy, the Vietnam episodes, and especially the campaign of 1970 had made the two wings of the Republican party more conscious of their bargaining relationship to the President. They had become partially strategized, and each in its own way began to threaten to withhold its support from Nixon should he not direct his policies and attention their way.

During the spring of 1971 a group of progressive Republicans who had objected strenuously to the administration's regressive policies on civil rights and its unwillingness to cut its ties with the Thieu government in Vietnam started talking publicly of forming a Republican insurgency. "The party of Lincoln is now fiddling with a 'southern strategy' of sophisticated racism that appeals to the baser instincts of the American people," former Senator Charles Goodell wrote in the *New York Times* on May 14. "The President must face the reality that a Republican movement is arising that wishes him to be a great and progressive President, but will shake his political foundation if he is unresponsive." Buoyed by an enthusiastic Republican reception in Minnesota, Goodell joined with Congressmen Donald Riegle of Michigan and Paul McCloskey of California in a series of antiwar speeches around the country. They counted heavily on enlisting New York Mayor John Lindsay in their cause. But well before he switched parties in October, Lindsay revealed his disinterest in challenging the President from within the GOP. Ultimately it was McCloskey who made the decision to test Nixon's policies in the New Hampshire primary.

But the conservatives were also in open revolt by 1971. From the beginning the Republican right wing had voiced concern over Nixon's more progressive policies. The July 1970 issue of *Battle Line*, a publication of the American Conservative Union, warned that liberals inside the administration were in the process of taking over: "Conservatives are dwindling from the White House staff and few were ever in evidence in the departments. Rumor has it that the few that remain have finally come to the realization that they have been outflanked on every side by Ripon liberals and dedicated 'moderate' Republicans of the Rockefeller-Javits variety. Calls have gone out for outside conservative help — pressure, noise — anything to swing the balance away from the left." In January 1971, representatives of the ACU, *National Review,* and *Human Events* held a "conservative summit meeting" to draw up plans for swinging the administration to the right. By midsummer *Human Events* had escalated its anti-Nixon position, claiming on July 17 that he was "severely weakening the philosophically conservative underpinnings of the GOP." On July 26, nine days after the President announced his plans to visit the People's Republic of China in 1972, twelve conservatives including representatives of *Human Events,* the ACU, the Young Americans for Freedom, and *National Review*'s William Buckley announced their decision to suspend support of the President. Besides the new China policy, they listed as grievances the Family Assistance Plan, deficit spending, and inadequate defense appropriations. Like the insurgent Republicans on the Left, they hinted at the prospect of fielding a presidential candidate in the 1972 primaries. (Details of their activities appear in Chapter 14.)

The administration response to public criticism from both wings of the party was instructive. Having carefully built up the China breakthrough over a two-year period, Nixon could hardly back away from an initiative that he felt was crucial to a settlement in Vietnam.

So the President offered a sop to the right wing by reviving, in dramatic form, his opposition to school busing. Significantly he made this move at the critical juncture between the announcement of his new China policy and the announcement of his new economic policy, with its reliance on wage and price controls, which he must have recognized would enrage traditional conservatives. On April 20, 1971, the Supreme Court had ruled unanimously (*Swann* v. *Charlotte-Mecklenburg Board of Education*) that busing was a legitimate tool to end desegregation and, more specifically, it struck down the administration's support of the neighborhood school concept. Despite the fact that the Swann decision offered the possibility of extensive crosstown busing in the North as well as the South, the President did not initially contest the court's interpretation as he had in the past. Instead he told Mitchell and his new secretary of HEW, Elliot Richardson, to stress cooperation with the South but to complete the job of eliminating the dual school system before the 1972 campaign started. By midsummer HEW had warned sixty-four school districts that they should move to increase the desegregation of their classes before they opened in the fall. Noting Mitchell's approval for an extensive busing plan for Austin, Texas, the *Washington Post*'s Peter Milius speculated on May 20, "It may just be that, in the field of school desegregation, at least, the southern strategy is a thing of the past." But on August 3, the President denounced his own administration's plan for desegregating Austin's schools. He announced that the Justice Department would intervene against the HEW plan in Austin, and that he was instructing HEW Secretary Richardson, who had already been embarrassed by the reversal of policy, to submit legislation to Congress expressly prohibiting the expenditure of desegregation funds for busing. The President, in a highly symbolic act, also authorized his press secretary to warn government officials to conform to the administration's anti-busing policy or face the loss of their jobs.

In August came the dramatic economic announcement of Phase I. At last the President was pursuing a *policy*, and there was a substantial upturn in his popularity ratings. But the conservative threat still seemed both real and extensive, and the administration moved to meet it. The Ashbrook candidacy was largely symbolic, but behind it on the Right loomed the imponderable of Wallace. In quick succession came a series of concessions to Ronald Reagan on welfare, the veto of the OEO extension bill with its child-care provision, and a near-endorsement of Vice President Agnew for renomination. The conservatives pressed their attack, reasoning that the more pressure they put on the President, the more he would move in their direction. The *New Guard* summarized their policies in a March 1972 editorial:

> The President has generally given the liberals the action and the conservatives the rhetoric, and last year we didn't get much of that. From a foreign policy that includes deteriorating national defenses and the China disaster, to a domestic policy that includes FAP and wage and price controls, the President has fulfilled some of the wildest fantasies of liberal dreamers. . . . A major part of the Ashbrook strategy is not so much to defeat the President — in San Diego or November — as it is to pressure him to conservative action. . . . The President responds not to behind the scenes pressure, but to public, vehement disagreement. It is in every conservative's interest to see that things like the veto of the Child Development Act and the decision to keep Agnew on the ticket continue to happen, and the Ashbrook candidacy is the best means of doing so.

Basically the President seemed to be in a serious dilemma. With conservatives and liberals within his own party challenging him on domestic and foreign policies respectively and with his domestic program largely shelved for a return to symbolic and rhetorical strategies, his political position seemed precarious indeed. He saved himself only by the most spectacular exercise of foreign policy. His dramatic journey to Peking, coincident with the New Hampshire primary, his successful mining of Haiphong Harbor, and the mission to Moscow all sharply propped up his public position and helped quiet Left and Right simultaneously. Holding the political initiative with these dramatic events, he was able to snuff out the McCloskey and Ashbrook candidacies and present the image, at any rate, of a united party.

Significantly, however, the President continued to tailor his public image not to long-range considerations but to the political expediencies of the moment, which were dictated increasingly by the candidacy of George McGovern. First, the President, after reviving his drive for welfare reform in the spring of 1972, abandoned his position after McGovern managed to hang himself on the issue. Then, when the White

House learned in advance of the Eagleton problem, the President made one of his most fateful decisions — to keep Vice-President Agnew on the ticket. In the end, it was the foreign policy achievements of the administration, the proficiency of CREEP, and especially the weaknesses of McGovern that enabled the President to overcome the liabilities of his approach to governing. The reckoning came afterward.

When President Nixon faced George McGovern in the fall of 1972, he had established a highly consistent and dramatic foreign policy and an extraordinarily checkered domestic record where progressive policies had been proposed, but not pushed, and conservative rhetoric had been employed, but not embodied extensively in concrete legislation or practice. As Jeffrey Bell wrote in the *New Guard*,

> To the American electorate, and not just conservatives, the Nixon administration projects radical uncertainty if not outright schizophrenia. A special Nixon quirk which accentuates this impression is his tendency to clothe liberal policies in conservative rhetoric, and conservative policies in liberal rhetoric.

This discontinuity between policy and politics on the domestic level was a confession that the administration had found it necessary to patch together an ad hoc and probably temporary coalition with a series of short-term tactical maneuvers. No coherent domestic political strategy or performance was devised that could deliver either to a Republican constituency or to a larger constituency, as the 1972 party platform revealed. Dictated to the delegates in Miami by John Ehrlichman and his staff, it enhanced the contradiction between progressive policies and conservative rhetoric by embracing both elements. It included, as expected, a full litany of Nixon achievements, including the new China policy, the Nixon doctrine, the volunteer army, revenue sharing, welfare reform, minority enterprise, and "hometown plans" for minority employment in the building trades. Also included, however, were passages in the Agnew style lashing out at McGovern as the "radiclib" target of 1972, a man guilty of wanting to get out of Vietnam even if it meant turning it over to the communists, who wanted to reduce military spending below the peril point, who was weak and permissive on law and order, and who voted inflationary appropriations to domestic spending bills: "We categorically reject the slash-now, beg-later approach to defense policy. . . . We declare ourselves unalterably opposed to a unilateral slash of our military power, and we reject a whimpering 'come back America' retreat into isolationism." Once again a voter could read into the GOP statement

46

what he wanted. He could have largely progressive policies or largely conservative rhetoric.

These practices of the Nixon administration are instructive. It came forth with grand schemes, new alignments, new revolutions, new majorities, and other genuinely innovative proposals but then quickly shelved them when their public relations value declined. Often it reverted to them again, but seldom did it stick to a given policy or set of policies with persistence; its priorities were forever changing. The Nixon people failed to realize that the creation of a genuine New Alignment, New Majority, or whatever, is a very difficult task. It is not impossible to achieve, but it requires a great deal of coherence and persistence. Building a majority is not the kind of enterprise that can succeed when a set of policies is promulgated, popularized, shelved, repromulgated, repopularized, and reshelved with alternative approaches and sheer rhetoric sandwiched between each move. The only way a lasting majority can be built is when the members of that majority have sufficient time to settle down with it on the basis of a lasting and continuous delivery to their interests on terms that in the long run also reflect the interests of the country as a whole.

What is happening in America is the reverse. By responding on an ad hoc basis to the opportunities of the moment, political strategists at all levels are increasing the fluidity of the electorate. The more the politician bounces back and forth the more he encourages the voter to do so as well. If the electorate has no fixed set of policies to respond to, no consistent set of practices to evaluate, or no philosophically coherent doctrines to identify with, then no lasting or stable arrangement can occur. By definition, a new majority requires a focal point for its loyalties. But that focal point can never be a shifting set of strategies and it can never be a set of largely incompatible policies made possible by emphasizing one at one time, another at another, or both simultaneously to different audiences. Neither the record of the first four years nor the campaign for reelection provided the necessary foundation for a lasting majority since both were dominated by highly strategic approaches to politics.

Even more important has been the effect on the government itself. The commitment to short-term strategies and the open-ended perspective gave a decided advantage to the public relations expert in his contest with the policymaker, who had to look at more long-range objectives and who had to live with the results of his efforts. Policymaking has a long time lag from initial decision to final implementation. Public relations has comparatively no time lag at all. If immediate success is needed, public relations is the answer; it is so much easier to manipulate appearances than to manipulate realities.

But realities come home in the long run, and the longer the wait the worse the awakening. There is such an artificiality about strategic game playing that it bears little resemblance to what the government ought to be doing. The initial advantage that the game player has over the policy-maker will disappear in the long run — when those realities come home. The problem for the strategic politician is that his games will be increasingly reminiscent of Renaissance politics, court intrigues, and Fourth Republic decadence: long on schemes and strategies, short on actual accomplishments. He will earn the contempt, not the respect, of the country. With the ability of the White House to perform called seriously into question, power will gravitate to those who can perform, namely, the permanent bureaucracies. They have already been the beneficiary of Watergate. They will be the future beneficiaries of further political game playing. It is terribly ironic, but attempts by the Nixon White House to accrue power by augmenting its image resulted instead in a diminution of its authority. All its narrow strategies failed either to build a political majority or to establish a power base from which to govern. Instead, they contributed to its decline as an institution of democratic government. And that is the real tragedy of the Nixon presidency.

3

The Logic of CREEP

If governing is rapidly becoming a gigantic game justified by the logic of strategic thinking, then elections are becoming even more so. Nineteen seventy-two was certainly quite a year for the players on both sides.

It may seem surprising to refer to an electoral contest as simply a game, and when that contest is for the presidency of the United States it may seem all the more surprising. But this is, in fact, the case. The candidate himself and many of his followers may take a more exalted view of their activities, but the managers and strategists who run the campaign suffer from no illusions about the object of their employment. They are hired (or recruited) to engineer a win.

This is certainly not all bad, but it does raise the question of what an election campaign is for in the first place. To the voters, presumably, it is an opportunity to familiarize themselves with the candidates and the issues so that they can make a judgment on election day. It is also an opportunity to receive an education about the conditions of the country. It is good entertainment, and participation of any sort can be enormous fun.

Although theorists of democracy may not totally agree, there is one more dimension to the contest that is a healthy thing. In America, and only in America, an election is a test of the skill, resourcefulness, stamina, and strategic capacity of the candidate. It is a very open enterprise, and it should remain so. It is a classic example of the adversary process at work and it remains a symbol of a free-wheeling society that has become regimented in so many other ways. A political campaign without some game playing and maybe even a bit of chicanery would be downright un-American.

But there must be limits. Strategy run rampant can lead to sordid practices as it did in 1972. Adversary relationships that go beyond the bounds of democratic practice can subvert democracy. The problem is that some equivalence of opportunity must be maintained between the candidates and some modicum of honesty must be preserved if the campaign is to retain its value as a source of information for the voter. Within these limits, strategy can, and should, play a central role in modern politics. If these limits are transgressed — as they were in 1972 — then the whole enterprise ceases to be an exercise in democracy.

How did strategic thinking dominate the campaigns of 1972? In this chapter and the next we will examine the strategies of the Nixon campaign and will show how the legal practices of 1972 were logical outgrowths of these strategies. We discuss the illegal activities in Chapter 5; McGovern gets his due in Chapters 6 and 7.

There is one overall caveat, however. Reality is never as neat as logic would have it. Many of the strategic approaches were the product of subconscious as well as conscious mental activity. But there was nevertheless an underlying logic to what happened. That is the most important fact to remember about the politics of 1972: it was unreasonable but not at all illogical.

The Strategy of Reelection

THE STRATEGIC REQUIREMENTS

When two candidates or organizations are pitted against each other in conflict, the laws of strategy give decided advantages to the team that has the largest number of organizational options: the ability to be flexible in the face of changing events and the ability to score points in a vast range of separate subcontests across the larger chessboard. Presidential politics is a game played in many different arenas. There is a media contest, an issues contest, and a voter contact contest. There are interest group contests, geographic contests, and demographic contests. Limits to the number of contests are set only by the capacity of each organization and by the tolerance of the public. Sometimes an organization will fight its battles in one or two areas of selected conflict, but such a strategy may leave it at a serious disadvantage if the other organization has the capacity to win numerous small contests in other areas. The point is that good political strategy often requires that a campaign plan provide for the flexibility to contest the opponent in all possible areas if the resources are available to do so.

50

Traditional Republican approaches to past presidential elections severely constrained the options of the central decisionmakers. Their instrumentalities were limited to control over the candidate's schedule, the speeches or pronouncements of the ticket, and the national media programs that presumably orchestrated the issues and styles of the presidential and vice presidential contestants. They occasionally set up special divisions for certain purposes, but these often came into conflict with local party officials and created more trouble than they were worth. For voter contact, for appeals to special groups, for election day activities, and for the performance of many other functions, the central managers had to rely upon the competence and enthusiasm of the vastly differing state and local party structures.

The Democrats enjoyed advantages in this respect. In 1960 Kennedy created an organization of some size and central control, but even this famed machine relied on the local parties and the abilities of a few men like Robert Kennedy, Larry O'Brien, and their staffers to compensate where possible for vast ranges of organizational incompetence. The union effort of 1968 was also a more centralized operation, but it too had severe limits and was effectively outside the control of the Humphrey central managers.

As the campaign of 1972 unfolded and McGovern became the probable nominee of the Democrats, the Nixon managers feared that the senator's organization, with its large lists of enthusiastic supporters, might well achieve a strategic advantage and create for the first time a truly centralized national campaign effort. It did not do so, but the fear that it might was the primary incentive for the Nixon managers to anticipate this eventuality by creating a national machine that would operate with a very high degree of organizational flexibility. When the McGovern nomination became a certainty in early summer, these managers decided to create a vast series of instrumentalities so that they could wage a contest in many arenas and could mix their strategies to suit their requirements.

It was the creation of these strategic instrumentalities that enabled CREEP at its lower levels to engage in massive and aggressive warfare against George McGovern (which the extant party organizations in most cases could not have done) while the President and vice president waged a very nonaggressive, above-it-all noncampaign. Without the option of effective aggression at the lower levels, the managers would have been in a very difficult position at the higher levels when they came to define their media and issues strategy. This was why CREEP seemed logically necessary.

On a more specific level, what were the strategic requirements for victory? The candidacy of George McGovern presented CREEP with some very interesting possibilities, but there were risks as well as opportunities. McGovern, after all, had been the upset victor of a long and fascinating nominating process that had focused the attention of the politically aware for several months. He had come to power on a protest movement and he seemed to represent to both followers and public the kind of strength, freshness, honesty, and hope that the country had longed for during the entire spring. The fact that he was relatively unknown to the larger public was not necessarily a liability either, as he thereby had a relatively clean slate upon which to write his image. His record, to be sure, had some skeletons in it, but the public in July was largely unaware of them and competent management might turn some of them into assets. His supporters knew where he stood. Those who did not support him largely did not know him.

Furthermore, the President's own polls, as well as the surveys of the prestigious polling companies, indicated that the President's *firm* support still hovered around the low to mid-40s, where it had been for the previous three and a half years. The surge toward Nixon in the spring surveys was read as coming more from McGovern's unfamiliarity than from any single negative perception about the South Dakotan or any single positive perception about the President.

Also, McGovern boasted a large and efficient organization, a superb collection of competent, experienced, and dedicated workers who had just succeeded in parlaying a thin base of support into a dramatic convention victory by means of tactical and organizational superlatives. The risk was that McGovern could win a personality contest with the President while his organization skillfully manipulated the real discontent that had been so extensively catalogued over the past few years. Could his managers reassemble the Democratic coalition by means of timely and well-placed concessions? Could McGovern capitalize on the Wallace phenomenon, on the elusive peace, on the continuing unemployment rate, or on the youth revolt? Could he capitalize on black dissatisfaction, on the aspirations of Mexican Americans, or on distrust in government? Could the obviously gifted strategists in the McGovern camp somehow find a means of exploiting for their candidate the issues of crime, drugs, and racial discontent that the President's managers had counted on for theirs?

Yet the opportunities were also vast from the standpoint of Republican strategists. Every McGovern asset seemed to have an attendant liability. The fact that McGovern was unknown could well create a sense of uneasiness and mistrust. The fact that his movement seemed well organized and highly disciplined undercut his image of a warm personality. His candor, a definite asset, might become a liability if it led him to take positions that ran against the perceived interests of voting blocs. Most of all, however, the dedication of his supporters had been purchased at the price of extreme dissatisfaction among many members of his own party. If played right by the Nixon strategists and if misplayed by the Mc-

Govern camp, the circumstances of McGovern's nomination and the nature of his support might cleave the Democratic party in half and destroy once and for all the Roosevelt coalition, whose persistent refusal to die had been the wonder of politicians and observers alike in 1968 and 1970. The Nixon managers, however, were aware that their own record in exploiting such cleavages was not impressive. The rather clumsy attempts at dividing the Democrats in 1970 had served only to unite them, and the high-road policy of ignoring them in 1968 had done so little to destroy them that they had come within a hair of winning. Considering the potential in each of these two years, the results had been disastrous. Hence a genuine sense of caution mitigated to some extent the optimism of the Committee to Re-elect the President.

Confronting this melange of risks and opportunities, the President's managers made three fundamental strategic decisions. First, the image "asymmetry" between the President and the South Dakotan could be exploited and should be preserved. Second, the senator's positions on issues made him extremely vulnerable with large segments of his own party, but this vulnerability could be exploited if and only if these positions could be driven home to selected Democrats in a highly targeted way. Third, the McGovern organization was formidable and had to be neutralized with a large and effective counterorganization. The President's managers also made a number of decisions about their geographic allocation of emphasis and their relationship to certain friendly Democrats, but these three basic strategies governed the campaign from July to November. Even when it became apparent that they had overestimated the strength of the McGovern organization, they continued to act upon the presumption that they had a major organizational antagonist. Each strategy, in turn, was developed with a high degree of sophistication.

STRATEGY #1. *Preserve the image asymmetry and exploit it wherever possible.*

There was, to say the least, a high degree of asymmetry between the images of George McGovern and Richard Nixon: one wore the mantle of populism, the other of establishmentarianism; one had the gift of evangelism, the other the skill of pragmatism; one seemed compassionate, the other tough; one claimed to be "Honest George," the other avoided the designation of "Tricky Dick." One was new and promised change; the other was familiar and promised four more years of the same. Indeed, it seemed a choice.

Initially there was a real question about who would benefit from this asymmetry, for each set of attributes, if well developed, could become a decided asset, and if successfully exploited by the opposition, a decided liability. Populism, evangelism, compassion, candor, and freshness of spirit are issues that can form the basis of a successful political campaign against those who appear to be the opposite, as Democrats like Reubin Askew, Dale Bumpers, John Tunney, Adlai Stevenson, and others had demonstrated. Yet, on the other hand, under certain circumstances populism translates to radicalism, evangelism to extremism, compassion to weakness, candor to naïveté, freshness and the promise of change into undependability and the fear of change. Simultaneously, establishmentarianism can turn to patriotism, pragmatism to common sense, toughness to tenacity, shiftiness to cleverness, familiarity to security and the promise of stability. Quite often a subtle or symbolic sense of whether a man is or is not "worthy" or "good" makes the difference to such image perception and the entire set of values can shift very easily from positive to negative or from neutral to either in this most subtle game of image maneuvering. It is clear in retrospect that the Eagleton affair permanently shifted the electorate's mind on the question of McGovern in the negative direction, and at the time, both Nixon and McGovern managers easily measured this shift. Neither, however, could be certain of its permanence, especially in light of the vast image shifts that have been so highly documented in recent years. The memory of wide fluctuations in the popular image of Romney, Muskie, Kennedy, Humphrey, and Johnson, as well as Agnew and the President himself, had to dominate everyone's calculations.

After the Eagleton affair, the asymmetry of images was decidedly working to the President's advantage, although neither side could tell for how long. The major strategic task, therefore, was to preserve and reinforce this situation. By mid-August, McGovern was perceived as an extremist and a radical, as weak and naïve, as undependable and (a large bonus) incompetent as well. This negative image tended to reinforce the positive asymmetrical image of the President as voters, finding no alternative in McGovern, attempted to self-justify their only other logical option.

Reinforcing an opponent's negative image is not easy. The lessons of 1970 were very much in the minds of Republican strategists. The President's "campaign for sheriff," as John Mitchell had put it, and the vice president's campaign for hangman had alienated as many voters as they had attracted. A frontal attack on McGovern by either Nixon or Agnew was deemed dangerous. Such an attack might have led to two results: (1) It might have destroyed the image asymmetry and raised a credibility problem for the President. Nixon's own image was not secure at the time, and strong attacks on McGovern might not have appeared entirely plausible. McGovern himself had this problem later when, from a noncredible position, he attacked the President. Also, a reduction of the campaign to a slugfest or to a mud-slinging contest could also have easily destroyed the asymmetry of the situation and could have driven voters away in droves from both candidates. When a President appears to be a mere campaigner, he has lost significant ground. (2) Even more serious, the indiscriminate use of attacks by the President might have pre-

54

served the asymmetry but reversed its impact had the South Dakotan remained the calm and cool campaigner of the spring primaries. Mc-Govern might have emerged once more as populistic, evangelistic, candid, and fresh, while the President reverted to the negative dimension of the asymmetry. A reversal of this sort would have been very serious and not impossible in the age of television. It is well known how difficult television is to master and how imperfectly President Nixon has mastered it. A slashing attack can make the attacker himself seem extreme and noncredible. A slanting attack can make him seem silly. Under some circumstances, the attacked can even become ennobled.

Nor did it seem wise to let Agnew loose extensively. President Nixon may have difficulties with television, but the former vice president makes him look like Johnny Carson by comparison. Agnew is harsh and wooden. To many he has a nasty face and a cold, hard image. He angers and scares. On the tube he holds his constituency but risks alienating other constituencies. Television is not his medium and the extent to which he used it during the campaign was probably counterproductive. The episodes where he blew whistles at demonstrators looked downright silly, and the wisdom of those who "kept him on a leash" was confirmed by a Harris poll taken just before the election that showed Kennedy beating Agnew in a projected presidential confrontation.

The logic of the situation, then, required a very low key and almost nonexistent campaign by the President with a somewhat more visible, but still subdued, vice-presidential effort. A series of Nixon radio speeches, a few foreign policy accomplishments, and a series of optimistic White House releases on the state of the nation were all that were deemed necessary to preserve the President's favorable image. A gaggle of surrogate speakers was dispatched throughout the land to attack the South Dakotan, but the national ticket played the game very close to the vest.

Even though the Nixon strategists correctly declared it inadvisable to use the President and the vice president in exploiting the advantages of image asymmetry, the obvious vulnerabilities of McGovern cried out for special attention. The decision to pursue a very low key strategy with respect to presidential and vice presidential appearances was matched by the decision to pursue an aggressive advertising campaign and an even more aggressive organizational attack upon the image and the positions of the South Dakotan.

Although a frontal attack in advertising is somewhat less dangerous than a frontal attack by a President, there are still lurking problems. The possibility of a counterproductive sympathetic reaction is real, if more subdued. Furthermore, any attack upon a candidate is always dangerous unless highly credible, as McGovern was soon to learn. The Nixon strategists had learned this in 1970 from their disastrous attempt to portray the opposition as un-American, and in 1968 from their attempt to superimpose the picture of a jocular Hubert Humphrey over scenes of disaster and destruction.

The strategic task for the advertising campaign was twofold: to undermine McGovern's credibility and to detach him from Democratic loyalties. These mutually supporting strategies worked very well with the preservation of image asymmetry and also reached out to support the massive attack upon the Democratic party that CREEP mounted in its organizational activities.

The advertising strategy was almost entirely negative. It focused on issues, not personalities, but the issues were carefully selected to have a major impact on the image of McGovern. One of the most effective ads showed McGovern's face flipping and flopping back and forth as the narrator revealed the inconsistencies in several of his positions. Another displayed a number of toy soldiers, ships, and planes. As the narrator detailed McGovern's plans to cut the defense establishment, dozens of these toys were swept away, while President Nixon was shown majestically surveying the fleet. Yet another hammered away at McGovern's alleged extravagance on welfare and the resulting increase in taxes for the workingman. Each of these was tied to a specific issue, but the overall thesis of irresponsibility and naïveté gave the ads a strong personality impact as well, preserving the asymmetry of the situation to the advantage of the President. The use of *issues* as the vehicle for attacks, rather than *personalities,* minimized the risks.

There was also the question of loyalty. Loyalty had been one of the most important ingredients holding the Democratic party together. The worst nightmare for Republican strategists was the "return to the fold" scenario that had nearly cost Richard Nixon the election in 1968. The pollsters agreed, after all, that Nixon's basic support remained in the low- to mid-40 percent range: his inflated showings were fueled by anti-McGovern, not pro-Nixon, perceptions. If the strategic contest could be turned from a contest of personalities into a contest of party loyalty, for example, the return surge of 1948 and 1968 might well cause trouble. Therefore it was necessary to destroy the basic loyalty to the Democratic party that many groups still held and to counter the sporadic attempts that McGovern made to associate himself with it.

To accomplish this, Nixon strategists selected John Connally to lecture his fellow Democrats on the meaning and nature of loyalty. Despite the fact that he looks like and talks like Lyndon Johnson, Connally has a considerable magnetism on television. He comes across as a man who could make a fortune selling refrigerators to Eskimos. Moreover, the logic of Connally's message was sound: McGovern had disassociated himself from large portions of the Democratic party and hence he could be portrayed as disloyal. In a personal sense his disloyalty to Eagleton underscored his deficiency on the question. Therefore Democrats as Democrats should owe no loyalty to McGovern. Furthermore, he had disassociated himself so much from the party that it could almost become an act of loyalty to vote against him. This was the theme of the Democrats for Nixon, and the message, when coupled with McGovern's negative image, was very effective. Quotations from Humphrey and Jackson were used in the advertising of the Connally group to underscore the thesis that "the man is not a Democrat."

It is too much to suggest that the loyalty question was intended to branch out to other areas of loyalty — to white flags and Hanoi trips, to amnesty and criminal coddling — but these subtle psychological associations certainly worked well together with the basic image asymmetry that the organization strove so successfully to maintain.

STRATEGY #2. *Destroy the Democratic coalition by compartmentalizing the appeals.*

The exploitation of asymmetrical images and the Connally attack upon Democratic loyalties dominated the nationwide public relations strategy of the Nixon campaign. These were relatively safe issues; they had universal appeal and they were very effective. But to restrict a campaign to these areas would have been to miss many excellent opportunities to destroy the Democratic coalition, which seemed to have had surprising resiliency as recently as 1970. It is one thing to exploit the deficiencies of personality; it is another to undercut political alignment.

The Democratic party, with its diverse elements, had all sorts of potential for destruction in 1972, but the elements of each faction's discontent were so diverse that a general appeal or even a series of specific appeals broadcast nationwide would have had only limited impact. For instance, had CREEP emphasized the "social issues," such as drugs, patriotism, crime and busing, with sufficient virulence to shake loose large numbers of "hard hats" and traditional ethnics, it would have risked driving back to McGovern many of those liberal suburbanites in the Northeast who had deserted him on the competence issue. Or, had Nixon wished to emphasize with young voters the termination of the draft, the seeming end to the war, the China visit, and other innovations with sufficient strength to shake loose large numbers of young people from their alleged loyalties to McGovern, or at least their presumed predilection for him, then many conservative voters might have been driven to stay at home or to vote for Schmitz, or whatever. Or, had CREEP wished to emphasize a number of pro-labor positions with sufficient detail to shake loose large numbers of union members from their traditional loyalties, it might have risked the alienation and financial support of some members of the business community, especially in the South. Strategists could have detailed many other conflicts: farmer vs. consumer, farmer vs. migrant worker or Chicano, black vs. white, and others that underline the zero-sum nature of so many group configurations.

The problem is that with such configurations general appeals on almost any issue are, by definition, less efficient than compartmentalized or targeted appeals, since a general appeal of sufficient strength to move some voters in one direction will probably move others in the opposite direction. Of course, good strategy will ensure a net gain, but the potentials for gain remain much less for broad-scale appeals than for targeted appeals. This is the paradox of cutting issues.

In recent national campaigns the trend has been away from targeted appeals for several reasons. For one, press coverage of candidates is so intense that it guarantees a widespread degree of awareness on many issues and personalities. "His every word" is listened to. Any inconsistencies in statements or positions will be widely trumpeted by a press that considers it a special duty to report the foibles and failures of various candidates. When Henry Cabot Lodge delivered a speech in Harlem in 1960, for example, it was not unheralded in Georgia. Also, any attempts to localize or compartmentalize advertising will become widely known because such strategies are "news" and will be pointed out by the press or the opposition. And further, in presidential campaigns the economics of network media buys and the imperatives of stylistic and thematic unity dictate that a national advertising campaign focus upon a very narrow message or set of narrowly integrated messages developed from one posture. There are several diseconomies from what advertising experts call "scattering your fire." There is also at work here an iron law of specificity: when a candidate is very specific about an issue, those negatively affected will probably be more aware of the position than those positively affected, and it is usually easier to move people initially on a negative issue than on a positive one. It has become bad strategy to be specific because of this law and also because specific commitments limit your future options.

The point is that different groups are moved by different issues, and even if a menu of such issues was not internally inconsistent (in policy realization), the simultaneous emphasis of the entire menu would lead either to a "scattering of fire" or to a severe diminution of impact as the negative response in one area canceled out the positive response in another. The requirement is compartmentalization of emphasis — but can it be implemented? In 1970 a unimodal campaign was disastrous because it repelled almost as many as it attracted. The nature of the approach was itself ill-advised, if not downright reprehensible, but part of its failure was due to the fact that the requirements of national advertising and campaigning precluded compartmentalizing the appeal. The advertising and the campaign pronouncements then had to be directed at the total audience since there was no alternative. The party itself was not used for this purpose in 1970 because it was regarded by the White House as highly fragmented, incompetent, and incapable of carrying on the kind of targeted appeals necessary to break large numbers of Democrats away from the traditions of the past.

It was clear to the Nixon strategists that if a presidential campaign could compartmentalize its appeals, its strategic options would be vastly increased. If it could emphasize one issue with one group of voters, another with a second, and yet another with a third, it could select the salient issue to move each group and it would be vastly less troubled by either the iron law of specificity or the paradox of cutting issues. Of course, there could be no blatant inconsistencies between the various positions, for that would become publicized almost immediately, but if a certain level of consistency were maintained, then vast payoffs might occur because the efficiency of each appeal (voters moved per effort made) would be vastly increased.

In presidential politics, then, if the speeches of candidates and the appeals of media cannot be used to compartmentalize an appeal, what alternatives can be used to achieve this eminently desirable goal? First, the political power of the White House behind the scenes can be quite effective. Money can be spent selectively. Businesses and unions can be bought off by various concessions of the IRS or the antitrust division of the Justice Department. Quiet and selective legislation can be fostered. Yet direct and overt appeals are risky. The use of the White House in a blatant way to secure a President's reelection is still frowned upon by many voters. Such appeals may be politically counterproductive.

Second, the traditional parties that remain so decentralized might well be used, but they too have a number of liabilities. Their competence and discretion vary widely from state to state. Central control is effectively lacking. Furthermore, if the purpose of compartmentalization is to break loose Democrats from their party affiliation, a traditional Republican organization is not necessarily the best instrument for that enterprise. Therefore the logic of the situation required a new instrument of strategy, a highly organized and centrally directed machine that could target appeals and compartmentalize issues efficiently so that a strong message could be conveyed to one group while other groups were not annoyed by a conflicting interest or bored by a barrage of politics. This was the logic of CREEP: to create an instrument of strategy that could effectively compartmentalize appeals. Its numerous divisions and extensive departments are discussed below. Their rationale, however, was simply to provide the central strategists with the ability to have access to various voting groups in a direct, targeted fashion.

What groups were targeted, and what was the nature of each appeal? Table 1 indicates targeted groups, the issues emphasized and deemphasized, together with the tactics employed. The necessity for compartmentalization is made strikingly clear by the range of the appeals.

TARGETED GROUP	ISSUES EMPHASIZED	ISSUES DEEMPHASIZED	TACTICS EMPLOYED
Labor and "Ethnics"	Special favors to selected labor leaders; symbolic retreats on 14b and other related issues. Patriotism, the "social issue," the three A's of amnesty, acid, and abortion. McGovern's welfare stand	The economy, unemployment, cost of living, wage controls, Nixon's Family Assistance Plan, tax reform	Active "heritage groups," creating publicity and opinion leader conversions; targeted issues through speeches and pronouncements of group leaders, word of mouth, direct mail, special events, and ethnic advertising
Jews	Nixon support of Israel: McGovern's softness; law and order to some extent; the competence issue	Civil rights record; lack of Jewish appointments to office, to the Supreme Court, etc.	The Jewish division of CREEP to target voters in similar fashion to the "ethnic" division. Use of prominent Jewish supporters as surrogates (Kissinger, Max Fischer)
Blacks	Nixon initiatives for minority business; appointments of blacks to federal posts, federal aid to black colleges, and sickle cell anemia research	Civil rights record; Supreme Court appointments	Recruitment of black personalities by various means to create media events to show black support of Nixon. Pitch made to middle-class blacks
Spanish-speaking	Appointments of Chicanos to high government positions and conscious recruitment into middle-range positions (in contrast to Jews)	The economy; the plight of lower-class Chicanos	Middle-class Chicanos targeted with an aggressive "Hispanic" organization. Peer pressure, literature, and speeches by Nixon appointees
Youth	End to draft, end to war, China; lack of credibility of McGovern	Amnesty, acid, abortion	Aggressive group activity on campuses and in high schools; countering of peer

Group			
Elderly	Social Security; patriotism, stability, and continuity	Cost of living; veto of Social Security bill	Mailings to Social Security recipients; visits to nursing homes by groups of campaigners
Consumers	*Existence* of controls; *attempts* to solve inflation; *war* (war vs. peace economy); decrease of rate of increase of inflation	*Performance* of controls; inflation; farm prices	National media, nonemphasized
Farmers	Farm price increase; inflation of wholesale prices; wheat deal	Scandal aspects of milk subsidy rise and wheat deal	Medium target priority. "Farmers for the President" direct mail
Environmentalists	Creation of Environmental Protection Agency	Nixon opposition to much antipollution spending	Low target priority
Business	McGovern's instability, economic schemes, tax reform. Advantages of wage-price freeze. "Corporatism", and support for large failing businesses (Lockheed, etc.)	Stagnant economy; laissez-faire capitalism, inflation	White House, Justice Department and IRS activity; also the Business Division's recruitment drive
Traditional Liberals	McGovern's competence; China; Family Assistance Plan	Civil Fights; amnesty, acid, abortion; war's continuation	National media (nontargeted)
Traditional Conservatives	McGovern's positions; amnesty, acid, abortion; war's continuation	China; Family Assistance Plan	National media (nontargeted)
Veterans	Amnesty	China; veterans' benefits not being significantly increased	Targeted mailings and speeches

TABLE 1.
Nature of Appeals to Targeted Groups

This table reveals not just the advantages of compartmentalization but its total necessity if issues are to remain a part of modern strategic campaigning. The zero-sum dimensions of so many political issues and the inability of broad-based media campaigns to overcome such deficiencies will require massive organizations in the future in order to target issues. With such organizations, issues will remain a part of campaigns since they can be used to strategic advantage.

The table also reveals the basic vulnerability of the Nixon 1972 coalition. Had McGovern created the capacity to compartmentalize his appeals and had he not suffered from image problems, a massive counterattack could have been mounted. With labor and ethnics he could have emphasized unemployment; with Jews, Nixon's appointments and record on civil rights; with blacks, just about anything; with Chicanos, the economy; with youth, the war; with the elderly, the cost of living; with the farmer, scandal; with the environmentalist, the ravages of business; with business, the stagnant economy; with liberals, Nixon's civil rights record; with conservatives, reduction of the size of government, and so forth. Whether these appeals would have succeeded is another question, but McGovern was at a vast strategic disadvantage because his organization was never really equipped to make them. In the age of media, the direct, targeted, one-to-one appeal is still an extremely important instrument of strategy, and perhaps once more a dominant one. The creation of CREEP surmounted the problem of "his every word."

STRATEGY #3. *Match the McGovern organization with an effective counterorganization.*

The one great fear of the Nixon managers was that somehow McGovern would outorganize the President. They needed an effective organization not just to compartmentalize their appeals but also to match the Democrats doorbell for doorbell, phone call for phone call, brochure for brochure. Traditionally Republicans have relied upon the local parties for this sort of effort, but CREEP's managers concluded that the parties were generally inefficient, outmoded, and totally unreliable. Hence it was necessary to create a party to supersede the party. This strategy provided the second major justification for the massive CREEP effort.

In July the McGovern organization seemed to be monolithic, so a monolith was required to match it. The McGovern organization also appeared to be well disciplined, so good discipline was required to match it. The McGovern workers might have been amateurs to start with, but by then their middle management had acquired sufficient experience to be called professionals. So professionals were needed to match them.

When Clark MacGregor replaced John Mitchell as campaign director during the summer, he reallocated three million dollars that had been designated for media to build a grass roots organization. There were many other reasons why this move was considered sound. The issue of big money influence in the Nixon administration threatened to work in the Democratic nominee's favor. The Watergate affair put the spotlight on the role of fat cats in the Nixon campaign. A lavish use of television advertising by the Nixon effort would have risked generating a backlash and sympathy for McGovern as a "poor man's candidate." Moreover, McGovern had gained considerable mileage in the preconvention maneuvering from his people-oriented organization. By investing heavily in paid staff who would outwardly look the same as the McGovern volunteers and the subsistence salary McGovern employees, CREEP could neutralize both the organizational advantage and the emotional appeal of the McGovern movement.

CREEP, then, was created apart from and totally separate from the party except for several states, such as New York, where the party machinery was sufficiently competent to run the show itself. This created a problem of resentment in traditional party circles since CREEP and the local party came into conflict over scarce resources such as money and competent personnel. But the soothing abilities and compensating efforts of a sitting President solved for the Republicans the problems of competence vs. loyalty that the Democrats could never solve.

The Organization
to Implement the Strategy

To many on the outside, the Committee to Re-elect the President resembled a huge juggernaut, a machine well fueled by Maurice Stans's enormously productive, if sometimes embarrassing, fund-raising efforts. This impression was undoubtedly heightened by the contrast between the public facade of imperturbability that the Nixon organization presented and the all-too-visible backbiting and jockeying for position in the postconvention McGovern campaign.

In sheer size, massiveness of funding, and staff resources, the 1972 Nixon campaign organization was qualitatively different from anything that had been seen before in American presidential politics. The various Nixon committees raised over $60 million by the end of the campaign, and, in what must have been a political first, ended with both a surplus of several million dollars and a flock of money-starved, losing Republican candidates for various offices.

In fulfillment of Parkinson's law, Nixon's campaign expenditures rose to meet the opulent flow of Stans's fund-raisers. The CREEP bureaucracy in Washington reached a paid staff of about six hundred with countless additional junior executives serving at no cost while drawing full salaries from Washington banks, corporations, or trade associations. These full-time political employees and volunteers were but a portion of the Nixon campaign effort. The White House staff, political appointees throughout the government, and a fair number of middle level civil servants spent much of 1972 generating projects and publicity that would produce direct campaign benefits to the administration. This use of incumbency for campaign purposes was no innovation, but the Nixon team was much more thorough than any previous administration in exploiting its many possibilities.

Yet, despite the landslide election results, the formal 1972 Nixon campaign organization was hardly a model of efficiency. The Byzantine intrigues of various Nixon aides seeking to maneuver for power in the second term resulted in numerous delays and considerable confusion in organizing the campaign. The caliber and political knowledgeability of the campaign officials ranged from superb to laughable, and in the early stages of the campaign informed Republican politicians whispered their misgivings nervously to each other. Despite all its problems, however, the Committee to Re-elect the President was a masterful example of the new strategic politics.

CREEP began in late 1971 as a skeletal operation staffed by comparatively junior White House aides. Jeb Magruder, Harry Flemming, and Bob Odle were dispatched to the new headquarters one block from 1600 Pennsylvania Avenue, but the overall direction of the operation clearly resided with Attorney General John Mitchell, who ran CREEP while continuing his efforts to restructure the criminal justice system. Flemming, a confidant of Mitchell, traveled regularly to see the attorney general on virtually all important matters. The son of former HEW Secretary Arthur Flemming and the 1968 Virginia chairman for Nixon, he had been close to John Mitchell during the 1968 campaign. As a result of this friendship and his demonstrated reliability, Flemming was the first person assigned by the administration to the very important role of personnel recruitment and patronage dispensing. By 1971, his standing within the White House had slipped from its 1969 peak, but the young Virginian still enjoyed cordial relations with Mitchell.

Magruder and Odle both came to the campaign from Herb Klein's White House communications staff. Magruder, a graduate of Williams College and the University of Chicago Business School, had served under Klein as deputy director of communications, but was regarded as a protégé of Haldeman. Odle, another Klein aide and a social friend of the Nixon daughters, had earned his spurs in 1968 preparing delegate books.

Under the original setup, Flemming headed the "outside" or "people" portion of the organization. This included the storefront and other volunteer-oriented operations. Magruder was responsible for the "inside" operations such as media, telephone banks, and advertising. Mitchell resigned from the cabinet to become the director of CREEP, but the

Watergate episode forced his resignation shortly thereafter. Mitchell's fall completely scrambled the power relations within Nixon's campaign organization. Flemming, whose position had been the result of his relationship with Mitchell, sank into obscurity. He was given the unedifying role (particularly in this campaign) of being CREEP's liaison with Republican congressional and gubernatorial campaigns.

Mitchell's nominal successor as director of CREEP was Clark MacGregor. A Minnesota congressman, popular among his Hill colleagues, MacGregor had been chosen to direct White House–congressional relations after the 1970 election fiasco (when White House relations with Capitol Hill had hit rock bottom). He had managed during his year and a half in this post to melt some of the ice between the White House and Capitol Hill. Yet his role, unlike Mitchell's, was largely devoted to being a public spokesman and surrogate for Nixon. An articulate and intelligent man, MacGregor had shown his mettle in a spirited, losing, 1970 Senate campaign against Hubert Humphrey. Unfortunately for him, however, as soon as he assumed his new post, he was besieged with questions from the press about CREEP's involvement in the Watergate break-in. MacGregor's innocence concerning any of the Watergate plotting was a factor in his being chosen director, since he was about the only major White House politico who could tell the press truthfully that he knew nothing of the affair.

Although MacGregor was nominally in charge of CREEP and was in a position to make some significant decisions (such as the reallocation of media money to organizational efforts), he was mainly concerned with public relations and various "front" activities. After Mitchell left, the real power in the reelection effort remained at the White House and at the management levels just below MacGregor.

The role of the White House was understandably very extensive. The President himself, together with John Ehrlichman, H. R. Haldeman, sometimes Charles Colson, and usually John Mitchell, was responsible for the major strategic decisions such as the one to preserve a low presidential profile while waging aggressive organizational warfare against McGovern. The White House staff was mobilized for the campaign and large segments of the White House operation were involved with the massive use of federal resources to target areas of political potential.

A former head of the J. Walter Thompson advertising agency's Los Angeles office and a veteran of Nixon's California and national campaigns, Haldeman served as White House staff chief. He controlled all access to the President: the memos that reached the Oval Office and the all-important appointments schedule. His protégé and fellow Christian Scientist, John Ehrlichman, had become a power in his own right as the chief of staff to the increasingly powerful Domestic Council.

His staff reviewed and cleared both the advertising that concerned domestic policy issues and the domestic policy statements made by

65

administration campaign spokesmen. This was to ensure that they were accurate and consistent with the official administration line.

Colson was a Massachusetts Yankee lawyer-politician with all the kindly instincts of an enraged Boston dockworker. He enjoyed a warm relationship with the President, possibly because Nixon has an affinity for a natural gut fighter, but his record was somewhat spotty. In 1970 he had played a critical part in the disastrous effort to elect a Republican Congress. In fact, a Republican candidate in Utah had to apologize on television for a Colson-inspired advertisement. His one major success had been the peddling of a story to *Life* magazine that had helped to defeat Senator Joseph Tydings of Maryland. In 1972 he circulated a memorandum suggesting that he would do violence to his own grandmother if it would garner votes for Nixon.

The White House was responsible for the entire strategy of image maintenance and the whole panoply of public relations efforts that went with it.

First, the day-to-day management of the campaign was directed by an ad hoc committee called the Attack Group. Colson was its most influential member. The group was composed of an ideologically diverse but politically proficient group of operatives. In addition to Colson were Ken W. Clawson, who had been a first-rate *Washington Post* reporter until February 1972, when he was recruited by Colson to become the White House's deputy director of communications; Pat Buchanan, the conservative Nixon speechwriter who was the source of many of Agnew's more famous alliterations; Albert Abrahams, a political pro who in the mid-sixties had run Republicans for Progress (an attempt by progressives to reshape the party). Abrahams participated in his capacity as director of communications for CREEP. The chief White House Hill lobbyist, Bill Timmons, was represented in the Attack Group through an aide, Wallace Johnson, and Ed Failor, an Iowan who for years was a power in the conservative "Syndicate" faction of the Young Republicans, sat in for Clark MacGregor.

Meeting every morning at 9:15 A.M., the Attack Group meticulously tracked every McGovern statement and sought to arrange an immediate and devastating reply — through a surrogate speaker, a high level government official, or a news leak. McGovern was kept on the defensive through most of the campaign, and while the senator could claim much personal credit for this situation, the persistence and competence of the Attack Group was also a major contribution. The group masterfully maneuvered the surrogate speakers to dominate the local press. A Nixon surrogate would be sent to a city the day before McGovern was scheduled to speak. Thus when McGovern arrived the headlines in the local press would feature the surrogate's attack from the previous day. McGovern would then spend his time rebutting the Nixon charges rather than pressing his own attack.

The White House's closest contact at CREEP was Jeb Magruder, who retained, under MacGregor, the supervision of the in-house activities: administration, polling, press relations, the surrogate speakers bureau, advertising, telephone and direct mail operations, and nominally Democrats for Nixon. The very nature of most of these activities, however, meant that very little authority or power could accrue to Magruder.

1. The polling operation was a full-time and extraordinarily comprehensive enterprise under the direction of Bob Teeter from Michigan's Market Opinion Research. Polling continuously in all the major states as well as periodically nationwide, the Teeter operation was quite independent of CREEP direction and reported directly to the White House strategists. This was the most extensive polling operation in Republican history, but was not significantly different in scope from the McGovern polling effort.

2. The press relations that Magruder supervised were largely administrative, not substantive, since the White House press operations handled that part of the campaign very effectively. The Speakers Bureau, which supervised the surrogates, was handled administratively by Magruder's staff, but the content of their statements was supplied largely by the Attack Group.

3. For campaign advertising CREEP created its own agency, the November Group. This organization, unique in presidential politics, was an innovation of Haldeman. During the 1968 campaign, Nixon had been burned badly when Joe McGinniss infiltrated the campaign's advertising division to write a book entitled *The Selling of the President*, which detailed in very unflattering terms the merchandising of Nixon's image. This episode created a security consciousness concerning the advertising operation, and the Nixon high command sought an ad agency completely under its control. No existing private firm could meet this criterion. The White House also felt that the agency should be based in Washington, but there were no agencies in Washington of sufficient size to handle the campaign.

By creating an in-house ad agency for the purpose of reelecting the President, Haldeman apparently hoped to hire the best available individuals from a variety of ad agencies, meld them into a loyal and single-minded team, and save some of the normal 15 percent commission on placement in the process.

Peter Dailey, a dynamic West Coast advertising executive, was recruited in November 1971 to head the agency. By February 1, 1972, he had assembled a staff of sixty professionals in New York and ten in Washington. The Washington operation established policy and served as a liaison to the White House while the New Yorkers handled the creative and placement efforts. As with the polling operation, the November Group operated largely independently of CREEP and reported directly to the White House.

67

4. Also under Magruder on the organizational charts were the telephone and direct mail operations, supervised by Nancy Brataas and Bob Morgan. These were also semi-independent operations but they were much more integrated into CREEP. Finally, Magruder was "responsible" for the Democrats for Nixon, John Connally's public relations and fundraising operation, whose total independence from the entire CREEP operation was a foregone conclusion by the nature of its leader and the peculiarity of its mission.

MacGregor's other deputy was Fred Malek, who was responsible for implementing strategies two and three discussed above: The organizational attack and compartmentalized appeals. A no-nonsense managerial type, Malek was a graduate of West Point and the Harvard Business School. He had become a millionaire rebuilding a floundering tool company in South Carolina and then went on to government service. He served for a while as a deputy undersecretary of HEW, then moved to the White House. He first attracted national attention and the reputation of a man with ice water in his veins when he served as "executioner" in late 1970 for a number of Hickel associates in the Interior Department. Nixon reportedly had had a very uncomfortable time telling Walter Hickel that he was fired. Malek, according to most accounts, settled in at the Interior Department and in a few hours had individually informed six top Hickel aides that they were fired and that they should have their desks cleaned out by the end of the day. The archetype of a "peripheral urban ethnic" (a favorite term around CREEP headquarters), Malek was an upwardly mobile Chicagoan of Czech ancestry. He was a strong believer in the application of modern and efficient management principles to political organizations and he viewed with disdain the more "political" types around CREEP. He instituted an incredibly demanding reporting system to keep close control upon the vast range of enterprises beneath him, a practice culminating in the postelection reports that each state chairman had to submit to CREEP. These documents constituted a vast evaluative encyclopedia on the competence and merit of all campaign workers and volunteers across the country.

For the first time in American politics, a completely centralized national political machine was created, with direct lines of command coming from Washington that did not rely at all on local political parties or on local power centers for its operational efficiency. Malek, with his impressive managerial skills, created this machine, and to him must go the enormous credit or blame for its institution. Under Malek were two major areas of responsibility: the very powerful Political Division, which sought to wage organizational warfare to match McGovern's volunteer effort, and the Special Voter Group Division, whose primary mission was the strategy of compartmentalizing appeals.

Under Malek in the Political Division were a deputy, Jerry Jones (a Texan with a Harvard B.A. and M.B.A. who had worked for Malek at the

White House) and ten regional directors of varying political experience. Beneath each of these directors was a CREEP state chairman under whom were the city or county chairmen who were directly responsible for the activities in their region. At the local level the organization usually centered around a storefront operation that served as a headquarters for door-to-door canvassing, telephoning, and the distribution of literature, buttons, bumper stickers, and other materials. These operations usually had a paid professional in charge, with volunteer or quasi-volunteer staffing. Many of these people were recruited into CREEP from the ranks of the local party organization, but the chains of command in most states went directly to Washington and circumvented the state party structure. In this way very close supervision could be maintained and the central organization could assure itself that calls were actually being made and doorbells rung without relying upon the word or the competence of the local Republican party chiefs. With this centralized, disciplined structure, the volunteers fanned out to match the McGovern effort, and in the actual election they far surpassed them in volume of delivered tasks.

The Special Voter Group divisions were much more decentralized, but were still under Malek's control. These organizations were designed to compartmentalize the appeals to various groups targeted for special attention by CREEP. They included farmers under Clayton Yeutter, who eventually became regional director for the Farm Belt states; businessmen staffed by Paul Kayser, an associate of Pepsico's Don Kendall and a former executive director of the National Alliance of Businessmen; blacks, headed by Paul Jones, a former government employee with little previous political experience; Jews under Larry Goldberg, a Rhode Island attorney and Harvard Law School alumnus who was a close friend of Jewish philanthropist Max Fischer; older Americans under Danny Todd, who had served ably as executive director of the White House Conference on the Aging and whose trademark in the campaign was a bow tie and a corncob pipe; and labor under Bernard DeLury, a Rockefeller recommendation and son of John DeLury, head of the New York Sanitation Workers Union. Other Special Voter Group divisions included the Lawyers' Committee under Dan Piliero, a very congenial Fordham Law alumnus (and one of the few division heads to finesse Malek's daily reporting system) and the Physicians Committee under Bill Stover, a Swarthmore and Stanford Law School alumnus who had served as executive assistant to former Senator George Murphy.

The Nationalities Division was headed by Taras G. Szmagala, who had been a special assistant to Ohio Senator Robert Taft. Although the thirty-one different ethnic group buttons distributed by the division have become collector's items retailing at two dollars a piece, the organization focused largely on three: Italians, Poles, and Slavs, totaling about twelve million voters. An effective Special Vote Division head was Alex Armendariz, who directed the Spanish-speaking Americans Division. Richard F.

McAdoo, a member of a California family well known in Democratic politics, directed a Transient Voter or Special Ballots Division.

Finally, one of the more controversial division heads was Ken Rietz, organizer of the Young Voters for the President. A Wisconsinite who had served as campaign manager for Congressman William Steiger in 1966 and 1968, Rietz had created a youth operation of major significance for Senator William E. Brock in 1970.

CREEP vs. the Party:
A Model for the Future?

This very brief outline of the overt and legal activities of the Committee to Re-elect the President gives only a flavor of the vast and intricate mechanisms of a modern campaign. It would be the work of a lifetime to detail its complete range of operations, its management techniques, its substrategies, and its personnel. In the next chapter we offer case studies of three CREEP divisions to provide a more detailed example of its activities, but even these must be brief at best. It is possible, however, to look at CREEP as a whole and see a number of implications for the future.

In many ways CREEP was a unique force in American political history. In its overt and legal aspects it was the sort of organization that others have attempted in vain to build before, and it is the kind of enterprise that the McGovern managers sought unsuccessfully to build in 1972. Many of its more acceptable characteristics will provide a model for future campaigns.

First, there is the tendency to move away from the political toward the technical and managerial. CREEP was made up of technicians and managers who phased out the traditional party loyalists and "political types." (A parallel phaseout of ideologues and "issues types," incidentally, occurred in the McGovern organization.) Also, there was the concurrent tendency to replace politics with public relations. (This also occurred with McGovern.) As a result of these two tendencies, the focus on strategy and tactics intensified.

Today, the professional decisionmaker is hired to make management, not political, decisions. He is hired to persuade and coerce, not to accommodate and adjust. Efficiency is his aim. The practices and methods of modern campaigning, therefore, are rapidly becoming the kind of practices that are most readily accomplished in a managerial way. The managers were hired originally to make the old practices more efficient and rational. Now they are tailoring the practices to suit their own efficiency requirements.

Another result of these tendencies is the increased reliance on paid personnel and on those men and women whose ambitions for advancement motivate them to work on the campaign. In traditional Republican politics a sense of participation and a personal contact with the candidate were often adequate rewards for most middle and lower level workers. But such rewards no longer seem sufficient to motivate people unless some great cause is presented to them. The day of the volunteer in the management level of Republican politics is fast disappearing.

All of these tendencies put together show why the party is being phased out in American electoral practice. It may have a PR value and it might be retained for this purpose, but its role in a campaign is fast disappearing. CREEP was a monument to its demise. We have discussed many strategic reasons for this tendency, such as the need to target groups outside the party, to become more efficient, and to attain more flexibility. But there is an obvious managerial reason as well. CREEP's managers could reason quite soundly that their rewards would come from a presidential victory, not a party victory, and that the greater the victory, the more the reward. Their interests lay with the White House, not the party. They used the party for their own purposes; they exploited its loyalties to the President, but they showed no loyalty to it.

Party disunity provided no excuse for such activities. Only a tiny handful of Republican conservatives marched to the tune of the witty, acid-tongued Congressman John Schmitz, the presidential nominee of the American Independent party. Republican conservatives were so apprehensive of McGovern that many would probably still have supported Nixon even if he had endorsed free love, free abortion, and free marijuana distribution. Liberal, antiwar Republicans who might have flirted with supporting McGovern were so taken aback by the incompetence and amateurishness of the McGovern campaign that the majority stayed with Nixon.

Yet as the campaign unfolded, it gradually became clear that the organization of Richard Nixon, an old party man, had minimal concern for the success of the other Republican candidates. Campaign strategy seemed devoted almost exclusively to maximizing the electoral and popular vote mandate for the President and his running mate. The argument was that if the President did well, all Republicans would do well. Such an argument might have been valid if the President had run as a strong party man. But if the President had to be divorced from the party to "do well," then it is difficult to see how the party could expect to benefit from the President's performance.

In certain areas of the country the efforts of CREEP were actually directed *against* the Republican party in *support* of the Democratic nominee for a congressional or senatorial post. According to *U.S. News and World Report,* on January 1, 1973, "More than 50 congressional seats held by Democrats reportedly were listed by the White House as 'protected,' that is, seats which the Nixon administration wanted to be retained by incumbents who had supported the President on key legislative issues. The 'protected' districts are said to have been scattered all over the U.S. and were not just in the South. If reports are accurate, the list included about one-fifth of the Democratic incumbents who sought reelection."

There is no question that the White House did go to considerable lengths to aid certain Democratic legislators who had protected the administration from embarrassment. Mississippi Democrat James O. Eastland, who as chairman of the Senate Judiciary Committee had run interference for the administration during judicial confirmation hearings and during several inquiries on potentially explosive scandals, was nearly canonized by Attorney General Kleindienst and Vice President Agnew.

In Alabama Winton Blount, who had served Nixon loyally for many years in a variety of capacities, found his Senate campaign written off by White House aides uneager to topple or offend Senator Sparkman. Blount's loyal service in undertaking the reorganization of the whole postal system counted for naught in these calculations. He received little more than lip-service support from the White House and found even this effectively washed out by a complimentary letter to Sparkman from President Nixon.

It seems probable that administration strategists decided at an early stage either that the Democrats would retain control of the House and Senate in any case, so White House efforts should be concentrated on currying favor with the Democratic committee chairmen, or that a Republican victory in either the House or the Senate would be of no particular value to the Nixon administration over the next four years. Some Nixon strategists believed that the President's hold over the Republican party would be weakened should Republicans gain control of either House of Congress. Republican control over committee chairmanships and the accompanying increased staff resources might allow Capitol Hill to become an alternative source of Republican power and initiatives. The prospect might not have pleased certain key White House strategists whose source of power had been their ability to deal with *minority* Republican congressmen.

This "flexibility" with respect to supporting Republicans (together with the Goodell episode of 1970) served to increase the power of CREEP and the influence of the White House within the structure of the party. It served even more the interests of those managers at the top whose own personal positions were strongly enhanced or made more secure by the policy of "this is the *President's* party."

But that was not the end of the story. After these managers had aggregated all the power to themselves, after they had exploited extensively the party's loyalty to the President, after they had actively campaigned against Republicans around the country, after they had siphoned away the party's money and resources to augment their own positions, they then proceeded to involve the image of the party in the biggest political scandal of the century. The Republican party as a party was about as remote from CREEP as it could have been and it had absolutely nothing to do with Watergate; if the *politicians*, not the *technicians*, had been in charge Watergate could never have occurred. But the Republican party must now bear the full impact of that sordid mess which was really not its fault. There is one thing for which the party *is* accountable, however, and that is the nomination of Richard Nixon.

4

Targeting the Fluids and the Solids

No discussion of CREEP's grand strategy and organizational logic can begin to give a complete picture of its activities and the methods it used to wage aggressive warfare on the Democratic coalition. We discuss the illegal — and more famous — dimensions of this "aggression" in Chapter 5. But the legal, normal, and quite legitimate procedures of strategic campaigning deserve serious attention, since these new practices are changing the nature of American politics by altering the relationship between a constituency and its representative.

To illustrate how CREEP operated we examine three very different, but highly successful, divisions of the organization. The task assigned to the first was to break loose a significant part of the Democratic coalition. The Hispanic voter was chosen, but other ethnic groups would have served as equally good examples. The purpose of the second division was coalition maintenance: holding a bloc within the coalition whose interests conflicted with a bloc being attracted by other parts of the coalition. The Business and Industry Division of CREEP was chosen. Not that there was much danger of business defection, but the techniques employed provide an interesting case study in "organizing for the sake of organizing" and foreclosing any possible activities by the opposition. The purpose of the third division was to target a highly "fluid" constituency, the young voter, whom both sides made extensive efforts to attract.

Each of these operations was technically sound; each was an excellent example of how a modern campaign can be run with managerial proficiency. With the exception of a few practices listed below, each was run in a commendable way, and no one can complain about the aims of the organizations or the methods used. There is one fundamental question, however, that future strategists and tacticians might ponder: can these approaches to politics be used to create a genuine constituency or a lasting political power base? There is certainly nothing wrong with tactical proficiency, but when technique is confused with substance the result is not always advantageous in the long run. Politics is more than technique; constituency-building is much more than a mechanical exercise.

Case Number One:
The Hispanic-American Voter

The Nixon effort to attract Spanish-speaking voters to his bandwagon is an excellent example of strategic politics at work. This group of Americans is about 70 percent of Mexican ancestry, 20 percent of Puerto Rican ancestry, and about 10 percent of Cuban and other Latin American antecedence. Although the Cuban Americans tend to vote Republican because of their strong anticommunism, the bulk of Hispanic-Americans are Democrats. The Mexican Americans voted 85 percent for Kennedy in 1960, 70 percent for Johnson in 1964, and 87 percent for Humphrey in 1968. The Puerto Rican presidential vote has been similarly one-sided for years.

The Democrats have taken these voters for granted. Kennedy may have given them some symbolic satisfaction, but Johnson delivered very little at all. The Democratic party in Texas from which he came had been dominated by conservatives for many years and the federal funds that flowed into Texas went more to Johnson's friends and to his type of Democrat than to the Mexican Americans. Because these voters had been taken for granted for so long, Republican strategists early in the Nixon administration flirted with the possibility of wooing a significant slice of the Spanish American vote from the Democratic party.

The importance of this vote was clear. In 1970, for example, Democrats had won impressive senatorial victories in Illinois, Texas, and California, states with large concentrations of Mexican American and Puerto Rican voters. Nixon's narrow Illinois and California margins in 1968 and his close defeat in Texas placed these states at the very top of his reelection calculations. If only the Democratic margin in the Spanish-speaking counties and precincts could be seriously reduced, the Democrats would have a great deal of difficulty in carrying these crucial states.

The administration began a concerted effort to break these voters away from the Democrats in 1971. Their first strategy was to appoint Hispanic-Americans to a number of important governmental posts. Phillip Sanchez, a young Californian, was chosen to head the Office of Economic Opportunity. Carlos Villareal from Texas was chosen to be the administrator of the Urban Mass Transit Administration. Romana Bañuelos, a California businesswoman, became the treasurer of the United States. Meanwhile scores of Spanish Americans were recruited for middle level positions in the government.

The administration strategy seemed to be aimed principally at the middle class among each of the Spanish American groups; somewhere in the neighborhood of 40 percent of the Mexican Americans and 30 percent of the mainland Puerto Ricans had attained such a status, according to Republican calculations. An emphasis on minority business opportunities and on high level Spanish American appointments in the executive branch were made a part of the appeal to the middle class. Some Nixon administration programs, however, had a more generalized appeal to Spanish Americans. Bilingual education funds cut across class lines as did increased grants to rural Mexican Americans in such areas as South Texas.

At about the same time that the administration was making these moves, a number of groups of varying ideological persuasion in the Mexican American community became particularly vocal in insisting that they should no longer allow themselves to be taken for granted by one political party. Nixon strategists worked expertly to fan this growing independence. Militant Spanish American organizations that were promoting the idea of separatist, Spanish-interest political parties at the state level found a cordial reception from the Nixon strategists. These groups, insisting that they would hold the balance of power between the two parties, were most useful to the administration since their objectives fit very well with those of the reelection campaign. This was especially true when a noncredible and obviously losing Democrat appeared and the strategy of demonstrating that they could not be taken for granted could be implemented at little perceived cost.

The McGovern candidacy gave the Nixon managers the chance they had been looking for. In his zeal to win the California primary by attracting Mexican American voters away from Humphrey, McGovern had promised to appoint a Chicano to the cabinet and had suggested the same concerning the Supreme Court, should a vacancy occur. Yet the intense heat generated over the quota issue following the Democratic convention made McGovern back down on promises related to quotas. His increasingly shaky promises then had to compete with the reality of Nixon Spanish-speaking appointees.

On July 17, right after McGovern won the nomination, Jean Westwood, the newly elected chairman of the Democratic National Committee, called the Spanish-speaking division of the committee a ghetto and abolished it, firing Director Polly Baca Barrigan. When McGovern learned that Mrs. Barrigan was threatening a public denunciation of his activities, he offered her a job as deputy director of the committee. Mrs. Barrigan quit rather than accept the offer.

McGovern also dismally failed to incorporate the Spanish-speaking into his own campaign staff. Nat Chavira, an exceptionally capable Mexican American who played a vital role in McGovern's California primary victory, finally left the McGovern campaign in disgust. In an unusually incisive confidential memo addressed to Gary Hart (dated August 7, 1972), Chavira had suggested the integration of Mexican Americans into all phases of the McGovern campaign, including press and scheduling. Chavira noted:

> I have now had five days of difficult conversations with people who helped me in California, Arizona, and Texas. Several have indicated they are no longer willing to work for the senator. The point they make is "if the McGovern campaign organization does not include Mexican Americans now, what makes you think the McGovern administration will be any different? With the exception of the last two weeks of the campaign in California when he needed us and we delivered, the senator has not made any remarks or personal efforts to show his concern or even interest in the Mexican American people."

Yet Chavira's memo, copies of which were sent to Frank Mankiewicz, Jean Westwood, Rick Stearns, Lawrence O'Brien, Gordon Weil, and Fred Dutton, fell on deaf ears. Democratic voter registration campaigns in the Mexican American communities of California fell well below their potential. Meanwhile La Raza Unida, a militant Chicano organization, strongest in South Texas, urged Mexican Americans to support neither McGovern nor Nixon and to vote for its own selection of candidates for statewide office in Texas.

This internal feuding provided a tremendous opportunity, but it could never have been capitalized on if the Committee to Re-elect the President had failed to target and compartmentalize its appeals to the Spanish-speaking voters in an organized and effective way.

First of all, CREEP had the good fortune to locate a top-flight Republican professional who happened to be of Spanish ancestry. Alex Armendariz, an Indianan who had once headed that state's Young Republicans, had established himself during the past four years as a rising young professional. He had managed the successful campaigns of Lloyd Allan for mayor of South Bend, Indiana, and Jack Kemp for Congress in a Buffalo, New York, district. He also ran the strong, though losing, campaign of Donald "Buz" Lukens for the 1970 Republican gubernatorial nomination in Ohio. He had been recruited by Bailey, Deardourff, and Bowen to run the campaign of Jack Nevius in the District of Columbia in 1971. Unlike most politicians employed by both parties to run their special voter appeal campaigns, Armendariz was a campaign professional more than a Spanish vote specialist.

Second, a White House Spanish-speaking Constituent Group Task Force was set up to mobilize the resources of the executive branch behind the Nixon campaign effort. This group had considerable say in Spanish American personnel appointments and federal grants. Finally, a relatively loose Spanish-speaking Citizens for the Re-election of the President organization was established. In the last weeks of the campaign Ed Hidalgo became chairman of this committee and succeeded in snaring as members a number of Spanish American celebrities, including golfer Chichi Rodriguez, athletes Alex Olmedo, Pancho Segura, and Mike Cuellar, actors Anthony Quinn, Cesar Romero and Desi Arnaz, and actress Lita Baron.

The Nixon Spanish campaign concentrated on the four swing states of California, Texas, New York, and Illinois. (Over half of the Spanish-speaking population in the United States resides in these four states.) The Nixon effort aimed at the Spanish-speaking middle class, which was much more likely to vote than the rural migrant populations. The McGovern campaign's preoccupation with the lettuce boycott and the Cesar Chavez movement very likely drove some of the moderate middle-class Mexican Americans to Nixon.

The administration spared no effort to publicize the President's considerable accomplishments for the Spanish-speaking. The very shabby treatment that Spanish Americans had received from previous presidents of both parties made Nixon's initiatives all the more impressive. This publicity presented the President's achievements in nonpartisan terms in full recognition of the still-strong Democratic leanings of most Spanish-speaking voters.

Especially significant in the execution of Nixon campaign strategy was a masterful use of the power of incumbency to gain endorsements and favorable publicity for the President among Spanish Americans. Federal grants flowed in unprecedented volume to areas of South Texas with large Spanish populations. Spanish Americans were appointed to positions in all departments of the executive with considerable attendant fanfare. Furthermore, the large public relations staff of all the federal departments could ensure that reams of publicity concerning administration efforts for the Spanish-speaking would be distributed at no cost to CREEP.

The Nixon campaign used as surrogate speakers for the President such Spanish personalities as Phillip Sanchez, Henry Ramirez, Romana Bañuelos, Carlos Villareal, Lita Baron, and Ed Hidalgo. From October 16 to 21 several of these surrogates blitzed five southwestern states, attracting modest crowds but considerable press. A number of regional federal officials also served as administration surrogates in their areas.

The most important Spanish-oriented national advertising in the Nixon campaign was an insert in *Selecciones,* the Spanish-language edition of the *Reader's Digest*. The ad, designed by the November Group, presented the President's record in housing, education, health, economic opportunities, drugs, and federal appointments. The advertisement was considered so effective that reprints of it were used as the main campaign brochure. A million reprints were ordered, 700,000 in English, 300,000 in Spanish. Spanish-oriented television ads were used only in California. A Mexican American media consultant firm prepared three television commercials focusing on bilingual education, Spanish-speaking presidential appointees, and job opportunities. Several different sixty-second radio spots directed at the Spanish-speaking were aired repeatedly in California.

This entire operation is a classic example of voter targeting. The White House used its considerable political and economic power to target certain areas for the receipt of federal moneys and it used its appointment power to create an extensive source of excellent public relations. All this would have been in vain had there not been a first-class organization to convey these messages to the voters in a directed fashion.

The results were dramatic. Nixon did not carry the Hispanic vote but cut heavily into this Democratic bastion, creating a much more fluid situation for the future, and giving the organizers of Hispanic voting blocs some leverage that they can use with respect to both parties. The Spanish American voter can no longer be taken for granted.

Case Number Two: The Business and Industry Division of CREEP

The Business and Industry Division of CREEP was a highly successful operation designed to target and compartmentalize the business community just as the Hispanic Division had been created to target its constituency. It provides another example of the benefits of a compartmentalized appeal, since the Nixon strategists used the fear of union political activities to create business solidarity at the very time that other tactics by the White House and CREEP were neutralizing the effects of these union activities.

On the surface, at any rate, it would seem that the business community would be the last conceivable constituency that CREEP would have to organize in 1972. The McGovern candidacy was regarded as a threat by so many businessmen that business was more politically united than it had been for several elections. Yet an effort of sizable proportions was made, not necessarily to convert Democrats, but instead to activate those businessmen who had traditionally taken a very hands-off attitude toward politics.

Sophisticated corporate executives have usually stayed away from political commitments or have pursued a policy of evenhandedness. For about a decade there has been a decline in the traditional role of business as a Republican bastion. The business community has become somewhat more fluid, especially since the Goldwater debacle in 1964, when many major business executives for the first time supported a Democrat for President. (Fluid is perhaps too strong here — the word is discreet.) In 1972, however, CREEP made a conscious effort to exploit McGovern's weakness and reverse the drift.

The President himself asked Don Kendall of Pepsico if there was some way to mobilize more effectively the normal Republican sentiments in the business community and to create a strong political instrument for the 1972 campaign. Kendall, a man active in public interest organizations, had spent a year as head of the National Alliance of Businessmen. Drawing upon his experience there, he organized the Business and Industry Division along almost identical lines.

In the words of its organizer, "The operation was a tremendous success. Our original goal was to organize 200 cities, but we ended up with 500 cities in the organization." According to Kendall, approximately 160,000 businessmen were enlisted in his campaign. These volunteers organized meetings, served as regional, state, and city chairmen, wrote letters, and gave talks in support of the President. Each city was organized along industry lines, so that the metropolitan chairmen and co-chairmen had a dozen or more industry chairmen working for them. "In a couple of cities, we even had barbershop divisions," Kendall recalled.

The organizing directive of the Business and Industry Division was a *City Chairman's Guide,* a 131-page looseleaf notebook describing the logic of the division's organization and containing tips on how to spread the word. Volunteer city directors were instructed to establish a business advisory council representing every major segment of the business, industrial, and professional community. This council, in turn, served to bring the message to all employers in the city. The major segments to be represented on the various advisory councils included minorities, women, and small businesses. According to the *Guide,* the advisory council was to be a "representative cross-section of the entire business community . . . the basis for reaching out to all businesses in your area, large and small, who, in turn, can bring the message to their stockholders and employees."

A persistent theme was the need to offset the activities of the AFL-CIO and its political fund-raising organization, COPE (Committee on Political Education). According to the *Guide,* COPE "has proved highly effective in having elected persons favorable to labor. This year, the efforts of COPE will be concentrated toward defeating the President. The number of businessmen you reach, the number of effective meetings you hold, and the quality of your presentations will be major steps in offsetting the activities of COPE." The "sample nonpartisan speech" for businessmen to give to their listeners contained the following "nonpartisan" peroration:

> Most recently, Mr. George Meany, president of the AFL-CIO, declared that his organization would work for the defeat of the President and that

they would work to have someone elected who feels more favorable to their cause.

No one argues their right to do this, and I am sure it is generally agreed that they do it well. But I ask you — don't *we* have the same right? Don't *we* have the same responsibility?

As the campaign wore on this approach became less relevant, but the necessity to create an organization to offset COPE was a recurring theme.

The Business and Industry Division was established to organize businessmen, not to raise money. However, fund-raising kits prepared by the Finance Committee to Re-elect the President were sent to businessmen in order to help them solicit political funds from their firms. Sporting a large, friendly shot of the President's face on the cover, the slick, folder-type kit also had the following words in bold white-on-black type:

THE RESPONSIBILITY OF EVERY AMERICAN . . .
SUPPORT THE CANDIDATE OF YOUR CHOICE

The kit included analyses of the McGovern budget, sample partisan and nonpartisan letters (the latter recommended for use by government contractors); partisan and nonpartisan pledge cards, a copy of the laws governing campaign giving, and a "by-the-numbers" sheet explaining how to set up a solicitation program for employee and stockholder groups. The sample letter to every chief executive officer suggested a range of giving (1 percent to 2 percent of salary, or $100 to $1000 for salaried officers who were not important stockholders). It warned that "it is most important to give careful consideration to selection of the group to be solicited. Most companies that have participated in this program have directed their letters to all salaried employees from top executives down to those in the salary range of $12,000 per annum."

The implication of this warning is that a partisan campaign or a campaign whose proceeds would be controlled by one or two corporate officers is likely to backfire if it reaches too far down the corporate ladder. Such a campaign, they pointed out, is effective only with those who cannot afford to step out of line. In one company interviewed for this book (which was setting up a new giving program in 1972), the appeal was limited to the employees who earned $30,000 and above. This same company also said that the decision to hold a partisan campaign or a campaign whose proceeds were tightly controlled had to be weighed against a decision to open the campaign to more people, make it non-partisan, and still hope to receive more money for the candidate of the board of directors' choice.

Kendall's success surprised him, since he had originally viewed the business community as being traditionally aloof politically. In describing to us the problem he felt he had to work against, Kendall stated that the business community used to be more actively involved when it contained a heavier proportion of entrepreneurs and owners. "As the country changed," Kendall continued, "more and more professional management crept in who were not identified with the original company. Historically, the professionals have covered both sides, and as a result the business community had almost no political clout at all."

This point of view was also reflected in the decision of some executives to become leaders in the division. "When I considered taking this position," said Stewart S. Cort, Bethlehem Steel chairman and head of the Pennsylvania Business and Industry Division, "I weighed very carefully my responsibility to the owners of this corporation."

The experience of the division's organizers provides an interesting commentary on the influence of business on party politics. As a general rule, according to the division's staff, the bigger the company and the more sophisticated its management, the less inclined it was to become involved. Bankers as a group were the most difficult, although there were exceptions (Chemical Bank Chairman William S. Renchard chaired the New York division). Executives in the regulated industries were also reluctant to participate, although Georgia Power Company President Harlee Branch, Jr., for example, served as state chairman in Georgia.

A possible reason for the reluctance of larger companies to become involved is their traditional standoffish attitude, usually backed up by company regulations that discourage politicking during business hours generally. The chairman of one of the top three hundred American firms, a midwestern corporation, stated to us that his firm had strict rules against using company time and facilities for partisan purposes. This was originally directed at union activities, but would have applied to speeches to employees by the chairman himself for the purpose of promoting the reelection of President Nixon. The chairman confessed that he circumnavigated this rule by warning employees during company time about the dangers of supporting any candidate who picked out corporations as an object for attack and who proposed restrictions on corporate activity.

To the extent that business executives could be weaned from their increasingly cautious policy of nonalignment, there were many bonuses that could be gained. One was the use of stockholder lists to reach an expanded, but potentially friendly, audience. This was a sensitive issue. The tactic was made legally possible by the Federal Election Campaign Act of 1971, which specifically permitted communications by a corporation to its stockholders and their families. In the congressional debate on that issue, the sponsors of the measure pointed out that prohibitions on this kind of conduct could quite possibly run afoul of the First Amendment right of free speech. However, the division found a reluctance by many businessmen to take advantage of this provision on the belief that sales would suffer.

The most publicized incident of communications with stockholders involved the president of Liggett and Myers. Milton Harrington sent a letter to his 47,000 shareholders urging the reelection of the President. The *New York Times* described the mailing as "a rare move" and played up the size of Liggett and Myers and its large number of stockholders. According to division insiders, however, the uniqueness of this event was overemphasized. "We had hundreds of such communications — I would say thousands," one Washington staff member said. Kendall was even more specific. "I sent the first one out early in the summer," he said, "partly in order to show what would happen to sales." According to him, the mailing did not hurt Pepsico's business and generated only eleven adverse replies. "I could have written something about apple pie," said Kendall, "and received a bigger reaction."

Liggett and Myers told us that, according to a special survey by its vice president for marketing, its mailing had had no effect on sales. L & M received letters from only 145 of its 47,000 shareholders; 69 were favorable, 76 were critical. According to an L & M spokesman, some of the critical letters showed clearly that the writers had not read the original letter very closely; others pointed out that it was inappropriate for a consumer business to engage in this sort of activity. Criticism notwithstanding, L & M's President Harrington was reported as favorable to trying the same tactic in 1976, should the need arise.

By organizing 160,000 businessmen and encouraging them to reach out to their stockholders, CREEP created a powerful instrument and wealthy constituency. It set a precedent for campaigning within the business community and reversed the trend toward nonalignment that managers had begun to favor with increasing consistency. In the future it may be possible to make direct, immediate, and effective communications to this constituency without relying on more traditional and less efficient methods of appeal.

The lines of communication are being kept open. After the election, Kendall's organization received a number of letters inquiring whether there was some way to serve in the same kind of organization during the intervening four years. An October 28, 1972, *Business Week* article indicates that the success of the Business and Industry Division has prompted Kendall and others to keep it active. For example, the organization had been used to lobby for a White House spending ceiling proposal.

Yet it is not totally clear that this organization is necessarily the wave of the future. "There was enthusiasm for this particular assignment," said the president of a large Ohio firm, a city chairman for the division. "Most people felt the format was a good one, and would do it again if asked. But I don't think that the exercise fundamentally changed the attitudes of businessmen toward being active in politics generally."

All respondents agreed that the threat that Senator McGovern seemed to pose to business made the job of finding businessmen-volunteers relatively easy. It also made easy the "radical" decision to communicate with employees and stockholders. In fact, at least one of the state chairmen of the division was a Democrat. The one-sided nature of the choice, so far as business was concerned, makes any assessment about future participation by businessmen in the same kind of campaigning very difficult. It is entirely possible that there will be a reversion to increasing discretion, and it is even more possible that the Democrats will begin to think in similar terms themselves.

Case Number Three:
Young Voters for the President

The conventional wisdom of 1972 was that youth, especially college youth, was either "owned" by George McGovern or was so anti-Nixon in sentiment that it would eventually choose McGovern over the President by a decisive margin. If this conclusion were true, the reasoning ran, the reelection campaign would have several serious obstacles. One, a sizable number of votes would be lost in an area where increased suffrage had created a large potential vote. Also, volunteers, a sizable proportion of whom are young people, would be much more readily available to the Democrats than to Nixon. This would create an organizational problem. Finally, to the extent that long-range calculations were made, the concession of young voters to the opposition would create a demographic imbalance that would be very dangerous in the future.

CREEP strategists felt that it would be advantageous to deny the Democrats a free ride among young voters partly for the above reasons and partly to force the Democratic campaign to devote some resources to an area hitherto regarded as an inviolable sanctuary. Since the issues that appeal to young voters often conflict with the issues that appeal to everyone else, a media-oriented approach would have been ineffective at best. Hence the decision was made to wage organizational warfare on the Democrats' position. As it became increasingly clear that McGovern would be the opposition, the challenge seemed all the more worthwhile.

While the objective of countering the opposition's efforts seemed admirable, there were serious questions about the Republicans' capabilities. There was, however, one encouraging precedent. In 1970, William Brock's successful U.S. Senate race made extensive use of a youth operation under the direction of Ken Reitz. The Brock-Reitz operation had demonstrated that in an Outer South state, at any rate, Republican young people could be effectively mobilized. Brock and Reitz suggested to the CREEP hierarchy that their experience showed wide possibilities for 1972. CREEP decided to test-market the idea in New Hampshire — and the test was very successful.

In the 1972 New Hampshire primary hundreds of high school and college students from New York and New England circulated Nixon petitions, planned and executed comprehensive door-to-door canvassing in most of the state's communities, and finally carried out a "call-back" telephone canvass on the weekend before primary day. The success of these projects (and of several enthusiastic and highly visible youth rallies) resulted in the formation of the Young Voters for the President, a permanent division of the Committee to Re-elect the President. From New Hampshire through the rest of the primary states, the YVP grew into a million-dollar operation with 100 full-time staffers, branch offices in forty-seven states, and a separate college program in all fifty.

There were originally two principal missions envisioned for the YVP: to destroy the "peer group pressure" that was assumed to be working against the President and to recruit personnel to work in other divisions of CREEP. To accomplish these tasks, an important third mission was added: publicity.

Young Voters, then, was supposed to take its place as part of the total campaign. Its workers were to knock on doors, attend rallies, make calls, stuff envelopes, and fulfill all the other roles played by campaign staffers. But in addition it had the total responsibility for reaching its own age group. This twofold function demanded an immense resource development since the YVP frequently had to meet the personnel demands of CREEP as well as its own requirements. To carry out its missions, a workable organization was created that allowed enough flexibility for the dual roles of YVP, but that still avoided the confusion and duplication that came from working on two levels. The problem of finding competent personnel was also compounded by the stipulation that they had to be young. Most of the top staff was under twenty-five although the top age limit was thirty-one, corresponding to that of Reitz himself.

The YVP had three principal divisions: the Nixonette Division, the Speakers Division, and the College Division. In most states this three-way split was preserved down to the local levels, with each state chairman and each regional chairman having three deputies corresponding to the three divisions. At the head of the operation was Ken Reitz, with deputies Ken Smith, Angie Miller, and George Gorton, respectively, chairing each division.

NIXONETTE DIVISION

The principal function of the Nixonettes was to supply young women to perform at rallies, receptions, and other public events. When the need arose, a group of young women (appropriately attired in red, white, and blue) were available to greet one of the President's surrogate speakers, to escort touring members of the first family, and to lead rallies in singing

"Nixon Now More Than Ever." The girls who participated in this aspect of the Nixonette program were very often high school cheerleaders.

But much more than the cheerleader identity was stressed. Nixonettes actively engaged in factual advance work for the visits of campaign speakers. In New York State they did the groundwork planning for a tour of prominent Republican women. Throughout the country they also visited hospitals and nursing homes. Here, politics was reduced to a very soft level. They sought to show senior citizens that someone cared enough to take the time to visit with them and so hoped to get across the message that the President cared as well. A subdivision of the program, Nixonaries, took its volunteers from the ranks of airline stewardesses. These young women, whose profession gave them great mobility, spent their off-duty hours serving the Nixon cause.

THE SPEAKERS DIVISION

The aim of the Speakers Bureau was to supply young speakers who would bring the Nixon message to the public. Armed with a weighty volume of facts on the administration and reinforced by periodic "update sheets" supplied by Ken Smith's office of researchers, speakers chairmen on the state, regional, and local levels recruited and trained high school, college, and working youths to speak for Richard Nixon. Their purpose was to show other young people not only that Nixon had young supporters, but also that these supporters were committed enough to come out and debate issues with their peers.

In many states the YVP Speakers Bureau worked in concert with the various CREEP surrogates and often had to take on responsibilities in conjunction with the CREEP speakers program. The New York City CREEP speakers office was inundated by calls from religious and civic clubs requesting the appearance of Nixon spokesmen. With the opening of schools in September, requests came for Nixon advocates to appear before class assemblies, debates, and forums. In many cases the Nixon representatives at these school debates were younger and looked more like the stereotyped vision of a McGovern supporter than the young lawyer types sent to represent the Democratic cause.

THE COLLEGE DIVISION

The College Division was perhaps the most active, since colleges remained the best source of young people. Its enthusiastic, hard-sell staffers moved into every state, and achieved a presence not only on college campuses but in high schools as well. The tacticians targeted the younger youth who were more fluid than upperclassmen. "Many older

86

kids had preconceived anti-Nixon feelings — and had had them too long to change them," explained George Gorton. "That's why many of our efforts were geared to high school and early college students."

The YVP, in its quest for young people, employed many techniques. The pervading feeling on campus was that being for Nixon was treason itself. Therefore the YVP college recruiters appealed to the notion that sympathy for the Nixon cause was, in the campus community, an almost subversive act. The radical cause was so prevalent that on many campuses it had become the establishment. Being for Nixon, the YVP recruiters preached with the fervor of revolutionaries, was indeed being different.

The tactics of the New Left were adopted in many fields. First, to deal with recruitment, one or two people on campus would be found to start a core group. These people (with the help of "outside agitators" from YVP) would usually set up a recruitment table in a conspicuous place and begin to attract attention. They would create as much activity around their table as possible. They would approach every individual they could, block his path, and ask him directly to work for Nixon. This method led to large numbers of recruits — along with equally large numbers of vehement opponents, outraged that their "turf" was being invaded. In New York over 4,000 college students were recruited in this manner. Large amounts of printed material were also distributed at the recruitment table. The stated goals were: (1) to reach as many prospective workers as possible; (2) to reach as many prospective voters as possible, (3) to be visible and confront the McGovern campaign at the center of its strength.

Second, large amounts of written propaganda were used. The sources were the CREEP research office, the Republican National Committee, and the local Nixon headquarters. Several pieces were tailored to YVP. A recruitment brochure was printed with a postcard on the back for prospective members to return. There were some imaginative handouts describing the President's record printed on a letterhead attributing them to "The Committee to Investigate Richard Nixon." For the most part a conscious effort was made to avoid slick Madison Avenue advertising. Written material was printed to look like the cheap handbills of a subversive organization. In California an "underground" newspaper was printed on a monthly basis.

Third, Gorton's office used direct mail extensively. A number of key colleges in each state were targeted that seemed to be good prospects for bringing the message across. It was then the responsibility of the state college organization to obtain a mailing list of the members of the incoming freshman class, the most "fluid" and hence the most targeted group. Such a mailing consisted of a letter to freshmen, welcoming them to the campus and encouraging them to join the new and blossoming Nixon youth movement; a YVP college-oriented brochure printed on recycled paper and showing on its cover the President at the Great Wall of China; an "involvement card" together with a return envelope through which the freshmen could sign up for the campaign. This material, the return envelopes, and the postage were supplied to the state organization by Washington in large enough quantities to reach each freshman in the targeted schools. Once the state organization received the mailing material its job was to personalize each letter.

All of these are time-honored techniques and are identical to those of the McGovern movement. The interesting thing is that the YVP demonstrated that youth or student movements do not necessarily hinge on philosophy but on technique and training. Youth had been successfully motivated and organized before for what Sidney Hyman calls "event politics." They created moratoriums, marches, and strikes. But for the first time on a national level they were organized from the Right and Center for "nonradical" politics. Eugene McCarthy's campaign had shown what impact youth could have on normal-process politics. The YVP showed that they did not need a strong, liberal, or popular cause to carry out such a project. And it showed that a national effort could be generated without benefit of a popular national issue.

The groups of the Left had had the benefits of strong issues that students could easily identify with. They also used effective motivational and organizational techniques. YVP had a President with a 14 percent campus popularity and a total lack of charisma. Yet it used the same techniques and equaled the success of its liberal predecessors. It was a triumph of tactics.

Thus YVP legitimized the youth area of the new strategic politics. Its relations with the Republican party, its goals, and its methods paralleled those of CREEP. After the campaign of 1972 no national candidate will dare run without paying strict attention to his youth organization. Another legacy of the YVP is a sizable group of individuals under twenty-five on the local, state, and national levels with experience and expertise in political functions. These people will be valuable tools in future campaigns.

5

Watergate

To those who took part in its planning and execution, Watergate was a rational and logical enterprise. It was not the product of haphazard planning, of disciplinary breakdowns, or of misplaced exuberance by a few enthusiasts. Nor was it the brainchild of crackpots and amateurs. Rather, it was the creation of professional strategists who had been active in electoral politics for a long time and who had been running the country for several years. It was directed from the top and was executed with all the discipline and rigor that characterized the style of the Nixon White House during the Haldeman-Ehrlichman administration. It could not have been otherwise in a regime that prided itself on a tight ship. The burglaries and buggings, the espionage and sabotage, the systematic use of extortion, and the deployment of sophisticated deception were all authorized by intelligent men in pursuit of what seemed to them legitimate objectives.

Furthermore, these decisions were not made casually. The Watergate constellation of episodes was the product of sober reflection over a considerable period of time. The strategists and decisionmakers recognized that their projects were illegal, dangerous, and potentially counterproductive. They knew that they might get caught. Still they persisted because they judged that the payoffs were worth the risks, that the potential rewards exceeded the dangers, and that these various enterprises constituted a rational set of procedures.

Of course the decisions that led to Watergate were not the responsibility of any single individual. They were the product of a bureaucracy and cannot be fully understood outside the bureaucratic context. For example, the operatives at the lowest levels no doubt had an inflated estimate of their own competence and an ability to convey their optimism and enthusiasm upward. Also, group-think and the dynamics of group decisionmaking certainly played a role. Most of all, the inner politics of the administration, especially the antagonism between Mitchell and Haldeman, was intimately involved with the whole affair. In many ways Watergate was used by the Haldeman faction to discredit the Mitchell faction and it may even have been so regarded *in advance*. But there is really nothing unusual about such bureaucratic affairs. They are part of any organizational process and their existence detracts neither from the logical approach used by the Nixon strategists nor from the perceived rationality of the attempt.

The point is that Watergate should not have been a surprise. It was simply the culminating episode of a politics that employed the same kind of hyperstrategic thinking that was responsible for the government-by-game plan and campaign-by-targeting that have already been discussed. It was a classic case of taking things to their logical conclusion. To its perpetrators Watergate was not a departure from normal political practice but the supreme expression of what politics is all about.

On the surface it should not be surprising that anyone who looks at politics primarily in strategic terms should behave as the Watergate conspirators did. After all, if winning is the supreme strategic objective, then why should any tactic that contributes to winning not be desirable and permissible? Why should the campaign not be a "total" campaign in which all the assets, organizational resources, and strategic reserves of the antagonist become legitimate targets? Why should any sanctuaries remain free from disruption and interdiction? What is wrong with securing one's own position by destroying the position of another? As long as the practices themselves do not become self-defeating and counterproductive to their goals, why should they not be tried? So runs the argument. On the international level, where the science of strategy has been developed to a high degree of sophistication, all these questions are part of the normal operating calculus and it should not be unexpected that a domestic employment could be found for espionage, sabotage, deterrence, preemption, escalation, and the other stratagems that have been used so extensively abroad.

Watergate, then, should not be viewed as a sequence of bizarre events, as a "normal" set of corrupt practices, or even as a traditional conspiracy. It is just one of the more spectacular examples of the "new politics," of the new patterns of strategic politics that are beginning to prevail in modern America. It is thus important to examine in some detail the nature of the strategies employed, their logical foundations, and their accompanying psychology.

The Watergate Mentality

Watergate and its attendant scandals were the product of a hyperstrategic mentality that many modern politicians and their managers are beginning to adopt. Where does this mentality come from? What are its logical assumptions? What kinds of people are most prone to adopt it? Why is it becoming so prevalent? We shall first examine its logical underpinnings and then its psychological dimensions.

DOMINOES AND GAME PLANS

A New Domino Theory?

About ten years ago commentators began to use the image of a row of dominoes to illustrate their expectation that the fall of South Vietnam to communist rule would cause other states in the region to collapse in rapid succession as the first domino crashed against the second, and the second fell against the third, until finally the whole row lay flat upon the geopolitical table. This image was subsequently subjected to some ridicule, perhaps unjustly, and it dropped out of our strategic vocabulary without its validity being demonstrated or refuted.

In a slightly different form, however, the domino theory is still very much alive. The deterministic image of one rectangular block crashing into another may no longer be very useful, but the concept of a series of items linked together in a linear fashion is perfectly reasonable, and in this sense dominoes are on the mind of almost every strategist. There is a common perception that events are linked in causal chains, like a row of dominoes, where one thing leads to another, the second to a third, and thus downward, as people proceed through the time frames of their existence.

Strategists and decisionmakers are especially attracted to this view of reality because they tend to look at the future as a chain of possible events leading to alternative objectives. They see life in terms of scenarios or game plans with a series of means that leads to an end, like a row of dominoes that leads to the last domino on the table. Viewed this way, each situation, each short-run objective, is simply a means of reaching the next situation or objective, and that, in turn, is a means to yet a further position in the line. Although the Watergate defendants did not use this image explicitly in their testimony, their repeated references to scenarios, game plans, time frames, and contingencies showed that they were thinking very much in these terms.

There is an air of plausibility to this image, and as long as the last domino is clearly in view, the strategist who wants to reach it can have a very good idea of where he is, how far away his goal is, and the sequence of means that will get him there. The problem is, however, that there is never a last domino for all practical purposes. Time frames don't stop. History is open-ended. Even when objectives are reached and goals are fulfilled, there are still new worlds to conquer, new problems to solve. Where one is at any given moment is really only relevant to where one soon may be.

Most decisionmakers are not bothered by this. They may realize that life will continue after a specific goal is attained, but they conclude that the achievement of specific goals will take precedence over what might come later. But the hyperstrategist, wedded to his dominoes and time frames, sees no visible end to the chain. Furthermore, all the dominoes begin to look alike to him and it becomes increasingly difficult to say which are means and which are ends. There may well be an end somewhere down the line, but for all practical purposes each concrete objective is simply a means of reaching the next objective, not an end in itself. Each time frame of his existence appears to be but a way station on the path to the next.

Because of this, he begins to lose sight of his goals, ever receding down the line; he focuses instead on augmenting his means. In this way the domino perspective of open-ended time frames leads to a focus on *process,* not on concrete *goals* and *objectives;* success is measured not by the *worth* of a goal achieved, but by *how well* the process is proceeding. As in the game of domino rows that children play, the whole point is to keep it going as long as possible, not to bring it to a purposeful conclusion.

Since this whole perspective destroys the traditional concept of a goal, it is easy to see how winning *per se* becomes the only possible remaining objective for the hyperstrategist. As the campaign motto in Fred Malek's office succinctly stated it, "Winning isn't everything, it is the only thing there is."

It was this domino perspective that was responsible for the practices of the Nixon administration that we examined in Chapter 2. Good Gallup ratings, image augmentation, power accrual, and electoral performance are all instrumental objectives. They stand in sharp contrast to the more concrete governmental objectives of cleaning up the environment, solving the welfare mess, lowering the crime rate, and reorganizing the government that were quickly shelved when the hyperstrategists came to power.

The Nixon managers, of course, were not the only people with hyperstrategic tendencies. The Kennedy administration was filled with them. Richard Neustadt, its leading domestic theorist, might well be called the patron saint of strategic politics. In the opening pages of *Presidential Power* (called the Bible of the Kennedy administration), he illustrates dramatically the distinction between a goal-oriented employment of strategy and a use that focuses on process and success instead of on purpose:

There are two ways to study "presidential power." One way is to focus on the tactics, so to speak, of influencing certain men in given situations: how to get a bill through Congress, how to settle a strike, how to quiet a Cabinet feud or how to stop a Suez. The other way is to step back from tactics on those "givens" and to deal with influence in more strategic terms: what is its nature and what are its sources? What can *this* man accomplish to improve the prospect that he will have influence when he wants it? Strategically, the question is not how he masters Congress in a peculiar instance, but what he does to boost his chance for mastery in any instance, looking toward tomorrow from today.

(In all fairness to Neustadt, he hoped that his recipes for power could be used for concrete objectives, but that is another tale.)

Another classic example of the focus on process instead of objectives is the idea of a "movement," a concept employed by both Left and Right to symbolize their motion down the open-ended time frames of their existence. Although both would insist that the "movement" has an "end," their practices say otherwise. As with so many other aspects of modern politics, the continuation of the process itself becomes the goal; movement itself becomes the end.

This linear perspective, then, is beginning to change the nature of our politics as we focus on succession and Success, procession and Process, movement and Movement. It is creating a situation where strategy is employed not to attain objectives, but to define them, a condition where the strategist supplies the goals and the politician the means, rather than vice versa. This is what a commitment to process does to politics, but it is only the first step in the logical path to Watergate.

The Problem of Risk

The domino image of reality is not completely accurate because a person does not view the future in terms of a single chain of events, but in terms of many alternative chains of events. There are several rows of dominoes between which he can choose. He calls them contingencies because, true to the domino image, each event in them is contingent or dependent on a prior event in the chain.

On what basis does he choose? Normally most people choose on the basis of their principles and life styles. But a hyperstrategist views things differently. Winning is his goal, so he must develop a winning strategy. This is difficult because he cannot see very far down his domino rows. Life is not only open-ended, but it is filled with chance and risk. To change the analogy somewhat, life is like a game of chess where the possible outcomes diverge with astronomical rapidity as the number of projected moves increases. Because this is the case, the more a strategist ponders his situation, the more he becomes aware that he is operating in a condition of great uncertainty.

Under these circumstances he is tempted to procrastinate. But he

93

knows that "not to decide is to decide." He recognizes the need for doctrine and choice. Therefore he is caught in a serious dilemma. By the very nature of contingency planning he must base his decisions on projected outcomes, yet he is unable either to predict very well where these outcomes will lead or to formulate stable goals in this open-ended world. He is thus continually forced down his time frames, forever trying to predict the results of his actions in a situation that precludes the possibility of such predictions being very accurate.

Faced with uncertainty, risk, and the necessity for choice, what is his logical course of action? Clearly it is to remain as flexible as possible in the face of unknown contingencies, to keep options open so there is always a reasonable set of alternatives. Only in this way can he be relatively sure that he can keep the game going well and preserve his winning streak.

The best means of keeping options open, however, is to acquire power and to create as many instruments of power as possible. (Power in a social context can be equated with a wide range of options.) But continually preserving options is the antithesis of commitment. Whenever commitments to follow a certain course of action are made, a diminution of options and of bargaining power results, since the more a strategist commits himself, the more others can take strategic advantage of his commitments. Therefore, as with the simple domino image, the only logical goal of the hyperstrategist is found in the process itself, in keeping the process going by preserving options and acquiring power.

This perception provided yet another justification for the game-plan governing discussed in Chapter 2 and also explains many of the activities discussed in Chapters 4 and 5, since the logic of the reelection campaign was based on a commitment to avoid commitments. The refusal to make specific pronouncements, the preservation of image flexibility, the creation of vast instrumentalities to combat McGovern in any area that he might show strength, the recognition of the iron law of specificity, the compartmentalization of appeals, and the decision to emphasize organization rather than media are all examples of a grand strategy committed to flexible response in the face of an unknown situation. CREEP knew well how to minimize risk by preserving options.

Anticipation and Preemption

If the only logical goal for the hyperstrategist is some form of winning or success, what if another strategist is at work in the vicinity? Certainly if both strategists are thinking in the terms outlined so far, each will be looking at contingencies, choices, and options. Therefore each will begin to become part of the risk factor of the other, and each could be logically regarded by the other as a threat. This is especially true if "winning" requires concurrent "losing" as it so clearly does in electoral politics. To people who view each other this way, their relationship increasingly resembles that of players in a game. But the stakes are so high and the game so important that it becomes difficult for it to remain friendly. The opposition soon becomes the enemy in the analogy of the international game of diplomacy and warfare.

Further, the more the hyperstrategist looks at other people in strategic terms, the more he realizes that there are a wide range of things that they *might* do to him in order to win. If they are also strategists, he cannot assume that they have overlooked their opportunities, and the farther he can peer down his diverging rows of dominoes the more possibilities there appear to be. He simply cannot afford to ignore all the things that the opposition — now the enemy — just might do. He must try to anticipate every possible contingency and to forestall it by preemptions, otherwise the antagonist would have an advantage and just might win. As Secretary McNamara stated in an international context, "A strategic planner must be conservative in his calculations; that is, he must prepare for the worst plausible case and not be content to hope and prepare for the most probable." To put it another way, the strategist must assume that the other side has its strategists, and that they are trying to think up every possible means of attacking him. Therefore, he must provide against every possible contingency that they might think up — and all this justifies his thinking up every possible contingency to use against them!

It is easy to see how this form of strategic thinking leads directly to an excessive concentration on security measures and even on intelligence and counterintelligence operations to forestall the *possible* plots and measures that the opposition might be dreaming up, even if, in fact, they are not thinking in these terms.

This extreme form of contingency thinking was widespread throughout the hierarchy of CREEP. People like Colson, Mitchell, Magruder and Dean were continually thinking up ways the opposition might attack them and ways they might attack the opposition. These concerns led to an excessive desire to have a vast range of intelligence capabilities. The first Liddy proposal for a special operations group is an example of this mentality at work. As John Dean described it,

> The plans called for mugging squads, kidnaping teams, prostitutes to compromise the opposition and electronic surveillance. . . . I recall Liddy saying that the girls would be high-class and the best in the business. . . . I recall Mitchell's reaction to the "Mission Impossible" plan. When the presentation was complete, he took a few long puffs on his pipe and told Liddy that the plan he had developed was not quite what he had had in mind, and the cost was out of the question.

Although Mitchell found that this scheme was a bit excessive, a toned-down version was eventually adopted and the Watergate bugging was the result.

Politics and Warfare

There is a seductive logic to all of these calculations, especially if the relationship between the policymakers and strategists on both sides is one of fundamental antagonism. The problem is that these calculations tend to create antagonisms. They depersonalize politics and in the process of doing so make it possible for politicians to regard other people in highly coercive and manipulative ways. The hyperstrategist perceives the people around him not in human but in strategic terms: they are either allies of convenience or enemies. Herbert Kalmbach stated it rather well: "If you are not with us, we must assume that you are against us." Furthermore, it is very easy for the hyperstrategist to forget that not everyone around is also a hyperstrategist. Some may be playing another game altogether, some may be acting more from tradition and custom, some may be trying to achieve concrete political objectives. If the hyperstrategist could be convinced that everyone around him is not out to "get" him, then he *might* be induced to think of his fellows in more normal terms; but he probably would just regard them with contempt (since he would be certain that his view of reality was superior to their obviously naïve perceptions) and he would proceed to exploit their "weakness" to his advantage.

It is easy to see how this depersonalized view of politics leads to an emphasis on deterrence as the normal political operating procedure. In this world of sticks and carrots, the stick seems more like a sure thing. During the last decade or so, domestic "deterrence and compulsion," as the game theorists say, have been on the increase in American politics, but the White House staff has carried these doctrines further than any of its predecessors. In the relationship between the Nixon White House and the Congress, the press, and the bureaucracy, explicit deterrence policies were pursued that replaced the more general, and hitherto more widely used, forms of political bargaining and compromise. In part it was the source of Nixon's downfall.

We can now begin to see the full implications of a hyperstrategic mentality turned loose upon our political system. As calculation becomes the primary basis for human interaction, trust and loyalty disappear and the foundations of political stability are thereby seriously undermined. As politics is increasingly viewed as game playing, serious governmental objectives are quickly and quietly subverted. As the strategic mentality begins to dominate the political process, conflict is created where none existed before. As people are regarded in strategic terms they quickly become treated as enemies. As risk becomes a major category of calculation, security-consciousness becomes the order of the day. As more and more people think in these terms the whole process escalates and its own logic takes on the aspect of a self-fulfilling prophecy.

And if this all goes too far, politics will no longer be the art of accommodation and compromise, the art of conflict resolution. It will no longer be the arena where a sense of loyalty and mutuality greases the squeaky wheel and provides for the constituency. It will increasingly become a state of war. And that is what Watergate is all about.

The hyperstrategist described above, of course, is a caricature. He does not exist outside of lunatic asylums and research institutes. Nobody runs around thinking of the future exclusively in terms of dominoes, chess moves, and preemptive strikes. And very few people sit down to calculate all their actions in terms of risks and payoffs. Yet all these perceptions do form the basis of a certain mentality that in a more general way tends to perceive the world in highly strategic categories. Games and war-gaming, contingencies and options, capabilities and deployments, are all concepts and expressions that betray the kind of mentality that lies beneath them. There is nothing wrong with a strategic mentality, as we have said repeatedly, as long as it does not subvert larger values and goals. But there is a tendency for this way of thinking to get the upper hand. And to create a Watergate, it is not necessary that a strategist calculate everything according to the domino perspective; he simply must have this overall approach to things, where a sense of winning games comes first and deeper values are destroyed. There are many psychological by-products of this view of reality, and they are quite important in the case of Watergate.

Most important among these by-products is insecurity. It is not surprising that the domino perspective, with all its risks and uncertainties, is highly compatible with a sense of insecurity, if not paranoia; the more that people think in terms of games, strategies, and contingencies, the more they are prone to expect the possibility of some form of attack. And as they ponder all the possibilities it is little wonder that they tend to believe almost anything suggested to them about a potential adversary — and to act upon it. There is thus a tendency to scare easily, to mistrust their own instincts, and to feel that the world is conspiring against them — as well it may if they act upon their conclusions and start trying to anticipate all eventualities by accruing as much power to themselves as possible. Risk and insecurity go together very well indeed.

The hyperstrategist also tends to suffer from the insecurity created by an erosion of values. As process becomes the focus, no intrinsic goals or purposes remain, just winning per se. But the goal of winning cannot provide the psychological security that a sense of larger purpose can. In this situation the hyperstrategist is susceptible to two psychological tendencies: the self-righteous justification of his enterprise in moralistic categories or its ideological justification in grand eternal verities, both of which substitute for a sense of purpose. The Nixon strategists gave evidence of the first tendency, the McGovern strategists of the second.

A third source of insecurity is what happens when hyperstrategists regard all other human beings in rational and strategic terms. They thus lose the sense of security provided by normal human relations, a sense that the traditional politician values and cherishes. Trust and loyalty disappear, and with them so many points of reference that are normally sources of security. Loyalty and friendship among game players denote something different from their common adult meaning, though they are not unlike the restless liaisons of small children and the insecure conformism of adolescents. Shifting alliances replace friendships, and party-line orthodoxy substitutes for principled loyalty. For the hyperstrategist there can be no such thing as a friendly game player whose interests diverge from his own: loyalty must be total and unquestioning. There can be no such thing as "loyal opposition" or "friendly criticism." Any deviation from the line of the moment may be a sign of diverging interests. To the puerile, paranoid, restive hyperstrategist, any member of the crew who is too critical may seem to be ready to jump ship; and if he, too, is a hyperstrategist, the chances are he may.

So it is easy to understand the peculiar form of loyalty and "team spirit" that characterized the first Nixon administration — and the incredible disloyalties that the same people exhibited when the Watergate scandal broke. In the absence of personal loyalties, the attempt to create a team spirit turned out to be a facade since the strategic mentality, with its incredible emphasis on the short-run interests of the strategists, tends to preclude any form of loyalty in the face of strong adversity. The hyperstrategic mentality thus tended to destroy a sense of loyalty either to principles or to people, and with these two fundamental points of reference eroded, it is little wonder that a sense of insecurity prevailed.

If insecurity is the first psychological by-product of the hyperstrategic mentality, then a lack of tenacity is the second. This condition in part is the result of having loyalties to neither people nor principles; it also comes from keeping options open and avoiding commitments. But its principal source is the extrapolative view of reality that the domino image provides. The hyperstrategist tends to have a very short-range perspective because he is continually dealing with current contingencies. Peering down his various rows of possibilities he is given to extremes of bullishness and bearishness with the slight ups and downs of momentary reverses. He lacks the long-range perspectives of a person committed to causes and principles: his major objective is to extend a winning streak, and when that winning streak is over, he has a strong tendency to quit the game. The hawks of the Johnson administration provide a striking example of this phenomenon. Those who were committed anticommunists, such as Rusk and Rostow, stuck it out to the end. Those who were game players, such as Bundy, McNaughton, and McNamara, were ready to quit when the game began to go against them. Having gotten the country into the situation as a result of their short-run extrapolations, they wanted us to get out as a result of similar perspectives. The problem was that the war was more than just a game to most people and it was not easy simply to pick up the chips and go home. There were many examples of a lack of tenacity in the Nixon administration, but the Watergate episode was the crowning illustration. When the whole thing broke, very few remained on board and those that did in most cases were responding to momentary necessity, not to long-range commitments or deeper loyalties.

The third important psychological implication of the hyperstrategic perspective is its appeal to the juvenile mind. A mature decisionmaker has a long-range view of things. He knows the meaning of a responsible decision; he recognizes the worth of personal relationships and concrete goals. He respects a solid reputation. He knows that narrow stratagems are often counterproductive and that short-run expediencies can create long-range problems. He trusts his instincts. Because he has a stable attitude, he is not upset by small reverses. His long-range perspective allows him to make sound judgments.

But what image does the hyperstrategist present, this person who has such an undue fascination with games and stratagems, who tends to be so insecure and labile, who prefers coercion and deterrence to accommodation and mutuality, who enjoys conspiracies, who exuberates in conflict, and who is so insecure that he must justify his actions in the excesses of self-righteousness? He tends to resemble a juvenile or an adolescent with no sense of responsibility or tradition, a petty revolutionary who has few qualms about violating the customs of political procedure, but who fortunately lacks the tenacity to make fundamental changes in them. His values are so shallow that he must justify them within the process of winning itself, so his games become very important to him. He must make them into grand adventures, just as children fantasize about the importance of their games. And when the game is presidential politics all these tendencies become even more exaggerated.

Because the hyperstrategist tends to think in terms of conflict, the military analogy easily comes to mind. It is little wonder that 1972 saw such a fascination with grand strategies, war games, attack groups, logistical deployments, sabotage operations, intelligence and espionage projects, clandestine maneuvers, strategic deceptions, and even the hardware of military security — the paper shredders, the walkie-talkies, the burn bags, the badges, and other surface paraphernalia of heroics. It was all a grand game of cowboys and Indians or, more accurately, of cops and robbers. Some symptoms of the immature mentality were found at the highest levels in both campaigns, but the juvenile delinquency was more pronounced in the operation of CREEP because the ideological basis of the McGovern campaign was consciously antimilitaristic.

One great irony of this whole attempt to mimic military operations is that the great historical tradition of the American military does not emphasize the values of hyperstrategic thinking. It emphasizes tenacity, service, loyalty, honor, maturity, and other moral qualities that have given its past leaders the ability to withstand short-term reverses and to overcome the short-range dexterities of the opposition. Washington, Jackson, Lee, Grant, Pershing, Marshall, and Eisenhower were not hyper-strategists, but men endowed with those moral qualities that the hyper-strategic view of reality tends to destroy. All these men were *strategists,* but they never lost sight of the more fundamental values that they served, and they never forgot how to deal with *people.*

We can now see the full extent of the Watergate mentality: the domino perspective, the commitment to short-range objectives, the erosion of a sense of purpose, the focus on winning and process, the unwillingness to make solid commitments, the desire to accumulate power for its own sake, the ploy of keeping options open, the perception of others as either potential enemies or allies of convenience, the fascination with a politics of coercion and conflict, the depersonalized view of politics, the decline of a sense of trust and loyalty, the assumption that politics is a form of warfare, the doctrines of anticipation and preemption, the great sense of insecurity that leads to a lack of tenacity, and, finally, the juvenile atti-tude with its game plans, war games, and paramilitary concepts and hardware. This is the kind of mentality that threatens to take over our politics and makes a mockery of our democratic institutions. It is the kind of mentality that has such a manipulative dimension that its perpetrators regard the public with contempt and each other with suspicion. It is the kind of mentality that revels in deception and subterfuge and treats politics as if it were a not-so-cold war. Not everyone who worked for the President's reelection shared these perspectives, but, then, not everyone who worked for the President's reelection was responsible for Watergate.

The Logic of Watergate

THE INSECURE POSITION

Planning for the various Watergate episodes took place early in 1972, during which time the Nixon managers had many reasons to conclude that their strategic position was insecure. To begin with, they seemed to be in trouble with the electorate. The President's approval rating in the Gallup poll on the average had been much lower than that of his prede-cessors, and its trend in early 1972 was generally down. In trial heats with Muskie, the Democrats' front-runner, Nixon usually ran only a few points ahead, a very poor performance for an incumbent. His firm support in public and private surveys hovered in the low 40s, very close to his 43 percent support in the 1968 election.

Furthermore, there were good reasons for the electorate to be dissatisfied. The economy was not in good shape and the newly inaugurated Phase II was off to an unsteady start. George Meany seemed quite dissatisfied and was threatening to lead a labor crusade against the President the way he had done in 1968, with quite a bit of success. The war had been wound down, but it was far from over, and there was always the threat that the North Vietnamese might upset things dramatically, especially if they had a chance to influence the election of a more pliable alternative to Nixon. Also, with three years' emphasis on public relations, the administration had little to show the voter in terms of concrete results. The welfare program had stalled. Revenue sharing had not gone through yet. The government reorganization program had never been taken seriously by anyone. Only in foreign policy could the administration claim credit for accomplishment, but even the projected diplomatic triumphs in Moscow and Peking were in danger of being eclipsed by some flare-up in Southeast Asia.

Looking over the opposition, the administration had further cause for alarm. Not only was Muskie a threat, but Humphrey was coming on strong at the time and no one had forgotten October 1968, when he closed a gap much larger than the one Nixon enjoyed during early 1972. There was the great imponderable of Ted Kennedy, always regarded as a major threat. And George Wallace was again demonstrating his appeal to the voters and exploiting the busing issue with rhetorical skill. Wallace as a third-party candidate would have been acutely embarrassing and perhaps fatal to the President's reelection.

There were other causes for alarm. Most important, the money was not flowing in. Contrary to popular assumptions, the McGovern camp was raising much more money than the Nixon camp throughout April and May of 1972. The disclosed Nixon donations of $100 and more — a good thermometer of enthusiastic support — did not exceed the McGovern donations until the middle of June (see Figure 5). Nixon had raised a lot of money clandestinely before April, but that was from a few large contributors, many of whom had been pressured into donating. The best indicator — the solicited but voluntary middle-range contribution — was not encouraging during the period when Watergate was being planned. There was much cash on hand, but the future did not look promising.

Not only did the administration strategists feel that they were in political trouble generally, they also felt that they were under attack by powerful forces that sought their destruction. The press was a constant source of irritation, giving rise to a widespread feeling that it would do what it could to embarrass the President. In an election year the normal hostility of the press was of increased significance and the lessons of George Romney and especially Lyndon Johnson were not forgotten. One of the most annoying problems with the press was the leak. The administration leaked like a sieve, and there had been a number of very embarrassing disclosures; there were to be more as the spring wore on. The Pentagon papers may have been a spectacular example of these leaks, but there were others too, and the Nixon managers were getting a trifle annoyed at finding so many of their machinations disclosed on the front page of the *Washington Post*. More to the point, they felt that these leaks might be a threat to their political position. In the hands of a hostile press, they might become a means of destroying the President.

The administration managers also felt that they were being threatened from within the government. In their attempts to gain control of the federal bureaucracy, the White House operatives had made extensive and often clumsy use of deterrence logic. They had tried to coerce bureaucrats into compliance with their dictates by making spectacles out of those who failed to join the team. The "with us or against us" mentality had created vast reservoirs of resentment in many powerful agencies, notably in the Justice Department, in Hoover's FBI, in the IRS, and especially in HEW. Some of this resentment came from policy disagreements, some from the simple fear of being fired, and some from the recognition that the White House was posing a threat to the institutional integrity of the agency. For whatever reason, this condition of hostility led to a gulf between the White House and parts of the bureaucracy that deepened into suspicion and mistrust. The White House began to suspect that powerful agencies were reasoning that they had an interest in the Democrats' return to power, and that they were acting on behalf of the opposition. The leaks to the press did not dispel these suspicions.

The demonstrators appeared to be equally threatening. In 1968 they had been an acute embarrassment to the Democrats, and some argued that they were responsible for Humphrey's defeat. While the President had found that he could use them to score political points, nevertheless there was the constant worry that they might disrupt the convention and the campaign, thereby ruining the image of quiet effectiveness that the Nixon managers wanted to project. The memory of a beleaguered Johnson haunted them constantly. Furthermore, they knew that the demonstrators got under Nixon's skin, and they were worried that he might lose his temper at some point and create a media spectacle that might ruin his image. But the demonstrators seemed to represent still a larger threat. Somehow they appeared to be part of a conspiracy to attack the administration in so many vague, yet portentous, ways. Perhaps they were in league with the press, perhaps with a foreign power, perhaps with the Democrats. At any rate they seemed but one element in a large array of potential antagonists.

As the McGovern candidacy became more probable, new fears arose about the security of Nixon's position. McGovern was an unknown quantity. His movement was filled with people who seemed to be linked to the demonstrators and who had (it appeared) the support of the press. His organization was obviously run by excellent strategists, and there seemed to be a conspiratorial flavor about the whole business. And since the Nixon managers themselves had considered a whole range of options and stratagems, it seemed only reasonable that the McGovern strategists might be considering similar tactics, hence these had to be guarded against, discovered, and foiled.

In light of these assessments and suspicions, it is not surprising that the Nixon managers felt insecure. Not only did they feel that their electoral position was in danger, they also felt that the press, certain agencies of government, the demonstrators, the Democrats in general, and especially the McGovern movement might all be cooperating in an effort to discredit and destroy them. They also felt frustrated by so much opposition, and a climate of suspicion and fear developed that was fed by all the psychological considerations discussed above. Magruder, in his testimony before the Watergate committee, described this condition as a "certain atmosphere that had developed in my working at the White House," an atmosphere that led to the Watergate decision: "[T]hat is basically, I think, the reason why that decision was made, because of that atmosphere that had occurred, and to all of us who had worked in the White House, there was that feeling of resentment and of frustration at being unable to deal with issues on a legal basis."

When this sense of insecurity is felt by a person with a strategic mentality, a person committed to gaming and winning, the result is likely to be an outpouring of countermeasures; this was the case with Watergate. CREEP wanted to provide for every contingency and to exploit every possible opportunity, so its plans were drawn to a large scale. There seemed to be two basic strategic requirements. One, the various interest groups that were sources of opposition had to be neutralized and the enemies among them deterred from further anti-administration activities. This strategy had been put into operation long before the opening months of 1972 and was part of a continuing policy of domestic deterrence. The second strategy was to wage organizational warfare on the opposition and thereby to cut down its potential for winning. This was put into full operation at the beginning of 1972.

Two subsidiary requirements were needed to make these strategies work. The first was a good intelligence system to identify the enemies, to find out their weaknesses, and to learn in advance about any moves they might be making against the President's position. The second was the obvious requirement for money — clandestine money and large amounts of it.

Long before the 1972 presidential campaign began in any formal way, the Nixon administration had been dealing with its enemies. Because its staff tended to be hyperstrategists, they rejected the normal political procedures of dealing with dissidents. Instead of ignoring them, compromising with them, accommodating them, or even isolating them by cutting them off from their own sources of support, the administration relied on a policy of domestic deterrence. If the demonstrators, the press, the bureaucracy, and certain Democratic opponents all seemed to threaten the administration, then, the Nixon strategists reasoned, these potential threats had to be neutralized by counterthreats. The methods and tactics varied somewhat, but the basic strategies were the same for all groups.

The Demonstrators. The demonstrators were handled in two ways. First the administration tried deterrence. The FBI and the Justice Department conducted extensive investigations and left the protesters under spectacular surveillance to serve as a deterrent. There were physical confrontations, difficulties over permits, and hassles over parade routes. There were lockups, preventive detentions, and other forms of official harassment. There were beatings. Since the demonstrators, too, were organized by strategic politicians who wanted to make the administration look either brutal or silly, many of these confrontations were regarded with pleasure by the leadership of both sides. Looking back on these spectacles, the Watergate defendants claimed that the tactics of the demonstrators justified their use of countertactics. This assertion was both a tacit acknowledgment that these officials had lowered themselves to the level of street demonstrators, and, more to the point, that they had recognized the moral parity of two sets of strategic politicians interacting with each other.

Deterrence, however, did not work very well. It led to defiance, as it usually does in the absence of authority, and the administration felt the need to change its strategies. It attempted, therefore, to neutralize the protesters' threat by exploiting their demonstrations to its own political advantage. It argued quite plausibly that the demonstrations were counterproductive for the demonstrators, and before long it was actively promoting them. For example, the Nixon strategists encouraged a demonstration at the Statue of Liberty so that the President could denounce it, and, when they heard that demonstrators in North Carolina were planning to shout obscenities at Billy Graham, they reacted ecstatically. This policy was successful on the whole because the strategists on both sides came to the same conclusion: the administration could get more mileage out of the demonstrations than the opposition could. Score one point for the administration.

The Press and the Media. Although the Nixon strategists tried to neutralize the hostility of the press and media in the same way it had neutralized the demonstrators — by generating public opinion against them — this policy was far less successful. Agnew's attacks hit home to some extent, but they were far less telling than they had been against the demonstrators. The unwashed, unkempt protester may have been turned into an object of contempt and hatred, but despite administration efforts to create similar contempt and hatred for the press, Walter Cronkite was never dislodged from his secure position as "the most trusted man in America." Since neutralization had failed, the strategists turned to deterrence. The government's licensing power was employed to threaten individual stations and the networks. Newspapers and reporters were singled out for special attention; passes were denied to press conferences and White House functions. The refusal to hold press conferences itself became part of the deterrence game. Individuals were marked for special investigations. And then there was the list of enemies. Aside from a number of politicians and political contributors the main thrust of the list was against media people in the largest sense of the word. Newspapermen, TV reporters, advertising executives, and entertainment figures were given undue attention. The strategists involved envisioned using the IRS (which the IRS resisted), government contracts, and embarrassing personal material to blackmail or otherwise force these people into a more reasonable frame of mind.

This policy had mixed results. The national networks were cowed to some extent and there was a noticeable softening of their attitude toward the administration during the campaign. Whether this was a result of Nixon pressures or McGovern convulsions, however, is difficult to say. But the next round of the contest clearly went to the press, who reacted to the administration's measures with a policy of long-range defiance. As Katharine Graham, publisher of the *Washington Post,* succinctly stated in a television interview, "If they had left us alone we would probably have dropped the whole [Watergate] investigation, but the more they put the pressure on us, the more we knew they had something to hide." When Watergate broke, the press, smarting from the policies of the previous years, found a means of striking back — and retaliate it did. The Nixon managers might well have taken to heart the advice Machiavelli gave to the hyperstrategists of his century, "Never injure an antagonist lightly." More realistically, the administration might have considered the New England adage that more flies are caught with molasses than with vinegar. But it stuck instead to its disastrous and narrow strategic perceptions. Score one point for the administration and five points for the press.

The Bureaucracy. The administration employed many varieties of deterrence strategy in its attempts to neutralize the antagonism of various elements in the bureaucracy. Naturally it made extensive use of the power to hire — and especially to fire — and it made a number of examples out of bureaucrats who didn't conform to its policies, as we have said.

An interesting twist to the war with the bureaucracy was the famous "plumbers" unit designed to stop leaks. This collection of unusual individuals was hired by the White House with the President's approval for the purpose of coercing the bureaucracy. They were employed partly because the President could not get other agencies (notably the FBI) to do the job for him. This unit was not concerned with the leaks themselves as much as it was concerned with the leakers, and it was worried about them not because their leaks were hurting the process of government or the security of the country, but because they were political threats to the administration. Leaks were simply politically embarrassing. The point of the plumbers was to get information that could be used to discredit current and former government employees and thereby to deter them from conspiring against the administration. The Ellsberg burglary was one of many famous examples.

There were other attempts to prevent agencies from harming the administration politically. There was the overall administrative move to centralize power in the White House that we have already discussed. After the election, open warfare was declared on various agencies; funds were withheld and whole structures were liquidated.

But again deterrence resulted in defiance. The White House created an atmosphere where the bureaucracy felt massively threatened. When Watergate occurred, the bureaucracy strove to maintain its security position by forcing the White House to back down on all fronts, and it succeeded. It forced the appointment of careerists in the CIA and FBI. It forced the White House to acquiesce in a "depoliticization" of the Justice Department. It inspired suits to make the courts release the funds that the President had impounded and to preserve agencies that he was in the process of liquidating. It sought to bolster its connections to allies and potential allies in Congress. Most of all, it used the petty inanities and corrupt practices of the administration to discredit the role of the White House in the governmental process and tried to secure for itself an almost independent role in the conduct of affairs. And the leaks became a torrent. Score ten points for the bureaucracy.

Political Opponents. Political opponents are not quite in the same category as the demonstrators, the press, and the bureaucrats, although the administration tried to find evidence that all four were conspiring together and allegedly tried to determine that all four (except, perhaps, the press) were conspiring with foreign powers. The political opposition should be fair game, though traditionally limits have been imposed by the canons of decency. For example, Dwight Eisenhower was informed by the FBI that a minor employee of Adlai Stevenson's campaign had a communist background. When he heard this, he did the normal and decent thing. He quietly called Stevenson and told him, so that Stevenson could take care of the matter. One has the feeling that Charles Colson would have handled the matter differently.

The attempts to neutralize the opposition by finding dirt on them were extensive but not systematic. One major target was Kennedy. The Chappaquiddick episode provided a golden opportunity, which was followed very closely with agents on the scene. Surveillance was considered but rejected on the grounds that the agents might be suspected of being part of an assassination plot. And then there were the telegrams: a bizarre plot to fabricate some State Department cables that would have implicated John Kennedy in Diem's murder and thereby reduced the Kennedy mystique. Other politicians received such attention — Thomas Eagleton most effectively — but these examples are sufficient to make the point. The opposition bided its time and then had a field day. Score all this as you will.

Before the election, then, the administration scored a number of victories in its attempt to neutralize those elements that it considered dangerous. After the election it had to reap the results of its policy as these enemies struck back, each in proportion to the amount of deterrence that the administration had inflicted on it. Although a discussion of the relationship between the White House and Congress is beyond our scope, this, too, conformed to the overall pattern despite Congress's incredible display of institutional weakness.

ORGANIZATIONAL WARFARE

In early 1972, the Nixon strategists decided to supplement their deterrence policy with a program of sabotage. The campaigns of the opposition were targeted in an extensive but not highly systematic way. Some of their inspiration came from a Democratic prankster named Dick Tuck who had been playing jokes on Richard Nixon for years. Among his pranks were: getting an orchestra to play "Mack the Knife" when Nixon walked into an auditorium; having a sign painted with "What about the Hughes Loan?" in Chinese and held behind Nixon's head during a visit to Chinatown; putting on an engineer's cap and signaling a train to depart while Nixon spoke from its rear platform; getting a number of obviously pregnant welfare women to carry some signs proclaiming "Nixon's the ONE." Most of Tuck's operations were not very serious, and all of them had an element of humor about them.

A more important precedent for this kind of activity was the Goldwater campaign of 1964, and especially the San Francisco convention that year, where extreme operators had installed equipment to interrupt the communications system of their fellow Republicans, to smoke-bomb Governor Scranton as he went to the microphone, and to harass the supporters of opposition candidates. Many of these projects failed to come to fruition because they were not necessary. In 1972, however, the necessity seemed to be there.

The strategy of sabotage was directed first against Senator Muskie, the Democratic front-runner and the man considered by the administration to be their biggest November threat. Some Muskie fund-raisers were put on the enemy list and some sources of funds were cut off. (The cutting off of funds is an old technique. Kennedy, for example, used it against Humphrey during the 1960 primary season.) Literature was put out on Muskie stationery that accused both Senators Jackson and Humphrey of sexual misconduct. And then there was the famous letter to the *Manchester Union Leader* that Muskie reacted to in a staged performance that triggered his downfall.

After Muskie's fall, the administration did not pursue a consistent strategy with respect to the opposition. Contrary to popular belief, it did not encourage the nomination of McGovern. In fact McGovern, when he became a real possibility, was regarded as a bigger threat than Humphrey, not because his chances of winning were any greater, but because the possibility of his winning was considered nightmarish. Only Kennedy would have been worse, and maybe not even he. After Muskie's fall sabotage was conducted against all the major survivors.

After McGovern's nomination the administration allegedly leaked the Eagleton information. The impact of this was even more dramatic than the Muskie letter, but the fact that the administration leaked it is not of fundamental significance since the story would have broken on its own very quickly anyway.

Besides these two spectaculars, there were many "normal" sabotage events carried on by the Segretti operation, as it subsequently was called. Here are some examples.

- Calls made to New Hampshire voters by "Harlem" Muskie supporters at unusual hours of the night.
- A telephone call from "Gary Hart" to George Meany insulting him.
- Calls made to people who leased auditoriums either reserving the hall or canceling the reservation to create financial embarrassment or just the general impression of incompetence.
- Canceling schedules that were supposed to continue.
- Jamming communications.
- Interfering with the amplifying equipment at rallies.
- Manufacturing "letters to the editor" on a grand scale.
- Generating telegrams of support for positions signed with phony names.
- Getting unkempt people with McGovern buttons to behave rudely to the President so he could make an example out of them.

All of these events constitute a sordid tale. They are examples of sheer organizational warfare where one group uses tactics to embarrass or destroy another. They have no place in a democratic society; there is no conceivable justification for them in terms of informing the voters, organizing supporters, or in any other rationale for a political campaign. However, it should be recognized that in 1972 these practices did not constitute a political Armageddon. They were extensive, but not systematic enough to be sinister. They were innovative, but not revolutionary enough to be frightening. They were effective, but not enough so to alter the outcome. They were the product of the juvenile mentality that we examined above, the puerile commitment to the paraphernalia of conflict. Their roots in strategy are clear, but they were much more the product of those psychological deficiencies that a hyperstrategic mentality produces.

INTELLIGENCE AND ESPIONAGE

It is not surprising that the Nixon strategists demanded an extensive intelligence-gathering operation. Their sense of insecurity, their feeling that others were acting against them, and their need to achieve a strategic edge over their opponents all provided strong justifications for spending money extensively on intelligence. Intelligence is a crucial concept in any conflict situation, and in the game of presidential politics it has taken on tremendous significance in recent years. The more strategic our politics becomes, the more political resources will have to be allocated to intelligence and espionage.

There are many aboveboard intelligence activities that are standard operating procedure in almost any campaign run by the new politicians. Where does information come from? From clipping services, from monitoring speeches and advertisements by the opposition, from friendly newspaper reporters attached to the opposition camp, from mailings and other public documents issued by the opposition, from the political grapevine, and from many other public sources. On another level, survey research provides a form of intelligence as does door-to-door canvassing by workers. If a campaign is to use such information effectively it needs skilled personnel to process it into workable form. CREEP had some excellent analysts and they supplied such agencies as the Attack Group with solid information gathered from legitimate public sources.

But the managers wanted more. They wanted to find out exactly what was going on in the enemy camp. They did not trust their public sources; their repeated suspicions, coming from their sense of insecurity, made them reject normal explanations of their opponent's behavior. Just as the administration refused to believe its own FBI reports that said the demonstrators were *not* associated with any foreign power, it also refused to believe that the McGovernites and the Democrats in general were not involved in some plots to undercut the administration.

The clandestine intelligence-gathering operation had four basic missions. First, it was to identify the supporters of the opposition camp, so that they could be added to the enemy list and dealt with accordingly. This would enable the Nixon strategists to shut off funds or to withhold favors from those who were against them. The second mission was to get information about the opposition strategy that was not available from public sources. This was not a major consideration because much was known anyway and additional information could not be expected to be "actionable" quickly. Third was the search for plots. There was a great deal of interest in the relationship between the Democrats and the "enemies." Were the Democrats in contact with the demonstrators, the leakers in the bureaucracy, and perhaps some hostile members of the press? Also, what dirt did the Democrats have on them? Did Chairman O'Brien have information on ITT, for example? Last, and most important, was the mission of finding usable information to discredit the opposition camp or any key member of it. If the Democrats could be linked to the demonstrators, if their finances were irregular, if some of their officials had been indiscreet in any way, if some notorious character had made a contribution, if some potentially embarrassing political promise had been extended, or if some rather unsavory campaign practice was being carried out, it would be possible to exploit this for public political mileage, for private persuasion, or for preventing the opposition from using similar tidbits that they might have found.

This was the kind of logic that justified the Watergate bugging and other operations. The methods used and the specific nature of the operation were a result of the operating procedures developed by the plumbers and the rest of the bizarre crew that the White House engaged for the caper; the go-ahead — the actual decision to bug — remains shrouded in the mysteries of bureaucratic decisionmaking at this writing.

SECRET MONEY

These grand schemes all depended on a comfortable flow of clandestine cash, hence the logistical support for the entire operation centered on CREEP's ability to raise it, launder it, and distribute it secretly. We say a lot about fund-raising elsewhere in this book, so it is not necessary to go into detail here about the many imaginative fund-raising schemes that Secretary Stans and his cohorts concocted. There is, however, one important dimension to their activities that needs to be mentioned, the use of the power of incumbency to raise money. Just as the instruments of the state were used to deter the enemies of the administration, so the instruments of the state were used to coerce its "friends." The power to grant and withhold contracts, the power to influence rulings by administrative agencies, the ability to construe antitrust legislation, the power to license, the power to investigate and examine, and other governmental powers were used by the Nixon fund-raisers to extort large sums of money from major corporations and interest groups. All this was highly illegal as well as unethical. But again, it was placed in the category of the ends justifying the means. Winning the election was simply ranked above everything else and those agencies of government that could be coerced were forced to join the team.

The Cover-up Game Plan

When the Watergate burglars were arrested, the White House had a problem on its hands. It was clear that a massive cover-up was required — no one seriously thought of an alternative. As Magruder stated it, "I do not think there was ever any discussion that there would not be a cover-up." Since there was so much to hide, it seemed absolutely necessary to prevent the truth from coming out, and the Nixon managers proceeded to this new strategic problem with energy and dispatch.

DENIAL

The first and most obvious strategy was to deny everything. After the break-in, officials at all levels issued statements reassuring the public that the White House was not involved in any way. The tone was one of controlled whimsicality and the initial ploy was to dismiss the whole episode as trivial. There was even a rumor started that Watergate was a Democratic plot to embarrass the President.

The initial denials were not entirely credible, since it was soon learned that Watergate conspirator E. Howard Hunt had been connected to the White House and James McCord was an employee of CREEP. With embarrassing questions becoming frequent, the President decided to put his credibility on the line by delivering in August 1972 the first of many carefully worked out denials that were to continue for over a year.

Drawing on his reservoir of public trust — at a time when he was at the peak of his popularity — Nixon announced that he had conducted an investigation of the whole affair and that the results were negative. He assured the country that his special counsel, John Dean, had presented him with a report that exonerated the White House from any involvement in the episode. This statement, which was pure public relations (there had never been any investigation), seemed to satisfy the public. For the rest of the election campaign, self-righteous denunciations of the press and other skeptics were sufficient. (Some of these statements make inter-

111

esting reading today, especially those by poor Clark MacGregor, who probably believed what he was saying.) George McGovern's attacks on the Watergate episode were largely ineffective because the President at the time had much more credibility than his opponent.

To deny the truth in a complex and extended situation, however, is a major strategic problem and it requires an extensive effort, especially if there are others who are determined to prove your lie. An alternative scenario of reality has to be formulated that squares with a large number of known variables and preserves enough flexibility for the fabricator to deal with the uncovering of new evidence. It is very difficult to build up a believable cover story incrementally over time, because each newly uncovered fact has to be fitted into an existing story that is at variance with reality and hence almost always at variance with the newly uncovered fact. This set of propositions is strongly reminiscent of the old rhyme: "What a tangled web we weave,/When first we practice to deceive." With care, however, some of these difficulties can be overcome by clever strategists who build in backups to their fabrications. The practice of formulating statements on the basis of their *utility,* not their *veracity,* is now widespread and this science is relatively well developed.

With the Watergate cover-up, the original stories were so patently fraudulent to begin with and the backups so carelessly created that the entire structure of denial collapsed at the first break in the chain when Judge John Sirica forced James McCord "to tell all." From then on, so many stories collapsed so quickly that the entire structure of the White House was shaken to its foundations in the course of a few months. The denials of White House involvement shifted to denials of presidential involvement, since it was relatively easy for everyone simply to agree that no one had ever told the President anything about anything on any date — and at this inner citadel the story held for quite a while. The President began to "discover" what was going on and asserted that a man who had been fascinated by politics and little else all his life knew nothing about the political activities on his behalf conducted by his close associates. He maintained repeatedly that he had been systematically lied to, deceived, and betrayed by those men upon whom he relied so much before the episode occurred and upon whom he continued to rely after the "betrayals" became public.

THE JUDICIAL STRATEGY

The most difficult antagonist faced by the administration was the independent judiciary. The options here were narrower and the risks vastly more dangerous than in the looser arena of public opinion. Furthermore, the rules of the game were not subject to administration manipulation to the degree they were elsewhere.

The White House strategists faced an honest and untouchable judge. Sirica had no price and they probably had no desire to approach him anyway in light of their unsuccessful attempts to deal with the Ellsberg judge. They had to resort to alternative methods, and there were several. First, they attempted to buy off the defendants in the burglary case with cash and promises of clemency. Second, they tried to water down the efforts of the prosecution during the original trial. Both strategies backfired, with exposure in the first case and suspicion by the judge in the second. A third alternative had been planned as a backup: the diversion of the blame to the CIA and FBI. Several high officials in these agencies were compromised, but the institutional integrity of both departments made it very awkward indeed for the White House to go much further in this direction. A fourth strategy was to deny the courts as much evidence as possible. An enormous quantity of evidence was destroyed at the beginning of the affair and much more was destroyed selectively as the affair progressed. Evidence not destroyed was in many cases withheld. Doctrines of executive privilege were evoked in extensive, but selective, ways and the affirmation or renunciation of this doctrine became a strategic instrument of some importance.

After the story broke with all its fury in April 1973, the President seemed to face both mounting demands for a cleanup and the possibility of congressional action. Giving in to these pressures, he appointed Elliot Richardson attorney general; Richardson, in turn, appointed a special prosecutor, Archibald Cox, as a condition of his own confirmation by the Senate.

This strategy seemed sound because it quelled suspicions, satisfied the Congress, and created the impression that the administration wanted to clean house. It left open the option of getting rid of Richardson and Cox if they became too troublesome. They did. The problem was that both Richardson and Cox took their mission seriously. Their assignment had been to get to the bottom of the affair and this was what they proceeded to do. These two lawyers had been hired because they *appeared to be* honest. Unfortunately for the administration's game plan, they turned out *actually to be* honest. It is easy to see how a judicial mentality and a strategic mentality will conflict with one another. The former is given a set of special tasks to be carried out according to certain procedures. The latter, however, focuses on the immediate impact of certain activities. Cox, pursuing his mission of finding the truth, soon began to interfere with the administration's game plan of covering up the truth. He therefore became an enemy, a man not playing on the team. It became imperative to dispose of him and this was carried out with dispatch.

Congressional Hesitance
Although it may have had some nervous moments, the administration could rely on one solid factor: the Congress of the United States in affairs

of great importance had no sense of institutional integrity whatsoever. Individual congressmen might be alarmed or disgusted, individual senators might be annoyed at presidential practices, and even a large majority in both houses might privately favor the removal of the President. But all of this would be of little relevance, because Congress *as an institution* could never be persuaded to act in its institutional interests. Ironically, this whole affair exposed more about Congress than it did about the President. It showed that no Congress will impeach a President, no matter what his offenses, unless it is forced to do so by overwhelming and sustained public pressures. Gone are the days when a Sam Rayburn, a Robert Taft, or an Alben Barkley would stand up for the institutional prerogatives of what used to be the greatest legislative body in the world. The shoes of these giants have been filled by genial, but not resolute, successors, men bent on avoiding conflict with the Executive at all costs, leaders who look to a policy of appeasement even when faced by antagonists willing to use ultimate weapons to achieve nearly unlimited objectives. It remained for the judiciary and to some extent the bureaucracy to curb the excesses of presidential transgressions; the Congress limited itself merely to exposing some of them. To be sure, an extraordinarily hesitant Congress was finally forced into impeachment proceedings, but few institutions have ever been more reluctant to do their duty.

Thus, the strategic politics of the Nixon administration brought on the disasters of 1973. When the counterattack on the administration was launched, it found itself in a totally untenable position. It needed trust, but none was forthcoming. It needed a constituency to sustain itself; none was there. It needed political support, but it had to purchase what little it could get out of its dwindling resources. It needed a rationale for staying in office, but little could be found of its own making. It needed a sense of conviction to sustain its efforts, but its game plans were not sufficient to provide one. Above all, it needed to restore its authority, but its strategies could not do so. For four solid years it had been pursuing a consistent policy of undercutting its own intrinsic power position as a result of its hyperstrategic perception of reality. It was a dramatic example of men bent on rational suicide.

6

Strategic Triumph: The McGovern Nomination

The Movement and the Man

The movement that nominated George McGovern provides a different example of strategic politics and illustrates what can happen when ideal-istic people try to achieve their political goals through highly tactical methods. The origins of this fascinating aggregation of men, women, ideas, money, and political experience are found in the turbulent sixties, in the civil rights movement, the Vietnam protests, and especially in the McCarthy and Kennedy candidacies of 1968. It is well known how these episodes brought together a large number of activists into a loose but extensive network of associations, and it is not necessary to discuss at length either its origins or dimensions, since they are familiar to most and the myths that surround it are essentially correct. Like its conservative counterpart, it is elitist and narrowly based geographically; its activists pride themselves on their sophistication and intellectuality, and its ad-herents enjoy a strong measure of self-confidence and self-righteousness. It is wealthy and has a claim on many inherited fortunes, but its members are largely upper middle class in origin. Its personalities have become ce-lebrities — all the way from the leaders who write the speeches and man-age the campaign of its candidates to the volunteers, often young, always "dedicated," who ring the doorbells and man the telephones. Its files and mailing lists constitute powerful political instruments and its publications are widespread and influential. The nature of its power has been more intellectual than financial or "political" in the traditional sense of the word and its leaders have found that ideas and causes can move men and women as much as other forms of influence. To this movement belong

115

some of the most astute minds and some of the most energetic people in the country. Someday they may govern the Republic.

The adherents of the movement were brought together by visions of a better, happier, and freer world than their surroundings seemed to offer, but these visions were rapidly translated into specific political objectives: pass certain legislation, force the government out of the Vietnam war, deny Lyndon Johnson renomination, block the passage of ABM, and many others. It makes a great deal of sense to everyone but utopians for moral commitments to be embodied in concrete political aims, but this embodiment is purchased at a severe cost. The more practical an idealist becomes, the more he must commit himself to political strategy and tactics, and the more he commits himself to these, the more his idealistic aims will recede and mere tactical considerations will become paramount.

In a movement of idealists this phenomenon becomes very pronounced, since the movement itself — its cultivation and perpetuation — becomes the focus, if not the goal, of its adherents. Furthermore, as the requirements of the movement and its immediate strategic considerations become more and more important, the ideologically committed are phased out by the tactically proficient. As long as the ultimate vision persists, however, its presence serves to reinforce, not to limit, the strategic nature of the movement, since the vision gives its adherents a strong justification to use the kind of highly strategic methods that would not be employed by the more traditional politician. This is why the new conservatives and the new liberals often appear so much more expedient than the old politicians.

On the surface, at any rate, George McGovern was no stranger to the movement. He had run for President briefly in 1968 after Robert Kennedy's assassination and had served as a focal point for those Kennedy supporters who did not wish to vote for Eugene McCarthy at the convention. In 1970 he had campaigned for liberal Democrats and had raised a large amount of money by means of a mailing list that eventually grew into the famous list that figured so prominently in his 1972 fundraising efforts. Most important, McGovern had come into close contact with the left wing of his party when he chaired the commission that drew up the reform rules that became so controversial — and so useful to the movement — in 1972. He was on good terms with the leading movement figures and they were on good terms with him.

Yet in another sense McGovern and the movement were profound strangers to each other, and as distant as New York City and Berkeley, California, are from the plains of South Dakota. Their backgrounds were so diverse and the sources of their protests were so different that it is doubtful that either really understood the other. McGovern's genuine, firsthand experience of poverty is far different than the movement's vicarious appreciation of its significance; McGovern's deep-seated moral conviction about justice is far different than the movement's symbolic rage of ideological fervor, and McGovern's stubborn persistence is far different than the movement's tactical flexibility.

George Stanley McGovern's personality and character are crucial factors in the politics of 1972, but relatively little has been written about them. He came from a humble, devout home that had a profound influence upon his life and politics. His father, Joseph C. McGovern, was a fundamentalist Wesleyan Methodist minister whose calling and devotion shaped his son's life more than any other element. George McGovern's style, his speech, his tremendous inner resources, his idealism, his self-sufficiency, his distance from intimates, his concealment of emotions, and his discipline come directly from his upbringing.

The McGoverns were a self-contained, self-sustaining family, quite apart socially from the other townspeople in Mitchell, South Dakota, but knit together by a deep faith in God. Pastor McGovern had family devotions, daily Bible reading, and prayer. The McGoverns worshiped twice or three times on Sunday and went to prayer meeting on Wednesday night. Their social life was completely within the confines of the church. "We didn't go out much at night," remembers McGovern's sister Olive, now Mrs. Phil Briles of Sisseton, South Dakota. "The things we did, we did at home." George McGovern has always been an intense and solitary figure. Father William Wendt, a fellow high school debater, acknowledged hell-raiser, now a radical Episcopal clergyman in a Washington ghetto, says that McGovern was never seen in the evenings downtown at the drugstore, the closest thing Mitchell had to a youth hangout. He didn't move with the rest of the gang or have any intimate friends. Always he kept to himself, friendly, cordial, but alone. Wendt observes, "George was a keen thinker, studious, rather attractive as a person, neat, well-mannered, an outstanding student, respected, terribly cautious, inquisitive, very sharp. He didn't run with a clique. He was busy collecting himself. He was comfortable where he was. He had a reserve and a strong sense of family. He didn't let many people into his privacy. He was terribly respected, but I can't say that he was loved in any sense."

This solitude and self-containment has continued throughout his life. McGovern solicits expert opinion, then makes up his own mind. When he decided to leave the ministry and transfer to a doctoral program in history and political science at Northwestern University — surely one of the two or three most momentous decisions in his life — he did not consult his wife, Eleanor, or her sister and brother-in-law who were living with them at the time in Evanston, Illinois. McGovern merely announced it one night at the supper table. To this day he makes decisions much the same way, and he did throughout his campaign. He is not part of the Senate establishment; he has probably fewer than a half dozen close

117

friends among his colleagues. His staff has said that in McGovern's early days in Washington he used to go, not to the Carroll Arms watering spot, but on walks alone. The "court of last resort" for finding him was Trover's bookstore, where he would be browsing.

As with so many self-contained individuals, there is a streak of arrogance in George McGovern. The story is told that when he was a first-grader the teacher mistook his timidity in volunteering to recite for slowness of mind. She found out later that young George was looking at his classmates and thinking what idiots they were, for he knew he could have read the whole book while they were stumbling over the first few pages. A reporter traveling with the 1972 campaign said that sometimes he wondered whether McGovern was thinking the same thing when dealing with his associates.

Despite his personal distance from individuals, McGovern developed a strong social conscience. Several years ago he confided, "In our home and church there was a constant reiteration that matters of the spirit and heart are more significant than material considerations. I suspect that almost assured that I would go into a career of teaching, or the clergy, or public service — and those are the careers that I considered." On another occasion he recalled, "I suppose I picked up from my parents a deep sense of responsibility for trying to do what I could to make the world a better place to live. I can remember my father speaking in those terms when I was a little boy — of the concept of service, of investing one's life to advance worthwhile causes."

But the source of these social convictions was religious belief, not political doctrine, and McGovern adhered to it with an intensity and tenacity that matched the enormity of his solitude. Robert Pearson, McGovern's debate coach and a strong influence upon him, recalls that he "always placed the highest priority on human values. He would not compromise between what was good for people and what was practical or pragmatic. . . . George was disinclined to take a side just for the excuse of taking that side. He wanted to debate either the affirmative or the negative for the sake of convictions." And these convictions were grounded in a very strong Christian theology that never came across to the voter.

In his philosophy and theology McGovern tried to bridge the age-old gap between introspection and activism, personal salvation and social commitment, the inner journey and the outer journey. During his presidential campaign, at Wheaton College on October 11 he delivered what he considered to be one of his most important speeches, a statement of his fundamental beliefs. He concluded, "Some Christians believe that we are condemned to live with man's inhumanity to man, with poverty, war and injustice — and that we cannot end these evils because they are inevitable. But I have not found that view in the Bible. Changed men can change society, and the words of Scripture clearly assign to us the ministry and the mission of fundamental change. While we know that the kingdom of God will not come from a political party's platform, we also know that if someone is hungry, we should give him food; if he is thirsty, we should give him drink; if he is a stranger, we should take him in; if he is naked, we should clothe him; if he is sick, we should care for him; and if he is in prison, we should visit."

Michael McIntire, McGovern's religious affairs coordinator, wrote sympathetically about McGovern after the election in the ecumenical *Christian Century,* saying that reporters were never able to grasp the essential theme of morality that permeated McGovern the man and his message. When McGovern began talking about morality and corruption, they yawned, grinned in embarrassment for him, and put away their notebooks. After the Wheaton speech McGovern had a meeting in Chicago that was relatively insignificant. But that meeting was the story covered that day; the three networks and one wire service ignored the Wheaton talk completely. Yet without question it was one of the most significant and revealing speeches of his campaign.

From start to finish, McGovern based his case for the presidency on a plea for moral leadership and a return to the values that he felt had made America great. His tone was usually calm and pastoral, but his words frequently carried the fury of an Old Testament prophet. Indeed, he quoted Isaiah most often. It is not surprising that McGovern gained his national platform through a long and impassioned opposition to the Vietnam war. To McGovern, the war was wrong not merely because it killed American boys, but because it killed Vietnamese as well. As he said repeatedly, "They, too, are children of God."

McGovern's convictions were also strongly influenced by the South Dakota of his youth, a state not too distant in time or living memory from the homesteaders who settled it, yet a state gripped by the Depression of the 1930s with its awesome poverty.

The early homesteaders of the South Dakota plains had to fight not only the elements but the railroads and the milling companies who manipulated the hauling rates and price of grain. These powerful interests controlled the statehouse and the county courthouses for many years, and in reaction to them the populist movement swept across the region in the late nineteenth century, influencing the politics of South Dakota as much as that of any state.

During those years, for instance, the South Dakota government proposed, and the voters endorsed in referenda, direct primary laws to make officials more responsible. State-owned enterprises were authorized: a cement plant, a coal mine, grain elevators, stockyards, and waterpower sites on the Missouri River. Not all came to fruition. Some that did, such as the coal site, were established and subsequently disposed of, heavily in debt. But the state cement plant in Rapid City continues to this day. One governor even ordered the state to sell gasoline at low rates to force the oil companies to reduce theirs.

Dr. Robert Pennington, a native of Redfield, South Dakota, and George McGovern's brother-in-law, says that although the present generation of South Dakotans may not be pioneers, they knew people who were. "Our grandparents homesteaded the state," he says, "and we knew our grandparents." George McGovern did not have to depend on other people's memories of what the pioneer plainsmen were like. His father had come to South Dakota as a pioneer preacher and McGovern grew up among them. He had personal knowledge of the dust and the Depression, for he saw their effects around him. Reverend McGovern's parishioners were especially hard hit because they were poor townspeople and farmhands for the most part.

George McGovern wrote later: "My most vivid boyhood memories go back to those difficult days in windswept, drought-ridden South Dakota during the Depression. I remember seeing dry, parched topsoil swept into the air by winds that sometimes made the noonday sun as black as midnight. I remember the discouragement of farmers receiving checks for a shipment of hogs that did not cover the trucking expenses of taking the hogs to market. That was the first time I ever saw a grown man cry. I'm sure it was those boyhood experiences that first got me to thinking about the injustice and hardships of life on the farm. My determination to tell the farmer's story to the city dwellers and my feeling that the farmer is entitled to the attention of his government go back to those bleak days."

George V. Cunningham, McGovern's 1972 deputy campaign manager and political aide from the very beginning, says that though some of the issues have changed, McGovern "is saying the same thing today with amazing consistency. His views are an intellectual, logical extension of populism. He is speaking in the tradition of Peter Norbeck of South Dakota, George Norris of Nebraska, Robert La Follette of Wisconsin, the Non-Partisan League of North Dakota, and the Democratic Farmer-Labor Party of Minnesota."

It is easy to see that the movement and the man from South Dakota made an interesting pair. They were far from mismatched, since both shared common convictions about the war and about many domestic social issues, even though the sources of these convictions were quite different. Furthermore, there were some striking similarities between the ideological fervor of the movement communicant and the moral convictions of the senator. Both were willing to engage in tactical maneuvers to attain their objectives, although McGovern's flexibility was considerably less than that of the movement leaders. Both were committed to dealing with people on the basis of abstraction, not political intuition or insight. And arrogance was a stranger to neither man nor movement.

Yet there was always a great distance between them, in contrast to the relationship that the Kennedys or Eugene McCarthy enjoyed to the earlier versions of the movement. This distance was partly the result of McGovern's own solitude and contempt for politics, partly the result of a divergence of background and life styles, and partly the result of hyperstrategists not understanding the limits to tactical flexibility that a man of conviction insists upon.

It is important to understand this distance because throughout the campaign it was never clear whether the movement was using McGovern for its purposes or McGovern was using the movement for his. It *was* clear, however, that the man himself did not figure extensively in the nomination campaign. Others would have served the movement as well, and it was the movement, not the man, that won the nomination. Ironically, George McGovern had practically nothing to do with his own greatest triumph. After the nomination he was never able to control the movement or effectively direct its activities, and it in turn had a negligible amount of influence on him. Each went a separate way to disaster.

Strategy and Tactics

The nomination of George McGovern was one of the greatest strategic masterpieces in the history of American politics. By parlaying less than 20 percent of the rank-and-file Democrats and less than 30 percent of the primary vote into a majority of convention delegates, the McGovern managers demonstrated the incredible advantages of technical expertise as they mobilized and maneuvered a small but ready-made constituency through a maze of legally fluid and politically unstable situations. Although their triumph was made possible by the folly of their adversaries, their ability to exploit this folly was the crucial ingredient of their success.

The McGovern strategists began with a very simple scenario. A long time before the season opened, they noted with some satisfaction that the sequence of primaries in New Hampshire, Wisconsin, and Massachusetts gave them an excellent opportunity for bringing their candidate into serious contention without spreading their resources too thinly. New Hampshire was small and seemed well suited to their candidate's personal style of campaigning, and the McCarthy experience of 1968 had demonstrated that a liberal, antiwar candidate could attract enough organizational support around New England to wage a credible, if not winning, campaign in that conservative state. Wisconsin, the high water mark of McCarthy's efforts, provided even more solid opportunities for organizing a victory. The files of names existed, the volunteers were there, and the potential list of competing candidates seemed long enough to enable a minority candidate to win. The ancient isolationist and antiwar

121

populism of middle America ran strongest in Wisconsin and this combination dictated a heavy concentration of effort for the April 5 primary.

Finally, Massachusetts seemed to offer the best chance of all. The most dovish state in the nation (whose legislature had made it illegal for its citizens to serve in the Vietnam war), the most academic state in the nation (with the highest per capita college enrollment), and the most professional state in the nation (with its extraordinary concentration of medical and scientific research centers), Massachusetts provided the largest proportion of potential McGovern supporters of any primary state. Hence a modest showing in New Hampshire, a win in Wisconsin, and a triumph in Massachusetts, each building on the other, was the domino theory to which the McGovern strategists committed themselves several months before the season opened. They felt that strong performances in these "movement states" would give their candidate the credibility and visibility that could, in turn, create a popular upsurge for him and enable him to win further primaries in less friendly states. Since credibility was the purpose of the first part of the game, they reasoned that it was in their interest to avoid potentially damaging contests in Florida, Tennessee, North Carolina, West Virginia, and Indiana.

The McGovern managers' two major worries in late 1971 were that Muskie would create such a large bandwagon that his strong appeal to politicians could be translated into a decisive appeal to primary voters and that the candidacy of John Lindsay would split the liberal antiwar vote in half and destroy their scenario before it could reach Massachusetts. Humphrey, an obvious contender, was not an immediate threat, since he appealed to a different constituency, and Wallace was only vaguely appreciated by the McGovern strategists in late 1971.

The scenario worked out rather well, but it could never have worked without the blunders of the Muskie and Lindsay strategists. Things started out rather poorly. In January, Lindsay began to move rapidly and showed some signs of delegate strength in Arizona, of all places. Muskie was cresting on his wave of popularity and the prestigious Becker poll in the *Boston Globe* predicted a New Hampshire triumph of major proportions for him. In fact, it looked as if he might receive a higher percentage of the vote than the President would in the Republican primary. But the White House came to McGovern's aid. William Loeb, the conservative publisher of the *Manchester Union Leader,* had been spearheading a crusade against Muskie with front-page editorials that savaged the front-runner with great frequency. "Flip-flop Muskie Is a Phony" and "Muskie and the Freaks" are examples of the headlines that culminated in the now famous "Muskie Insults Franco-Americans," a front-page editorial commenting on a letter that the paper purported to have received that said Muskie had laughed at the use of the ethnic slur "Canuck" in a Florida motel.

122

This letter later turned out to have been a White House plant. Muskie's strategists had largely ignored Loeb's attacks because their lead in the polls was high. But the reaction to the editorial among the still ethnically conscious French-Canadian mill towns of New Hampshire was severe and Muskie's polls picked it up immediately. A reply was needed to this fraud that had begun to have such an impact. The Muskie strategists set their candidate up in front of the *Union Leader* building and created a "pseudo-event," a media exclusive in which the candidate blasted the absent publisher in front of his office. This staged performance led to the famous crying scene that marked the beginning of Muskie's rapid decline. The interesting question is whether or not the display of emotion was in the original script. The performance was so out of character for Muskie that one strongly suspects that he was counseled in advance to "show emotion." If so, this tactical blunder must rank very high in the long catalogue of mistakes that spotted the 1972 season.

Within two weeks Muskie had dropped about twenty points in the Becker survey. The beneficiary was McGovern, who was the only other viable candidate with a credible New Hampshire organization. Loeb had not attacked McGovern extensively (since he had discounted his chances) and the voting results showed that McGovern's areas of greatest strength (aside from the campuses) were in the conservative and hawkish Manchester area that the Loeb newspaper blankets. The liberal Massachusetts border towns on which McGovern had counted went comfortably for Muskie. Hence the New Hampshire result was more the product of Loeb's editorials and Muskie's mistakes than of McGovern's efforts, but had these efforts not been made the advantage would have gone elsewhere.

The *early* decision by the McGovern managers to concentrate in New Hampshire and Wisconsin together with *early* and solid activities in these states also created a vast strategic problem for John Lindsay. He could not enter either area massively without being a "spoiler" of the liberal cause, and if he couldn't score points in these states, where could he turn? The McGovern strategy forced him into a calculated risk that turned out to be a fatal trap, a trap that removed him from the game and solidified McGovern's position with the Left.

Florida followed New Hampshire by a week and Florida was an unknown. Populated by Southerners and Northerners, retirees and entrepreneurs, Cubans and blacks, the second primary state was described by the national media as a microcosm of America, a correct observation if it meant that all kinds of Americans lived there; an incorrect observation if it meant that they were there in similar proportions to the rest of the country. Lindsay managers noted with satisfaction that Florida was a classic "media state," and the domination of television seemed well suited to the needs of their supposedly media-sophisticated candidate. Unfortunately for them, they confused style with substance, and their massive campaign and media effort in a politically hostile environment got absolutely nowhere.

The McGovern strategists were much more shrewd. They did not ignore Florida, but they put virtually all of their efforts into organizational activities, which are inherently less visible than the overt kind of media campaign that the Lindsay strategists were running. Hence a poor showing by McGovern would appear considerably less damaging than a poor showing by Lindsay, while a good showing by McGovern would appear all the more spectacular. They thereby kept their options open and maintained a high degree of flexibility. After the New Hampshire showing, the strategists decided that they had an unexpected chance to embarrass Lindsay seriously and they sent the senator into Florida for the express purpose of matching the Lindsay effort. Good organization proved to be more advantageous than clever advertising, as is so often the case in primaries, and the objective was attained. McGovern's 78,232 votes approximated Lindsay's 82,386, and the New Yorker, embarrassed by a poor showing, in effect quit the race. The Lindsay strategists, who had no political purpose aside from winning per se, gave up very easily. Their dominoes were scattered in the first round, and with their scenario interrupted, they totally lost interest in the game. Having no underlying commitments, no political objectives, and no mission to fulfill, they cashed in their few remaining chips and went home. Lindsay himself went to Wisconsin to wrap up affairs, but there was really no effort made after Florida. This is an excellent example of what happens when politics is reduced to sheer gamesmanship: when there is no longer a purpose or a cause to be served, any significant setback will induce the strategists to quit. The McGovern managers themselves behaved this way after the Eagleton affair, but the man himself never did because his motives and his sense of mission always transcended narrow strategic considerations.

Florida was a major turning point. By committing themselves in a limited way, the McGovern tacticians had averted a loss of credibility and the Wallace triumph (42 percent of the vote) minimized the effect of their fourth-place finish since everyone else looked poor. Lindsay had been eliminated, and Muskie, with 9 percent of the vote, was effectively finished. Most of all, the fall of the front-runner necessarily created great instability, and in unstable situations the highly organized have tremendous advantages. The confusions of Florida made possible the victory in Wisconsin.

The McGovern organization had been preparing for over a year in Wisconsin. They had reassembled a large part of the McCarthy organization and had received the support of a number of elected officials. The state had been poised like an ambush along the primary route for a long time. The decline of Muskie brought Humphrey and Wallace to the forefront and each of these candidates had historical support in Wisconsin. Humphrey, however, was still looking very much like a loser and the voters were tired of him. Wallace had done very little organizational work and hardly any survey research, so he did not know where to place his emphasis. In this political and organizational vacuum the McGovern forces consolidated 29 percent of the vote to achieve a statewide victory. With the benefit of hindsight, it is easy to see that Wisconsin was more a demonstration of weakness by Muskie and Humphrey than of strength by McGovern, but at the time it looked otherwise. The scenario was working. Massachusetts and Pennsylvania were next. Muskie and Humphrey let McGovern have the former by default and the McGovern tacticians, repeating the logic of Florida, left their candidate largely out of the Pennsylvania fray, leaving the effort in that state up to the organization.

With 52 percent of the vote in Massachusetts and a credible showing in Pennsylvania, the McGovern campaign reached a major milestone. Until that point the primaries had been carefully selected for their psychological impact, not for their delegates. No-win situations had been carefully avoided, and the temptation to get involved extensively in states like Florida and Illinois had been resisted. But by mid-April the delegate selection process had netted such concrete results in so many nonprimary states that the McGovern tacticians could begin to envision the possibility of a first-ballot victory.

The effort in the nonprimary states provides an excellent example of how well ideological commitment and campaign strategy go together. The intricate system of caucus-packing and rules manipulation, under the supervision of Rick Stearns and Gary Hart, was certainly the most impressive tactical triumph of 1972. Conceptually the operation was very simple. First identify every supporter or potential supporter and then turn that person out at the delegate selection caucus. These supporters, to begin with, were committed to a cause, not a candidate, and McGovern became merely a symbol for that cause and a reason for their activity. But because they were strongly committed to the movement, supporters would turn out in fantastically higher proportions than the rest of the party electorate. All the organization had to do was master the rules (here they had a head start) and be proficient managers. They did not have to be politicians or even to associate with politicians. All they had to do was organize their ready-made constituency effectively and apply the reform rules that they themselves had written. This they did very well. In state after state the faithful were manufactured into delegates with a great deal of proficiency. Even such unlikely places as Virginia, South Carolina, and Georgia produced a modest number of McGovern convention supporters. The managers were not universally successful — they suffered setbacks in Kentucky and Missouri, for example — but the net effect was phenomenal.

This grass roots effort, carried out in strict accordance with the party reform rules, became one of the most controversial operations of the entire campaign. The reform rules had been designed to open up the party and to make it more representative. The commission that drew up the reforms had been mandated to find means of including people in the nominating process who had been excluded by the traditional practices of the party organization. There was a genuine commitment to reform, and these rules constituted a milestone in the direction of representative democracy. However, in the hands of the McGovern strategists they soon became political instruments of major proportions. They had been designed to change the basis of power within the party and this they did. They not only opened up the party, however; they provided such a fluid situation that the tacticians of the movement had a tremendous advantage over the more traditional politicians. With the old practices set aside, the delegate selection process became a strategist's paradise as well as an exercise in party reform.

Although this process was still far from complete in April, the central command realized that its potential put them in a possible win situation. Their delegate projections, however, showed them that without sizable blocks of votes from Ohio, Michigan, and California, they could be stopped. Immediately after Massachusetts and Pennsylvania they decided to take a calculated risk and strongly contest the Ohio primary. This was the most important strategic decision of the nominating campaign. The risk of a decisive defeat by Humphrey was obvious. This was the first head-on confrontation between the two, since Wallace supporters were not seriously contesting the situation. The unions were presumably for Humphrey and were reputed to be strong in Ohio. There was no long-standing McGovern effort to build on. A decisive defeat would be psychologically fatal, but a close match would give them crucial delegates and real credibility. Moreover, Humphrey seemed weak despite his Pennsylvania victory, and he was bogged down with Wallace in Indiana and West Virginia, dividing his time and resources between several states. The delegates were necessary, the decision was made, and the results were impressive. Impressive performances in working-class areas gave McGovern an almost even split with Humphrey in Ohio and paved the way to victory.

The Democratic establishment had not taken McGovern very seriously until the Ohio primary — since they had not done their mathematics very well. After Ohio, their hasty calculations showed very alarming projections. Complacency was replaced by intense activity and they set out to stop McGovern by every possible means. His left-wing orientation became the obvious target and the remaining candidates pitched in to stop him. The Nebraska primary provides an excellent example of the strange twilight politics that occurred after McGovern became the front-runner for the nomination.

Countertactics and Their Failure

The plains were turning green and tractors were in the field when George McGovern brought his flourishing campaign for President back home to the country where many of his ideas were formed and so much of his style was shaped. He hopped across Nebraska in an ancient Martin 404 during a week-long blitz and wound it up with a whistle-stop train tour along the Platte River two-thirds of the way across the state. Returning to his plane just before midnight, McGovern peeled off his suit coat, took off his shoes, and rested a stocking foot on the rear wall of the pilot's cabin. He was asked if he was satisfied with his burgeoning national image of a quiet man of strength and conviction. He nodded quickly and said, "That's exactly what I think this country is looking for . . . the most valuable talent I have is to be able to present progressive ideas in a moderate manner."

But the counterattack was already in evidence. In McGovern's backyard his opponents began to destroy this moderate image that had enabled him to present so many progressive ideas so plausibly to so many nonsympathizers.

While McGovern, Humphrey, and Muskie had concentrated on Massachusetts and Pennsylvania, Scoop Jackson had spent nearly all his time in Ohio, and he had focused on McGovern. In a series of hard-hitting speeches, he charged that McGovern had become "the spokesman for some of the dangerous and destructive currents in American politics," adding that "his endorsement of amnesty for draft dodgers and deserters is good news for those who have encouraged the most ignoble and irresponsible forms of resistance to the Vietnam war." Stating that two members of the Chicago Seven, Abbie Hoffman and Jerry Rubin, had endorsed McGovern, Jackson concluded, "It is perfectly fair to ask why these two 'hate-America' leftist extremists, who have been in the forefront of violent demonstrations, should find Senator McGovern's candidacy congenial to their own problems." To clinch the argument, he recalled that McGovern had supported Henry A. Wallace in 1948, the candidate of "communist appeasement."

McGovern replied, in Ohio, that if the nation had listened to Henry Wallace it might have avoided tragedies like the Vietnam war, and added weakly, "I have grown and changed a lot since then."

By the time McGovern got to Nebraska the radical charges were waiting. For instance, a large advertisement in *The True Voice*, a statewide Catholic archdiocesan weekly, asked: "How do you stand? Are you for legalization of marijuana? Amnesty for deserters? This is the McGovern record." The ad was signed by Citizens Concerned for the Preservation of Life, an organization with only a telephone number and a post office box, headed by one Michael Fauhast. "I've been in Nebraska politics forty years and I've never heard of him," remarked former Democratic Governor Frank B. Morrison, head of Nebraska Citizens for McGovern.

On the plane over Nebraska that Saturday night, McGovern said that if he had answered Jackson head-on, he would have won Ohio. He tried to do so in Nebraska. He told reporters standing along the machines at the Tip-Top Products plant in Omaha that Jackson had done "a hatchet job on me." He gave the main task of answering the charges to two popular elected Democrats, Morrison and his own confidant, South Dakota Governor Bill Dougherty. Morrison called the Fauhast ad "last-minute smear charges"; Dougherty, a cotton buyer from Sioux Falls, standing on a street in Hartington, Nebraska, in front of five hundred men in bib overalls, said of McGovern; "He's our kind of people. He's midwestern brand of people."

McGovern took out a signed newspaper ad seeking to clarify his views: that he favored no federal action over abortion, that he advocated reducing the penalty for marijuana from a felony to a misdemeanor, and, in the tradition of presidents after every war, that he supported amnesty for those who refused to serve. He told the Hartington audience, "I have the faith to believe that, despite the false charges, with the kind of people we have supporting us, we will be victorious on Tuesday. In South Dakota, where the registration is two-to-one Republican, it's hard for a left-wing radical to get elected. These old moth-eaten tactics are a thing of the past. They didn't fool anyone in South Dakota, Wisconsin, and Massachusetts, and they won't here." But they did. McGovern edged Humphrey by only six points in his neighboring state after a very hard campaign effort.

Columnist Tom Braden, a former associate of Frank Mankiewicz, McGovern's political director, and a reporter whose writings often mirrored Mankiewicz's own thinking, sat on the press bus as it drove through the prairie and wrote: "Nebraska in mudtime is talking about marijuana and amnesty and whether George McGovern is a 'left-winger' as much as it is talking about the issues of war and taxation which are McGovern's principal themes. It is a dangerous omen." After Nebraska the charges became more precise and things came to a head in California.

One problem that began to plague McGovern was the specificity of his positions. His camp had issued various papers and he had presented a number of specific propositions to comply with his wish for an open campaign in which the voters would know his positions. In the early part of the campaign, McGovern needed to contrast his point of view with that of front-runner Muskie, and later with that of his centrist successor, Humphrey. There was also press value to the detailed reports. But at some point precise positions can become a hazard.

In California, Humphrey attacked McGovern's welfare and defense proposals during a series of television debates and exposed them as imprecise, poorly thought out, and in some cases unwise and unworkable.

Instead of answering in broad, antiestablishment exhortative strokes, McGovern defended his positions detail by detail and became increasingly involved with minor points and seeming inconsistencies. This practice put him on the defensive.

The Humphrey attacks were very painful. Humphrey was a native South Dakotan and was McGovern's political mentor at the start of his career in the mid-1950s. He had been his next-door neighbor in suburban Chevy Chase for years. He may have been acting out of pique because McGovern challenged his presidential candidacy in 1968 or out of desperation to salvage his fleeting final hopes. In either case, he did a job on McGovern and he did so with all the credibility of a liberal Democrat attacking another liberal Democrat. He put McGovern on the defensive and cast what became an ever-lengthening shadow on his competence.

McGovern saw his Field poll margin of 20 percent in California shrink to a 5 percent victory. The *New York Times* reported two days afterward that 40 percent of the Humphrey Democrats would defect to Nixon if McGovern became the nominee, and William V. Shannon of the *Times* editorial board concluded: "McGovern, in my judgment, has committed a major political blunder because his proposals have evoked distracting controversy when the Democrats ought to be focusing attention exclusively on the failures and weaknesses in the Nixon record."

Despite McGovern's tarnished image, it was simply too late to stop him after California. States like New York, New Jersey, and Rhode Island either had gone or were about to go to McGovern by default, and the completion of the delegate selection process in the nonprimary states put the movement over the top in projected delegate strength. The California challenge lay ahead, but the nomination was relatively secure.

It seems incredible, retrospectively, that the Democratic establishment could have let this happen. After all, they too could read rules, and presumably they had the support of a large number of rank-and-file Democrats who did not want McGovern. To be sure they had problems with candidates. The Muskie collapse caught them unawares, but at least they had Humphrey to fall back on. Humphrey's greatest problem was that he inherited all the liabilities of the centrist position that had plagued Muskie without the advantages of the front-runner status that Muskie had squandered. He was unwilling to move either in the direction of Wallace or of McGovern; the former tack would have lost him the support of the labor leadership and the latter the support of the rank and file. Lacking any place to go and unable to create any issues himself, he ran on his past record — and his past record was a losing one. For a while he wavered, and then launched into McGovern. But by then it was too late and his attacks, while hurting McGovern, never established his own position on a positive basis. With more advanced planning he might have created a viable organization, but his lack of personal charisma and political cause put severe limits on his organization potential. His support

Figure 1

Total of Disclosed Contributions of $100 or More to Democratic Candidates by Week

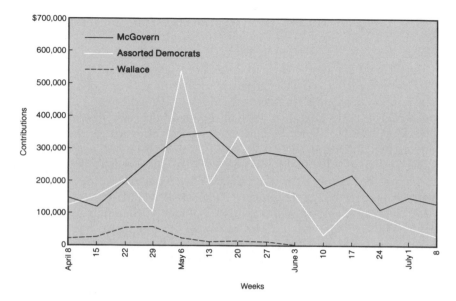

was desultory. It was larger than McGovern's but much weaker, and it never could be mobilized to turn out in the decisive numbers necessary to give McGovern a knockout blow. With no really exciting alternative, the moderate Democrats stayed at home. Intensity of support can be measured to some extent by willingness to contribute money to candidates, and the strong edge McGovern enjoyed in this category is illustrated in Figures 1 and 2. We conducted a computer analysis of the financial disclosure information from the General Accounting Office, and found that for the period of April 7 (when disclosures were made legally mandatory) through the convention, McGovern's dollar contributions (in amounts of $100 or more) ran ahead of those of his combined opposition many weeks and the *number* of contributions far exceeded those of his opponents. This information provides striking evidence of the enthusiasm generated by the movement for its candidate compared to the level of support given the other candidates by *individual* contributors. Further details are provided in Appendix 1.

If it is surprising that Humphrey did not stop McGovern before the convention, it is even more surprising that George Wallace did not. The Wallace candidacy was in many ways analogous to the McGovern candidacy: an antiestablishmentarian effort with an enthusiastic constituency at least as large as McGovern's. (In total primary votes cast in all con-

Figure 2

Number of People Making Disclosed Contributions of $100 or More to Democratic Candidates by Week

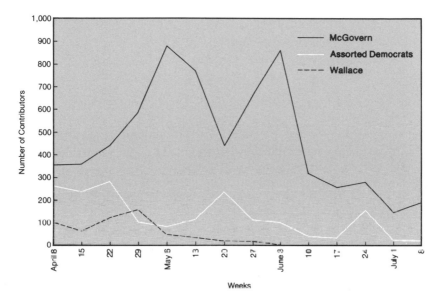

Weeks

tested primaries, McGovern, Wallace, and Humphrey received approximately the same number of votes.) What Wallace lacked was organization. His tactics were faulty and his tacticians were fourth-rate. Had he mounted McGovern's kind of organizational effort, he could have received far more convention votes than he ultimately won. He, too, could have packed caucuses all over the country and he could have received far more delegates in primary states. (In Pennsylvania, for example, he ran only four delegates while McGovern fielded an entire slate. He received more votes in the primary than McGovern did, but the movement ultimately obtained 81 of Pennsylvania's 182 votes for its candidate. Wallace got 2.) With good tacticians, Wallace might have received as much as a third of the convention delegates; at any rate he could have taken a sufficient number from McGovern to deny him the nomination. But he didn't, and nobody else did. McGovern won by virtue of the tactical deficiencies of his adversaries.

The Political Problem

This fascinating road to the nomination is all the more interesting because at no time did the McGovern forces find it necessary to define a

131

coherent political strategy at all. By maximizing the impact of their ready-made constituency and by exploiting the folly of their adversaries, they were able to win the nomination without expanding their *solid* base of support. In various primaries, to be sure, they did expand their voting base, but it was done on a very ad hoc basis and in such an incoherent way that new-found support remained very soft at best. They were never able to engage in the kind of politics that would have created an expanding and relatively solid power base. All they were able to do was assemble a series of fleeting coalitions in state after state; these were not lasting coalitions since many members became increasingly skeptical about the candidate's concern for their needs and interests. In some states they successfully courted potential Wallace supporters, in other states they successfully courted blacks. Elsewhere they won the Chicano vote. Occasionally they did very well with rank-and-file labor. Yet at no time did they ever convince these temporary supporters that either the candidate or the movement had a lasting concern for the needs of these groups. There are several reasons for this.

The McGovern followers, first of all, were motivated by their ideological commitment to certain concrete ends, such as Vietnam withdrawal. To accomplish these ends they were willing to engage in tactical compromise. But they were emphatically unwilling to engage in political compromise that might jeopardize the ends themselves. "Sellout" was a cardinal sin, and to avoid it they had to avoid dealing with the moderates of the middle. Ironically they were quite willing to deal with George Wallace and bid for his supporters because such maneuvers seemed *merely* tactical and there could be no danger of selling out. The great desire to preserve the distinction between tactical and political compromise made deals with the centrist Democrats much more suspect.

McGovern himself, however, approached politics in a somewhat different fashion. His was a genuine voice of reform, and his social gospel was a gospel of accomplishment. He recognized the need for compromise as an abstract principle, but he was very uneasy whenever a concrete opportunity presented itself. Lacking a good instinct for personal politics, but recognizing the necessity, he often came forth with unusual views on the nature of his political mission. A solitary figure in the midst of a high political situation, his sense of loss was compensated for by a moral outlook that justified his actions but compounded his problem. As is the case with so many moralists or decent men, when he compromised he looked much worse for having done so than others do who have less commitment to principle. And he didn't compromise very often.

McGovern's supporters, then, were committed to tactical, not political, compromise. The candidate himself was willing to make political compromises but was so uneasy about them that he looked for other options first. Hence political compromise and maneuvering would always come very late in any situation, if at all. This applied not only to politicians, but to the voters as well. Since this was the case, it seemed risky to trust him, however unfair this might really have been.

McGovern began his campaign with the support of just the movement, which was confined to a very narrow base: the Northeast suburbanites, the academic community, some young people, and many opponents of the war throughout the country. He had no support whatsoever among blacks or among white workingmen and women whose combined totals constituted an overwhelming numerical majority of his party. These groups belonged, in differing proportions, to Humphrey, Muskie, Jackson, and Wallace. Despite a much-celebrated claim by his managers that McGovern was getting the support of blue-collar workers, this was simply not the case on any *consistent* basis until well into the primary season. Even then this support, while significant, was soft.

To broaden the base of McGovern's constituency, one of two political strategies might have been adopted. He might have moved to the center of the road, made his peace with the Democratic establishment, and tried to attract the white-collar Democrat and a healthy percentage of union members. This course of action did not seem promising because so many other candidates occupied the middle and because, at the early stages, the movement was not so committed to McGovern that its support could easily be taken for granted. Had he appeared to make political compromises early, the fervor of his supporters would have disappeared.

Alternatively, McGovern might have moved decisively in the direction of the Wallace voter. If the traditional categories of Left and Right had truly disintegrated, then this intriguing alternative could have been fruitful. Could the obvious discontent and antiestablishmentarianism of the Wallace voter be exploited for McGovern's purposes? This strategy also presented enormous difficulties. Many white supporters of McGovern were willing, in the name of expediency, to wink at appeals to the Wallace voter as they were *not* willing to wink at appeals to the Muskie voter, but clearly McGovern could not employ the kind of racist appeal that had shaken these voters loose to Wallace. His own conscience forbade it; his own constituency would not stand for it. Also, the possibility of attracting such voters was limited by the nature of his own existing supporters, whose life styles were highly distrusted by the potential Wallace voter. Finally, the appeal to this constituency would have been made over the heads of the Democratic establishment and it would have thereby risked even further difficulties for the future.

While it is easy to sympathize with McGovern's dilemma, it is hard to understand why the campaign never confronted this question head-on. It never attempted to build a lasting political relationship with either the Democratic establishment or with discontented workingmen and women. It bounced back and forth between these two incompatible strategies as the tactics of the moment required so that no sense of confidence or reciprocity could be established with either. In this way —

and in a much briefer time span — the movement's politics bore a striking resemblance to the strategic politics of Nixon's first term.

Because both the candidate and his followers were so suspicious of the Democratic establishment, the Wallace flirtation seemed more acceptable. On the night of the Florida primary McGovern commented on the Wallace victory by saying that the governor's supporters were not racists but that they were just fed up with the way things were going. "In case anybody hasn't heard," he said, "I'm fed up with the way things are going too." Later on he was to make this very revealing statement about Wallace: "As I listened to the litany of frustration and anxieties ticked off by the governor from Alabama, the thought ran through my mind, why, these are the same things I've been saying! Both of us are painfully dissatisfied with the status quo."

Tom Wicker, the *New York Times* columnist who wrote frequently and favorably about McGovern in early 1972 while other writers were ignoring him, wrote just after the Wisconsin primary about the similarity of "the two Georges." Wicker noted that both McGovern and Wallace campaigned for tax reform and suggested that both ran well in blue-collar wards:

> Finally, whatever their difference on such questions as busing and pointy-headed intellectuals, it is clear that George McGovern and George Wallace were, indeed, what the professor said — antiestablishment candidates. Both campaigned boldly against things and politics as they are; neither has much "regular" Democratic support, and both depend heavily on the votes of people who, for whatever reasons, feel left out of or ill-represented in "mainstream" party politics.

Alternatively, however, McGovern in principle recognized the need for reaching out to the establishment. He told David Broder of the *Washington Post* in April: "Some of the more rigid purists in my camp don't even want me to talk to those [establishment] people. But they're just going to have to take me on my own terms. They've got to understand that I'm a politician, and if I'm going to be the leader of this country, I've got to have communications with all segments of this country."

McGovern told Broder that he would never change his fundamental convictions on Vietnam, tax reform, and a cut in defense spending. But he also said that he was not totally tied to his staff. It was a sign both of his independence and of his desire to reach out beyond the "new coalition." But he was never able to accomplish this goal either. He remained aloof from the Democratic establishment until well after the convention, and by then it was too late.

7

Political Failure: The McGovern Campaign

Disaster

By the time George McGovern's presidential campaign officially began on Labor Day, there was a universal agreement that he had lost; the pollsters differed only about the size of Nixon's lead. The pundits, after a bit of hedging on the possibility of a return surge, were nearly unanimous in their judgments. Only George McGovern, supremely confident in the righteousness of his cause, seriously believed that he had a chance.

There are many theories about how the McGovern candidacy reached this state. Some suggest that Hubert Humphrey's California charges destroyed McGovern by exposing to a nationwide audience the weakness of his stands on controversial issues. Others theorize that the Democratic convention was the decisive factor in McGovern's fall, with millions of Democrats watching a convocation of delegates "who are not our kind of people." Some experts suggest it was the Eagleton affair, while others speculate that McGovern's handling of the issues during August and his inability to pull together a postconvention organization were decisive. All of these situations may have contributed to McGovern's difficulties, but the evidence indicates overwhemingly that the Eagleton affair was, by far, the most decisive factor.

Using survey research materials from a number of sources, it is now possible to piece together a fairly complete and accurate picture of voter attitudes toward George McGovern throughout 1972.

It is not surprising that the South Dakota senator remained largely an unknown quantity during the early months of the year; his relatively strong performance against President Nixon in the Gallup polls in the early spring was the result more of anti-Nixon respondents than of pro-McGovern sentiments.

As his streak of primary victories continued through April and May and his candidacy became more credible, the war opponents began moving to him in large numbers. With Muskie and Kennedy receding as alternatives, McGovern picked up strength as he collected almost all the antiwar support during those months of intensified activity in Vietnam. Until June the rest of the public was less aware of his views either on the war or anything else, although some growing awareness tended to create a small negative reaction during this pre-California period.

The California primary campaign and the sudden realization that McGovern was the probable nominee brought a much greater awareness of the man, but still a much lower degree of awareness about his positions. Sindlinger reports a leveling off of support, and even a slight decline, after the California primary. The Humphrey attacks and union suspicions prevented him from increasing his support among Democrats, and the campaign entered a period of hesitation and uncertainty until the convention. McGovern's chances of winning the election, however, remained quite good during this period. Patrick Caddell of Cambridge Survey Research, McGovern's own pollster, reported a standing of Nixon 52 percent, McGovern 38 percent, balance undecided, in early July just before the convention, when Gallup was reporting McGovern at 37 percent, *up* three points from his post-California showing. The softness of the Nixon support in the Caddell survey (43 percent firm, 9 percent soft) gave the McGovern managers reason to be optimistic.

The Caddell figures showed, however, that the McGovern totals included a comfortable percentage of Republicans (15 percent), while the Nixon totals included a disproportionate number of Democrats. The Independents during this period were trending toward Nixon but without a strong degree of commitment. Retrospectively, it appears that in early July it was still possible for McGovern to erase Nixon's significant, but soft, lead and to win the election.

The convention had a surprising impact upon the voters. First, there is evidence that it tended to confirm the suspicion of many Democrats that McGovern was not their man. Polling the week after the convention, Sindlinger found that among Democrats McGovern led Nixon 55 percent to 31.8 percent, an astoundingly low margin for a Democratic candidate following a Democratic convention. Nixon was performing very strongly among male Democrats, with 38.6 percent of them indicating support for him, while McGovern was holding a 54.1 percent to 25.7 percent lead among female Democrats. Even more dramatic was McGovern's very slight lead among union households — 47.5 percent to 40.1 percent — a remarkably poor performance for a Democrat.

On the basis of these immediate postconvention findings, we can conclude that the Humphrey California exposure, the Democratic convention, and the general increase in the level of voter awareness had created serious trouble for McGovern among male union Democrats.

The convention also sent Republicans scurrying back to Nixon. McGovern had had some support in this category before the convention and it disappeared just afterward. Sindlinger reports the President holding a decisive 92.8 percent to 4.4 percent edge among Republicans.

But the Independents were strongly for McGovern and the convention boosted his position dramatically in this category. Immediately after the Miami victory, his support in this vital swing area was 54 percent to 43 percent, according to Sindlinger. Since in this survey Independents made up the largest single category of voters (35.7 percent of the electorate), the overall Nixon-McGovern showing for the two-week period after the convention was 51.4 percent Nixon, 42.2 percent McGovern, with a low 5.3 percent undecided.

McGovern was making major cuts into the Independent voters and a fascinating situation was developing. On the basis of these figures it appears that the loss among Democrats, while significant, was offset largely by appeals to Independents. After the convention, McGovern reached the high water mark of his entire campaign. Some polls showed McGovern and Nixon neck and neck in Texas!

And then there was Eagleton. The Sindlinger week-by-week figures are overwhelming. Starting with the week after the convention, McGovern stood at 44.5 percent. The Eagleton affair broke during the second week after the convention; McGovern dropped to 38.1 percent while the fate of the Missouri senator was still being debated. Nixon did not rise during the period, but the undecideds took a giant leap. Then Eagleton was removed from the ticket and McGovern was without a running mate for about a week. During that fateful period, McGovern dropped almost 15 percentage points in the Sindlinger survey. Somewhere in the vicinity of 12 million voters deserted him. The President picked up some of these, but most were moved for the time being into the undecided column. McGovern was left with the basic support he had had before California — about 23 percent — but all the gains he had made among Independents were wiped out and female Democrats deserted him in droves. In Sindlinger's survey, McGovern remained in the low twenties until late October, when some of the Independents and Democrats returned. His final prognostication was within 1 percent of the actual results. These post-Eagleton findings are confirmed by the Yankelovich poll, which is also a telephone survey. Gallup and Harris, who rely on personal interviews, had fewer undecideds and hence slightly higher figures for contenders.

An equally dramatic piece of evidence is Figure 3, the political awareness diagram. The Eagleton affair was the most talked-about political event of the entire summer and fall. Not until just before the election itself did public awareness reach the peak that it did during those two

Figure 3

Political Awareness in the Country

DAILY TALK ABOUT POLITICS — Among All U.S. Adults

Question: When was the last time you recall having any conversations or discussions with anyone — at home or away from home — where you talked about politics or anything about the current election campaign?
IF WITHIN PAST WEEK, ASK: What was discussed? Anything else?

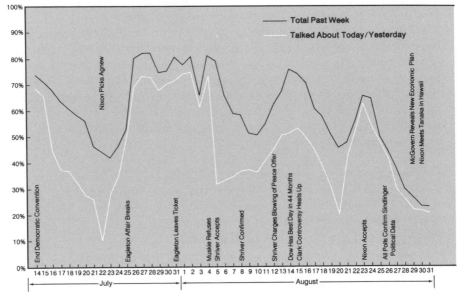

fateful weeks. The American electorate had not known much about McGovern, and except for a significant number of disaffected Democrats, it had liked what it saw of the convention. It was during the Eagleton affair that the public took its first good look at McGovern and it really never looked very hard again, as the awareness chart so dramatically illustrates.

Why the catastrophe in the first place? Who was to blame? It can be argued that the McGovern staff should have checked out Eagleton more carefully, and indeed they should have. It can be argued that McGovern should have kept Eagleton on the ticket; perhaps he should have. It can be argued that McGovern should not have pasted his "1,000 percent" support statement to the press room window at the Hi Ho Best Western Motel in Custer, South Dakota, and then gone table-hopping among reporters in the dining room at the Sylvan Lake Lodge the next night, inviting speculation that he was reevaluating the matter. But when all is said and done, the blame rests with Thomas F. Eagleton for deceiving George McGovern knowingly and with calculation.

Eagleton, despite his relative youth at forty-three, was a big city politician who had waged three statewide races in the relatively populous state of Missouri. He was not naïve. Frank Mankiewicz may have not asked

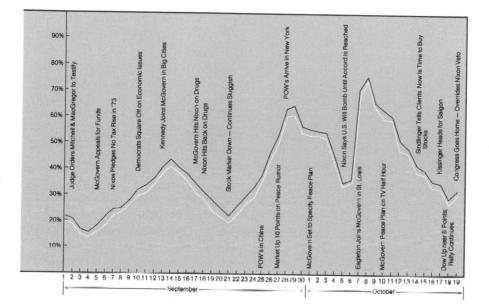

precisely the right questions of him ("Are there any skeletons in your closet?"); Gordon Weil may not have checked thoroughly enough (Weil said he thought looking into Eagleton's "background" meant checking out the senator's father!); and, if McGovern had been on more intimate terms with more colleagues in the Senate, he too might have heard the rumors. No one knew what or whom to ask. Eagleton, however, knew what to tell, and he was silent.

In a revealing interview in *Newsweek* the week after he was dropped, Eagleton acknowledged that he and his wife had talked about his history of mental illness and shock treatment. This is what he told Mel Elfin:

When we got to Miami Beach, Barbara and I discussed the possibility of my being chosen as McGovern's No. 2, and she said: "Tom, you realize that you're running the risk that if you go into a national campaign that there will be a public disclosure of your hospitalization." And I replied: "Yes, I realize that. It's quite possible, in fact."

So when I thought about the possibility of a national campaign, the two things that went through my mind about the hospitalization experience were that I would take a *calculated risk* that the story would not leak out, at least not in the form it ultimately did. I thought it would be sort of a general story that I once suffered from a fatigue problem . . . and even if it did leak, I thought I had proved to the world during my four

139

years in the Senate and during the '68 campaign that I can hack it [italics added].

After the initial disclosure (leaked by the White House), he played games with the McGovern staff to make it all the more difficult for them to drop him. He tried to justify staying on the ticket by stating that his reception during his travels across the country following the disclosure had been "warm, supportive, and cordial." And still later Eagleton's staff passed word that True Davis, a former political opponent, had passed his Eagleton folder to columnist Jack Anderson in a deal in which Anderson promised not to write about Davis and his bank, the National Bank of Washington, which is controlled by the United Mine Workers. Anderson denied it. Finally, when it appeared that he would have to go, he refused to do so gracefully until he had obtained the pledge that he would have a veto power over McGovern's statement announcing the decision.

When the story first broke, the McGovern staff, smarting from what they regarded as massive betrayal, checked further into the affair while McGovern came to the support of his ticket. This was McGovern's own decision and was regarded by him as an act of loyalty. Perhaps Eagleton's explanations had seemed adequate. But the staff dug further and then suggested to McGovern that he talk to Eagleton's doctor. Although the doctor would not comment extensively, he did tell McGovern in a private phone conversation that if he had been consulted in advance by Eagleton, he would have suggested that he remain in the Senate. Assembling all the evidence they could find, the McGovern high command concluded that, medically speaking, Eagleton simply was not fit to be President of the United States. McGovern had to make the decision, and again, he made it alone. Dropping the Missouri opportunist was his only responsible alternative.

So six excruciating days after the tense news conference in the lodge at Sylvan Lake that broke the story, the two senators made public their decision in an emotional news conference in the Senate Caucus Room where the Kennedy brothers had announced for the presidency. Eagleton, as columnist Mary McGrory put it, was a sort of cocker spaniel who became a national folk hero and television celebrity.

George McGovern was still largely unknown to the American people at the time of his nomination. He had been on the covers of *Time* and *Newsweek* in May, and a wire service finally assigned a reporter to him that month. But few people had seen him on television and most had missed his eloquent acceptance speech in Miami Beach. Their first glimpse of him was standing serenely beside a perspiring Eagleton in the Black Hills and then alongside a sobered Eagleton in the Senate Caucus Room. It didn't help his image at all.

Then followed six more excruciating days as McGovern suffered the indignity of not being able to persuade anyone to run with him. Again, the McGovern staff erred in not having a running mate to announce immediately upon Eagleton's withdrawal; instead, names were trotted out for reporters each day, and each day the refusals came — from Humphrey, from Gaylord Nelson, and from Muskie. Finally, choice number 7, R. Sargent Shriver, ebulliently accepted and three days later was gratefully nominated.

A few weeks later, McGovern stopped at the Caterpillar plant in Peoria, Illinois, to talk to workers in the cafeteria during their twenty-minute supper break. A young worker, Jack Blanton, pressed McGovern about the Eagleton matter as the two sat across the table from each other in hard hats. McGovern patiently explained again that mental illness was not the question, but that controversy about it threatened to dominate the campaign.

"I don't feel a man's past should be held against him," Blanton said, mentioning Senator Harold E. Hughes's conquering of alcohol. "He never made any effort to hide it, did he?" McGovern said quietly, his hands folded in front of him.

During the first part of September, when their condition was so obvi-ously dire, several members of the McGovern staff suggested that they leak to the news media the entire amount of evidence they had amassed, including the physician's remark. Recognizing that Eagleton was the source of their trouble, they felt that discrediting him might indirectly serve their candidate's cause. But McGovern had previously vetoed such suggestions — to save Eagleton from further humiliation. If someone in the campaign had broken the news, he would have faced both McGovern's anger and Eagleton's countercharges. In the end no one leaked the full truth on the man who had done so much to destroy both McGovern and the movement. After the Eagleton affair the campaign never recovered. The question is, could it have?

Recovery?

As soon as the convention was over, the expert strategists who had engi-neered McGovern's nomination triumph faced a series of political, not tactical, problems: how to deal with a disunited party, how to deal with a potentially skeptical public, how to create a winning *political* coalition, how to appeal to groups who were being pirated by the Republicans, and above all, how to hold hands and conciliate, how to know when to com-promise and when not to compromise; how to know whom to reconcile with threats and whom to reconcile with more positive incentives. To maximize the political impact of an existing constituency is a tactical problem, but to *create* a constituency is a political problem. To turn out a ready-made constituency on primary day or caucus evening is a tactical problem, but to get the support of former opponents is a political task. Strategists and tacticians do not always make good politicians, and moralists make even worse ones. Hence neither the staff nor the candidate was equipped to solve political problems. The staff's own experience had been limited to manipulating those who were willing to be manipulated; and the candidate himself, this solitary moralist who had rarely participated in the politics of the Senate, approached problems and people more from the standpoint of abstract principle than from the sureness of political intuition. Neither was able to operate effectively in the highly personalized atmosphere of traditional democratic politics. The old organizations and the labor movement both operated within a very stylized code of procedure quite alien to the highly tactical maneuvers of the movement or the abstract moral principles of the candidate. The intensely personal and human relationships of the old politics were rejected by both McGovern and his movement because they felt that these people, trained in the old practices, could not be trusted. The traditional politicians, alternatively, felt that the movement managers, trained in the new manipulative practices, could not be trusted either. This fundamental cleavage was never resolved.

For the McGovern candidacy to recover from the Eagleton disaster there were at least three political problems it had to solve. It had to confront its own internal political difficulties, which mounted daily. It had to deal with the Democratic party. And it had to straighten out the mess in which the Eagleton affair had left it; it had to regain credibility in order to establish a viable political coalition with which it could win.

PROBLEMS WITH THE ORGANIZATION

After the convention, the campaign chieftains were so emotionally and physically drained that all of them scattered. Hart and Mankiewicz went to the Virgin Islands; McGovern left for the Black Hills back home. The intention was to gather again at the Sylvan Lake Lodge in a few days to make plans. Then came the Eagleton affair, and as a result, the master plan for the general election was not fleshed out until late August. The momentum of the campaign was lost and the advantage of a month's barnstorming before the GOP convention was forfeited.

The confusions of August were deeply felt in the central command of the McGovern organization. The movement tacticians who had engineered the convention victory felt that they had a strong claim to continue directing the effort. The party regulars, brought in to solve some of the political problems that the campaign obviously had, were resented by those who had been in charge all along. And the regulars, in turn, distrusted the movement personnel with whom they had been at war for years and whose political life style was alien to their instincts. The result was a prolonged series of highly counterproductive organizational battles that focused the energy of the high command inward upon itself, rather than outward upon the Republicans. For example, Jean Westwood, the controversial party chairman, tried to get Gary Hart removed as campaign manager. Hart succeeded in retaining his post through the intercession of McGovern, but proceeded himself to get rid of Representative Frank Thompson of New Jersey, an old friend of McGovern's, who was supposed to set up a voter registration drive. Larry O'Brien was brought into the organization to mollify the party regulars and to compensate for the lack of political expertise, but his authority was never clearly defined and his relationship to political director Frank Mankiewicz was somewhat strained whenever they had anything to do with each other. There are many other examples of this kind of infighting.

To compound the difficulties, the overall structure of the campaign was never really defined. The nomination effort had been highly decentralized to conform to the localized nature of the nominating process. The middle and lower ranges of the organization were therefore highly state-oriented and relatively independent of central control. But a national campaign can be much more efficient if it is centralized. The effort to centralize, however, created further difficulties. The whole organization degenerated rapidly into a series of vertical and horizontal baronies that proceeded to feud with each other. At least twice after the convention McGovern summoned his key staff together and tried to clarify the lines of authority. During one Saturday session at Sylvan Lake, according to Matt Troy, Queens County Democratic leader and McGovern's first big-name supporter in New York City, the nominee responded angrily to reports that his preconvention staff was discounting O'Brien's role in the fall campaign. Troy, himself blunt-spoken and highly critical of the youthful staff, said McGovern told them he would tolerate no undercutting of O'Brien and concluded, "I don't want any more nonsense."

But McGovern was a man experienced neither in organizational management nor in the kind of head-knocking that the situation required. The movement managers, a law unto themselves until July, and the candidate, a law unto himself always, had never really come to terms with each other. The cause, not the candidate, had been the principal motivation for many staff members before the convention, and they felt that he was as much their creation as he felt that they were his. As a result, he was never able to control the organization or really deal with it.

What was needed most was a czar who could command the confidence of the candidate, the respect of the preconvention managers, and the affection of the party. No such person may have existed, and certainly none was found. The candidate himself tried to run his own campaign from afar — always a dangerous practice — and in the end he accomplished only an occasional interference in a chaotic situation. As the campaign proceeded and the polls continued to forecast disaster, morale dropped even further, the process fed upon itself, and the organization was never able to mount the kind of effort that was necesssary to match the Committee to Re-elect the President.

If McGovern could not solve his organizational problems at the center, neither could his organization solve its problems with the party. The situation was simple. The McGovern organization that had existed from the beginning of the year regarded itself justifiably as an extremely competent organization, state by state. It felt that it could make the telephone calls and pass out the literature better than the regulars ever did or could. There were some exceptions to this superiority. In Chicago, for instance, voters were influenced by other means than ringing door-bells, but in most areas their success in the spring had instilled in the McGovern workers a supreme confidence in their own methods.

Not only did many McGovern middle-range organizers on the state level mistrust the competence of the party regulars, but they questioned their motives as well. It seemed foolish to entrust the fate of a campaign to men and women of less technical competence whose own party position might well be enhanced by the defeat of the candidate. But *not* to entrust these politicians with the conduct of the campaign would be politically very dangerous because their constituency was crucial on election day. If bringing the party back together was necessary to win, then some gestures were necessary. But if these gestures created further organizational chaos, then their net effectiveness would be very small. These paradoxes were never resolved and the relationship between the old McGovern organization and the Democratic regulars became, in most states, a relationship of high expediency, not campaign loyalty. The McGovern movement, looking to November, regarded the party as an enemy because it was incompetent, unenthusiastic, and perhaps disloyal. The party regulars, looking beyond November, regarded the movement as the enemy because they wished to regain control of the party from it. This led to some interesting, if not amusing, episodes.

• In Illinois, Mayor Daley, despite his humiliation at the convention, quickly came to McGovern's support because he needed him. The mayor and the Democratic slate, including the State's attorney Edward V. Hanrahan, appeared many times with McGovern when he came to Chicago, and Daley put the Cook County Democratic machine to work for him as best he could.

Daley needed McGovern for a number of reasons. He wanted a Democratic President to replace the incumbent U.S. attorney for northern Illinois, Republican James Thompson, who almost daily was obtaining

144

indictments against the mayor's machine. He also needed some solid straight-ticket voting to help reelect Edward Hanrahan and keep the State's attorney's office out of Republican hands. In neither of these endeavors was he successful, but his marriage of convenience to the McGovern ticket produced some amusing episodes.

The campaign's most embarrassing moment must have occurred in the Sherman House Hotel in Chicago on September 12 when McGovern found himself sitting alongside Daley, the symbol of the chaotic 1968 Chicago convention, and Hanrahan, the alleged oppressor of the Black Panthers. McGovern gave a speech comparing his start in politics as an organizer of South Dakota Democrats to the Cook County Central Committee's organizing activities. One could almost sense the committeemen giving one another an elbow, a wink, and a knowing grin.

• In New Mexico, Eric McCrossen of the *Albuquerque Journal* described what happened to William Byatt, McGovern's state coordinator since early 1970. Byatt had a summer teaching job in Chile in 1972, returning to learn that Senator Joseph M. Montoya had been named McGovern's New Mexico coordinator as a gesture to the regulars. Byatt, the report went, was offered the "honor" of serving McGovern a plate of beans at the Indian Chicano really in Espanola, New Mexico, on September 10. He withdrew from active participation in the campaign organization and started closing down the Citizens for McGovern headquarters. But the gesture to the regulars didn't work either because Governor Bruce King was snubbed inadvertently when he tried to see McGovern, who was spending a Saturday afternoon relaxing at the Albuquerque Hilton. The *Journal* front-paged the story and the damage was done.

• In Texas, where some polls showed McGovern doing well (until the Eagleton affair), Agriculture Secretary John White and Lands Commissioner Bob Armstrong were the only Democratic officeholders or candidates who took leadership roles in the McGovern campaign. Even Frances "Sissy" Farenthold, who waged a strong race for the Democratic gubernatorial nomination and appealed to the same groups that McGovern did, was out of the country until almost the time of the election. Barefoot Sanders, the candidate for senator, and Dolph Briscoe, who was elected governor, never appeared with him.

• In New Jersey, special attention was given by both McGovern and Shriver to the Hudson County machine — or that part of it that was still out of jail — but Hudson County went for a Republican President for the first time since the Depression.

• In Indiana, Democratic regulars were so uncommitteed that a precinct vice committeeman in Terre Haute showed local voters how to vote for Nixon and how to stay with the regular ticket locally. The precinct went overwhelmingly for Nixon and McGovern ran far behind the other Democrats.

• And in Rhode Island, the Democratic state chairman suggested he was behind McGovern — 1,000 percent.

The failure of the McGovern managers to deal with themselves and with the party destroyed their ability to deal effectively with the public. After the Eagleton affair they had the solid support of some blacks, some youth, some suburban antiwar voters, and some hard-core Democratic diehards — little more than 20 percent of the electorate. Their inability to create a wider political base before the convention hurt them severely afterward since they had to more than double their constituency. In August, they faced two major political tasks: coalition repair and public conversion.

With respect to the first task, the organization's effort was extraordinarily clumsy. Initially it decided to take the youth, the Hispanic-Americans, and the blacks for granted. We have seen in Chapter 4 how CREEP exploited this neglect among youth and Hispanic-Americans. The neglect of blacks was equally disastrous. Despite the convention quota system, there were very few blacks in the McGovern organization. It had been upper-middle-class white to begin with and it remained upper-middle-class white to the end. Attempts to reach out to the black community were half-hearted and appeared to be acts of expediency. The aims of the movement and of the blacks have not always been identical and a great deal of suspicion about McGovern's ultimate practices was never removed. The organization rightly reasoned that the blacks would not go to Nixon, but they did not realize how extensively a lack of enthusiasm would lower the voter turnout in black areas.

There were other lapses. It wasn't until mid-September that someone bothered to create an ethnic division, and this effort was so late that it seemed to be a desperation tactic in response to Nixon's organizing. McGovern's effort with labor is detailed in Chapter 8, but it was a case study in how not to restore a coalition. Sargent Shriver was dispatched to mend fences, but his ploys were so blatant that they didn't seem credible at all. The organization simply got nowhere in its efforts to rebuild the old Democratic coalition and nowhere in its attempts to build a new one.

With respect to the larger public, results were equally chaotic. Much attention was devoted to clarifying past positions — which meant that McGovern's most embarrassing issues were, by definition, the ones most talked about: welfare, abortion, marijuana, defense spending, and amnesty. Although this clarification would have been necessary to restore the old coalition, an early emphasis led both to a charge of inconsistency and to a focus upon McGovern's weakest areas.

By the time McGovern returned to more positive questions, it was too late to make much headway. When his specific policies began to tumble forth from the issues task force it was September and the candidate himself was engaged in a massive attack upon the administration. His positive positions were buried on the back pages of the papers.

McGovern also failed to exploit the issues effectively. For example, he spoke out against the Vietnam war in every speech, which unfailingly drew the greatest response. But he did not focus sharply on the issue of tax reform that had brought him so much currency in the Wisconsin and Nebraska primaries because he feared that it would bring to mind the ill-fated $1,000 minimum grant proposal.

The fundamental difficulty was that neither the staff nor the candidate realized before it was too late that their problems were political; they could not bring the party back together without creating a sense of trust or a spirit of good will and they could not bring the public back without restoring some confidence in their candidate. Blatant tactical moves with respect to the party served only to increase suspicion, and the escalating rhetoric of the fall served only to confirm the electorate's loss of confidence. Issues did not destroy McGovern, image did. His was a genuine crisis of confidence and the tactics of the fall campaign served to undermine that confidence further, not to restore it.

Desperation

August simply disappeared with the Eagleton affair, the staff problems, and the Republican convention. Suddenly it was Labor Day and the campaign had about two months to go — eight weeks to erase a 30- or 40-point deficit. The situation was desperate and a strategy of desperation was devised to meet it. With the organization in relative disrepair, the campaign managers had only two major resources available: the candidate's time and a large amount of movement money that was just beginning to flow in their direction during early September (see Figures 5 and 6). With these resources available, the managers envisioned a threefold strategy: (1) maximize the quantity of hard news coverage by using the candidate's schedule optimally; (2) focus on an electoral college majority, not on a popular mandate; (3) repair the candidate's image by use of *paid* media time. While the managers were carrying out these policies, the candidate, impelled partly by his own convictions and partly by the situation he found himself in, engaged in his own desperation move — a full-fledged and very shrill attack upon the President of the United States.

UNPAID MEDIA STRATEGY

McGovern began a whirlwind campaign on Labor Day to maximize his media coverage nationwide. The strategy was to visit on the average

147

three major media markets a day until November 7. These "media stops," which involved a relatively small amount of campaign time and a relatively large amount of travel time, were designed to ensure two or three minutes of key television coverage and a front-page newspaper story in each city. Meeting people, attracting crowds, holding organizational hands, and even making serious speeches were largely sacrificed to the imperative of maximizing the quantity of media coverage.

Day after day, week after week, McGovern and his entourage traveled in two Boeing 727s leased from United Air Lines at a base cost of $70,700 a week plus 8 percent transportation, plus $350 for each hour in flight, plus $250 for each takeoff and landing. The lead plane was named *Dakota Queen II*, after McGovern's World War II B-24 bomber; the second was affectionately called *The Zoo*.

The schedulers showed imagination. For instance, McGovern went to a warehouse that was distributing food to the unemployed in Seattle and to facilities for the aged near Portland, Oregon. He flew all the way to Duluth-Superior in northern Minnesota to make a speech at a grain terminal about the Nixon administration's grain sale to the Soviet Union. Such stops provided some footage for the network evening news, some copy for the wire services, and material for specials. More important, they permitted McGovern to be interviewed and written about by reporters and newscasters well known to their local audiences. Occasionally there were statewide telethons, as in Illinois and Michigan on the last weekend of the campaign.

Frequently McGovern spoke to unexpectedly large and enthusiastic audiences: at the Seattle Hilton Hotel Labor Day night, when he gave one of the most effective speeches of his campaign; in the darkness of the Rockford airport; and outside the posh new Fairmont Hotel in Dallas where he talked about "John Connally and his billionaire friends" and said, "I don't mind being called 'radical' by that crowd."

The second week of September, Ted Kennedy joined him for three days — another media draw. Kennedy, however, overshadowed him and McGovern always thanked him with the self-deprecating remark, "He's a hard act to follow." McGovern told 20,000 persons jamming Broad and Chestnut streets in Philadelphia that "this noon in Pittsburgh two women almost knocked me over to see Senator Kennedy and one of them said, 'Oh, we just can't wait until 1976.' " It was another embarrassing moment in the campaign.

It was a grueling pace, and after the campaign McGovern told Margaret Scherf of the Associated Press that he doubted if anyone would ever run for the presidency again by trying to cover three or four widely separated cities in a day. "I don't know how I did it," he said, "and Nixon never left the White House."

The candidate's extensive schedule also reflected the campaign's electoral college strategy, another act of desperation whereby McGovern managers wrote off the entire country except for a few large states where they placed nearly all of their effort. They reasoned that they might win the election in the electoral college while losing it in the popular column.

A presidential election campaign is a contest of resource allocation, with both sides deciding where to place their resources to receive the highest expected payoff. The McGovern forces reasoned that they had a potential advantage; their supporters were located primarily in a handful of large states whose voters lived in highly populated megalopolises with concentrations of urban poor, blacks, colleges, suburbanites, and traditional Democratic voters. By limiting (in effect) their voter registration efforts to these states (which also have large and concentrated liberal college populations), and by devoting much of the candidate's campaign time to metropolitan areas (where he could cover a lot of concentrated population in relatively short distances), the McGovern strategists reasoned that they could be very efficient and redress some of the imbalance in popular support.

This strategy of concentration was also dictated by the fact that the President had such a large advantage in so many other states that the costs to McGovern of wresting these states from him exceeded the costs to the President of retaining them. The McGovern forces were compelled to concentrate in the most likely configuration of states that would add up to 270 electoral votes.

But such a concentration worked to the strategic advantage of the President, not of McGovern. Secure in so many areas that were not being contested at all, the President could concentrate *his* efforts and those of his surrogates in the very states where McGovern had concentrated his. Simply by denying McGovern a few of his targeted states, the President could almost guarantee his own victory. In fact, the President's polls always showed sufficient margins in most of the big states, and he never had to concentrate. But even had the election been close, McGovern's strategy of concentration would not have gained him any inherent advantage over Nixon. As it was, the strange spectacle of a populist candidate, opposed in principle to the electoral college, yet employing an acknowledged electoral college strategy to thwart the popular will, served only to weaken his image in many knowledgeable quarters.

ADVERTISING STRATEGY

Even the McGovern advertising effort reflected a sense of desperation. The campaign took to the air massively in September and by November it had spent approximately half again as much for advertising as the Republicans had. The initial television placements were addressed specifically to issues: the war, jobs, prices, and taxes. They featured the candidate discussing problems with voters and citizens. They were low key and soft-sell in an attempt to create an image of strength and to restore some sense of confidence in the candidate. Supplemented by half-hour shows which were also low key and image-restorative, these spots were an attempt to overcome the damage done by the Eagleton affair and to put the campaign onto an issue-oriented basis. The advertising experts believed that McGovern, a former college teacher, could communicate more effectively before small groups than at mass rallies and would come across better in the quiet setting of a TV "fireside chat." The half-dozen half-hour programs included a biography and talks on economics, morality, and Vietnam. These television appearances were probably McGovern's most effective tools of the fall and the only ones really addressed to resolving his image problem.

By the time that these advertisements were operating at maximum coverage, however, the candidate himself had launched his massive and negative attacks upon the President. Because there was little image consistency between the behavior of the candidate and the style of the advertising, a serious anomaly occurred, so the media campaign was changed in mid-program to a series of shrill attacks upon the President that appeared to be what they were — desperation tactics.

ESCALATION

The final act of desperation was McGovern's own decision to attack the administration on a massive scale. The candidate plunged into this self-defeating enterprise with a missionary zeal. There was, of course, plenty to attack: ITT, Watergate, grain deals, dairy deals, and sabotage. The ever-increasing list of malfeasance and corruption was disgusting to most voters. There were also plenty of traditional areas of administration vulnerability; the economy, the war, corruption, and credibility, for example. But shrill attacks that appear to be the flailings of a desperate man injure the attacker as much as the attacked and the escalating rhetoric of McGovern served only to undermine his own position, not the President's. Had he been able to establish himself on a positive basis as a credible and viable candidate before he began the attacks, and if the attacks had then been less shrill, he could have scored on the administration with devastating effect. But the source and nature of the attacks condemned them to failure from the very start. His one hope was that Richard Nixon could be baited into a counterattack that would make him look foolish. But with a huge lead in the polls, the President was playing his cards very close to the vest.

The examples of McGovern's attacks are extensive:

- He accused the President of "taking the low road by remote control" (Washington, D.C., 8/14).

- He said that "Mr. Nixon has been manipulating Mr. Kissinger and he has manipulated American public opinion to appear to be negotiating seriously when actually he has been stalling to prop up . . . Saigon" (Racine, Wisconsin, 8/18).

- He called the President "Tricky Dick" (Portland, Oregon, 9/6).

- He said that "President Nixon treats women's rights as a joke" (Washington, D.C., 9/26).

- He said that if President Nixon was reelected he would ask for a national right-to-work law (San Francisco, 9/27).

- He said, "The President would have you believe that we are staying there and bombing to secure the release of our prisoners. That is a lie" (Baltimore, 9/30).

- He called President Nixon "the worst leader in U.S. history" (Washington, D.C., 10/3).

- He said that President Nixon conducted "the most ruthless, most opportunistic" of campaigns; he called it "a strategy of fear" (Austin, Tex.).

- He accused the President of presiding over "the most corrupt regime in recent American history" and "the most morally bankrupt administration in the entire history of the country" (Washington, D.C., 10/12).

- He compared the Republican party to the KKK: "I think a Republican politician who would approach a black man or a Mexican American — and say, in effect, we're going to bribe you to spread the word [that] it doesn't make any difference whether you register or vote, is just as immoral as a man who puts on a white sheet and tries to scare people out of voting" (Chicago, 10/17).

- He accused the White House of being "a cutthroat crew," and said that it was having "all the families of the [Democratic] candidates followed" (Essington, Pa., 10/19).

- He said that "a President who will send his agents over to wiretap [the] Democratic National Committee, a President who will send saboteurs inside Democratic ranks to try to sabotage another national party, that is the kind of man who won't hesitate to wiretap your union hall, or your law office, or your university, your church, or even your home" (New York, 10/19).

151

In the light of the Watergate revelations, many of these charges seem rather tame. But at the time they appeared incredible. McGovern went further. He said the Vietnamese war was the worst atrocity since Nazi Germany and the Republicans promptly accused him of comparing Nixon to Hitler, only a slight distortion. But in Lordstown, Ohio, on August 14, McGovern referred to Watergate and said, "Now this is the kind of thing you expect from a person like Hitler." In Espanola, New Mexico, on September 10, he said that anyone who works with his hands and votes for Nixon "is too confused to know which end is up." On the last weekend of the campaign, dog-tired, he told an airport heckler in Michigan to "kiss my ass." All this led James J. Kilpatrick to write: "He and Vice President Agnew are passing like ships in the night."

President Nixon was not baited by the attacks, and as soon as the Republicans were able to translate the McGovern charges from substantive attacks upon themselves to demonstrations of McGovern's alleged personality defects, then the game was over. With no positive thesis to build on, with the negative campaign neutralized, with the party divorced and fragmented, the landslide became eminently predictable.

A Case of Credibility

In the Gallup poll that was taken just after the Republican convention in August, an interesting set of statistics appears. The polling firm asked its respondents, "In general, would you say that you are satisfied or dissatisfied with the direction in which the nation is going?" Fifty-eight percent of those interviewed said that they were dissatisfied, while only 35 percent said that they were satisfied. Yet in that very same poll 64 percent of the respondents said that they would vote for the incumbent President of the United States, while only 30 percent said that they would vote for the alternative choice. Taken by themselves these figures appear unbelievable, but they are simply a stark testimony to McGovern's inability to present himself as a *credible* alternative to the administration.

Much has been heard recently about "credibility" and it is often used simply as a euphemism for telling the truth. But the word has a far more useful meaning: believability, viability, being "for real." It is this quality that George McGovern ultimately lacked and it was the lack of this quality, more than anything else, that cost him the election.

This fascinating and often decisive imponderable is a very subtle concept in presidential elections. Those who are perceived as extremists will find it very difficult to obtain "credibility," but it is not the issues on which candidates run or the pronouncements that candidates make that establish or destroy their credibility. Teddy Kennedy, for instance, has made so many "extreme" statements on so many issues that by any rational comparison George McGovern is a moderate. Yet a Kennedy can do it and get away with it because he is a Kennedy. Kennedys are for real. They are not believed to lack substance, whatever the realities of the situation. They always appear credible, and it would take an extraordinarily egregious statement or event to destroy this viability. There are others who enjoy this valuable commodity, and some who actually deserve it. Nelson Rockefeller is for real. His viability and credibility have never been denied by even his strongest opponents. He fights back. He is substantial. And, although this quality creates enemies, no one episode nor any one statement has ever permanently destroyed him. During his first term as President, Nixon also earned this image in the public view. It is difficult to say what gives a man credibility, but it is possible to suggest that weeping in public over a silly newspaper charge, or claiming that one has been brainwashed, or acting in a very indecisive manner in reaching a critical decision can easily destroy the credibility, viability, and believability of a candidate. Somehow it is related to an image of toughness, honesty, and sincerity — but also to the ability to do things, to make good on one's promises, and to stand for no nonsense. This perceived personal qualification is the starting point in most voters' evaluation of a candidate, especially a candidate for the presidency of the United States.

It is difficult to say whether George McGovern ever reached a high level of credibility in the eyes of the voters, but probably not. As he became known in April and May, the electorate responded negatively to his stands on many issues but positively to his personal characteristics. Virtually all surveys confirm this. People did perceive George McGovern as a moderate, calm, decent human being, compassionate and concerned. They admired his courage to speak his mind on the issues. They perceived a variance from their own position, but in the presence of a sense of trust, people will forgive such a variance until they are directly and adversely affected by it. It is not easy to win a campaign on character alone — especially if the candidate is a relatively unknown quantity — but it is possible if the issues' variance between that candidate and the electorate is skillfully handled.

If a candidate's personal image is destroyed, however, it is very difficult indeed to save him unless the opposition is similarly flawed. When McGovern lost his credibility over the Eagleton affair, he never could have won an election until he restored that credibility, no matter how positively his stands on issues might have been received — and they were not received positively at all by most Americans. The electorate demands that a candidate be able to deliver, and the expectation that a candidate will deliver is based upon an evaluation of his motives, his competence, and his platform: "*Will he try* to do what he says he will do? *Is he able* to do what he says he will do? *Do I want him* to do what he says he will do?"

The Eagleton affair destroyed McGovern's credibility on the first two questions and his issues' clarifications confirmed the electorate's hesitations about the third. This confirmation, in turn, reinforced their perceptions on the first two. The evidence is striking. On the question of sincerity, the August Gallup poll reported that President Nixon was considered more sincere or believable than George McGovern by a margin of 59 percent to 20 percent, with 21 percent having no opinion. On the question of competence the evidence is even more striking. McGovern's own polls, taken by Pat Caddell, indicated that by September 41 percent of the electorate felt that McGovern was "unqualified" to be President and 50 percent agreed with the statement: "George McGovern doesn't understand enough about how things work to solve the country's problems." Caddell also discovered that 46 percent of the voters had changed their minds between July and September on the competence question — negatively. Using a sophisticated regression analysis of factors most influencing voters' negative perceptions of McGovern, he concluded that the competence issue was, by far, the most important factor.

When these perceptions of capability were combined with McGovern's stands on issues, the result was political catastrophe. Let one example suffice. Louis Harris reported in August that "by 76 percent to 21 percent the country overwhelmingly wants to 'bring home all the U.S. troops, naval and air forces from Vietnam.'" But by the same token, he continued, "an equally overwhelming 74 percent to 19 percent of the voters do not think that George McGovern would be able to fulfill his pledge to 'have all U.S. troops and prisoners of war out of Vietnam three months after he is in the White House.'"

McGovern simply ceased to be credible as a candidate. He could not deliver, it appeared, no matter what he *promised* to deliver on, no matter what he *intended* to deliver on. With such a perception of a candidate's competence, issues become almost irrelevant in a positive sense. If you can't deliver on your platform, of what relevance is your platform — except that negatively it can confirm the suspicions of your competence. In this negative sense issues and personality did become intertwined and the extremism charge became real in the minds of the voters.

If George McGovern had been strongly tied to his party, then some of these difficulties would have been removed, since party association itself conveys a sense of credibility and believability to a candidate. There is still some expectation that Democrats will do certain things and that Republicans will do other things, although this attitude is diminishing in the age of strategic politics. The closer a candidate is to a viable party situation, the more the party itself can be counted on to aid in the delivery process — through its other elected officials and through its own demands upon the elected candidate in question. But McGovern had no such prop, and the movement with which he was associated, far from providing a substitute for a party, tended to reinforce the voters' perceptions of his alleged extremism. Divorced from his party, alone, and without credibility, he had to build a coalition with very little to offer people for their support. In such a situation issues pale in significance, but his apparent vacillation on issues simply destroyed their relevance altogether. The only remaining credible issues were the war and the President, but on both of these he had to build a negative coalition, not a positive one. This ultimately was what he attempted to do, but things have to be dire indeed for the country to repudiate the status quo in order to embrace a totally noncredible alternative. With his charges echoing back and forth among a disbelieving public, George McGovern, like Barry Goldwater before him, left the country with no choice at all.

The President and his image were the dramatic beneficiaries of this state of affairs. As voters began to compare George McGovern with Richard Nixon, the President began to appear all the more favorable. On issue after issue Nixon was perceived as considerably more competent than the South Dakotan. Who can deal better with Vietnam? Nixon, 58 percent to 26 percent. Who can deal better with inflation? Nixon, 46 percent to 32 percent. Who can deal better with crime and lawlessness? Nixon, 50 percent to 26 percent. These September Gallup figures are decisive.

President Nixon had not been doing too well on these issues as late as July, but the comparison to McGovern began to reinforce his image. The voters began to feel the need for self-justifying their choice, and as this need grew, so did the voters' evaluation of Richard Nixon.

The most interesting fact that emerges from the survey research data during the fall is that on the concrete issues per se, the electorate was not enthusiastic about the President's policies. Gallup reported, for instance, that the public disapproved of the bombing of North Vietnam. Harris reported that the public favored defense *cuts;* Gallup reported a great deal of skepticism about the war ending by January. Harris reported that a majority of Americans did not feel that Nixon had kept his promise to end the war. Gallup reported that the country was dissatisfied with the looseness of the wage and price controls.

Furthermore, the country as a whole remained dissatisfied by the large margins quoted. According to Gallup, every age group, every income bracket, every occupational category, every educational level, and every region of the country reported that it was more *dissatisfied* than *satisfied* with the direction in which the nation was going in the August survey. Only Republicans were satisfied, and these by a margin of 52 percent to 43 percent. With such a high level of dissatisfaction and with such a landslide for the incumbent, the only viable conclusion that can be drawn is that the challenger must have been in an extraordinarily sorry condition. The light turnout of voters and the high number of people who told Gallup that they were voting against, not for, a candidate indicates that large portions of the electorate were disgusted by what they saw.

It would be inaccurate to suggest that the electorate was a monolith or that it moved decisively in large blocs to the President and remained with him through November. This was not the case at all. Throughout the summer there was tremendous voter fluidity, although shifts in both directions tended to cancel each other out. The McGovern organization took a poll in July, going back to the same sample in September. The size and procedures enabled them to examine actual shifts in the electorate, not just net shifts. Caddell found that 31 percent of the electorate had changed its mind during the summer, 14 percent moving from one candidate directly to another and 17 percent moving toward or away from the undecided column. These are minimum figures and do not reflect other changes that may have taken place within the time period or after it. Gallup in 1968 reported that 17 percent of the electorate changed its mind during the entire preelection period, but he did not include the undecided category in his figures. Since the 1968 race was a three-way contest in which most of the movement was the result of brief flirtations with a third-party alternative, the 1972 figures for July–September are remarkably high.

Table 2 indicates the amount of movement, where it came from, and where it went. The categories are very interesting.

	NIXON	MCGOVERN	UNDECIDED
Position in July	52	37	11
Stayed in category	43	24	2
To Nixon	8 ←——————— 8		
	5 ←——————————————— 5		
To McGovern	6 ———————→ 6		
		4 ←————————— 4	
To undecided	3 ————————————————→ 3		
		5 ————————→ 5	
Position in September	56	34	10

TABLE 2.
Candidate Shifts within the Electorate

- The 8 percent who moved from McGovern to Nixon contained a very high proportion of young people; 46 percent of this category was under the age of thirty. Young suburban families and young blue-collar Wallace Democrats were the major categories to shift; the reasons given were primarily Eagleton and credibility.

- The 6 percent who moved from Nixon to McGovern were chiefly low-income Democrats moved by the economy and the war, together with some upper-income suburbanites influenced by Watergate.
- The 3 percent who moved from Nixon to undecided were largely middle- and upper-income suburbanites moving on the Watergate issue.
- The 5 percent who moved from McGovern to undecided were generally younger Democrats who were strongly anti-Nixon, but who became increasingly disillusioned by McGovern on the competence question.
- The 5 percent from the undecided column who moved to Nixon and the 4 percent who moved to McGovern were largely traditional Democrats, Catholics, and blue-collar workers who were generally both anti-Nixon and anti-McGovern to begin with, and who stayed that way through the election.

These figures are simply phenomenal. They show that Watergate did have an impact upon the voter and that the economy had not disappeared as an issue. They show that the issues that McGovern stood for were not the most decisive factor in his difficulties. They show that party designations are still of some value, but that they are not overwhelming among a very large segment of the electorate. These figures also show how fluid the electorate really is and they illustrate the paradox of cutting issues discussed in Chapter 3. Had the competence issue not intervened but the Watergate and the economic concerns persisted, there would have been a horse race. There was plenty of movement in the last month of 1968, but that was a "return to the fold" and a reassertion of political alignment. Nineteen seventy-two's movement was away from the party alignment in the direction of nonalignment. The electorate is increasingly becoming unhinged by events, by candidates, and by the strategies of the various campaigns.

In 1972 it was also angry — angry at the administration for its policies, angry at the Democrats for nominating McGovern, angry at McGovern for not providing an alternative choice, angry at the political process and politicians in general. Despite its anger it made what it felt to be a responsible choice. The problems of this society cannot be blamed on the irresponsibility or lack of judgment of the electorate, which — so far — remains sober, stable. intelligent, and responsible even when angered by the conduct of its officials and its politicians. And in 1972, according to George Gallup, 60 percent of that electorate split its ticket.

Many commentators have reflected upon the similarities of George McGovern and Barry Goldwater: their movements, their alleged extremism, and their massive defeats at the hands of "pragmatic" opponents. What is less recognized is that these two men are throwbacks to the two dominant political and social influences of nineteenth-century America, the small-town businessman and the small-town preacher, both of whom for better or for worse shaped the lives and the thoughts of the Republic in another era. The peddler's grandson and the preacher's son, themselves products of small-town American society, were never really able to grasp the sophistications and the depersonalizations of modern American culture. The one, gregarious and easy-going in the style of his background, the other solitary, yet intense, in the traditions of his — neither was ever at ease with the manipulations, the strategies, the tactics, and the power plays of contemporary politics.

The basic question that will forever remain unanswered is, did America reject these men because it understood them or because it misunderstood them? Barry Goldwater, for all his idiosyncrasies, is a decent, honest, sincere, and competent man. George McGovern, for all his problems, is also a decent, honest, and sincere human being, probably much more competent than his image would suggest. It is doubtful that voters perceived these qualities in either man and the conduct of both was to blame for this misunderstanding as much as any other factor. Yet Americans also may have grasped the fact that neither man is *of this century*, with its enormous complexities, its massive disillusionments, and its growing inhumanities. The country might well be convinced that the image of the world envisioned by each of these men would be better than the conditions of the present, but Americans had no illusions about either man's ability to recreate the past or to use the homilies of the past to deal with the future. Twice they rejected the appeals of the nostalgic visionary and placed their trust in what seemed to be a more credible alternative — and twice they saw that trust betrayed.

8

The Agony of Labor

If George McGovern's major problem was his political credibility, there was no more striking example of this than his relationship to organized labor. For years the Democratic party had enjoyed a very close and warm association with the labor movement; this relationship had been defined by the personal ties and intensely "political" practices of the "old politics." It was based on a sense of mutuality if not trust, and it had created a condition of relative stability where both politician and labor official knew where they stood.

The McGovern candidacy, however, seemed to pose a massive threat to this whole arrangement. To be sure, McGovern was strongly pro-labor as far as his specific policies were concerned. His voting record was sound in this respect and his official positions left little room for labor complaint. But neither McGovern nor his staff enjoyed the kind of personal relationship with organized labor that could become the basis of a solid association of mutual confidence. The candidate and his followers may have had a very sophisticated sense of issues and ideology, but they had an extraordinarily naïve sense of constituency. They assumed that symbols, ideals, and positions could by themselves create the basis of solid and lasting support. They were never able to perceive that labor's association with the Democratic party went far beyond issues and ideology, that it involved a whole way of doing business.

Labor and the Democratic Party

The labor movement has always insisted, that, in theory, alignment with neither party would perpetually increase its bargaining position with both parties. Samuel Gompers, effective founder of the American labor movement, was basically nonpartisan, though not by any means apolitical. At the first meeting of the American Federation of Labor held in Pittsburgh nearly a century ago twelve of the fourteen resolutions passed had to do with prospective legislation and Gompers was well aware that electoral politics was a necessary complement to any legislative strategy. He made his point clearly in a letter to Theodore Roosevelt in 1906, warning that labor "will stand by our friends and administer a stinging rebuke to men or parties who are our enemies, and wherever opportunity affords [we will] secure the election of intelligent, honest, earnest trade unionists with clear unblemished union cards in their possession." But Gompers consistently opposed the concept of either a separate Labor party or a permanent alliance between labor and any political party, insisting that unions could most effectively ply their influence as independent bodies. The AF of L's only presidential endorsement under Gompers – of Progressive Robert La Follette in 1924 – was justifiably consistent with this policy of nonalignment.

In 1936, however, after four years of unprecedented labor activity and legislative gains, the leadership of the AF of L, under a new president, William Green, supported Franklin Roosevelt for reelection and John L. Lewis persuaded the nonmember industrial unions to commit $750,000 to the campaign. Although the theory of nonalignment was never abandoned, 1936 was the start of a warm rapport between labor and the Democratic party on the national level. Since that time, until 1972, organized labor has united behind every Democratic candidate for President. To be sure, there have been a handful of defections under extraordinary circumstances. In 1940, for instance, at the height of a bitter feud, John L. Lewis, then president of the CIO, endorsed Willkie over FDR; and twenty years later, at the height of his feud with the Kennedy clan, Jimmy Hoffa endorsed Richard Nixon. But otherwise labor has had little difficulty supporting the Democratic ticket.

This has been a close relationship not only on paper but in spirit. Throughout the last thirty-five years, nearly 70 percent of union members have maintained a basic attachment to the Democratic party, and in a loose sense this remains true today. In some areas union groups became synonymous with the Democratic organizations. In *The Making of the President 1960*, Theodore White explained that "the UAW are to Michigan Democrats what the Chase Manhattan Bank is to New York Republicans"; and in a later volume he was to observe that the Humphrey campaign organization in '68 was synonymous with the AFL-CIO. What started as rapport became a sort of marriage. Organized labor's basic constituency and the Democratic party's basic constituency became one.

For thirty-five years, at both the national level and at most nonsouthern local levels, the Democratic party delivered to the labor movement and the labor movement delivered to the Democratic party. The old notion of bargaining between parties was replaced by a more advantageous arrangement of mutual reciprocity, trust, and accommodation.

In a recent interview with *Washington Post* reporter Haynes Johnson, George Meany described the special relationship of reciprocity that came to exist in the industrial states between the workingman and the Democratic party long before any special arrangements occurred at the national level. "Now in New York, where I was brought up," the former Bronx plumber explained, "all we knew was the Democratic party. I recall as a kid where there'd be baseball teams backed by the Democratic party in my district. They'd be passing out Thanksgiving turkeys to people. You could go to the Democratic club . . . this was an area where there were a lot of poor people, although it certainly wasn't a slum — you could go to the Democratic club every few weeks and get an order for a half a ton of coal. And there were jobs. I remember the thousands of people who we put on snow removal in the dead of winter. Five dollars a day for snow removal. Shoveling snow, thousands of people. People'd be out of work in the winter, you know. Well, all right. Who gave them the tickets to go out and report for the jobs? The Democratic club. Now there was a lovely avenue in the neighborhood, the finest in the neighborhood. It had some three-story brownstones; one of those was the Republican club. I remember the green shades and the initials of the club were in gold letters I remember that. And those shades were never raised and nobody ever saw a sign of life in the club except on election night every two years, when the club would be lit up, especially for the election. And that was the only contact the people had with the Republican party. Now this is our traditional business with the Democratic party." What has this "traditional business" done for the Democratic party?

It has done a lot. Members of labor unions compose approximately a seventh of the adult population of the United States. They and their families make up about a quarter of the potential American electorate, and because they are more likely to vote than average citizens are, they comprise nearly 30 percent of the voters. Out of a total labor force of 86 million, 22 percent — 19 million workers — are members of the 185 national unions in the United States. Of these, about 14½ million are members of AFL–CIO unions. Approximately 20 percent are women, 10 percent are black. A third of all union members are concentrated in the three most important electoral states: New York, California, and Pennsylvania; and as a percentage of the work force, organized labor is most *significant* in Wisconsin, Michigan, and West Virginia, representing over 40 percent of workingmen and women in each.

COPE

There are many ways in which these statistics are translated into political results. The most illustrative modern techniques are those employed by COPE, the AFL–CIO Committee on Political Education that came into existence in 1955 when the two unions merged. Operating with a budget of over $2 million a year (not including special funds for campaign contributions), COPE engages in several efforts.

Using volunteers provided by member unions and affiliates, COPE has conducted massive voter registration campaigns every two years since 1960. In 1968 and 1970 COPE director Al Barkan reported to President Meany that 65 percent of the membership was registered, in many instances as a result of its efforts. This year, with the introduction of court rulings that simplified the registration process, the figure rose to the 80 percent range. While registration is in some sense a good government effort, it is also the backbone of the unions' political clout, since their influence depends on an ability to show that they have a deliverable voting constituency in as many districts as possible. These programs are also used to cement their relationship to the Democratic party, since "85 percent of them are registered Democrats," according to Meany.

Furthermore, these efforts can become a strategic political tool. In 1968, for instance, Walter Reuther cut off an effort aimed at registering normally Democratic blue-collar wards, where Wallace sentiment appeared strong, and emphasized instead the registration of blacks in Detroit's inner city, where Humphrey was expected to have extremely large margins.

To complement moves aimed at getting its members to register, COPE works with its state affiliates on "Get Out the Vote" programs. In 1968, 1970, and again in 1972, labor had 100,000 volunteers getting out "its" vote on election day. Often these workers are paid for their time under contract provisions permitting leave for "union business." Says one Chrysler vice president, "It just happens that on election day there's an awful lot of leave for union business."

One aspect of this operation that will have significant long-term implications for COPE's effectiveness is its voter identification program. This is a continuous project in cooperation with state and local COPEs to pull together a computerized file on all its members in a format compatible for use as a political tool. COPE has such a file on over 8 million members in two dozen states. There are another fifteen states in which the data processing is partially complete and another eight states where a manual filing system is in operation. The result of this effort, which will cost COPE several million dollars, is clear. For instance, COPE can use this file as the basis of a mailing list or a sophisticated canvassing operation to target and compartmentalize its appeal to selected elements of its constituency, and it can be used for very effective organizational work on primary and election day. For example, in Pennsylvania, Mike Johnson, vice president and political director for the Pennsylvania AFL–CIO, is now able to provide favored campaigns with a list of 900,000 names of workers, their wives, their children of voting age, and other vital statistics broken down accurately in terms of Democrats, Republicans, and Independents, all complete with their latest home addresses.

Since the Taft-Hartley Act forbids unions to contribute directly to federal elections out of members' dues, COPE has two separate funds of money. First, regular dues paid by the members through their internationals are used for educational efforts such as registration drives and for other programs not strictly partisan in nature. Second, voluntary contributions solicited by the unions from the membership go directly to selected candidates. The candidate fund, which raised well over a million dollars in 1972, is ostensibly divided between national COPE and its state and local affiliates. Its voluntary contributions are generated by an appeal from Al Barkan through the internationals that each member contribute $2. Some unions ask for more. The Machinists, for example, suggest $5. Of course, not everybody contributes, but the funds still do generate a significant amount of money for the unions' own use and for candidates' war chests. COPE also has a large number of political experts and consultants that are loaned to campaigns. In 1972, for example, it had 500 full-time people assigned to marginal House and Senate races and another 8,000 full-time precinct workers on election day.

The Humphrey campaign of 1968 is a classic example of what labor can do — and has done — for the Democratic party. That year, the AFL–CIO registered 4.6 million (presumably Democratic) voters, printed and distributed 55 million pamphlets (20 million of which were anti-Wallace pieces), canvassed 72,225 homes, produced 94,457 volunteers on election day, and probably spent around $5 million. All this effort was made for a presidential candidate who "was as close to a Labor party candidate for President as there has ever been," according to one Meany staffer. Equipped with ancient credentials associated with the Great Society, which was nearly a Labor party platform, and running against Richard Nixon, who was, in the words of Al Barkan, "the same union-hater he's always been," Humphrey was precisely what labor wanted. Furthermore, the Democratic party machinery was in worse disarray than it had been at any time in the previous thirty years, so the unions, by choice and necessity, provided the party with a vehicle and a strategy. It is little wonder that when 1972 arrived, many in labor considered '68 the litmus test for loyalty and begrudged those on the Left who had sat it out. In his speech before the 1972 convention, I. W. Abel, president of the United Steelworkers — and Humphrey's labor chairman — confronted the assembled legions of the new politics with a bitter reminder when he said, "If some of these new politicians had worked as hard to support our party as they subsequently worked to reform our party, we would be

163

meeting here to renominate and lay plans to reelect President Hubert Humphrey."

Fragmentation of the Labor Movement

The labor movement has never been a monolith. It is probably less so now than it ever was. Despite many surface demonstrations of solidarity, it is beset by all manner of structural and political difficulties. It is becoming increasingly fragmented from within, and as it becomes so, it becomes all the more susceptible to fragmentation from without. Shrewd political strategy by the Nixon administration has exploited virtually every dimension of labor's increasing fragmentation: its structural deficiencies, its personality disputes, its policy conflicts, and its generation gaps.

Organized labor is broken down into "affiliated" and "independent" unions. Affiliated unions are part of the American Federation of Labor–Congress of Industrial Organizations (AFL–CIO). This organization, formed in 1955 as a coalition of the AF of L (representing primarily skilled or craft unions) and the CIO (representing primarily unskilled or industrial unions), today has 125 member unions, the largest of which are the United Steelworkers, the International Brotherhood of Electrical Workers, and the International Association of Machinists. Three and a half million workers are members of unions that are independent of the AFL–CIO. Most of these belong either to the International Brotherhood of Teamsters or the United Auto Workers.

AFL–CIO president George Meany, a former officer of the Plumbers' and Pipefitters' union, presides over the Executive Council, which is made up of representatives of thirty-three unions plus Meany and Lane Kirkland, his chosen secretary-treasurer. Except for Meany and Kirkland, all members of the Executive Council hold the title of vice president of the AFL–CIO. This conglomerate is broken down into 6 departments, 50 state bodies, and 175 local central bodies. The departments each relate to different categories of unions represented by the AFL–CIO: the Building and Construction Trades' Department, the Industrial Union Department, the Maritime Trades' Department, the Metal Trades' Department, the Railroad Employees' Department, and the Union Label and Service Trades' Department.

Despite a high degree of decentralization and autonomous decision-making, this aggregation of personalities and interests has been remarkably cohesive with a few exceptions, such as the expulsion of the Teamsters' union for corruption, the departure of the UAW on grounds of policy and personality, and the removal of the East and West Coast Dockworkers' unions on suspicion of communist sympathy. Yet there are

164

many divisions within the movement whose differences are beginning to become all the more apparent and exploitable.

• Occupational divisions are the most obvious. For instance, the Maritime and Transportation unions clearly have other interests at stake than those of the Steel and manufacturing unions in the debates over trade policy. There are many other examples of conflicting economic interests.

• There are regional divisions within the labor movement, based in part on the more generic political differences among the regions, in part on the strength of the union movement (which varies regionally), and in part on the basis of the local political climates they have had to contend with. For example, the New York State Building Trades' unions had little difficulty supporting President Nixon's reelection, for they have supported moderate Republicans often since Nelson Rockefeller came to power in 1958. The California Building Trades' unions have been presented with no such opportunity to support Republican candidates on a large scale and therefore tend to be closer to the Democratic party. The McGovern organization in California, for example, was chaired by building trades people.

• There are divisions of personality and factionalism. For instance, within the higher leadership of the AFL–CIO, internal politics centering around the succession crisis has become acute. Some of the most prominent figures in the debate over the organization's 1972 election strategy are also those mentioned most often as possible successors to Meany: Joe Bierne of the Communications Workers, Paul Hall of the Seafarers, and Lane Kirkland. There are many more such examples.

• There are divisions of ideology and policy. Within the AFL–CIO, the leadership of the Building and Construction Trades Division is concerned that labor's lobbyists are spending too much of their time on social questions. They would like to see the operation concentrate more of its energy on basic trade union policies. On the other hand, the leadership of the industrial unions and the government employee unions feels strongly that labor must now renew its commitment to social change and the quality-of-life issues. The UAW also agrees. During the 92d Congress, the UAW supported legislation designed to encourage industrialized housing to meet the nation's critical housing shortage, while the AFL–CIO, led by the Building Trades Department, opposed it. The Vietnam war was another issue on which labor has split along the same lines.

• Most of all there are increasing cleavages between the leadership of labor and its rank and file. The latter, particularly in the industrial unions, is becoming younger, blacker, and increasingly female, while labor's top leadership seems only to grow further away from its membership. With one exception, the Executive Council of the AFL–CIO is white and it is entirely male. Two-thirds of the board members are over sixty; more than a third are over seventy. Only one member is under forty-five.

Alternatively, the majority of the work force — for example, at the Big Three (GM, Chrysler, and Ford) — is under thirty-five. The impact of this experience gap could be seen clearly at the Democratic convention. Numerically there were more union delegates in Miami than there were at Chicago in 1968, but many of them were young, black, and female. Few had even heard of the Battle of River Rouge and none had been there. Few could remember the time that "Hubert" had come through in a pinch. Few really felt a major obligation to the leadership.

This does not mean that labor's new minions are "liberals"; in fact, it was the young trade unionists who made up the bulk of George Wallace's support outside the South in '68. Conversely, this is not to say that they are all reactionaries, either. It is clear, however, that there are significant enough changes occurring in the union constituency demographically and ideologically to create vast and exploitable rifts between the top leadership and the workingmen and women at the bottom.

With these potentials for fragmentation, the labor movement could not be expected to remain associated with one party exclusively for very long. But as long as labor's unity was sufficient to control the Democratic party and its nominating process, the unions had a strong excuse for remaining with that party. As long as they dominated one party and could not dominate the other, there remained many strong incentives to do so. But in 1972 they were cut loose from the ability to control one party and were enticed — but not embraced — by the other party. This situation has left the leadership in a very interesting position.

The "Disenfranchisement" of Union Power

The McGovern candidacy in effect destroyed — perhaps permanently — the power of organized labor to hold a veto over the selections of Democratic presidential candidates. This fact has incredible implications for the future of American presidential politics since it cuts the labor movement loose and accelerates the movement toward fluidity and party instability that 1972 saw so extensively.

Labor was represented on the McGovern commission that drafted the guidelines under which the nominating process operated. Both the independent United Auto Workers and the establishment AFL–CIO had a delegate. The UAW, represented by political director Bill Dodds, participated, but the AFL–CIO, represented by I. W. Abel, did not. The guidelines that were finally adopted contained quotas for women, blacks, and youth, but not for trade unionists or Democratic public officials. These guidelines, by encouraging primaries and open caucuses, placed barriers to the selection of delegates by state Democratic committees, and severely limited the influence of elected officials. The guidelines were written in order to open up the convention and in that sense to take power away from the establishment, the most powerful part of which was organized labor.

On the surface there appears to be a paradox. There were more labor leaders at the 1972 convention (5 percent) than there were at the '68 convention (4 percent). There were also, according to a CBS poll, more delegates carrying union cards at Miami (16 percent) than there were in Chicago (10 percent). In fact, labor had set a goal of having 500 union members at the convention and had fallen short of its goal by only 12 delegates. What the McGovern commission reforms really did to labor were, first, to make it more difficult for them to send their traditional group of loyal, white, middle-aged males, and second, to make it more difficult for the party establishment to handpick its delegations. The source of labor power at conventions has never been the number of union delegates. It has been the relationship between the union leadership and the party leadership. Traditionally elected officials and party officials controlled the convention and labor officials in turn dominated them. By breaking the control of the traditional leadership, the McGovern reformers destroyed labor's power, which had been exercised indirectly through traditional channels. The reforms resulted in the selection of fewer public and party officials than ever before in measurable history. That alone was sufficient to destroy labor's power. The number of union delegates or leaders on the floor was relatively unimportant.

Second, the rules also created a vastly different primary season than the regulars had ever known. Previously, primaries were only used as a forum where a candidate could prove whether or not he had "voter appeal." It was then up to him to go to the convention and negotiate for the nomination with the unions and the party kingmakers. His primary victories were important but not decisive. John Kennedy, for example, only ran in three contested primaries. In 1968 there were clear contests in only six primaries, five of them between McCarthy and Kennedy. But under the new guidelines, 1972 saw heated primary battles in nineteen states.

Primaries have always been the scourge of any established party leadership for two reasons. They tend to split that leadership into competing factions whose battles must be fought in the open, not in a quiet conference room. Further, they tend to split the rank and file away from the leadership.

In 1972, the leadership was also badly divided. There were three candidates who were acceptable to official labor: Muskie, Humphrey, and Jackson. Meany wanted Jackson first, Humphrey second, and Muskie third. The UAW wanted Muskie first — because he looked like a winner — with Humphrey a distant second and Jackson not very much at all. Other unions had other patterns of preference. The inability to agree on any one candidate and the confusions of the Muskie collapse delayed the conclusion that Humphrey was their alternative to McGovern until very late. Even had they agreed on a candidate, they still might have had many difficulties. Television and modern campaign techniques have severely reduced the impact that old-style organizations have on the electorate. Also, labor this year was simply "outgunned." The McGovern organization had as many staff people skilled in canvassing and precinct work as the COPE organization, and their young volunteers could easily match labor's body for body. With labor's changing constituency and the general alienation of its membership from the leadership, it is quite possible that labor will never again be the most organized constituency within the Democratic party.

If the primary season of 1972 was a harbinger of permanent change, and the party's nominee is now to be selected in local elections and packed caucuses, then the AFL–CIO will have to consider setting up an effective nationwide precinct operation in order to compete. In an interview, the political director of one of the AFL–CIO unions said, however, that the question was not "whether COPE would want to do something like that, but whether they could." He mused for a minute more and then added, "Now, Al Barkan is a friend and I think he's a very competent man. But he's never been a precinct captain. Precinct-level organization is not the kind of politics that those people in Washington know much about."

The point is that the structure of the nominating process will make it very difficult for labor to regain its traditional position within the Democratic party. Many commentators in 1973 felt that labor had staged an impressive comeback — and in one sense it had. It regained access to the inner councils of the party and it saw the repeal or modification of those rules it found so obnoxious in 1972. But its regained position will not be relevant in 1976 as long as the nomination itself is fought for in the open. The primary laws, if they are left on the books, define the nature of the nominating process and ensure that the contest will be fought in the arena least subject to the influence of union leadership. The Wallace, McGovern, and Nixon tacticians have detached many union members from the effective control of their leadership, and it is doubtful that they will be able to regain that control without the kind of vigorous activity the aging leadership can no longer provide. In any case, the old forms of power have been destroyed. If labor wants to nominate "its" candidate in 1976, it will have to focus largely on influencing the rank-and-file Democrat, not on influencing the party leadership. This it might succeed in doing, but the job will not be an easy one.

The Agony of 1972

Organized labor had supported George McGovern in his previous bids for public office and regarded him as a pro-labor senator. The relationship, however, between this aloof prairie politician and the union leaders had always been more correct than cordial, and McGovern had never felt at ease in the traditional atmosphere of political backscratching that characterized the mutuality between labor and its friends. His managers were even more uncomfortable in the traditional setting of Democratic-labor politics.

Yet McGovern had usually voted with COPE, and despite an episode or two in the past where Meany felt McGovern had let him down on a roll call, the union chieftain, as late as April 1972, had said that he would support McGovern if he were nominated. The events of late spring, however, undercut and destroyed this support. When labor finally made up its mind to back Humphrey, the McGovern forces were far along the road to the nomination and labor began to sense that it might be shut out of the nominating process altogether. Its hesitations had left it in an awkward position, and to restore the situation it began to embrace Humphrey, an old friend, with increasing enthusiasm. By midspring the top leadership began to look resentfully and suspiciously at the Mc-Govern supporters and managers, and the Humphrey campaign became a crusade to stop McGovern. Labor psyched itself up to fight the South Dakotan and boxed itself in with rhetoric and rationale that would, as one Meany staffer explained it, "sure as hell make it impossible for us to support McGovern now if we wanted to." The climax came in California. Labor virtually took over the Humphrey campaign, flooded the state with anti-McGovern material, and almost succeeded in erasing a 20-point deficit. McGovern reacted strongly to this activity and attacked the "labor bosses." His rhetoric, in turn, deepened the antagonism and seemed to confirm all the suspicions labor had accumulated.

At the convention labor continued to fight hard. It spearheaded the credentials fights and other floor fights. It circulated a devastating forty-six-page document researched and written by Tom Kahn, a Meany speechwriter, that analyzed McGovern's record on civil rights, the labor issue, amnesty and the draft, marijuana, crime and violent protest, the "basic assumptions" of his foreign policy (the Cold War, the USSR, Czechoslovakia, China, Vietnam and Israel), and his stand on military cuts. Meany himself came to Miami to buttonhole delegates. But they were dealing with as different a proposition as the establishment Republicans had encountered in 1964. They had no instruments of persuasion.

While the 1968 convention was 87 percent male, 95 percent white, and 97 percent over thirty, the 1972 Democratic Convention was 40 percent female, 24 percent youth, 15 percent black, 3 percent Chicano, and 1 percent American Indian. Eighty-three percent were attending for the first time. Meany described it as "the convention that nominated the candidate who chaired the commission that made up the rules that governed the selection of the delegates who selected the candidate." For labor, it was a convention of the elite. "Thirty-nine percent of the delegates at that convention held postgraduate college degrees. Not just college degrees, but postgraduate degrees, 39 percent," Meany said, almost disbelievingly. "Thirty-one percent had incomes of over $25,000 per year, according to the *Washington Post,* so this was really a classy convention." He was so astounded by the figure that he forgot for a moment about his own $90,000 a year paycheck. But to a union man all other measures are secondary to what a person does for a living. On that subject Meany referred to a July *Life* magazine spread on the Oregon delegation. "The reason," Meany explained, "that they selected the Oregon delegation was that they said this was the delegation to the convention that was nearly perfect, according to the so-called McGovern reformation. It had thirty-four delegates, consisting of the following: six students; five teachers; four businessmen; four lawyers; three writers; two bureaucrats; two editors; two officeholders; two homemakers; one social worker; one newspaper indexer; one retired army officer; and one secretary. No bricklayers, no steelworkers. And worst of all, no plumbers."

Between his primary victories and his caucus coups, McGovern was able to amass enough delegates to win the nomination without negotiating with anybody and without owing anything to labor, and labor was not pleased. It had been shut out of its own party and denied the role it had traditionally enjoyed by the very people it blamed for its 1968 defeat. Humphrey had lost, labor felt, because the liberals had sat it out four years before to show that the party couldn't take them for granted. Labor now decided to demonstrate the converse proposition. A veteran columnist described a chance encounter between Al Barkan and former Maryland Senator Joe Tydings as the angry COPE commander stormed out of the convention hall: "You so-called responsible leaders of this party seem to think the kids and the kooks and the Bella Abzugs can win you some elections. Well, we're going to let them try to do it for you this year. We're not."

MEANY AND MCGOVERN

Before Meany left Miami he announced that a special meeting of the federation's Executive Council had been called for July 19, the following Wednesday, to consider whether or not they would support the McGovern ticket. His position was clearly that they should not, and the council so voted. But to understand why this happened requires understanding George Meany.

One Meany associate said that he thought of the union leader while watching a scene in the film *Patton,* when the general is forced to attend a banquet hosted by the Russians. Throughout the festivities General Patton uses his rank and his glance to keep his men in line and at the end of the entertainment is invited to share a ceremonial toast with his commissar host. Patton then walks up to the Russian officer and tells him face to face that he wouldn't think of sharing a drink with any "communist s.o.b." (a favorite Meany expression). Maintaining his composure, the Soviet general tells Patton, through his interpreter, that he frankly doesn't wish to drink with any "American s.o.b. either," whereupon the two officers break into a smile and share the toast in a warm embrace, assured that they understand each other fully. Like Patton in the movie, George Meany is a strong, deadly honest, old-fashioned patriot who has a tremendous appreciation of those same characteristics in other people. His friend Abe Raskin of the *New York Times* has said that [like Patton] "his bluntness masks a considerable capacity for practical accommodation." For example, it is reported that Meany isn't so anticommunist that he won't smoke a good Havana cigar.

The neutrality decision was not an easy one for Meany to make because it virtually assured, in his eyes, the reelection of Richard Nixon. Contrary to the impression he gave during the campaign, it is a matter of faith within the AFL–CIO that Meany loathes the President. Raskin wrote a *New York Times Magazine* profile of the federation president at the beginning of 1972 in which he explained that "on Meany's irascibility chart the Pay Board ranks high enough, but it is a mere irritant compared to his obsessive goal: the defeat of Richard Nixon next November." But after the events of the spring, not even his basic dislike of the President was reason enough for Meany to back McGovern. In fact, when a reporter asked him why beating the President was no longer "the paramount issue of the election," Meany said clearly, "Because a man like George McGovern got the Democratic nomination." Practical accommodation had given way to unequivocal disgust. The old-fashioned traditionalist in Meany saw McGovern as a candidate "surrounded by gay lib people — you know, the people who want to legalize marriage between boys and boys and girls and girls and vice versa." The proud trade unionist and conventional liberal in him saw McGovern being advised by John Kenneth Galbraith, who "said a few months ago, and get this, that the American trade union movement is the most reactionary force in America," and then had "the colossal gall" to get on the Today show the morning after the convention and say that "we need labor. Not just the rank and file of labor; we need the leaders too because they have the political know-how."

The Cold Warrior in him, which prompted him to describe himself (pre–Ping-Pong) as the nation's "number two" anticommunist (and presumably leads him to view himself today as "number one"), saw McGovern as "an apologist for the communist world" who views communism as "all right for people who choose it." This is particularly important in his eyes. Meany is a "social Democrat," and he surrounds himself with such people. This faction of the trade union movement is best described as long-range socialist, class struggle–oriented, leaning toward labor, very liberal on social questions, definitely nonisolationist, and viewing communism as a dictatorship. It is this group within the movement that was most defensive during the McCarthy era and, to compensate, spearheaded a drive that purged eleven ostensibly communist-infiltrated labor organizations from the federation.

In one sense neutrality was the most honorable move the federation president could have made, considering that both his membership and the 158-member General Board were almost evenly divided on the question of endorsing the Democratic nominee. But his staunch support for school busing shows that Meany is a man who thinks for himself and who isn't afraid to disagree with his membership. After all, they supported Stevenson in '56 under similar circumstances. This decision represented far more than Meany simply riding the fence. He was fully committed to stopping McGovern and simultaneously to electing a favorable Congress.

McGovern never really understood. He was the only candidate who actually held an active union card and his COPE voting record was every bit as good as John Kennedy's, considerably better than Lyndon Johnson's, and seven times as good as Richard Nixon's. He was, therefore, in the Gompers tradition, entitled to the union nod. To the extent that he, like everyone else, had deviated from labor's path, he was more than willing to admit and repent. Although he had only spent a total of fifty minutes with Meany, he had no reason to think that the labor leader felt ill toward him. After all, he had backed his previous bids for public office. In his eyes the choice was a simple one:

> If I were the chairman of the board of a giant corporation thinking only of maximizing profits I would vote for Mr. Nixon and his party. But if I were a garment worker, anxious to rid America of profit callousness, of tax loopholes for the rich, of rising prices that rob food from the family table, of the haunting fear of crime in the lower ranks of our society triggered by moral laxity in its upper echelons — if I were determined to protect my job against sweatshop products made in our country or imported from abroad, and resolved to fight for a better life for all workingmen and women in a United States that can provide it but still doesn't — I would vote on November 7 for McGovern and Shriver and a ticket which on the record is committed to advance the welfare of America's workers.

Beyond the moral imperative he presented, the South Dakota Democrat also proposed an affirmative recruiting policy for ethnics, an end to wage controls, a compromise on future party reforms, and an overall platform that seemed to be taken right from the AFL–CIO's official program — certainly a lot closer than President Nixon's.

But Senator McGovern ran into a brick wall in many unions. In the spring, they didn't think he could win the nomination; by the time he proved that he could, they felt that he wasn't going to fall into line with labor and that they should peddle their influence elsewhere. When the convention came around there were no longer any bridges that could have been built betweeen Meany and McGovern. And finally, when the AFL–CIO decided to sit on the sidelines, McGovern lashed out in a frustrated attack on those he knew he could no longer convert, saying he would run a campaign to "test whether the union power brokers are alive or dead." The way to do that, he felt, was to make a big score among individual union leaders and among union voters on election day.

THE LABOR COMMITTEE FOR MCGOVERN-SHRIVER

He was successful only in the first category. By the end of the campaign McGovern had the endorsement of thirty-three international unions, representing all the unions that have traditionally been active in national politics, with the single exception of the Steelworkers'. These unions, as well as some local chapters of other unions, including some Steelworkers' and Teamsters' districts, were part of the Labor Committee for McGovern-Shriver. This committee came together in August to take labor relations out of the hands of McGovern's insensitive technicians, who had badly mishandled them.

The initial call for the formation of a labor committee came in July from a group of labor leaders headed by Jerry Wurf of the American Federation of State, County, and Municipal Employees. This committee included Presidents Rohan, Brown, Potofsky, Smith, and Woodcock. However, while Wurf vacationed in Morocco in the weeks that followed, some of the more traditional Labor Democrats who had decided to support the ticket balked at serving on a committee headed by Wurf and Woodcock. So in early August, Joe Bierne of the Communication Workers, then a Meany intimate (one of the few to openly challenge the neutrality decision), and Joe Keenan, secretary-treasurer of the International Brotherhood of Electrical Workers (also known to be close to Meany), called a meeting of McGovern's labor backers. This created a momentary dilemma for McGovern's earlier supporters. Bierne was more acceptable to a wider range of leadership than mavericks Wurf and Woodcock, but his sudden affinity for the "radical" senator raised some suspicions. It was decided, however, that if Bierne would assure his complete dedication to the effort and if they could come to a compromise on the troublesome war issue he would be ideal. (Both Bierne and Keenan, like Meany, backed the President's Vietnam policy.) It is interesting to note in the context of McGovern's apparently irresolvable split with Meany over foreign policy that these labor leaders had little difficulty simply "agreeing to disagree" on questions of American policy

173

abroad. They felt they had more than enough issues of domestic concern to bind them. "If you think Vietnam is the beginning and the end of the world you might wonder what I'm doing here," said Bierne at the announcement. "But I say it's a choice between Nixon and McGovern and it took me two seconds to wind up with McGovern. My issues are poverty and excess profits and the faceless men who control the economy of this country."

The committee saw its job as translating McGovern's positions into messages that made sense to union voters, building as large a coalition of labor groups as they could for an umbrella, and cultivating local labor manpower to perform COPE's functions. On a $250,000 budget they ended up with full-time staffs in thirteen key industrial states and a labor effort that even surprised them in its intensity. Bierne later suggested that the reason for this release of energy was that locals had become used to relying on COPE to do the job but this time they had to do it themselves. The national office was directed by Howard Samuel of the Amalgamated Clothing Workers, who coordinated the activities of four field representatives provided by member unions. They put out between 20 and 25 million pieces of literature and organized an October "blitz," where teams of union presidents spent a week on the road engaged in well-publicized plant and union hall visits. They put out a persuasive newsletter that accented the candidate's meetings with Johnson and Daley, a comparison of McGovern and Nixon on building trades' issues, polls on the Truman election, quotes from Humphrey on McGovern and from JFK on abortion, similarities between McGovern and Nixon on amnesty, and a comparison of Shriver and Agnew in the event . . .

Paul Jennings, president of the International Union of Electricians and a powerful figure in national labor, summed up the message of McGovern's trade union committee when he said that their job was to "get across to the rank-and-file members that the issue is not whether George Meany goes back and forth but what McGovern stands for, what Nixon stands for, and what the GOP stands for." One person who did hear the message and understood that he had become something of a campaign issue was George Meany himself, who, in an unusual move, bypassed national meetings of a number of his most important member unions for fear of personal attack.

In many ways, however, the opposition forces proved to be less of a hindrance to the labor committee's efforts than McGovern's own legions. Tom Turner, an old-line Democratic leader and head of Detroit's AFL–CIO Council, provides a revealing account of the reception he and presumably many like him got at local McGovern headquarters. "I've been out there and at their downriver headquarters and they've got young people running things that don't know up from down. They've got the damnedest attitude — they don't want to be aligned with labor leaders or leaders of the Democratic party. . . . I've visited a lot of their head-quarters and I have found that in most of them I'm just another face in the crowd; even when I tell them I'm Tom Turner they still don't know who the hell I am."

McGovern may have eventually picked up most of the active leader-ship, but he lost half of the rank and file in the largest defection of union members since the labor association with the Democratic party began in the 1930s. His candidacy thus became a vehicle for accentuating the division within the labor movement. Without a lot of repair work, the labor movement may well have to retreat to the role business now has within the Republican party: that of selective donor to, sympathizer for, and intensive lobbyist with elected officials on a secondhand, not a first-hand, basis. If so, the Democratic party will become more and more the vehicle and the victim of the professional strategist and political techni-cian who will move in quickly to fill the vacuum.

The Nixon Assault

Charles Harris, president of the Florida AFL–CIO, opened the biannual national federation gathering in November 1971 with a story. He told about a young fellow who had seen a well-dressed man fall from a yacht off the Florida Keys. Seeing that the man was drowning, the youngster pulled his motorboat alongside and jumped in to rescue him. When he pulled the drowning man aboard the luxurious yacht, he discovered that his catch was the President, Richard Nixon. The Chief Executive was very grateful to the young man, and offered to use his influence to help the boy in any way he could, whereupon the lad, now quite upset, asked the President if he could arrange a military funeral for him. The President was shocked. Why, he asked him, do you want to think about funerals; you're not even old enough for the draft. Because, the boy responded, "My father is a labor leader and when he finds out what I've done, he's going to kill me!"

It seemed perfectly natural for union men to talk that way about Richard Nixon. He first got elected to Congress on a platform that focused on smashing the union bosses. He served on the House Labor Committee where he helped draft Taft-Hartley. Later, as a senator, he voted for the injunction to force the striking steelworkers back to their jobs. As vice president he had cast the tie-breaking vote to cripple the Davis-Bacon prevailing wage protections, and in 1968 he beat labor in one of the most important political campaigns in its history. But once in office, the President and his strategists began a calculated effort to weaken, divide, and neutralize his old enemy.

President Nixon's relationship with organized labor was a shaky one at best. His appointment of George Shultz as secretary of labor (1969) started him off relatively well with labor leadership. Although election bitterness prevented them from admitting it right away, Shultz was considered a fair man in most labor circles, and he was (and still is) close to George Meany. The *AFL–CIO Newsletter* during the first administration looked almost as if it had been created by Shultz's personal public relations agency instead of Meany's. And it is on the strength of Meany's friendship with Shultz that so much of his relationship with the Republican administration rested. When the labor secretary moved over to the White House and was replaced by James Hodgson, former Lockheed Corporation executive, Meany refused to deal with him, calling him a "janitor," and continued to work through Shultz.

By September 1970 the President's relationship with most unions was cordial enough that he hosted a Labor Day dinner in their honor. He toasted George Meany as a "great American," and the federation chief admitted that this fellow "Tricky Dick" was really no trickier than labor's sainted Franklin D. Roosevelt.

But in 1971 Nixon and labor resumed their feuding. The battleground was economic policy. The President's game plan had failed, but not before it had added two million to the unemployment roles. He had the first foreign trade deficit in seventy-nine years and a budget deficit larger than the accumulated deficits of the past quarter century. To add insult to injury, American business managed their first $100 billion profit year in history. As a result, in a complete reversal of policy, Nixon responded to labor's call for wage and price controls. Rather than assuage his labor troubles, however, this decision served only to exacerbate them.

What labor wanted was an equitable wage-price freeze, but what it got, in its opinion, was "rank discrimination against those in lower economic circumstances in favor of big business." Every employer became the willing enforcer of a wage freeze while the Internal Revenue Service was asked to enforce the price freeze over the telephone. On top of that, labor saw a $3 billion investment tax credit for big business. On August 19, four days after the President announced the freeze, the Executive Council met and issued a statement that explained quite clearly that it had no confidence in the President's ability to manage the economy of the nation. But it added that it was still willing to participate in an equitable program following the three-month Phase I.

In late September the President agreed to set up a board to oversee prices and a tripartite wage board including representatives of labor, management, and "the public." Meany, Woodcock, Fitzsimmons of the Teamsters, Abel, and Floyd Smith of the Machinists agreed to serve as the five labor members. But beginning with the first meeting there was disagreement over the standards, the number of workers who would be covered, and the retroactive increases due under existing contracts. Furthermore, labor felt that Nixon had packed the delegation of "public" members with corporate and administration henchmen. They included the chairman, Federal Judge George Boldt; Arnold Weber, who had been on the administration payroll as associate director of the Office of Management and the Budget until the day he became a "public" representative; William Caples, who, aside from two years as a college president, spent his entire career in big business, including two years as a vice president of the National Association of Manufacturers; Dr. Neil Jacoby, a conservative economist and director of the Occidental Petroleum Company, who said when he was appointed that if wages were kept down that would take care of profits and prices; and Dr. Kermit Gordon of Brookings. In Meany's words, "It added up to playing with loaded dice."

Shortly after the Phase II board began its deliberations the federation had its biannual meeting in Miami. The President informed Meany at the last minute that he would like to address the group and did so. The address became a televised confrontation between the two leaders. Meany introduced the President perfunctorily and then tried his best to look bored during the speech. Nixon concentrated his talk on welfare, patriotism, and foreign policy. Then, in a surprise move, the Chief Executive descended from the podium to campaign among the delegates. Meany was incensed that Nixon would do this without clearing it with him in advance, and he called the delegates back to their seats as the President reached out to speak with them. When order was restored Meany ended the affair by announcing, "We will now proceed with Act II."

Enraged White House aides claimed that Meany had insulted the President. Charges and threats started flying back and forth, including a call for mandatory retirement of union officials at age seventy, and a plausible charge by Meany that the whole confrontation had been staged by Nixon for political mileage.

The conflict finally came to a head when four of the five labor members walked off the Pay Board after the public and business members voted to scale down an increase won by the West Coast dockworkers. The reasons for the walkoff, reaching beyond the nonfederated ILWU contract, included the whole Pay Board experience, the complete failure of the price commission in holding down food prices, and the needs of the union leaders as union politicians to get tough in order to keep their own houses united. This is not a new phenomenon. Every wage board ever set up by the government has run into precisely this problem.

177

Although the President's domestic policies met with little support from organized labor, his Vietnam policy was the key to beginning a significant political relationship with a large segment of organized labor leadership. This was most clearly visible in May 1970, when the President launched an incursion into Cambodia when most of the public was adjusting to his policy of gradual deescalation. There was a loud public outcry over the new turn of events in the wearisome Vietnam situation, and when White House aides were desperate to find support for the President's policy, they found it within labor. George Meany issued a welcome statement of support and a few days later the President made an unprecedented trip across Lafayette Park to update the labor chiefs on the war situation. But all this was overshadowed by Peter Brennan's now famous "Hard Hat March on Wall Street." The construction men marched downtown in support of President Nixon, the flag, the war, and the establishment. They marched against the demonstrators whose protests were much in the news. Brennan, a Nixon supporter and head of the State Building Trades Council, rallied nearly 100,000 construction workers in a loud, flag-waving extravaganza. One White House aide described the event later, recalling that "we were sitting around the White House feeling that the country was collapsing around us. Thousands of kids were marching in Washington and then that Kent State thing happened. Then we heard that 100,000 hard hats were marching on Wall Street in New York in support of the President. It had an electrifying effect on everybody, including the President. It struck him that those workers had the same feelings about the country that he did."

The realization that segments of organized labor and some of its leadership shared the Nixon view of the world triggered his political machine into active pursuit of a labor constituency for the first time in his career. The mainstay of the efforts was a White House operation under presidential aide Charles Colson, who bargained for support among labor's top leadership, using both the President's prestige and federal policies as chips. This was supplemented by a campaign effort aimed at securing support for the President among state and local labor leaders and a Nixon move within the Republican party to soften the labor relations plank in the '72 platform.

The easiest of these tasks by far was remodeling the platform. Nixon dispatched a number of senior White House aides, draft in hand, to see the platform committee officials. Peter Frelinghuysen, New Jersey congressman and chairman of the GOP Platform Committee, wrote the new language into the document. "This is the President's party," Frelinghuysen said as he blocked efforts by some committee members, including Senator Tower, to return to the previous support of right-to-work laws. The '68 platform stated explicitly that "we will assure those rights [the

178

right of workers *not* to join a union] through enforcement of present laws, including the Taft-Hartley Act, and the Landrum-Griffin Act, and the addition of new protection where needed." The 1972 platform made no such commitment. Rather, the labor plank followed closely its preamble, which began, "We salute the statesmanship of the labor union movement." This was not a year for labor-baiting.

The presidency is an enviable position to bargain from, but for a minority party it has definite limits. The Nixon strategists knew that there were only certain elements of organized labor who might risk breaking away from the majority Democrats. First, there was that portion of the movement that was leaning their way gratuitously — the building trades; and second, there were those elements they had been able to woo in the course of the first term — primarily the Teamsters and the Maritime unions. They realized that most of the other unions were either too liberal or too wedded to the Democratic party to be likely allies.

THE BUILDING TRADES

Nixon's courting among the building trades was executed shrewdly. To begin with, he knew he had a considerable base of support among the membership that had its roots in his foreign policy and his stands on welfare and busing — on non–trade union issues. Bill Dodds of the UAW, one of the Democrats' top labor technicians, eloquently described how Nixon "gnawed" around the edges of workers' lives: "He hasn't touched the central trade union part. But he gnaws a little at the Catholic part, a little at the Polish part, a little at the patriotic part and a little at the antihippie part. After a while he has an awful lot of worker."

Nixon's well-publicized Labor Day address epitomized this appeal: "The choice before the American workers is clear. The work ethic builds character and self-reliance, the welfare ethic destroys character and leads to a vicious cycle of dependency. The work ethic builds strong people, the welfare ethic breeds weak people. This year, you are not only to choose the kind of leadership you want, you are going to decide what kind of people Americans will be."

His campaign for support among the Building Trades' leadership emphasized a more basic commodity than issues: power. Objectively speaking, the Nixon administration had brought more than its share of disaster on the construction industry and its unions. He slashed federal construction spending during his first year in office. He refused to spend some $12.5 billion of congressionally appropriated funds for public works; he vetoed an additional $2 billion in emergency public works spending in '71; he created the highest unemployment for the industry in ten years; and he temporarily suspended Davis-Bacon, the mainstay of the construction union's ability to fix wages on federal projects. On economic grounds he was very weak.

However, the administration shrewdly recognized that the top leadership of the construction unions had a very strong desire to centralize in their organizations the power that now rested in local fiefdoms around the country. In the building trades, contracts are negotiated and wages set locally. Furthermore, the locals are clearinghouses for much of the hiring and therefore they exercise tremendous power independent of their internationals and central leadership. Five months before instituting controls on the overall economy, Nixon set up CISC, the Construction Industry Stabilization Committee. This group was a fascinating example of dual strategy. On the one hand it did an extraordinary job of keeping wages and costs down to less inflationary levels, and on the other it forced all the locals to clear their contracts through their international officers who served on the council. Wage increases dropped from 16 percent in 1970 to 11 percent in 1971 to 5.6 percent in 1972, but the presidents of nine building trades unions, satisfied with the additional power given them by the new arrangements, endorsed the Nixon reelection efforts. None of the *unions* that these men led endorsed the President, only their chiefs did. None of these unions has ever been politically significant on the national level, except in 1972. But their importance to Nixon cannot be underestimated. Probably the biggest obstacle he faced to receiving massive support from the rank and file of labor was his identification as a big business, and therefore antilabor, Republican. Visible support from even politically impotent union leaders was priceless under the circumstances.

THE TEAMSTERS

By far the largest union to endorse the President was the International Brotherhood of Teamsters, whose 2 million members make them the largest labor unit in the nation. They are the model of a union whose leadership was actively wooed by the White House. Frank Fitzsimmons ascended to the presidency of the Teamsters in 1966 when the brotherhood's czar, James Hoffa, entered federal prison on a jury-tampering conviction. Fitzsimmons had come up through the ranks with Hoffa and had always been right behind him. When "the little man" was put away he entrusted the leadership to the loyal Fitzsimmons, reportedly on the understanding that he would just keep the chair warm until Hoffa's return. Fitzsimmons apparently got to like the job and the opportunities it allowed him, the most attractive of which was the opportunity to hobnob with the President of the United States. Knowing this, Colson engineered the "full treatment" for him: meetings with the President and his family, invitations to state functions, service on presidential commissions, a chat with Kissinger — "the whole circus," as one labor official put it. And it wasn't just Frank Fitzsimmons that relished this first-class treatment from the Chief Executive; it went all the way down into the ranks because, like Nixon, the Teamsters had an image problem with labor. George Meany was personally instrumental in ousting them from the AFL–CIO for being the most visibly corrupt union in the country. For a decade the only direct contact that the brotherhood had with the government was through process servers. This public attention from the White House looked like a *Good Housekeeping* Seal of Approval. But the relationship went beyond just the courting stage. Like any good political marriage, it was consummated with an act of friendship and a little insurance.

The act of friendship was the withdrawal of the Crippling Strikes Prevention Act, an administration bill calling for a dispute-resolution mechanism regarded by labor as the equivalent of compulsory arbitration for transportation strikes. At the beginning of the 1972 legislative session, the White House told its sponsor, Republican Senator Packwood of Oregon, that it was at the top of its domestic legislative priorities; the week that the Teamsters' Executive Board endorsed the President's reelection Packwood received a call from Undersecretary of Labor Laurence H. Silberman telling him that the administration no longer planned to pursue the bill. The reason given was that it had no chance of passing despite the fact that Packwood claimed to have a hard count of 47 for passage, 45 against, and 7 uncommitted (6 of whom were Republicans).

The insurance was a kind of left-handed act of friendship. The White House interceded to obtain a parole for Jimmy Hoffa. This was good for Fitzsimmons as it demonstrated to his largely pro-Hoffa membership that it was beneficial to have a relationship with the President. It was also good politics for the President, as it "honorably" repaid his debt to the Teamsters' boss who had personally endorsed his election in 1960. But most of all it set President Nixon up as Hoffa's keeper. Knowing full well that Fitzsimmons's presidency was dependent on keeping Hoffa out of circulation, the terms of his release specifically placed the Justice Department in charge of seeing that the former boss stayed clear of union politics or face a return to prison. Hence Fitzsimmons's tenure is at Nixon's pleasure.

THE MARITIMES

The other significant catch Nixon brought into the Republican effort this year was his endorsement by three of the nation's five leading maritime unions: the Seafarers, the International Longshoreman's Association, and the Marine Engineers Beneficial Association. The Seafarers also sent a check for $100,000. The background of the formation of the National Maritime Committee to Re-elect the President is not as clear as some of the other arrangements, but it probably involved many of the same motivations. These unions, for example, are vociferously anticommunist in the Meany tradition and probably viewed McGovern as being tied to coexistence. Many times throughout the years they have refused to handle shipping to and from communist countries, and they remember George McGovern as the man who spoke out most visibly against their boycotts. Furthermore, they probably went with the President because McGovern never cultivated their support while Nixon spoke of setting as "our goal a sharp increase in the transport of United States trade aboard American flagships . . . and a building program to accomplish that objective." In an industry that once boasted 2,000 vessels flying the American flag and carrying large portions of the nation's trade, and that today can count less than 600 ships and only 5.6 percent of our trade, their support made the simplest political sense. However, in addition, a number of veteran labor columnists suggested that the Justice Department's dismissal of federal charges against Seafarers' President Hall (on a campaign finance indictment similar to that on which Mine Worker President Tony Boyle was convicted) just might have been a factor in lifelong Democrat Paul Hall's decision to come on board.

THE LABOR COMMITTEE TO RE-ELECT THE PRESIDENT

While Colson handled the bulk of President Nixon's labor relations out of the White House, CREEP had its own labor committee operating in the field. The Labor Committee to Re-elect the President was under the direction of Don Rodgers, a former associate of Peter Brennan and a veteran of a number of Nelson Rockefeller's labor efforts, and Bernard DeLury, Rockefeller's deputy commissioner of Industrial Relations and the son of one of New York's most powerful labor leaders. According to Rodgers, they "spent most of their time on the road doing one-night stands." He described how they relied on local representatives of some of the internationals that were supporting the President and state industrial commissions (where there were Republican administrations) to put together a list of labor leaders who might be favorable to endorsing the President. They would then set up a cocktail party where someone from the National Labor Committee would make a pitch. The line was simply that "you're going to vote for the President anyway, your membership is going to vote for the President, and the President is going to get reelected. But if you sit on the sidelines it isn't going to do you or your membership any good." Rodgers explained that the issue most often raised by the local union chief was the war. Then came busing and crime, but "the war was the overriding issue. After all," Rodgers continued, "these men have been at the bargaining table all of their lives and they know that today President Nixon is at the bargaining table with the communist world and they remember Munich." The next day those who would support the Nixon-Agnew ticket were encouraged to form a paper committee and hold a press conference or send a letter to the editor of a local paper. They were being asked to lend their names to the notion that Nixon had some friends among labor. The key was publicity, and nothing else was really expected of them. Since the President was starting at ground zero, any support they could muster among these state and local union officials was a plus that they would not have received otherwise and, in that sense, the $200,000 operation was, in Bernie DeLury's words, "a terrific success."

To a large extent, that success is owed to Nelson Rockefeller, who has had singular success in attracting New York labor to his own corner. The last time he ran, Rockefeller persuaded the state AFL–CIO to endorse him over Arthur Goldberg, a former counsel to the United Steelworkers and labor secretary under John F. Kennedy. It was Rockefeller who coached Nixon prior to his first appearance before his would-be union backers. He advised the President to "make no promises" but to tell them straight out that his was not going to be an antilabor administration. Tell them that they would have a friend in the White House who would do what he could to help them, but that they weren't going to agree on everything. And when they would reach an impasse and he felt they were wrong, "he would tell them so and that would be it." Rockefeller also instructed the President that labor operated on a quid pro quo basis, and that if he wanted to get their support a second time he was going to have to produce on jobs, public works, and labor legislation. The governor provided Nixon with his top labor staff people and even held a few informal dinners at his Pocantico Hills estate to soften up some of the union officials. "But the question to which no one in either camp has any answer," says Abe Raskin of the *Times*, "is how much of the Rockefeller formula Mr. Nixon intends to apply at the White House — whether he will go beyond effusive external expressions of cordiality to policy concessions in areas where labor and the GOP have traditionally collided."

Republicans and the Future of Labor

After the election many actions were taken to cultivate a continuing relationship between labor and the White House. The appointment of Peter Brennan as secretary of labor seemed to indicate that the President wanted to continue his appeal to the union rank and file on the basis of conservative policies. The office of Labor Adviser to the President was created within the White House to establish someone close to the President who could serve as a liaison with labor groups and as an expediter of labor's interests. Don Rodgers was appointed to this post after he completed his work at CREEP. Both men were building on the efforts of the past when the Watergate scandal broke and focused the attention of most Americans elsewhere.

As the country and the party begin to emerge from the thicket of scandals, the fundamental question remains: What is the future of the Republican party in the calculations of labor?

The answer involves a number of complex considerations. The first is the future of labor in the Democratic party. Since the election, COPE and the traditional elements of the party have been able to wrest back control of large pieces of the national machinery. Barkan played an active role in the fight to dump Jean Westwood and replace her with Lyndon Johnson's intimate and former party treasurer, Robert Strauss. With his help, "responsible" trade unionists should have more say in the workings of the party, and Meany, as one Nixon adviser contends, "with the Democratic party in his grasp, [will be] more inflexible in his dealings with the Republican administration." This antagonism has been very much in evidence since the election, as Meany's call for Nixon's impeachment clearly illustrated.

The "recapture," however, has complicated, not simplified, the relationship between labor and the Democrats. While the "centrists" were fighting Westwood, many of the most politically active members of the movement were supporting her. The Communication Workers, Auto Workers, Machinists, Oil, Chemical and Atomic Workers, Retail Clerks, and Amalgamated Clothing Workers were all active in the McGovern effort, and they are not at all sure that George Meany is the man they want back in the driver's seat of the Democratic party's labor wing.

The second consideration is whether splits in the union movement and concurrent power realignments will continue to provide opportunities for the Republicans. Will the Machinists leave the AFL–CIO and ally with the UAW? (They held a joint political conference after the election). If they do, will others join? Will they merge to form the largest labor organization in the nation? Or, more likely, will the UAW go back into the AFL–CIO as part of a political realignment within that body that will happen after Meany retires? Such a realignment might be a real possibility for a number of reasons. First, these two unions, and the fast-growing American Federation of State, County, and Municipal Employees and the rapidly expanding Teachers' unions are generally liberal. United they could soon emerge as a dominant force in the federation overshadowing Meany's current power base. Also, a possible merger between the Communication Workers' and the Postal Workers' unions would increase McGovern chairman Joe Bierne's influence. With such mergers and the reentry of the UAW, the AFL–CIO could become dominated by its liberal wing. Should this occur, however, an enormous backlash might well set in, not only among the building and maritime trades, but among many of the centrist organizations as well. Such a split would only serve to help

184

the Republicans and create further opportunity for strategic fragmentation.

The third factor is the future of the Democratic rank and file. Is "the uneasy coalition of the New Deal about to yield to the easy consensus of Middle America," as Gus Tyler suggests? What will happen to a movement, some of whose membership are becoming younger, blacker, and increasingly female, while other elements are becoming more affluent, suburban, and middle class? Or will "those who once marched against the war make a transition and start marching over inflation, health care, and taxes," as Bill Dodds suggests? Can the Republicans continue to attract sizable portions of the rank and file? Will the social question continue to dominate the calculations of many workers or will economic considerations resurface? What will be the impact of corruption? Will labor after Watergate put aside much of 1972's disunity in pursuit of the White House in 1976? The answers to these questions will be provided by the state of the economy, the performance of the government, and the shrewdness of the political strategist.

For the Republican party to transform its affair with labor into a more serious relationship, there are three major difficulties it must surmount, any one of which could prove fatal.

First, can it reconcile its historical relationship to business with its new affection for labor? The labor movement, after all, exists for the purpose of negotiating with business in a conflict pattern. There are means of avoiding the implications of this confrontation — but they require extraordinary dexterity.

Second, and equally important, can the Republican party permit the labor unions to exercise the same kind of influence in the party councils that the Democrats historically have? So far, according to Don Rodgers, none of the union leaders who endorsed the President's reelection has expressed any interest in becoming involved in the inner workings of the party. But to cement a lasting relationship such involvement would become necessary. Rockefeller has encouraged this form of influence in New York, but his own power position within the party made it possible. Will the traditional Republican party leaders and satraps throughout the country willingly share their authority with those union officials whom they have fought so long? Of course one solution to this problem is to render increasingly irrelevant the role of the party leader. In the strategic age the kind of relationship that the unions had with the Democrats may be simply obsolete. The loyalties and reciprocities may simply disappear, not be transferred. Bargaining may become the reality, not the myth, of the relationship, and political support may become increasingly the product of ad hoc negotiations. This is why the White House in its political strategies is increasingly finding the party to be a hindrance, not a help.

Finally, and most important, can the administration *deliver?* Watergate has seriously undercut the ability of any administration to play the kind of politics the Nixon managers played in 1972. As the White House begins to lose its grip on the bureaucracy, it will be less able to influence the award of special contracts, less able to play politics with the union leadership, and less able to get such agencies as the Justice Department to do special favors for its friends. More significantly, can the Republican party, as a party, perform on the fundamental issues of job security, inflation, and tax reform?

To hold onto the support of labor in the future, then, the party will have to make concessions and will have to produce the results that labor demands. It will have to embrace those whom it has found in the past to be strange and distant. It could perform, and it could make these concessions, which are as much social as political and economic, but the chances are that it won't. In the end, the epitaph for this brief flirtation will probably be taken from baritone George Meany's favorite refrain from *Galway Bay*:

> *For the strangers came and tried to teach us their way.*
> *They scorned us just for being what we are,*
> *But they might as well go chasing after moonbeams,*
> *Or light a penny candle from a star.*

9

The Politics
of Nonalignment

For nearly a century and a half the United States has had a two-party system. Sporadically a third party has risen to capture the imagination of a certain percentage of the electorate, and occasionally some great event has "realigned" the electorate and reversed the majority status of a party, but the overall structure of our system has remained the same. We have become quite comfortable with this image of politics and most observers still like to think in these terms. Alignments and realignments, aligning and realigning elections, majority and minority parties, dominant and subordinate coalitions — all remain very much a part of our political vocabulary. But events in recent years seem to indicate that politics is undergoing some basic structural changes and that it is no longer meaningful to talk in terms of traditional political alignment in America. To be sure, these changes are not occurring instantaneously, nor are they necessarily automatic and irreversible, but the evidence of recent elections (and especially that of 1972) shows that the new practices of strategic politics have not realigned the electorate, they have non-aligned it.

Now it is difficult to demonstrate that a trend is valid until it has held good for a reasonable amount of time. This trend against trends is no exception, and it has only just begun. Still we do think that the evidence is persuasive. There is a basic logic to what is going on and this revolution may go far indeed.

The New Structure of American Politics

The starting point for this structural revolution is the decline of parties. Everybody seems to agree that parties are in trouble and many excellent

187

books have been written to demonstrate this (David Broder's *The Party's Over* and Saloma and Sontag's *Parties* are two important expressions of this point of view). There are many reasons why parties are declining, but one of the most important is the rise of strategic politics, which induces candidates to adopt practices that are at variance with the traditional functions of a party and occasionally subversive of them. Strategic politics was probably not responsible for the start of party decline in the postwar period; in many ways it was a response to this decline. But it has now become a major accelerator of the trend. If other factors had not begun to undercut the position of the American political party, strategic politics would never have had the opportunity to operate, but if the practices of strategic politics had not been adopted by so many people, the collapse of our parties would not have gone so far. This feedback is fascinating.

Why are parties in such trouble? Some demographic and sociological causes are apparent. The young voter, historically more volatile, is now a significantly larger percentage of the voting-age population. New living patterns are having their effect. The country is becoming more mobile. The educational level of the electorate has risen sharply with the tremendous increase of the college-age population. Shifts in vocational patterns are having an impact. The rise of the professional class has created new voting patterns; a rise in the income levels of all classes has given many people the economic opportunity to become nonaligned. The generation gap has undercut the traditional tendency of children to vote like their parents. The black revolution has created new awareness.

The media have played an enormous role, since voters now have access to a vast amount of information about individual candidates that was never available before. Furthermore, the role of the party in the governmental process is changing dramatically. Parties no longer serve as the basis of patronage and financial largess. The "traditional business" that George Meany referred to in Chapter 8 is no longer relevant. Nor are they serving their historic function of resolving disputes between competing factions and interest groups: log-rolling today takes place outside of the party milieu. The permanent bureaucracies are now the source of government services while the courts, the regulatory agencies, and other nonpolitical institutions are serving as dispute settlers.

All these factors have influenced party decline. All are well known and all have been operating for many years. But the most important *current* factor in the eclipse of parties is strategic politics, the new political logic employed by today's candidate-oriented strategists. In Chapter 1 we saw that this logic led strategists to focus increasingly on the fluid voter, to reward him, and to try to create more of him if there weren't enough already. In subsequent chapters, we saw these principles put into practice with the southern strategy, the compartmentalized appeals of CREEP, the Democrats for Nixon, and the labor movement. In Chapter 1 we also suggested that the new strategic politics required that its practitioners selectively ignore their own party and take it largely for granted. In subsequent chapters we saw how the Nixon and McGovern teams, each in its own way, put this principle into practice. In Chapter 1 we also examined the destabilizing tendency for politicians to substitute symbols and rhetoric for hard, credible, deliverable, substantive accomplishment. And again we saw, both in the conduct of the Nixon administration and in the practices of the McGovern campaign, how these strategic politicians failed to create either the promise or the reality of performance.

These political practices are not unique to presidential politics. In constituency after constituency around the country they are being used by members of both parties in their normal pursuit of electoral success. This is especially true of senatorial and gubernatorial candidates in large industrial states, but it certainly goes further. And many times these practices are successful. Politicians all over the country are succeeding in loosening up the party commitments of the opposition camp, as CREEP did on a national basis in 1972. From a strategic standpoint, all this is very understandable, but the net result is an increase in the fluidity of voters nationwide. As politicians everywhere succeed in loosening up the opposition, more and more people are cut away from their traditional loyalties. After they split their ticket once, or make the big psychological jump of voting in the opposite party for the first time, they find it easier to do so again.

The candidate-oriented strategists are also trying to create a candidate-oriented electorate. "Vote for the man, not the party" is the cry of minority party candidates everywhere, and it is both a useful and plausible slogan. It has a "good government" ring to it. Two presidential landslides have helped this trend nationally: in 1964, many lifelong Republicans learned for the first time how to vote for the man (a Democrat); and in 1972 many lifelong Democrats learned the corresponding lesson. For similar reasons, such lessons are being learned on the local level all across the country. As the scythe sweeps back and forth, more voters each time remain less committed to their original party.

This increased emphasis on candidates is changing the structure of American politics. The party is no longer the most important variable or point of reference in our political system. It is the candidate who now fills this role and he is becoming highly strategic in ways that political parties never could be. He is much less constrained by institutions, personal relationships, old loyalties, and issues in the classic sense of the word. He can maneuver, and the more he does, the more the relationship between himself and other candidates will approximate a relationship of sheer contest, a condition unregulated by the constraints and styles that parties traditionally imposed upon their representatives. In this way our politics will become much more unstable than the stylized politics that character-ized the party system and its accompanying alignments.

In a situation of sheer contest there is nothing that constrains a candi-date to fight that contest on any given ground. In fact his first task is to define the grounds on which he will fight. Will the contest be fought on the basis of partisanship, issues, personality, competence, governmental performance, or what? How does each of these factors align the electo-rate? Where is he strong and his opponent weak? How can he maneuver his opponent into fighting a contest on terms favorable to himself? What is the appropriate mix between factors that will be to his advantage? The ability to maneuver among these questions — and the factors that they reflect — is what sets a candidate contest apart from a party contest, where the arena is much more fixed and the contestants much more constrained by their lack of flexibility. (This is one reason why candidate politics is taking precedent over party politics in our increasingly strategic age.)

There are, then, two levels operating here. There are the basic align-ments within each arena of contest and then there is the overall align-ment between the areas of contest. How do people break down on partisan questions? How important are partisan questions? How do people align on the race issue? How important is the race issue? How do people align between candidates on the factors of competence and per-formance, and how important are the factors of competence and per-formance? Given that the candidates can maneuver not only within these factors but between them, the possibilities for strategic manipulation are limitless. Because this is the case it is no longer possible to talk in terms of political alignment in America because there can be nothing stable around which to align.

This is not to say that issues don't align people. They do. But candi-dates can maneuver with respect to the issue and with respect to the emphasis placed on it. This is not to say that partisanship has dis-appeared. It remains a very important factor — if candidates make it important. This is not even to say that political changes cannot "realign" the electorate within a given category. They can, but such realignments are of temporary significance in the face of sound opposition strategies.

This dual set of strategic considerations makes possible a politics that never could have existed within the old party framework. It also creates a politics that cannot be analyzed in traditional political categories. For example, it is now possible to show simultaneously that (1) the Demo-cratic voter is becoming more fluid; (2) the Democratic coalition has been realigned on the racial and social welfare questions; (3) the Demo-cratic coalition remains intact. (We shall do this below.) The point is that the arena of contest defines the nature of alignment and that arena is constantly changing in an age of candidate politics. As it changes from election to election, the configuration of candidates and their strategies define and redefine the meaning of political alignment — but you can never truly align the electorate around a configuration of candidate strategies.

It is easy to see how ideological alignment is also very difficult to achieve in the new strategic age. Ideologies and slogans are slender things on which to build lasting alignments unless they are coherent and can lead to concrete performances that will benefit a large constituency in the long run. None so far have come close. We have seen a succession of realignments. The economic issue was the last truly aligning issue. As it became less important, the so-called social issue came to the surface. It lasted through Watergate, when it was replaced by the issue of governmental honesty and performance. No doubt another issue and symbol will arise. It is always in the interests of opposing candidates to find one, and they have the research techniques to do so. Because there are many constituencies nationwide and because the interests of each coincide on some issues and diverge on others, all sorts of strategic possibilities are created. Coalitions can be formed and re-formed on the model of city politics unless a coherent ideological basis can be created that covers a wide range of issues in such a way that its different adherents are aligned with it on most of the important issues. This is very difficult to do.

The Election of 1972 and the Trend Toward Nonalignment

The electorate is responding to the strategies of the candidates. During the last few years we have seen a remarkable increase in the overall fluidity of the voter, his willingness to move between parties with great frequency and decisiveness. We have also seen the alleged collapse of the New Deal coalition and attempts to replace it by new majorities, or whatever. And we have seen voters all over the country violate their historic party traditions and move into a condition of increasing political instability. Each of these trends is important for the future of our politics.

What is the evidence that the voter has become more fluid with respect to his party affiliation? First, there has been a dramatic increase in the amount of ticket-splitting during the last decade. Tarrance and DeVries demonstrated this point in their excellent book on ticket-splitting, but the evidence since they wrote has piled up even more. In 1972, Gallup reported that 60 percent of the country split its ticket (up from 54 percent in 1968, when the Wallace factor inflated the total). Nineteen seventy-two was also a record year for the number of states that elected candidates of both parties to statewide office. It was also a record for the percentage difference between the top vote-getter and the bottom vote-getter of a given party in statewide contests, a figure that has been steadily rising for two decades. Furthermore, ticket-splitting has spread to every conceivable socioeconomic group in the country. Tarrance and DeVries suggest that the suburbanite was the most likely voter to split his ticket, but the election of 1972 saw the propensity spread much further. Urban blacks in Chicago split their ticket in record numbers, as did rural blacks in Mississippi. Northern working-class Catholics split their tickets more than ever before. So did farmers in Iowa, laborers in Jacksonville, Florida, affluent upper-class WASPs in Massachusetts, lower-class Jews in New York City, poor whites in eastern North Carolina, and almost everybody in Arkansas, Kansas, and Utah. As far as ticket-splitting is concerned, there has been absolutely no year like 1972.

Second, there has been a great deal of shifting back and forth among certain groups between years. As it happened, suburbanites across the country were not the biggest ticket-splitters in 1972, although they had tended to be in 1968 and 1970; but suburbanites over the last few elections in many regions of the country have shifted back and forth in their support of parties. In 1970 Democrats carried such Republican strongholds as Bergen County, New Jersey, and Cook County *outside of* Chicago. These were typical of results across the country as the suburban professional — the natural constituent of the moderate and progressive Republican — was antagonized by the backlash appeal of Nixon-Agnew. The suburbanite is not alone. The shifts among blue-collar workers, farmers, and Southerners are equally dramatic. All across the country there seems to be an increase in the swings between elections for almost all voting constituencies.

Third, this volatility has been picked up by the pollsters. We saw in Chapter 7 how the patterns of support for Nixon and McGovern shifted over the course of the summer and how the Eagleton affair drove 12 million voters away from McGovern. The sixties and early seventies had many other examples of volatility. Nelson Rockefeller's 1966 rise from a trial heat reading of 18 percent in the spring to a November victory is a classic one. Romney's 1967 performance in trial heats against Lyndon Johnson is another. Presumably the Quayle poll, taken in 1973 at the height of the Watergate crisis showing that McGovern would beat the President nine months after his landslide loss, is still a third. In state elections similar fluidity is becoming commonplace, as any survey research expert will tell you. To be sure, "the people" are not the same as "the electorate," and their November voting habits are more stable than their popularity choices, but much more attention should be given to these fluctuations that seem to be on the increase in our politics.

Fourth, there seems to be an increase in the number of groups that are bargaining consciously with both parties from a nonparty or extraparty position. George Wallace is, of course, the egregious example. But blacks, Chicanos, certain labor groups, and public interest groups are successfully pursuing a conscious policy of divorcing their constituencies from a party context. The fact that they can succeed in doing so is a powerful piece of evidence to support the nonalignment thesis. The rise of group and interest consciousness has been demonstrated repeatedly in recent years. It is part of this overall pattern.

In short, it begins to appear that the voter is becoming more fluid, more flexible, and more nonaligned. This does not mean that he is becoming less responsible, less intelligent, or less decent — fluidity is not the same as febrility. It simply means that he cannot be taken for granted anymore by any party.

But this view is a very simplistic one. Party still is important in certain circumstances and it can be made the ground for contest between candidates. When it is, old alignments reemerge. To see the extent — and the limits — of this fluidity let us examine the current status of the New Deal coalition.

The Enigma of the New Deal

On the surface it appears that the New Deal finally collapsed in 1972. President Nixon's inroads among traditional Democratic voters were massive and historic, his performance much stronger than in 1968.

• Among blue-collar workers, Nixon's percentage of the vote rose from 33 percent in 1968 to 57 percent in 1972 according to an NBC indicator precinct analysis made available to us.

• Among union members the increase was even more dramatic. Gallup reports a jump from 29 to 54 percent between 1968 and 1972. This was the first time a Republican carried the union vote since the Depression. Young manual workers, incidentally, supported McGovern, but this group contains a high percentage of blacks.

• The northern Catholic ethnic votes also went strongly for Nixon. This group overlaps the first two to a great extent. NBC reported a Nixon jump from 34 to 55 percent among Italo-Americans between his two elections. Returns from the Chicago, Buffalo, and Detroit areas show massive swings among Polish-American voters in the same direction.

• The black vote went strongly for McGovern — 82 percent according to CBS, 90 percent according to NBC, 87 percent according to Gallup — although there were some exceptions to this overall performance. (In Louisville, Kentucky, Nixon hit 30 percent of the black vote, according to the Joint Center for Political Studies.) Yet a lack of enthusiasm for McGovern led to a remarkably light turnout this year. The JCPS reported that only 41 percent of voting-age blacks turned out to vote — compared to 55 percent of whites — down about 6 percent from 1968, which, in turn, was a low year compared to 1964. Black turnout was especially low in southern rural areas, where McGovern ran *substantially* behind Humphrey's 1968 totals.

193

• Jewish voters can no longer be taken for granted by the Democrats. According to NBC, Nixon's total among Jews jumped from 18 percent in 1968 to 37 percent in 1972, and surveys conducted during the course of the campaign indicated that this percentage was much higher in September and October. The Jewish vote has never been monolithic, and it is certainly not so today. Much of this change came from the lower-middle-class Jewish voter, who has traditionally been solidly Democratic and who moved toward Nixon in 1972.

•In 1963 about 83 percent of the Hispanic-American vote went to Hubert Humphrey, and Richard Nixon received about 17 percent. In 1972, according to NBC, the President's total reached approximately 31 percent.

• The South, needless to say, went massively for President Nixon.

On the surface these figures appear decisive. But let us take a closer look. Figure 4 portrays the voting habits of the elements in the Democratic coalition since 1952. The remarkable thing about this figure is that it shows both fluctuation in totals and stability in structure. The elements of the Democratic coalition move extensively, but they move together. With the exception of the South and the blacks, there is enormous consistency between the voting patterns of these groups. The only exceptions seem to be the realignment of Catholics in 1960, of the South during all the 1960s, of blacks in 1964, and of youth to a small extent in 1972. Except for the South, these realignments have taken place *toward* the Democrats.

This pattern is remarkable. Voters who have twice elected Richard Nixon are not divided along lines that are fundamentally different from those of 1960 and 1964 when they elected Kennedy and Johnson. From this perspective, the 1972 election looks no different in its underlying structure from the five elections that preceded it. In fact, hardly any realignment of groups or interests occurred in 1972. The Democratic party remains disproportionately attractive for people in the lower classes, for union and blue-collar workers, and for Catholics. The factors that caused McGovern's defeat did not repolarize the electorate or introduce a new set of divisions into politics. To be sure, McGovern received slightly fewer votes proportionately than he might have expected from blue-collar and union workers, 4 and 6 percent respectively. But this hardly bespeaks a massive realignment of political interest. It probably resulted more from McGovern's highly publicized relationship with the leaders of organized labor, although the race issue may have contributed to this marginal shift. Figure 4 makes quite clear that labor continued to be more Democratic in its voting behavior than the nation as a whole,

194

Figure 4
Elements of the Democratic Coalition

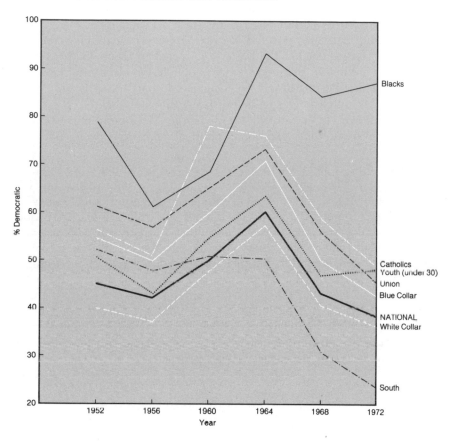

with the basic lines of cleavage continuing at about the same level as always.

The same can be said of Catholics. It is true that they gave the Republican candidate a majority of their votes for the first time since 1924. Yet it is also apparent that their voting behavior ran parallel to that of the whole nation: the trend merely came to rest at a point where Nixon received 52 percent of their votes. Catholics continued to be more Democratic in their political predispositions than most groups in the country, and the essential structure of the Protestant-Catholic cleavage remained unchanged in 1972.

This result is even more surprising because Catholics no longer have the same social and economic positions that they had when the New Deal coalition was forming: they are now every bit as middle class as their Protestant counterparts. Yet their economic and social gains have not resulted in a critical realignment of partisan behavior.

It seems as if the Democratic party has been able to hold on to the underlying loyalties of the basic elements in its coalition, probably because it has been able to adjust the nature of its political appeal. It simply expanded its middle-class emphasis as its constituency grew more affluent. Thus Catholics rejected George McGovern's candidacy because he did not represent what the party now meant to them. In this respect they were no different than most other people in the electorate. However, Catholic voters did not desert the Democratic party as a *group:* to the contrary, as a group they remained disproportionately loyal to the Democratic candidate. In a curious way, George McGovern moved so far beyond the party that traditional political affiliations were not reexamined.

We see, then, a situation in which voters are becoming more fluid, but not realigned. Their party loyalties remain largely unchanged, but they are less important. Other factors are now operating and "issues" of personality, competence, good government, and other nonpartisan questions may take precedence over those that formerly aligned voters in partisan ways. Hence the voters can remain aligned in one sense and increasingly nonaligned in another as candidates and their strategists attempt to render existing alignments increasingly irrelevant. In fact, it probably is much easier these days to render alignment irrelevant than it is to change it. As parties decline and candidates advance, all kinds of strategic possibilities present themselves. The 1972 returns from Chicago provide another illustration of what is happening to our politics as strategic maneuvering replaces party alignment.

THE CHICAGO CONFUSION: TICKET-SPLITTING AND CANDIDATE CONFIGURATIONS

Candidate configurations were very interesting in Illinois in 1972. The election matched a "conservative" Republican President against a noncredible liberal Democrat, a progressive Republican senator (Percy) against a conservative, backlash Democrat (Pucinski), and a moderate middle-of-the-road Republican governor who had a tax problem (Ogilvie) against a liberal populistic Democrat (Walker). In Chicago there was the additional spectacle of a machine Democrat, Hanrahan, who had been nominated in a primary over the opposition of the machine, who was a conservative, and who had been implicated in the raid on the Black Panther headquarters, matched against a progressive Republican reformer (Carey). These configurations split Chicago wide open.

The President, for example, carried 18 Chicago wards while Senator Percy carried 19, but only 4 of these were the same wards! In the presidential race, Nixon did very well in traditional white working-class ethnic areas of the city, while Senator Percy did well compared to past Republican performances, but nowhere nearly as well as the President. In the black wards, however, it was the other way around. Percy cut substantially into the traditionally Democratic totals, with the President far behind. Since Nixon was much further behind in the black wards than Percy was in the ethnic wards, the senator's totals were higher in the city than the President's.

In the Ogilvie-Walker race, Ogilvie did relatively well in the white working-class areas against the liberal populist. He even ran slightly ahead of Percy, who was running against an opponent with a special relationship to that constituency. But in the black wards Walker did remarkably well against Ogilvie, although not quite as well as McGovern did against Nixon. In the State's attorney race, the moderate Republican swept most of the black areas from Hanrahan, lost most of the white working-class areas, but by small margins, and held the Republican precincts sufficiently well to win the county. The vote in black and ethnic areas deserves special attention.

CANDIDATE	WARD 42 Pct. 4, 6, 9, 10, 12, 32, 39, 42, 51, 52 (very low income)	WARD 3 (low income)	WARD 17 (average black income)	WARD 2 Pct. 2, 25, 32 (highest black income)
Nixon	5	7	0	9
Ogilvie	12	11	15	29
Percy	27	31	49	80
Carey	42	60	61	81

TABLE 3.
Black Ticket-splitting in Chicago:
Republican (by percentages) Vote in Selected Areas

The Black Wards

Ticket-splitting was extensive in the black areas of Chicago, although it was certainly not uniform. Table 3 presents the Republican percentage of the vote for our four races in four black areas arranged in order of income levels from lowest to highest. The figures speak for themselves. The more liberal the Republican and the more conservative the Democrat, the higher the total Republican percentage in each area. Also, the higher the income level, the higher the Republican percentage in each race. It is interesting to note, however, that as income increased the President did only marginally better and the governor modestly better, while Percy and Carey received substantially more support. In the highest-income area (median income, $13,482; leading occupation, "professional"; average school years completed, 13.8), the ticket-splitting reached over 70 percent of the total. But even in the low-income, machine-dominated 42nd Ward, ticket-splitting approached 40 percent. Local polling results added the further conclusion that Hanrahan's vote was strongest among older blacks and weakest among younger ones, which says much about the future of fluidity.

A careful examination of this table will provide insights about the fluidity of the black vote. Obviously a Republican has to try harder than President Nixon did to move much of the black vote to the Republican column. Governor Ogilvie, a moderate, did relatively better against a liberal Democrat who was perceived generally as being much more competent than McGovern. Percy obviously tried harder. His opponent's "backlash" campaign was pitched to the white working-class ethnic voter on the strategic assumption that he was more fluid than the black voter. As it turned out, he was *less* fluid than the black, but sufficiently fluid to have created difficulties for Pucinski had he run as a liberal. Percy, in a centrist position, was strategically much more flexible, and was able to move in behind Pucinski in black areas with devastating results. Had Percy not been as "liberal" as he was, the total vote in black areas probably would have dropped at his expense; had he been more "liberal" his totals in ethnic areas might well have dropped more than they did.

The Ethnic Wards

Ticket-splitting was extensive in the white working-class ethnic areas of the city also, but the configurations were precisely the opposite of those in the black areas. Table 4 presents the Republican percentage of the vote

		Polish		Italian	Lithuanian
	WARD 12 Pct. 56, 59	WARD 22 Pct. 5, 24, 46, 59, 49, 60	WARD 36 Pct. 12, 40, 41	WARD 36 Pct. 16, 64, 75	WARD 15 Pct. 9, 56, 57, 58, 59
Nixon	62	66	61	73	77
Ogilvie	51	50	46	64	33
Percy	34	34	29	43	54
Carey	33	34	30	34	44

TABLE 4.
Working-Class Ethnic Whites:
Republican (by percentages) Vote in Selected Areas

for the four races in representative Polish, Italian, and Lithuanian areas of the city. Again, the figures speak for themselves. Here the Nixon-McGovern contrast provided the highest percentage for the Republicans, with Ogilvie second, Percy third, and Carey last — the precise opposite ranking from the black wards. Of course, Percy and Carey did not drop nearly as low in these areas as President Nixon did in the black areas — which is why, in part, Percy did much better citywide than the President did. Although we have not reproduced the figures, the Nixon totals in these areas were substantially higher in 1972 than in 1968, and virtually all Republican figures were higher than those for the 1970 Republican candidate for the Senate (Ralph T. Smith), who was buried by Adlai Stevenson in every Chicago ward.

The range of ticket-splitting here is much less than in the average black wards and shows that by and large, the white, working-class, ethnic Democrats are more attached to the Democratic party than the blacks are; they are less fluid, even though the President's inroads are very dramatic. The one exception to this seems to be in Italo-American areas, where it is possible to speak about trends in the Republican direction.

These Chicago returns seem to illustrate the importance of the "social issue" when candidates make it the basis of competition between them. It can certainly split up the Democratic coalition, although the Illinois governorship race demonstrates that the coalition can be reassembled when other issues (taxes, personality, population, etc.) are made the arena of competition between candidates. The social issue, however, is a very complicated one and the results of 1972 show that there is nothing automatic about this new realignment that so many observers have been publicizing.

TWO CUTTING ISSUES:
SOCIAL WELFARE AND RACE

Although the major factor in George McGovern's defeat was the perceived gap in competence between President Nixon and himself, the issues of social welfare and race were not totally absent from the campaign, and they remain questions of great relevance for the future. What was their impact in 1972? Every election since the New Deal has contained some aspect of the social welfare question, and George McGovern's proposals for income maintenance would have been part of a perfectly viable electoral strategy if the Democrats had maintained their traditionally favorable positions on such questions. A strong emphasis on social welfare would have served to mobilize the party faithful as it did in 1948.

However, the consensus that had operated on social welfare questions shifted gradually during the 1960s. This fundamental change of attitude began in 1964, at the time of Barry Goldwater's unsuccessful campaign against Lyndon Johnson's version of the New Deal. Goldwater challenged the entire New Deal in all of its manifestations and consequently tracked back and forth over policies that had genuinely become part of the governing consensus. The public was — and is — simply beyond debating whether or not the government should provide Social Security payments, unemployment insurance, and disability assistance, and it will not listen to arguments about the legitimacy of organized labor and government intervention in the economy. In the 1964 election, however, amid the triumphant reestablishment of the policies of the New Deal, Goldwater won points in terms of the social welfare question. Because of the radical nature of his candidacy, he was unable to cash in on these attitude shifts, but opinions changed nonetheless.

Goldwater himself simply didn't understand what he was doing. An ideological conservative, he merely spoke against everything that the New Deal had instituted, and in opposing everything, he stumbled across issues that were ripe for change. In concluding that the New Deal was not uniformly successful, however, Goldwater failed to notice that parts of it were terribly popular. In fact, his campaign had precisely the wrong emphasis on these social welfare issues. He singled out Social Security and health insurance as the targets of major policy revision and gave relatively little attention to welfare payments and issues associated with the urban unease. As a consequence, the 1964 election made it appear that the New Deal was reaffirmed overwhelmingly when, in fact, opinions had altered quite substantially on part of it. By attacking the New Deal in precisely those areas where it had succeeded, Goldwater quickly put himself outside the "mainstream" of public opinion, an unacceptable candidate for President, an extremist.

George McGovern did the same thing with his welfare program. The New Deal is in a very interesting position today. Some parts of it are so acceptable that they are no longer seriously debatable, while other parts of it are so controversial that they tend to split the Democratic party in half. There is no question that today federal school programs, urban renewal, and model cities are thought of increasingly as threats to personal values and jobs. There is also little question that "welfarism" is decisively rejected by vast sections of the Democratic coalition. In many respects, the New Deal has reached the point where its extension would be more costly to its constituency than the benefits would justify. McGovern, embracing the New Deal totally, emphasized those aspects of it that were potentially the most expensive — and least beneficial — to the traditional white northern Democratic voter. This was a strategic error of major proportions.

There is an important lesson in the logic of electoral competition here: incumbent administrations are most easily defeated in terms of their own performances, not on the basis of highly specialized appeals on "the issues." That is, the electorate is able to respond quite meaningfully when it is presented the question of whether or not it approves of the policies that have been governing it. People know what they have experienced and whether the policies of government have helped them or not. They are less able to judge the consequences of policy proposals in the abstract; and hence people process hypothetical alternatives at a different and more variable level.

In 1972, voters never got a chance to consider the issues that had emerged during the four years of the Nixon presidency: the performance of the economy, the administration's apparent involvement in scandal, the Watergate case, and the feeling that they weren't being told the truth about Vietnam. Instead, policy differences rooted in McGovern's ideas for social change became the essence of the election contest. This happened at first because McGovern had pushed them so hard in his struggle to win the nomination. It continued because Nixon would not let McGovern move away from these proposals. The more McGovern attempted to shift to performance issues, the more the administration spoke about the radical implications of the minimum income idea and how it posed a threat to basic American values. Many voters wanted a change of government, but did not want that change to include any new ideas about social welfare. Thus the campaign, in its early stages, was fought on McGovern's weakest ground as a result of his strategic decision to do so and Nixon's obvious strategic decision to keep him in his exposed position.

The paradox of the McGovern candidacy, then, was that it did not really give voters a choice, not the choice that voters wanted to make. McGovern made them choose on the grounds of social welfare. Even people who finally voted for McGovern didn't approve of the concept. The people who were unhappy with the economy, suspicious about Vietnam, and worried over corruption "in high places" should have voted for McGovern. In different circumstances they would have. But the "extremism" they saw in McGovern's emphasis on social welfare removed these sorts of issues from the campaign entirely, and the electorate was left to choose between Nixon and McGovern on other grounds.

In 1960, it was still possible to keep the Democratic party together on the racial issue, though just barely. The voting behavior of northern Democrats was not affected by the issue that year, since those who were for and against civil rights were equally likely to vote for Kennedy (see Table 5). The issue did affect the southern wing of the party, causing some damage there. But Lyndon Johnson served the ticket well and the losses were not as great as they might have been, given the distribution of opinion on the issue.

By 1968, the effects of the civil rights issue were quite visible in the North (see Table 6). Nonsouthern, white Democrats with opinions unfavorable to civil rights voted 30 percent less for Humphrey than did Democrats who were favorably disposed toward civil rights. Nor were these losses made up from Republicans who were sympathetic to civil rights; they voted 90 percent for Richard Nixon. These data also make

NONSOUTHERN DEMOCRATS	PRO (n = 179)	MIXED (n = 127)	CON (n = 42)
Kennedy	83	89	85
Nixon	17	11	14

SOUTHERN DEMOCRATS	PRO (n = 27)	MIXED (n = 113)	CON (n = 67)
Kennedy	78	65	66
Nixon	22	35	34

TABLE 5.
Voting in 1960 on Civil Rights Issues among
Northern and Southern White Democrats (by percentages)
This data comes from The Survey Research Center
at the University of Michigan.

NONSOUTHERN DEMOCRATS	PRO (n = 87)	MIXED (n = 145)	CON (n = 70)
Humphrey	82	71	53
Nixon	16	26	26
Wallace	2	3	21

SOUTHERN DEMOCRATS	PRO (n = 121)	MIXED (n = 18)	CON (n = 64)
Humphrey	83	51	28
Nixon	17	26	22
Wallace	0	39	50

TABLE 6.
Voting in 1968 on Civil Rights Issues among
Northern and Southern White Democrats (by percentages)
This data comes from The Survey Research Center
at the University of Michigan.

clear the critical function that Wallace performed in assisting anti–civil rights Democrats who wanted to leave their party. The 1972 election continued these trends, and the Wallace candidacy again served as a catalyst for Democrats unhappy over the race issue. The Yankelovich surveys show that Wallace voters, by and large, were satisfied with having Richard Nixon in the White House from the first.

While it is impossible to predict with certainty, it appears that the future of the Democratic party is not as bleak as some analysts would have it. Certainly the South has departed over the racial issue and now presidentially seems part of the Republican party. Not one state in the Deep South has voted for the Democratic presidential candidate since 1960. The race issue remains very real. But it is only one issue among many. It has realigned the political behavior of those who feel intensely about it, but race has yet to set group against group in the heartland of the Democratic coalition (blacks and southerners aside). Catholics, blue-collar workers, and union members have continued their pro-Democratic predispositions without serious exception. This is not to say that there have been no defections from election to election. Obviously there have been; but they have been defections of individuals in particular elections, not the erosion of group identifications in politics. This is why the behavior of these groups in the Democratic coalition have so closely paralleled the trend for the nation as a whole. The issue of race has undoubtedly been a factor in moving these votes around. But thus far it has been "merely" an issue, and has not attached itself to the various groups within the Democratic party with enough force to splinter the coalition.

Of course, everything depends on how the race issue continues in politics. Catholics, blue-collar workers, and union members have the very real potential for realigning their politics if the race issue is pushed. After all, the nonsouthern working class is a territory that Wallace has worked quite successfully. Yet, these groups have other interests in politics. And at least thus far into the seventies the race issue has not overpowered them. To the contrary, the drift of events seems such that the issues of the economy (jobs, prices), housing (interest rates, rents), and taxes are becoming more, not less, salient. The issues of honesty, competence, and performance are also replacing the racial question these days, and there is the strong possibility that the Democrats will make them "their" issues — as they did so successfully in New Jersey in 1973. Such issues can easily preserve traditional political loyalties and at the same time diminish the impact of racial tensions.

As these examples show, the Democratic coalition is still very much in existence, but its significance has changed. In one sense it has been realigned, in another it has not; but in a third sense it is not terribly relevant anymore whether or not it has. One configuration of candidates and strategies will bring about a certain alignment of voters, another configuration a different alignment. If partisanship and party-related issues become the ground for electoral combat, then the coalition will reappear; if race is the salient issue, new alignments will occur; if some other factor (such as personality) becomes important, that will dictate the alignment.

The whole situation is opening up rapidly, but it is not just the Democratic coalition that is in trouble, the whole electorate is being cut loose.

Difficulties in the Republicans' Backyard

While the Democratic coalition in the cities has been fluctuating spectacularly, the Republicans have been quietly losing their grip on the rural areas of the North that they have held solidly since the end of the Depression.

Kevin Phillips demonstrated in his *Emerging Republican Majority* that the monopoly that the Republican party has held in the rural Northeast is no longer there, although his conclusion that it is becoming a Democratic region is erroneous. It is becoming fluid, although a careful examination will show that it is less fluid than the suburbs of the region. It is an area plagued by chronic unemployment, and this factor is responsible for the Republican party's difficulties. In 1972 President Nixon swept the area — to refute Phillips's trend — but ticket-splitting was extensive.

In the rural Midwest, northern Ohio, northern Indiana, northern Illinois, and southern Michigan, the Republicans are holding strong. East of Nebraska and north of Kentucky this region was Goldwater's strongest area in 1964 — although he lost it — and Nixon's strongest in both 1968 and 1972. There is very low unemployment in the area, there is a relatively stable population, and there is a long tradition of Republican support. It is about the least volatile region in the country, and for the present, at any rate, it can be taken for granted by the Republicans.

The situation is not at all the same in the farm belt. Here the electorate over the last decade has become highly volatile, ticket-splitting is growing rapidly, and the Republicans who have dominated the region for twenty years are in serious trouble. They now must bargain for the area's support. This is the only region of the country (except for the Pacific Northwest and a few sections of Wallace country) where McGovern did as well as Humphrey in a large number of counties. Since both came from the area, it is hard to attribute this to local appeal. In the Scandinavian counties of Wisconsin, for example, McGovern's percentages were as high as or higher than Humphrey's. Humphrey ran a bit ahead of McGovern in his home state, but McGovern did as well in Minnesota as he did in any state west of Massachusetts. Democrats have been winning in the region — and winning in the rural areas of the region — over the last few years. Wisconsin, Minnesota, Iowa, and South Dakota all have two *liberal* Democratic senators. Nebraska has twice come very close to electing a liberal Democrat in the last two elections, and Democrats control the governorship in almost every farm belt state. Kansas alone can be taken for granted by the Republicans: its Democratic governor is a genuine anomaly. It could be argued that the region will remain *presidentially*

Republican, even though every other office seems to be highly contestable, but the election of so many liberal Democratic senators must mean otherwise, for senators too are elected on national issues.

The softening up of the Republican bastions in the northern countryside is not as dramatic as the convolutions of the Democratic coalition and the damage is easier to repair — if the agricultural crisis can be solved to the farmer's advantage. Here, as elsewhere, however, the party will have to work to achieve success.

The Volatile Northern Suburbs

Population shifts have given the northern suburbs tremendous political influence in the last decade and their voting patterns are crucial to any political calculation. There are many kinds of suburbs and each area has its own politics. But generally speaking, there are four major types. (1) Wealthy and usually established suburbs, such as Dover, Massachusetts; Darien, Connecticut; Ardmore, Pennsylvania; Chevy Chase, Maryland; Kenilworth, Illinois; Grosse Pointe, Michigan; and Shaker Heights, Ohio. These suburbs are solidly Republican, will vote Republican as long as there are viable candidates, and are definitely not swing areas. However, there are not very many of these communities, and the bulk of the suburban population lives in the other three categories. (2) Upper-middle-class professional suburbs — such as Lexington, Massachusetts; Teaneck, New Jersey, Glencoe, Illinois; and Bethesda, Maryland. (3) Middle-middle-class suburbs with white-collar clerical workers and junior executives — such as so many communities in Nassau County, New York; Bucks County, Pennsylvania; western Cook or southern Lake County, Illinois; and some areas of Oakland County, Michigan. (4) Working-class suburbs — such as Ward 20 of Boston; or the many Levittowns in New York, New Jersey, and Pennsylvania; Macomb County, Michigan; and countless others surrounding the large cities of the industrial states.

These three kinds of suburbs, which merge into each other, are volatile and fluid in different ways. Generally speaking, the upper-middle-class professional suburb is Republican, yet liberal, quite susceptible to moderate or progressive Democrats, and relatively skeptical about conservative Republicans. The middle-middle-class suburb is generally also Republican, much more Nixon-style, much less susceptible to liberal enticement, and much less skeptical about conservative Republicans. The lower-class suburb is marginally Democratic, generally conservative on the "social question," but very sensitive to economic problems.

Although there were some exceptions in Massachusetts and in other areas, every category of suburb went for Richard Nixon in 1972. Of the three kinds, the professional suburbs were stronger for McGovern, but he didn't carry very many of them and, outside of Massachusetts and California, virtually all that he did carry were college-oriented. The competence issue could be expected to rank high among suburbanites and there is little doubt that McGovern lost the suburbs on that question. But over the last decade the suburbs have been highly volatile and in 1970 the Democrats swept them in New Jersey, Pennsylvania, Maryland, Michigan, Ohio, Wisconsin, and even Illinois, whose Chicago suburbs are the least volatile and the most Republican of any surrounding a megacity. The Republicans held the northern suburbs in 1970 on a consistent basis only in New England and New York.

The point is simply that no one can take the suburbs for granted. The working-class suburb will generally remain Democratic and the professional suburb will generally remain Republican, but a backlash appeal to one will scare away the other and a frontlash appeal to the other may scare away the first. The middle-middle-class suburb will remain Republican in either case — which is why the Republicans generally hold the edge in the suburbs taken as a whole. The professional suburbs are smaller than the working-class suburbs in total number of voters, but are growing much faster and are probably more influential with the middle-middle-class suburbanite, who generally aspires to be a "professional." There is much opportunity here for the Republicans to firm up their position — and much opportunity for the Democrats to break open their position. The Republicans can put the professionals together with the "middle" by running moderates. The Republicans can put the backlashers together with the middle by running conservatives. But the Democrats can respond by putting the working class together with the professionals when the Republicans run conservatives, as they did in New Jersey and Pennsylvania in 1970. When the Republicans run moderates, it is not so easy for the Democrats.

Cycles in the Outer South

Nineteen seventy-two was an interesting year in the Outer South states of Virginia, North Carolina, Kentucky, Tennessee, Florida, Arkansas, Oklahoma, and Texas because it marked an advancement along a sort of cyclical politics that the region has been following for the last decade. Each of these states was traditionally Democratic, although Kentucky was an occasional exception. The Democratic party varied from state to state, but it was largely conservative, traditional, and entrenched. An occasional populist or liberal would emerge — such as Kefauver, Gore, or Yarborough — but generally speaking the last twenty years have seen few of them.

During the 1960s, however, the Republicans broke open the politics of the region. As a result of their more conservative national posture and their exploitation of voter reaction to the courthouse politics of the

Democrats, the Republicans began to capture these states in a massive way. But very recently a countertrend has set in that is moving the states, not back to the Democrats, but into a swing status. In some states, the Republican phase is longer than others, and here the Republicans have invariably worked to earn their rewards. Where this has not been the case, the swing to a fluid condition has come rather rapidly. Kentucky and Florida are the furthest advanced along this cycle. Tennessee is in the highest stage of the Republican phase. Virginia and North Carolina are entering their Republican period, while Arkansas and Oklahoma are well along the road to a swing category. Texas has yet to enter a Republican phase, but it may well soon.

1. Kentucky is an excellent case in point. In the 1950s it was largely Democratic except for the United States Senate. It had gone Republican, however, for President, and this performance soon carried over to the governorship. During the sixties the Republicans captured some additional congressional seats, won some impressive Senate victories, and seemed to be moving the state in a favorable direction. However, in the 1970s the trend seemed to reverse. They lost the governorship and a hard-fought Senate seat. So after a brief flirtation with the Republicans, the state is now up for grabs.

2. Florida is another state that has gone through the entire cycle in a shorter period of time. While it voted for Eisenhower twice, Nixon three times, and *almost* for Goldwater in 1964, Florida had never elected a statewide Republican in modern history until the mid-1960s when a gubernatorial victory in 1966, a Senate victory in 1968, and a number of gains in Congress seemed to predict a Republican trend. However, in 1970 the Republicans lost both a governorship and a Senate race to a pair of populist Democrats who were able to assemble a coalition of Miami "liberals" and Florida Wallace Democrats. The state can now easily go either way.

3. Virginia is in an early stage of the cycle: trending Republican, largely the result of a solid and still-growing Republican base in the Richmond suburbs. Virginia is demographically chaotic — with the strongly Democratic Norfolk area, its naval installations, and its black population; the swing suburbs of Washington; the Wallace counties of the southern region; the mixed mountain counties of the west; and Byrd country, conservative non-Wallace, central Virginia. Together with Richmond, these diverse areas should be a strategist's paradise, but so far the Republicans have had the edge because of their solid base in the Richmond area and the inability of the Democrats to find a candidate who can assemble a coherent coalition of minorities against them.

4. North Carolina is also in an early phase of the Republican cycle, and despite heavy ticket-splitting in 1972, should trend Republican for a few years. The state is divided into three or four regions: the mountain region, traditionally Republican; the Piedmont region in the middle of

the state dominated by new textile interests, previously Democratic but now trending strongly Republican; and the whole eastern half, largely rural, poor, divided between black and white, and never Republican until 1972. If Republicans can continue to cut into the eastern part of the state, they can win continuously in North Carolina; but here, much more than in Virginia, they are threatened by moderate, conservative, or populist Democrats who could easily pick up the eastern counties the way the populist Democrats have picked up Florida's northern counties against conservative Republicans. At present, the edge remains with the Republicans because of their novelty, but that will wear off. What they must do is establish a political base in the eastern part of the state and not simply rely upon ideological configurations to aid them in the future. The example of Tennessee should be learned throughout the entire region.

5. Tennessee is in a peak Republican phase — and it could well be a prolonged phase — because the party has been performing and building a political base, not simply an ideological one, throughout the state. Tennessee has three regions: an eastern region, Republican since — and because of — the Civil War; a central region, Democratic for a century, but grateful to the Democrats more recently because of TVA; and a western region, traditionally Democratic, conservative, now swing, and trending Republican. It is the swing of the western region toward the Republicans that is trending the state in their direction just as eastern North Carolina is swinging that state the same way. But the party has established a much firmer base in western Tennessee than in eastern North Carolina. The Republicans in Tennessee have put themselves into a very strong position, and only a poor performance by a governor, a factor of personality, or a competence issue can defeat them in the near future.

6. Arkansas and Oklahoma are interesting contrasts in border state politics, the one clearly trending Republican, the other seeming to trend Democratic. The Republican picture in Arkansas is grim indeed, with a populist governor, a conservative Democratic legislature, and an election debacle in 1972. It is probably still a swing state, and it holds the 1972 record for a high-low Republican split between presidential and gubernatorial candidates. But a Republican victory, as in the past, will have to be fashioned by a personality contest, not a party one. Oklahoma is the opposite as far as statewide contests are concerned, but its electorate is less one-sided and it still can swing Democratic as it did in 1970. Governors are always vulnerable, and that office, more than any other, seems to be responsible for the increasingly wide party swings everywhere west of the Mississippi.

7. Texas politics is extraordinarily complicated. The Democrats have a clear majority if they can hold the party together, but that is difficult. Divided into conservative, moderate, and liberal factions, it historically was unified by machine tactics and classically balanced slates. Despite its

current fragmentation, its blatant corruption, and its bad reputation, it still seems to win the races it wants to. Presidentially the Republicans carry Texas quite frequently, but Senator John Tower is the only other Republican ever to carry it in modern history. The conservative Democrats have been able to hold onto the countryside comfortably against conservative and moderate Republicans, especially in the governorship races. In 1964 the Democratic candidate received more than 60 percent of the vote in all but six counties (not large ones). In 1966, only two counties failed to give the Democrat more than 60 percent. But in 1968 the Republicans made inroads in the Houston area, the Panhandle (traditionally conservative and Republican), and in a few counties in central Texas. In 1970 they widened their performance in the Houston area, in southeastern Texas oil and space country, and in Dallas — to still lose 54 percent to 46 percent. In 1972, Senator Tower and President Nixon won comfortably. Running against a populist Democrat, Tower made big inroads in the countryside but lost ground significantly in the cities. Strategically speaking, the conservative Democrats can win primaries and outflank the Republicans. Liberal Democrats seem to lose both primaries and elections. Populist Democrats might either win or lose. We expect, however, to see more Republican victories in the future.

On the surface it has appeared that the Outer South is trending Republican, and in one sense it is: Republicans have been winning elections in the region in an increasing number. This performance, however, has not been the result of any grand swing or major trend. What it reflects is the movement of certain key areas or swing districts within each state that, in turn, have put the state into the Republican column. Louisville, Kentucky, northern Florida, certain regions of Virginia, eastern North Carolina, western Tennessee, and central Oklahoma have swung their states to the Republicans — and in the case of the first two, back to the Democrats. In Florida and Kentucky, the Republicans were unable to cement their political position in these regions sufficiently. In Tennessee they have. In North Carolina they now have the chance to follow the example of either Florida or Tennessee. In Virginia the configurations of the voting blocs are in their favor; in Texas they are not. Strategically speaking, this area is the least fluid in the country, yet careful political manipulations will retake it from the Republicans unless they firm up their constituencies with immediate and meaningful deliverance to their newfound supporters. Presidentially speaking, the Republicans can count on the region against a *liberal* Democrat more than other regions of the country — as a region. It will not go to a third party the way the Deep South might; it will not go to the Democrats as easily as the farm belt. If the Democrats run someone other than a liberal, things are much less clear.

Volatility in the Deep South

The Deep South can be treated as a unit for purposes of analysis. This is not to say that the politics of Louisiana, Mississippi, Alabama, and Georgia are identical, or even to say that South Carolina's politics resembles that of Georgia more than that of North Carolina or Virginia. Nor is it to suggest that the region is totally homogeneous. Atlanta and New Orleans give a flavor to their respective states; northern Alabama and Georgia are somewhat different from the rest of the region; the Yazoo Delta in Mississippi has its unique politics; South Carolina's Piedmont is coming to resemble North Carolina's; the black counties have their own voting patterns; and still other anomalies exist. Yet as far as the prevailing politics of each state is concerned — the politics that decides elections — these states can be treated as a unit, and most of the traditional intrastate distinctions have broken down in recent years.

With respect to parties the region would appear to be highly fluid, presidentially speaking. In the last twelve years, the Republican percentage has gone from 24 percent to 87 percent to 14 percent to 78 percent in Mississippi, for example. A similar pattern, although a less extreme one, exists in the other states as well. Of course, this swing reflects *ideological* stability: a decided preference for the more conservative candidate.

On the lower levels, where Democrats have no difficulty in finding conservative candidates, the states remain solidly non-Republican. Since Reconstruction none has had a Republican governor or legislature; only one has had a Republican congressional delegation. Republicans have only gained one Senate seat in the region — and that from a party switch by an incumbent Democrat. Except for this Democrat-turned-Republican, the Democrats won all the Senate races in these states in 1972 by comfortable margins against conservative Republicans.

As far as Republican prospects are concerned on the local level, there is a long, hard, party-building task ahead that most recognize but few have undertaken because the task seems so impossible. What is needed are local victories to form the base of a party, but the base of a party is generally needed to obtain local victories and the circle cannot be broken. Party-building from the top down has so far been largely unsuccessful.

For our purposes, however, the interesting question is presidential politics. How fluid is the Deep South? No liberal Democrat will carry the region unless there is a national political cataclysm so awesome that all speculations are now meaningless. A conservative, middle-of-the-road, or liberal Republican — as long as he is white, and especially if he is Protestant — will carry the region against any liberal Democrat in a two-way race. It is possible that a "populist" Democrat such as Askew could carry the area, but it is unlikely. To be sure, Askew carried the counties of northern Florida, which are politically indistinguishable from neighboring Alabama and Georgia, but if an Askew-style candidate were running for President and wanted to carry the Deep South, he would have to take a position so obscure on the racial question that he would risk losing the crucial northern black vote massively. It is doubtful, although not totally inconceivable, that a populist Democrat could ignore the black vote, move in the southern direction on the racial question, and win in the North by appealing to the white working-class and ultraconservative Republicans. In such a case, he might carry the Deep South. Should someone like Wallace become the standard-bearer of the Democrats, an unlikely but not impossible contingency, then he could take this region easily against any Republican, conservative or otherwise.

Because the Republicans depend totally upon the configuration of the candidates, there is nothing they can do about the region. In a two-way race they will either carry it massively or lose it massively, as indicated above. In a three-way race against a Wallaceite things might be a bit closer, especially if the Deep South voter saw that these states would make the difference nationally, but even here they are at the mercy of the third candidate. Strategically speaking, there is very little the Republicans can do to lose the region against one kind of Democrat (liberal) or to hold it against another (Wallaceite) in a two-way race. The South is so inflexible that it has no bargaining power in the absence of a third-party candidacy. It was the recognition of this situation that made the Wallace phenomenon real in 1968, and the symbolic pandering to the region during the first Nixon administration was a result of this Wallace threat. The irony is that the administration did not need to play this kind of game. Had Wallace run in 1972 he would have carried these states unquestionably (except, perhaps, for South Carolina); had he not run, Nixon would have carried them unquestionably. Furthermore, all the Nixon moves seemed to have had little, if any, effect upon the Alabama governor's own decisions, and hence the whole southern strategy, as a strategy, was simply a demonstration of a poor bargaining sense and an inability to understand one's own strategic position. We do not advocate taking the South for granted, since we are trying to get away from this entire high strategic approach to politics. All we are saying is that the southern strategy is not sound for those who like to play the strategic game.

The Mountain States

Despite an enormous amount of ticket-splitting in 1972, the Mountain states remain solidly Republican, presidentially speaking. It is undoubtedly the least fluid region of any in the country. Only Montana dipped below 60 percent in its support of the President and the other states averaged in the mid-60s. Nixon carried all the states in 1968, and with the exception of Colorado, Goldwater ran above his national average in all of them in 1964. He just missed carrying Idaho by less than 1 percent of the vote. The region sends a few liberals to Washington, and it also elects moderate Democrats. But presidentially the region will go solidly Republican for the foreseeable future — unless there is some major upheaval that brings a conservative Democrat to the ballot.

California and the West Coast

The politics of California has always had an element of instability about it, institutionalized instability associated with the Hiram Johnson reforms of another era. By and large the state has fluctuated from progressive Republican to liberal Democrat to conservative Republican, and it has fluctuated historically in a bloc. Yet in 1970 it elected a conservative Republican governor and a liberal Democratic senator. In 1972 it continued its departure from tradition by going Republican nationally and Democratic locally. Its brief flirtation with Reagan and his brand of conservatism seems to be over — it lasted about as long as its flirtation with Brownian liberalism.

Although anti-McGovern sentiment was the determining factor in the presidential election, a considerable amount of anti-Nixon feeling also existed in the electorate. It appears that many voters expressed their dissatisfaction with Nixon by voting against Republican candidates for legislative offices.

The Republican candidates for Congress and the state legislature did almost as poorly during the 1972 Nixon landslide as they did during the 1964 Johnson landslide. In 1972 GOP candidates for Congress won 47.2 percent of the two-party vote and GOP assembly candidates polled 46.9 percent; in 1964 Republican candidates for Congress polled 47.1 percent and Republican assembly candidates polled 46.4 percent. In 1972 GOP candidates for the state senate won 48.9 percent of the two-party vote, but this slightly better showing was because only half of the seats were contested — most of them in Republican areas.

In Oregon and Washington, the 1968 trends were reversed. McGovern ran significantly ahead of Humphrey's totals in the populated Willamette Valley counties and just about the same or slightly behind in the southern and western parts of the state. Overall, he improved Humphrey's total by about four percentage points — one of the very few states where this occurred. In Washington, however, McGovern lost where Humphrey had done very well. The more conservative Democrats of the Seattle area went for Richard Nixon.

But the coast can be carried by liberal Democrats if they don't run into image problems, and the region as a whole can, as with so many others, be classified as increasingly uncertain.

Alaska's politics is extremely volatile, in part a result of the small electorate; and Hawaii, traditionally Democratic, went very strongly for President Nixon in 1972.

All of these observations and statistics point to one disturbing conclusion: American politics is becoming very unstable. It is no longer given definition and shape by party structures and loyalties. It is losing all of its traditional form and coherence. Should these trends continue unchecked, what can we expect our politics to look like?

First, in national contests the candidate will become even more important than he now is. He will not really need the support of a party; he will need only an ideological following or a large amount of money to wage a credible, if not winning, campaign. In fact, he may not even need the party nomination. If the Republicans should insist on nominating a person far to the right of center and the Democrats insist on nominating a candidate far to the left of center, then there is no reason at all why a popular centrist couldn't run as an Independent and win. If the electoral college should be "reformed" and candidates given the opportunity to run nationally, we predict that the whole party situation would rapidly dissolve and there would be many candidates running for President — some perhaps successfully — outside the party context. This would emphatically be the case if there were a runoff arrangement because many aspirants would reason that they had a good possibility of coming in second during the first of the two trial heats. Because the removal of the electoral college would result in a national politics that might resemble the politics of a large city, with its coalitions, strategies, runoffs, and instabilities, we strongly suggest that those who advocate reform would examine the probable outcomes of their proposals in terms of the strategic calculations of ambitious politicians, not in the abstract terminology of political philosophy.

Second, our increasingly fluid politics might create an ideological reaction. The more the politician becomes strategic and the more the voter becomes disaffected, the more susceptible the electorate may become to an ideological counterattack. People do not want to be the victims of hypermanipulative politics, nor do they want a condition of political febrility. If an ideology can promise stability, then it will have a strong appeal — no matter whether it is an ideology of the Left or Right.

Third, what is to become of political parties? At the moment they seem headed for the antiquarian museum, shunned by politician and voter alike. It is difficult to say whether our increasing instability is a cause or an effect of the decline of political parties, but it is certain that the two phenomena go together. It seems that the only way to halt the degeneration of our politics in the direction of strategic categories is to restore the party — to make it a vital, living political animal once more, a creature relevant to the politics of the last quarter of the twentieth century. This cannot be done by managerial techniques or by ideological dexterity; it can only be done by re-creating the representative-constituency relationship. But this is a difficult undertaking in the age of strategic politics — although if it could be successfully done, the payoffs would be enormous.

But now the parties have neither organizational coherence, programmatic consistency, nor political proficiency. What are their chances of attaining any one or combination of them? To answer these questions it is necessary to look much closer at the current status of the parties, and for our purposes we will look at the current condition of the *Republican* party. But the crucial variable — and the starting point — of such an examination must be the power structure of the party and its potential future. Those who control a party presumably define its role and its activities. If the "new managers" control the Republican party it will evolve into one kind of organization. If the ideologues control it, another kind will emerge. If certain interests dominate the party, they will shape it to suit their own requirements. The point is that those who want to see the party revitalized must look to the power configurations within it, for only through these power configurations (or newly created ones) will such changes take place.

II

THE REPUBLICAN PARTY TODAY

10

Power in
a Divided Party

The first part of this book deals with strategy and its impact on the electoral process. This second part is also concerned with strategy, but strategy expressed as power.

Political power is a fascinating, very complicated, and often quite elusive commodity in modern America. Everyone seems to want it and some actually succeed in getting it. Progressive Republicans, however, never seem to be able to, and when occasionally they do, it slithers away from them very quickly. Why is this? It is tempting to dismiss their fate as the result of forces beyond their control, but this would be as naïve a view of reality as the presumption that if they wait long enough things eventually will fall into their laps.

There are two kinds of political games, each quite different from the other, but both of great relevance to any assessment of a power configuration: political games where the rules of power are clearly established and political games where they are not. In some ways the electoral process is an example of the former, although we have seen that this is less so than it used to be. The overall rules of the game have been traditionally set by the Constitution, by custom, or by state and federal legislation.

The party power situation, however, is an example of the latter. Here the rules of power are far less specified and the exercise of power can become very easily the result of a dual set of games and strategies rather than the single set that the electoral process traditionally enjoyed. There are not just the rules of the game, but more important these days, there is the game to define the rules of the game.

In a united and stable party this would not be the case. In a united party the rules of power can become fairly clear and widely acknowledged. The stability fostered by unity creates a sort of subconstitution so that stable and acknowledged rules of power create an analogous one-dimensional game.

In such a situation (and at state levels such situations still exist), tactical considerations dominate the acquisition of power and, within the stability of the situation, it is easy to see who is winning, who might win, who will lose, and the relative positions in the power hierarchy. The rules of political advancement in Chicago, New York State, Alabama, and Wisconsin, each in its very different way, are nevertheless sufficiently stable so that it is possible to define "where the power lies": who has it, who does not, who might get it, and who — in the short run, at any rate — could not dream of getting it. The national Republican party of the forties and fifties was very much the same way, as was the national Democratic party of the same period. Each was decentralized, if not fragmented, into varying power centers, but the rules of the game were clearly defined. Admission tickets to the councils of power in each party were not too difficult to obtain, but there were certain definite ways of *not* obtaining them. The rules of nomination were also relatively stable and the power relations between various factions of the party were easily definable.

Furthermore, the stability of the parties and the rules created through custom had their own self-sustaining dimension. Attempts to take over or exercise power within a party could easily be portrayed as attacks upon the party itself and this tended both to discourage such violations and to defeat the violators.

But in a divided party, such as the Republican party now is, things are very different. There are no set or lasting rules for acquiring power or exercising it effectively. The more divided a party, the less clear the nature of power at any given moment. In such a situation, strategy becomes very complicated. It is as much the science of shifting the *nature* of power to advantage rather than simply operating advantageously *within* the existing rules of power.

There are, then, two levels of analysis at work here. There is the game to define the nature of power and the game to be played within that definition. Power becomes, in effect, the ability to define and redefine what power is. Traditionally the practitioners of power performed these calculations by instinct and succeeded most often by luck. But now, the more politicians become aware of this set of interlocking strategies, the more the games become rationalized and strategized.

The problem is that the strategies of one game applied to the realities of another create serious disadvantages. The military analogy is tempting here. The American commanders in Vietnam were, for the most part, honorable, intelligent, and competent men employing the most advanced technological and strategic equipment that our society and war colleges could produce. Yet not only were they absolutely humiliated, they never understood why they were humiliated. (Some may have misread the situation so completely that they never understood that they were humiliated.) The point is that their strategic doctrines were so badly tailored to the kind of contest that they were engaged in (not to mention their hardware) that fantastic advantages and efficiencies accrued to the other side.

As in war, so in politics — strategic politics, that is. In 1940, Senator Vandenberg remarked somewhat plaintively after the convention, "The Willkie thing took us completely by surprise." What the senator was confessing to was an awareness that vast shifts had occurred in the nature of power within the Republican party — but why they had occurred or what had really happened, he confessed, was beyond his ken. What actually had happened was a decisive change in the rules of power within the party, removing Congress as an effective source of party governance and transferring power decisively to the famous eastern establishment, which could translate its connections within the financial, legal, and media communities into hard delegate votes. Not that many old forms of power were swept away at an instant, but their relevance was severely diminished.

The New York establishment, with its Philadelphia and Boston wings, was equally shocked in 1964. What had happened was clear: Goldwater had been nominated. How it had happened was also clear; one could study the various elements of F. Clifton White's strategies and tactics. But why it had happened was simply beyond, it seemed, rational ken. Most observers focused upon tactics and mechanics, blaming it on some one-shot coincidence, or referring to it as a whirlwind, thereby confessing their total lack of understanding. Others blamed it upon the sheer organizational abilities of White, a fallacy made clear in 1968. That a revolution had occurred was obvious to all; why it could succeed was less well understood. To focus upon tactics was ill advised, however, for such a focus could never come to grips with the meaning of ideological power that was so central to the phenomenon.

What the Goldwater people had done, consciously or otherwise, was to write a fundamental redefinition of the nature of power within the Republican party — as the McGovernites, somewhat more consciously, were to do later for the Democrats. They had, in effect, changed the rules of power. This is not the same thing as altering the actual rules of the nominating process, as the McGovern activists did. Such alterations may well change the rules of power, but the rules of power can be changed without altering the formal legal structure of the party. Even with the McGovern movement, the change in actual rules was not decisive. The original source of its power was not the mandate to examine and alter the rules of the nominating process. It was the ability to define the grounds on which the new rules would be based. The rules of power were decisively changed when the reformers induced the incumbents to accept "openness" as a criterion for party governance. From that point on the rest followed with inexorable logic.

As long as the conservative wing of the Republican party continues to define the current rules of power within the party, everybody else will be at a serious disadvantage. And if the rest of the party continues to focus upon *tactical* failure without understanding in any more than an instinctual fashion why so many defeats are suffered so often, it will remain at the mercy of the conservatives. Nelson Rockefeller has repeatedly misjudged the nature of party power in his several quests for the presidency. Other moderates may well do so in the future. As long as moderates continue to accept the conservatives' definition of the nature of political power, then the conservatives will enjoy a tremendous advantage.

Of course, the moderates might win party control as the result of tactical successes on their side and of tactical failures on the part of the conservatives. But can Republican moderates in fact change the *nature of political power* within this badly divided party in order to equalize their situation with respect to the conservatives? And, assuming that they can do this, should they do this, or will their efforts simply open up larger and more divisive splits within the party that will lead to increasingly frequent attempts to shift the rules? To answer these questions it is necessary to sketch some of the components of party power and then to analyze the nature and sources of the divisions within the party.

What are the sources of power within the Republican party? There is an endless list of actual and potential power categories. Power lies with elected officials, with party officials, with party regulars, and with various networks and associations of these. Power lies with interested and wealthy contributors, with the organizationally proficient, with the charismatic, and with the high priests of ideological orthodoxy. The list of greats, near-greats, and would-be greats of Republicandom is vast. But such a list is always incomplete, not because it must leave people out or ignore categories of power (as any list must), but because it does not address itself to why these people exercise power.

Why are some state chairmen more powerful than others? Why are virtually all state chairmen less powerful than their ancestors of a generation ago? Why is some minor functionary who works in the Executive Office Building more powerful than many congressmen when it comes to certain (but not all) party affairs? Why have governors less influence in party affairs now than a decade ago? What is the source of a vice president's political power? What can businessmen actually do to influence party and governmental affairs? What is the potential of an organized women's movement? And the great coalitions, networks, conspiracies or whatever, the Syndicate and the establishment — what is their power?

The normal approach to these questions — the approach of a traditional strategist — is to assess the relative power configurations of the moment and to create his various strategies around them. He decides who holds the power, the extent of that power, whether it is increasing or decreasing, and its relevance to his requirements. He then makes his strategic decisions. But the new strategists look at power configurations quite differently. To them the map of party power is simply a starting point for their calculations. Their task is to change the map itself to suit their own requirements. He who takes advantage of the present and changing nature of power configurations is a clever man, indeed. But he who changes the nature of power itself to suit his own positionings is a cleverer man yet.

In any sophisticated contest, the ability to shift favorably the grounds for deciding the outcome of that contest is a tremendous asset. Every good political strategist knows that if he can maneuver his opponent into a position where their dialogue is conducted in terms favorable to himself, it can be decisive. Every candidate, for instance, wishes the political debate to be carried on in an area of his strengths and his opponent's weaknesses. For example, if a liberal politician wants to win elections in a conservative district he will try to shift the political debate to issues that are not easily reduced to a conservative-liberal division or he may try to run a campaign on the "issue" of personality — anything to move the contest away from the arena in which he is most vulnerable. An opponent — if he is either a conservative or an opportunist — will try to shift the campaign back to the conservative liberal arena where the first politician is more vulnerable.

The same sort of logic applies to power in a wider context. The presidential nomination in recent years has been won in the different arenas of ideology, managerial competence, and organizational loyalty. If a candidate or party faction is stronger in any one of these areas and weaker in another, for example, it is sound strategy for him to augment the *relevance* to party power of his area of strength.

It is not difficult to list the components of power in the Republican party at any one time. The striking thing about such an exercise, however, is how often the list changes — and recently, how fast. One fascinating example of the fluidity of power is that under slightly different conditions, opposite characteristics can become sources of influence — in much the same fashion that the image asymmetries discussed in Chapter 3 could fluctuate between positive and negative. For instance, a reputation for honesty, decency, and civic-mindedness was a tremendous asset to Robert Taft, yet a reputation for deviousness, cleverness, and manipulative ability has been an asset to John Connally. A reputation for winning can be an asset, yet so can one for losing safely and comfortably. Public relations expertise can be an asset, yet so can be dedicated naïveté. Ideological orthodoxy conveys power to men like Goldwater and Brock, yet ideological flexibility conveys power to men like Nixon and Percy.

Intellectualism can be an asset, yet so can anti-intellectualism. Intelligence helps, but so does stolidity, which has its champions and conveys a sense of security to those who fear eminence, as Gerald Ford has illustrated. Self-righteousness is an asset, as Henry Cabot Lodge has often found, but so is self-effacement, as others have demonstrated. Association with various networks, syndicates, and establishments can bring tremendous advantage — as can the reputation for being clean and without obligation to networks, syndicates, or establishments. Sometimes ideological commitment is a great advantage, other times "pragmatism" or "electability" becomes a greater component of party power. Traditionally, "conservatives" have preached virtue, while "moderates" have preached success. To those who preach success, virtue is often regarded as "counterproductive," and to those who preach virtue, success (at the expense of virtue) is often a "sellout"; yet the ability to convince others that either "success" or "virtue" is the object of political activity is a very strong component of power.

The point is that the sources of power vary extensively and the nature of power can change very rapidly. Any candidate who wishes to enter the shifting arenas of national party politics would do well to examine not only the present configurations of power but the ways in which they can be changed. In this book we are not going to present a systematic picture of the power structure of the Republican party; to do so would be beyond the point. What we are presenting is an analysis of three kinds of power followed by a discussion of how they may relate to the overall situation. In each of these three examples we show how that particular element of power can be augmented or diminished either by accident or by design, and what would be the implications of such augmentations or diminutions. Our focus is the nomination of a national candidate — power to control the party nationally in the future. But our purpose is not to provide a chart of how our wing of the party can "take it over" (although such a chart could be compiled). Rather, our aim is to raise some questions about how all elements of the party can come together and produce on a national level the kind of candidates who will represent our party, who can win elections, and who can serve the country as it ought to be served.

The first element of party power is institutional power, the power of the party hierarchy and its relationship to the party's elected officials: the National Committee and its staff together with the state and local committees, party officials, and others who become formally and informally involved in party business. The new professionals, the pollsters, the campaign consultants, and the public relations experts are also relevant to this power configuration. All of these interact with each other, with the President, and with governors, senators, mayors, and other elected officials and their staffs.

Second, there is financial power, especially the influence of the business community in party circles. It is fashionable to focus on the negative effects of business influence in politics, and we shall do so to some extent. But it is only fair to examine some of the positive effects that business and finance can have when they exercise an influence in party affairs.

Third, there is ideological power; here we examine the role of the conservative wing of the party, its relationship to business, its internal divisions, and the nature of its influence.

These three influences are very important. In 1968, for example, Richard Nixon was the candidate of the party organization, Nelson Rockefeller was the candidate of a powerful segment of the business community (although certainly not the entire community), and Ronald Reagan was the choice of a large segment of the conservative wing (although not all conservatives supported him). The contest among these three candidates could be viewed in part as a contest among these influences. Their successes and failures in 1968 reflected the extent and limits of power that each could exercise. It is possible to imagine a similar configuration in 1976, if the nomination is seriously contested, and it is easy to see how various candidates would benefit from the strengthening of one or more of these influences within the party.

The overall point is that the party situation is so chaotic that no one can feel secure in his aspirations to be the party nominee for President in our bicentennial year. To be sure, the conservatives are regarded as having an edge in the control of the party machinery, and conservative candidates are often regarded as front-runners or front-runners-up. But this image of conservative dominance is illusory. Events, strategies, and redefinitions of power can intervene in sovereign ways.

For example, CREEP was given a continued existence by the White House in order to give its staff a major role in the nomination of President Nixon's successor. This was a calculated effort to change the rules of power within the party. But the Watergate scandal intervened and shattered — if only for a while — the role of the White House and its ability to use the ghost of CREEP as an instrument of party control.

For example, John Connally was given an inside edge by many observers in early 1972. The basis of his power was stated to be his close association with President Nixon, his relationship to the business community, and above all, his reputation for shrewdness and effectiveness in the corridors of power. His brief role in 1973 as counselor to the President, the facts surrounding his departure, and Nixon's own fate seriously impaired — if only for a while — all three of these power bases.

For example, to move away from Watergate and into the realm of potential shifts in the nature of party power, suppose that the business community really organized itself to act in concert and created an organization similar to the Business and Industry Division of CREEP. Some 160,000 businessmen were on its rolls in 1972. If only 10 percent of these could be mobilized around a "businessman's candidate" they still would constitute an awesome force in the party — if they could bring their influence to bear effectively.

For example, what would be the impact of a much-heightened activism on the part of Republican women? How would women's issues cut across traditional ideological lines? Could women become a major political force within the party beyond their current, and not insignificant, role? What impact would they have on the nomination?

For example, what influence will the large numbers of Republican young people have on party affairs in the future? The conservatives, who have controlled the Republican youth divisions for years, were to some extent watered down in 1972 by a large influx of less ideologically motivated young people. Will they remain active in 1976? What impact will they have upon the nomination?

For example, will the conservatives remain a monolith — if they are so now? Will the real disagreements over policy and ideology that are now papered over by the term "conservative" come to the surface as new issues come to dominate our political debates? What impact would such divisions have upon the nomination?

For example, will the party hierarchy be as strong in 1976 as it was in 1968? Or will the rank and file have more say? And if the rank and file has more say, who are the rank and file? Who can be motivated to pack a caucus — and on what grounds? Who can be motivated to vote in a primary — and for whom? Will Independents vote in Republican primaries if the Democrats appear to have no major contest? What new primary laws will be in effect? what new delegate selection rules?

Finally, how do all of these factors interact with each other? How would organized businessmen influence a primary? What effect does money have on a campaign — compared to ideological commitment? How do the various mathematical configurations of candidates in multiman primaries affect the outcome? It is easy to see why it has become impossible to predict the outcome of nomination processes much in advance of the events themselves. It is also easy to see why no one can count on winning with any degree of certainty either. In 1972, one cannot forget, the Democrats nominated a 50-to-1 long shot. In 1976 the Republicans may well do the same.

Despite all of this fluidity, however, there is one clear guide to party power that cuts through the maze of imponderables — the concept of *constituency*. Successful candidates for the presidential nomination for the last decade and a half in both parties have all had solid do-or-die constituencies that had a strong interest in each candidate's success. These constituencies have varied widely and the use made of them has shifted considerably over the years, but no one has been nominated without one since Adlai Stevenson — which takes us back into another political era. Kennedy's support among Catholics, Nixon's among the Republican party organization, Goldwater's among the conservative movement,

Humphrey's among labor, and McGovern's among his antiwar movement were all decisive. Candidates who relied on public relations, tactical maneuvers, and winning images were repeatedly destroyed by those with constituencies. This should be a sobering lesson for progressive Republicans.

11

The Managerial Party and the End-Run Game Plan

The Republican party organization is the logical starting point for an analysis of party power. After all, Richard Nixon won the nomination in 1968 partly because he was the candidate of the organization and the champion of so many party officials across the country. It is not clear that the organization could still nominate "its" candidate — assuming it could find one — since the whole party is now undergoing some massive upheavals. But the organization as an organization is still a force to be reckoned with in everyone's calculations.

We cannot begin to give an extensive description of the various party power centers in Washington and across the country. A brief sketch of the party and its recent history will suffice. Nor are we interested in momentary shifts of personnel and policies, since these ups and downs in surface relationships are of temporary significance. Instead we will examine some fundamental questions of party organization and purpose that have a direct bearing upon the future of the formal organization as a force in Republican politics: Should the party be centralized or decentralized, should the party be party- or candidate-oriented? That is, should it be a political party in the traditional sense of the word, or should it become a managerial party, an organization of competent managers, whose job is to select and service candidates to the best of its strategic ability? We will not state a set of preferences; our recommendations for the future come in Part III. Instead, we will simply look at the political implications of the various answers to these questions: Who will gain from centralization and who will benefit from continued decentralization? Who will gain from a philosophy of party orientation and who will benefit from a policy of candidate orientation? Above all, on what grounds might these decisions be made: winning in the short run, benefit to the party in the long run, or the interests of the country at large?

Before examining these questions in detail, let us briefly sketch the national and state party machinery to understand their context, since the questions of whether the organization should be more political, more orthodox, or more managerial have been the focus of a number of debates that have taken place in party circles over the last few years and since they reflect a set of struggles now going on — struggles between a number of party institutions to define the relationship between them, and struggles between champions of the party and champions of the new professionals. Sometimes these contests have been polite, subtle, and subdued. Other times they have not been so subtle. At all times, however, they have been important, since the debate to define what a party is can often resolve the question of who will control it.

The National Committee
and the White House

At the national level of the Republican party are several offices and organs of importance. Officially these are the National Committee, the national chairman, the National Committee staff, and the congressional campaign committees; unofficially there are the President, the White House staff, and the ghost of CREEP. Below them are the various state and local committees, their officers, and the many elected officials who take more than a passing interest in party affairs. There are also a series of auxiliary organizations such as the National Federation of Young Republicans and the Federation of Women's Clubs, which serve as important adjuncts to the regular organization. A party chart would be relatively succinct.

Legally speaking, the National Committee stands at the apex of party authority, subject only to the presidential nominating conventions that serve as quadrennial constitutional conventions for the party. The committee, composed of one committeeman and one committeewoman from each state together with the state chairman ex officio, is officially responsible for electing a national chairman and for maintaining the National Committee staff. Actually the National Committee has very little power at all and seldom interferes with the running of the party's national machinery. It meets only three or four times a year, and then usually just to ratify a series of proposals presented to it by either the national chairman or by the President when the Republicans control the White House. The staff of the National Committee, in effect, is managed by the national chairman and is loyal to him, not to the committee. This arrangement makes a lot of administrative sense, but it removes from the National Committee any effective possibilities for party governance. The committee has a few subcommittees, but with the exception of those that deal with convention rules and procedures, they have few responsibilities, no staff, and no power.

Furthermore, the one major responsibility of the committee — the selection of a national chairman — is traditionally exercised only when there is no sitting President and then just in times of controversy. The convention nominee traditionally selects the chairman and the committee ratifies his choice. Nixon's three national chairmen have been named by the White House without prior consultation with the National Committee and simply presented to it for ratification. Once in a great while — such as after the Goldwater debacle — the committee will replace a chairman, but this is a rare occurrence.

The chairman himself would appear to have some power. He is delegated to manage the central staff of the party and, on paper, he has wide latitude in the selection and management of that staff. During the first Nixon term, however, this was not the case and the White House was extremely influential in selecting key staffers, in supervising the direction of the staff, and in circumscribing the role of the chairman. Under Rogers Morton some degree of independence was maintained; under his successors, very little was possible until the Watergate scandal created the imperative of appearing to be independent of the White House.

The role of the national party machinery is a curious one when the party also occupies the White House. The President and his staff argue plausibly that the party is the President's party, that it exists to support and reelect him, and that it should aid him in any way possible. Since the President and his staff feel that they are the best judges of how the party can be of assistance, naturally they make a strong case that the national party machinery should be an adjunct of the White House operation.

On the other hand, the argument has been made that presidents come and go, but the party stays forever. Sometimes the long-range interests of the party may be at variance with the short-range requirements of the President. Shouldn't the national party machinery retain some independent existence for the sake of larger interests? Shouldn't the party be deferred to as a continuing institution? The President usually wins this argument, but the way he wins it is very instructive; the Nixon takeover of the national machinery and his treatment of it was in many ways unique.

Under Eisenhower the National Committee operation was small and its activities relatively limited. It was not the object of great interference by White House staff (who were far fewer in number than now), although deference to the office and veneration for the President certainly precluded any real independence of action. In a sense the National Headquarters and the White House each went its own separate way, but with very little, if any, friction between them.

In the early 1960s the National Committee continued in a somewhat expanded role and in 1964 the Goldwater forces briefly took control. Bill Miller, chairman at the time, was sympathetic to the conservative cause and became Goldwater's running mate. He was replaced by Dean Burch, a strong conservative who carried out a purge of sorts, filling key positions with other conservatives such as John Grenier of Alabama. After Goldwater's defeat, the National Committee convened and fired Burch. A group of moderates and pragmatists were instrumental in his removal and it is widely believed that Richard Nixon was very active behind the scenes in this operation. Burch was replaced by Ray Bliss, Ohio state chairman, an effective organizer and the articulator of some important organizational philosophies.

The Bliss approach to party organization was to strengthen the party as a party, to build up the power and effectiveness of its officials and to move it into the modern era by streamlining its operations and improving its machinery. In this sense, Bliss was very much an "old pro" who wanted to modernize the party, not a "new pro" who wanted to work *around* the party.

Bliss instituted many reforms. (1) He made a strong attempt to rebuild the party organization in the big cities and he put an enormous amount of effort into finding and training city chairmen. He had an extensive report prepared on the Republican position in large urban areas, and he encouraged them to build grass roots organizations. (2) He tried to strengthen the role of the state chairmen. He urged and insisted that all state chairmen work full-time. He encouraged them to develop adequate staffing. He made them ex officio members of the National Committee and set up training schools for party officials and campaign managers. (3) He attempted to make some of the tools of the "new politics" applicable to *party* functions. He recruited both public relations experts and statisticians to service the local organizations, and in a rudimentary way he began to use new professional managers within a party context. (4) He centralized and rationalized the National Committee's fund-raising procedures and instituted modern, direct-mail fundraising techniques.

His whole purpose was to strengthen the party as an institution. Bliss would not involve himself in candidate recruitment and took the position that the party organization should remain neutral in contests for the nomination. (He adhered to this policy faithfully during the presidential nominating process in 1968. For instance, Henry Bellmon, Nixon's campaign manager, came to Bliss early in the campaign and asked for a complete list of state and county chairmen. Bliss refused to give him one until he was prepared to give one to all contenders.) To him the role of the national party was to service the local parties and help them establish viable grass roots organizations on the Ohio model. The emphasis was on *parties,* not candidates, and on local, not centralized, organization. He did not neglect the methods of the new professionals, but he advocated their employment to strengthen, not weaken, the party.

After the election of 1968 Nixon fired Bliss. Originally he seemed to want Murray Chotiner to replace the Ohioan, but the moderates in the party hierarchy were very nervous about such a proposition and Rogers Morton was chosen instead. The Morton tenure was a sort of transition between Bliss's attempts to rebuild the party and Dole's subsequent anguished performance totally subservient to the interests of the White House.

Morton in many ways continued the party-building role that Bliss had begun, although he employed some different methods. He hired a number of new professionals to beef up the party's image nationally. Harry Treleaven and Ken Reitz were recruited to handle the advertising and press operations of the National Committee staff. Treleaven centralized the party's publications and started the now famous *Monday,* a sheet so popular with the President that the White House staff, in effect, snatched it away from the National Committee staff and put it under the control of John Lofton, who turned a credible and informative publication into a noncredible smear sheet — now defunct, ironically, because of a Watergate-instigated financial crunch at the National Committee. By and large, however, the new public relations functions were *party*-oriented. A second attempt at party-building was run by Elly Peterson, former Michigan state chairman. Called the Action Now program, it involved a series of Action Centers in a number of cities modeled after the highly successful storefront operations used by Romney, Lindsay, and Percy in their campaigns during the early and middle 1960s. This program was envisioned as a long-range party-building operation that would gain the confidence and eventually the votes of traditional Democrats by performing services for residents of the inner city. It attempted to refurbish the image of the Republican party in areas that had not gone Republican for years. Third, Morton continued many of Bliss's efforts at strengthening the local party machinery.

Morton departed from many Bliss practices, however. He began to pay as much attention to candidates as to party officials, and he began a conscious policy of encouraging candidates to employ the methods, if not the services, of the new politicians. This was the beginning of a shift from *party* strengthening to *candidate* recruitment, a policy that was articulated most loudly during the first few months of George Bush's tenure.

There had been quite a bit of liaison between the national headquarters staff and the White House during the first year of Morton's chairmanship — and some tension. But the campaign of 1970 opened a wide breach between the two. The National Committee staff shouldered a large part of the effort during the early phases of the campaign, but the White House moved in during the later stages and, in effect, replaced the committee staff as central organizer of the effort. The resulting friction — and the resulting disaster — were used ironically as a justification for more White House control of the National Committee staff operation, even though a good case could be made that the White House efforts in the campaign had been highly counterproductive. After the 1970 election, Rogers Morton went to the Interior Department and was succeeded by Senator Robert Dole of Kansas.

Dole's election to the chairmanship was unusual in one sense. For the first time in history someone campaigned for the position of National Committee chairman. Dole had people from Kansas write letters, make phone calls, and lobby with national committeemen. The President, a bit outmaneuvered, a bit amused, and a bit intrigued by Dole's credentials, indicated his support to the nominating committee. Anne Armstrong of Texas was suggested as assistant chairman, and the National Committee met to ratify the choice. Before they could do so, however, the telephone rang. John Mitchell, it seemed, had other ideas. He wanted to install one of his associates, Tom Evans, as co-chairman to watchdog Dole. Over many objections — including those of Ray Bliss — the signals were switched: Dole was elected chairman, and Evans was installed with Armstrong as co-chairmen. Evans later exercised some independence from his former associates at the White House, but from this point on the independence of the National Committee was severely circumscribed and the party-building efforts ceased to receive much priority. As the presidential election of 1972 grew nearer, the creation of CREEP further eclipsed the National Committee staff and it was given a series of perfunctory roles during the reelection campaign. When Watergate broke, many were retrospectively happy that this had been the case, but by the end of Dole's tenure both the independence and effectiveness of the organization had, despite many of his efforts, been destroyed by the White House.

George Bush was brought in to rebuild and recoup. He was given assurances by the White House that he would have a free hand in reorganizing the party and redefining its role. Some lively debates over the nature and purpose of the party organization took place during the opening months of his tenure, and we shall discuss them. But his efforts to rebuild the party were severely interrupted by the Watergate scandal, which ironically freed the National Committee machinery from White House control but at the same time dried up a lot of its funds so that it could not take advantage of its unexpected liberation. It remains ready for White House recapture. When the Watergate scandal is finally resolved, all the arguments about the "President's party" may well be resurrected and the White House's influence restored, if in a somewhat subdued form.

231

Decline of State Parties

While the national party machinery has been attempting to define its relationship to the White House, state committees have been operating with varying degrees of proficiency and success. Few generalizations about state parties are possible. In some states the party is organized and institutionally strong (Ohio, for example); in others it is disorganized and nearly nonexistent (Massachusetts and Washington State). In some states elected officials seem to be in the driver's seat (Connecticut, Iowa, Arizona). In other states, powerful party and satellite figures have tremendous influence (Oklahoma, Idaho). There are centrally controlled parties (New York), there are feudal parties (New Jersey), and there are loose traditional parties (Kansas and the Dakotas). There are southern parties that lack a broad base or a long tradition (Alabama, Arkansas), and there are parties in the same region that *do* have a solid base (Tennessee). There are parties deeply divided on grounds of ideology and policy (California) and parties divided on grounds of personality and policy (New Hampshire).

Despite these vast differences, however, there is an almost universal agreement among party officials across the country that the party organization, as an organization, is on the decline. These institutions, once the heart of our political system, are becoming increasingly irrelevant to the political process. There are many reasons for the decline in influence and importance, but one stands out above the others: in the age of strategic politics the party organization no longer seems to hold the key to electoral success.

When the most important piece of information a voter had about a candidate was his party affiliation, it became the principal ground for his choice on election day. Therefore the party label — the party blessing — was a coveted commodity and the key to victory. (The party was also the source of money, volunteers, and other important political instruments.) The party, therefore, had what the ambitious politician wanted: the key to electoral success. This put it in a good bargaining position with respect to the candidates, made the party organization the center of political calculations, and enabled it to dominate the patronage distribution that filled its offices and supplied its volunteers.

Today, however, in state after state, the party no longer holds these keys to victory. Voters do not need it as a source of information about political aspirants, primary laws have curtailed its ability to name candidates, elected officials and governmental bureaucracies have taken over its historical patronage and welfare functions, and the new strategists assert that they, not it, hold the coveted key to success, which seems to be the "professionally run campaign," not the "support of the organization." This shift has momentous implications for the future of party control.

To be sure, parties do still perform some important political functions.

All states have a party headquarters with at least an office and a secretary. Some state chairmen are full-time paid employees of the party. Every state has an executive director or an executive secretary; some have both a full-time chairman and an executive director. Many maintain an extensive staff between elections with offices in principal counties.

These personnel enable the state parties to perform a number of functions. For example, field organization of one form or another is common to almost all state organizations. In some states the chairman and executive director spend long hours on the road trying to pull together county and district organizations. In New York and California (as well as in other states), field men are continually on the move assisting county organizations in planning dinners, setting up meetings, recruiting candidates, and in helping to resolve patronage questions. Some states take responsibility for "get out the vote" drives that enable candidates to allocate resources elsewhere.

Furthermore, the state organizations are sources of publicity, especially when there are no prominent Republican elected officials. In some states the organization is responsible for shaping legislative strategies, although this function is on the decline everywhere. Many states have a research department to supply candidates and elected officials with information about their constituencies and about current issues. Some states have compiled centralized voting and mailing lists. And a number of parties have candidate training programs.

Most important, a few strong state parties have created systems of central fund-raising that enable them to provide the above services and many others. These strong parties still provide the key to electoral success in a few states, but by and large, the lack of effective centralized fund-raising in most states keeps the parties from playing the sovereign role on election day that they used to. Candidates, not parties, have become the central focus in most states and candidates have turned to the new professionals.

The Professional Alternative

The "professional" revolution in American politics is well known and there is no need to describe again how many young men and women in the 1960s began to sell their skills in political technology. It is interesting, however, to note that this new professionalism has always grown and prospered in an antiparty context.

The new politics may have come of age in the sixties, but it was born in California in the thirties when the public relations firm of Whitaker and Baxter began to accept political accounts to promote candidates and referenda. This application of what were later called "Madison Avenue techniques" was a natural outgrowth of the political situation in California. The progressive reforms of the first decade of this century destroyed the party organization in California by enacting laws that curtailed most of their traditional activities and gave the voter direct control over the selection of candidates and even the enactment of legislation. Because there were no parties left to speak of — no organizations to deliver the vote — and because referenda, initiatives, and other complexities appeared on every ballot, extensive advertising became the key to political success. The new politics of California was designed to replace the party and to perform its functions better. It is not surprising that the decline of parties in the East has brought forth a similar response. Today there are about 350 private firms with several thousand employees involved in politics for profit and about fifty of these are exclusively engaged in politics. They vary by size, by service offered, and by proficiency, but taken together they are a very important part of modern politics, and more often than not they operate apart from the parties.

Why do these professionals seem to hold the key to success more and more while the parties seem to hold it less and less? First of all, their collective list of services is impressive: campaign planning and management, organizational techniques, budgeting services, resource allocation analysis, demographic analysis, voter targeting, scheduling, advancing, event planning, issues research, speechwriting, electronic data processing, survey research (polling), direct mail techniques, telephone and door-to-door canvassing (both techniques and personnel), clipping services and newspaper analysis, press relations, fund-raising techniques, and advertising of all sorts and dimensions — theme, graphics, copy, production, and placement. No state party in America is equipped to provide all of these services and very few provide a substantial number of them. Some, such as Ohio's, have taken long strides in this direction, but even that model of a modern party has a long way to go. To the extent that candidates consider these services essential, they must go beyond the party.

Even when a party can provide these services, however, there are many reasons why a candidate will turn to the new professional. For example, the backbone of a party organization is the dedicated volunteer, but volunteers, while cheap, are less reliable than employees. They work their own hours, their motivations are different, it is difficult to fire them, and hence it is often difficult to control them. To the professional a volunteer who is not highly motivated by an ideological cause is a less efficient resource than a paid hand. Furthermore, the candidate and his immediate deputies find themselves much less obligated to hired professionals than to volunteers. When the campaign is over, if the bills are paid, that is the last the candidate need hear of the consultants and workers. That is hardly the case with volunteers. Also, it is generally acknowledged that the kind of personnel provided by the new professionals in that highly competitive business is of a much higher quality than the kind provided by the noncompetitive patronage atmosphere of a traditional party. Parties don't pay as well, they are often quite reluctant (on political grounds) to get rid of incompetents, because, as we said, you cannot fire a volunteer.

The new professionals also serve to "legitimize" a candidate's campaign and to help attract large-scale financial contributions. The candidate who needs money but relies strictly on old politics and the traditional party organization finds it difficult to convince business leaders that his effort should be supported. Many businessmen find it distasteful to contribute to a candidate whose operation appears to be masterminded by a Neanderthalic Boss Tweed. But the new professional creates a climate of confidence by speaking not only the language of the politician, but also the language of commercial enterprise — flow charts, market research, media buying, and a whole host of other business concepts. This climate of professionalism is a crucial element in fund-raising. A candidate with a rational, organized operation under the direction of a professional appears to be a good financial risk.

Finally, the new professional provides the candidate with strategic independence. He is candidate-oriented (because the candidate pays his fee) and hence is not fettered by party interests. He is willing to target Democrats as well as Republicans. He is willing to create organizations totally apart from the party. He is willing to take the party for granted in his attempts to create a new majority or coalition. In short, he is willing to use the party when it is useful to his candidate and to discard it when it is not. This independence can be a strong asset to a candidate.

It can also be an asset to an elected official. Concurrent with the rise of the new strategic politics has been a rise in the number of elected officials who keep their distance from party affairs and who rely on the advantage of incumbency and the advice of professionals to hold their office.

But what about the influence of the new professionals on intraparty affairs? If they hold the key to electoral success, it would seem that they could begin to exercise political power in this crucial area despite the fact that they often operate outside the party orbit. They have not done so yet because they are disorganized, because they can be hired and fired — it's a buyer's market — and because many are simply interested in monetary rewards. Their intraparty contributions have been limited to managing formal intraparty contests between candidates. But what if they got together? What if an organization were created for the very purpose of using this newfound influence to take over the party or to render it obsolete? What if the new professionals began to rewrite the fundamental definition of intraparty power that in so many states sits with the organization? The interesting thing is that such a scheme was being instituted when Watergate intervened and postponed everyone's plans. Its projections are instructive.

The End-Run Game Plan

After the election of 1972 and before the full fury of Watergate broke upon them, the Nixon managers engaged in some unusual postelection activity. They kept CREEP in full operation for several weeks, writing reports, assessing procedures, and evaluating thousands of personnel. They continued to solicit money. They installed some of their key workers at the National Committee headquarters to plan a 1974 campaign around a New Majority instead of Republican theme. Key CREEP personnel fanned out to assume positions in important government posts. The President himself began to talk in terms of 1974 and 1976. What was going on?

We will never know exactly what they had in mind, but everything indicates that they were planning a political revolution. They were trying to organize a large number of effective managers and technicians in order to dominate the process of selecting candidates for office in 1974 and especially in 1976. More specifically, it seems that they were trying to use the new "keys to success" to dominate the party in a centralized way and to change the rules of power within the party. What they seemed to have had in mind was the creation of the first national political machine in American history, an instrument of power that would enable them to make a dramatic end run around those existing party organizations that might resist their efforts to nominate a successor and perpetuate themselves in power.

To illustrate the need and rationale for such a machine, consider the problem of how a President and his staff can nominate a successor. (Even in pre-Watergate calculations this question was far from trivial.) Logically speaking, there are two parts to the problem: influencing the composition of the convention by intervening in the delegate selection process and influencing the delegates once they have been selected. The latter has been a traditional route and a President would not be at a total loss in this exercise. Nevertheless, the whole emphasis of convention politics is increasingly on the process of selecting delegates with prior commitments, and this trend would severely undercut the President's effectiveness if he were not involved. It would seem that the President and his staff would have to intervene in the delegate selection process or they would find themselves graciously abstaining from the fray and warmly endorsing the winner they did not want, or at least did not choose.

But how does a sitting President intervene in the delegate selection process? Of course he can name a choice and campaign for delegates committed to him in the primaries. An endorsement by a popular President certainly should count for something. But Nixon's record in convincing voters to support the candidate of his choice is spotty at best. It might be marginally better among Republican voters than among the electorate at large, but as events have shown, presidential popularity is a risky proposition to rely on. Nor can the President always deal effectively with the party in the closing months of his administration. Considerations of ideology and organization may intervene decisively. Despite the new primary laws and other reforms, the Republican party hierarchies in many states still play an active role in presidential nominations. It is one of the few important roles they have left and they guard it with jealousy. Attempts to influence this role directly or to subvert it openly would create enormous negative repercussions. What is needed is the means of getting around the party in a way that the party cannot stop.

Since their plans were interrupted at the earliest stage, we must enter the realm of conjecture; we can only ask how they might have proceeded. It is an interesting strategic problem: how to create an organizational (instead of ideological) revolution, how to change the rules of power so that the party could be rendered irrelevant, so that in 1976 a new managerial machine could nominate a President who would wear the legal label of "Republican."

To begin their organizational revolution, the Nixon strategists had a number of assets. There was more than $5 million left over from the 1972 campaign — an excellent starting point. Furthermore, there was the strong expectation that sizable funds could be raised in the future. The power of incumbency had been used to extort large sums of money from firms doing business with the government and there was no reason to feel that they could not go back to the well repeatedly. Moreover, the legitimate sources of funds could be stimulated by the professional techniques used in 1972. The theme of "Elect a Congress for the President" might not have raised the money that "Reelect the President" did, nevertheless it would have served for 1974. Other rationales could have been found for 1976. The power of incumbency also gave the strategists important leverage with party officials. The argument that "this is the President's party," so effectively used to take over the National Committee operations, could also have been used with lower party officials as a very strong asset.

Furthermore, their reputation for winning, their acknowledged managerial skills, their nationwide contacts, and their claim on the services of qualified technicians (media, survey research, canvassing, etc.) enabled them to make a strong case to party officials that they possessed the keys to electoral success. How would they have assembled all of these assets? Nineteen seventy-four would have been the starting point.

The Nixon strategists would probably have begun with the plausible argument that the 1974 campaign should be centralized because centralization seemed to provide advantages in 1972. Centralized fund-raising, centralized professional advice and skills, centralized advertising themes, and carefully coordinated campaigns by leading national figures might all have provided vast economies of scale. CREEP — no doubt with a new name — and working either independently or through a captive National

Committee, could easily have made offers to supply candidates with a vast range of services for free or at temptingly reduced rates. Money itself could have been channeled directly to candidates. Consider how far $10 million could go in direct contributions. It could provide a gift of $25,000 to each of *two hundred* targeted congressional candidates and $100,000 to each of fifty statewide candidates, presumably governors and senators. Even at today's inflated political prices, these are not trivial contributions. Enormous quids pro quo could be extracted for them in the future. An interesting sidelight is that this would be a very low-risk operation politically even if the electoral results were not spectacular. Those who won after receiving these services would be both grateful and in a position of power. Those who lost would presumably not be in a position of power and their ingratitude, if any, would not count for much.

If their resources permitted, the Nixon strategists might well have reinstated all the various agencies and subgroups of CREEP — the Business and Industry Division, the Heritage Division, the Young Voters Division, and so forth. These would have left the contacts active, the files updated, and the relationships intact. They could have been employed to help elect local candidates, but their lines of command would have been maintained vertically to Washington. Even the powerful Political Division of CREEP could have been reactivated to provide services to candidates all across the country — and to keep the organization intact.

The justification for all of this would have been that "we can provide the keys to electoral success." CREEP's managers, with their recent triumphs, certainly looked like winners regardless of their actual merits. They could have emphasized the team aspects of the effort, they could have used the name of the President to convince skeptical party managers, they could even have co-opted many professional consulting firms and driven others to the wall. They might also have co-opted funds as they did in 1972. "Give the United Way" would have been a promising theme.

And they could have been selective! They could have encouraged the election of candidates who would play ball with the team while discouraging the election of others. They could have engaged in an extensive candidate recruiting operation (this was actually in the planning stage). They could have used their influence with those they were underwriting to promote certain kinds of supporters to key party posts. Their extensive files and evaluations left over from 1972 and conscientiously updated would have provided them with quite a bit of information about who was with them and who most likely would not be. They might even have intervened early in primary contests.

Would they have used a persuasive ideology? Would the New Majority theme have worked? Would the coalition have held together? It is difficult to pursue this ghostly speculation much further and we shall revert to these questions when we discuss ideology and coalitions. But one thing is clear. Such an effort would have been quite feasible had Watergate not intervened. This instrument of power, this newly created national political machine, then could have proceeded to 1976. The candidate (or in the early stages the selected candidates) who received its blessing would have had enormous advantages over all rivals. The ability to pack caucuses, to round up support on primary day, and to influence key politicians would have been enormous. All the regular procedures of party discourse would have been superseded and the end run would have had a strong chance for success. Had this machine been erected, had it nominated and elected a candidate in 1976, and had it then had four more years to operate, the Republican party as a party would have been totally phased out. One by one pockets of resistance would have been snuffed out and politics would have entered another era. Although Watergate intervened decisively, removed many key personnel, discredited the political methods of CREEP, and compromised its fund-raising techniques, nevertheless this whole operation could appear again in modified form. But the key is money. Cut off the central funding and the whole operation would wither.

Alternative to Phaseout

There are several obstacles to the achievement of a centralized managerial candidate-oriented machine that would replace or supersede the party organization. One is the strong, healthy state party organization — and a few do exist. There are two ways in which such a party can avoid being phased out by those who now claim to hold the keys to electoral success: obtain similar keys or take the keys away from those who hold them. It can adopt the methods of the new professionals in an organized and proficient way; or it can render its rivals impotent by restricting severely the amount of money spent in a campaign.

The Ohio State party, organized by Ray Bliss in the fifties and welded into a fine political instrument, is a model of how the new methods of politics can be employed by a political organization. The Bliss organization was built on the twin principles of centralized fund-raising and a nonideological approach to candidates. These two principles continue today. The fund-raising operation is central to the entire organization. Bliss utilized some of the most modern fund-raising techniques and instituted a system of periodic giving by large and middle-range donors. (The Ohio party is still one of the most effective political fund-raisers in the country.)

The money raised by the party is used to support candidates, especially at the legislative and congressional levels. As new methods of politics become current, the party adopts them into its practices of candidate assistance. This assistance includes, for example, the preparation of detailed statistical analyses of the districts, their swing vote or split-ticket vote potential, their past voting history, and as many demographics as are available. This information is presented and explained to the candidate as soon as he or she becomes the nominee. Training schools for candidates are also held so they have some opportunity to familiarize themselves with experts in the field of campaign management, advertising, direct mail, and telephone campaigns.

The centralized fund-raising organization that Bliss built provides contributions directly to candidates. The amount varies with the importance of the race, the vulnerability of the Democrat, and the candidate's own resources. This distribution is a way to assure that virtually all candidates can wage a respectable campaign, and that candidates in marginal districts or in particularly important campaigns can be given the means to run the most effective campaign possible.

For several years the Ohio party has retained a political polling firm to conduct continuous polling on issues and candidates and to develop a voting data bank as the basis for the district-by-district analysis package given to candidates. The state committee has also developed, designed, printed, and distributed campaign literature tailored to fit the needs of candidates for the state legislature, complete with district maps, photographs, and other modern media attractions.

Although Bliss embraced modern methods and attempted to create an organization that would provide candidates with the keys to success, he did not neglect the interests of the party as a party. He fostered a spirit of unity, he used his influence to discourage statewide primary contests, and he created a situation of party-consciousness on the part of Ohio Republicans. He resisted attempts by ideologues to take over the party and he created an organization that was self-sustaining. In short, Bliss worked out a compromise position between candidate orientation and party orientation to the benefit of both. To be sure, there are a number of problems with this model. It tends to be closed; advancement is often regulated by the party and therefore it is slow. Young blood seldom reaches the top before it has been turned to old blood. But in a power contest — which is what we are looking at — the Ohio party is in a very strong position to resist attempts at outside influence because it is both united and relevant to the needs of its candidates.

There are several other states that have a strong and centralized party organization, but not many. At the moment the weaknesses in most state organizations are fully exploitable by the followers of a charismatic candidate, by the ideologically motivated, or by the organizationally proficient. It is very doubtful that the state party organizations will be able to resist the tremendous pressures put on them by these three forces in the future unless they adopt some of the methods of the Ohio-style party.

But what if they did? What if a large number of states centralized their finances, began to service candidates, and emphasized party-building?

This, too, would create some fundamental alterations in the nature of party power. Today the Republican party is a decentralized aggregation of mostly weak parties. An occasional strong party and an occasional governor who interests himself in party affairs create exceptions to this rule, but these are at the moment rare exceptions. If a large number of parties became strong again, then the party organization in each state would once more have a great deal to say about presidential politics, primary laws and reform rules not withstanding. They would be able to resist the pressures of Left and Right as well as the blandishments of the new managers. This new arrangement would have its attendant advantages and drawbacks, but it would create some fundamental changes in the nature of power within the party. Simultaneously it would reinforce the party's decentralized character.

Alternatively, the impetus to party-building might come from above. The Nixon managers, with their projected emphasis on organizational techniques, candidates, and new coalitions, did not view party-building as one of their tasks. Quite the contrary. But suppose that the National Committee attempted to use its influence and resources to encourage party-building in the various states? Suppose it could find the money to carry out the programs Bliss initiated when he was national chairman? This, too, would create an obviously different power pattern, but it is very unlikely that such an operation could occur without strong White House blessing and financing. Neither is likely to be forthcoming.

Most of these speculations about potential shifts in the nature and distribution of organizational power within the party have centered around finance and its use. It was financial potential that enabled the Nixon managers to plot their revolution. It is centralized financing that enables the Ohio party to retain its keys to electoral success. It is the lack of centralized finance that keeps so many other parties weak and ineffective. And it is their inability to raise money that keeps the National Committee bureaucracy weak and captive to White House staff members. There are certainly other components to organizational power, but this one is commanding.

It is therefore reasonable to ask what the impact on organizational power would be if campaign fund-raising activities were curtailed by legislation. There are many components to this complex problem, the method of curtailment being crucial to all calculations. But if massive curtailments were made, by whatever means, the whole nature of organizational power would be decisively altered. So many of the alleged keys to success that the new politics have created depend on money! Without money the whole CREEP style of politics would become impossible — and so would the Bliss model of party organization. The volunteer would once again become the center of political calculations, but a major by-product of this shift would be the strengthening of causes and movements that are best equipped to motivate volunteers. If, however, parties survived the initial onslaught of these imponderables — a big if — then they would be forced to go back to organizing and maintaining themselves on the basis of volunteers and on the more traditional forms of political activity. This would be a possible outcome, but a far less likely one than the proliferation of movement organizations, with all the instability that they imply.

Finance, then, plays a sovereign role in the calculations of party organizational power and in the ability to change the nature of that power. It is therefore necessary to look a lot more closely at the structure of Republican finance to understand many of the more subtle organizational changes and potential changes that are — and may be — taking place. Fortunately the disclosures of 1972 enable us to look closer at Republican finance than ever before.

12

The Structure of
Republican Finance

Before, during, and after the campaign of 1972, Richard Nixon raised a lot of money. It will never really be known just how much he raised since massive efforts were made to hide the figures, if not the money; and years of equally massive efforts would be necessary to pry loose the truth since much of the money was raised clandestinely, some of the money was raised illegally, and quite a bit of the hottest money was given back. A good working estimate would fall between $50 and $70 million, rounding off to the nearest $10 million. There were three principal kinds of donation to CREEP and its many receptacles: the small contribution of less than $100, which was not required by law to be disclosed on an individual basis; the *disclosed* contribution, which ranged from $100 up (but which included few donations above $10,000); and the large clandestine contributions made either legally before the disclosure law went into effect or illegally afterward. The first type raised over $10 million, the second, somewhat under $20 million, and the third, over $20 million — up to whatever figure can be imagined.

Since the campaign laws did not require the various committees to disclose the names, addresses, and occupations of the small contributors, very little is known about them. Much more is known about the large contributors, whose donations have been disclosed through the efforts of the Watergate investigators and Common Cause. Yet these particular contributions are of historical but not lasting interest because so many of them were one-shot affairs given by individuals for unique reasons that may never recur. But an analysis of the middle-range contributors, about whom a great deal is known, is of lasting value to a study of Republican

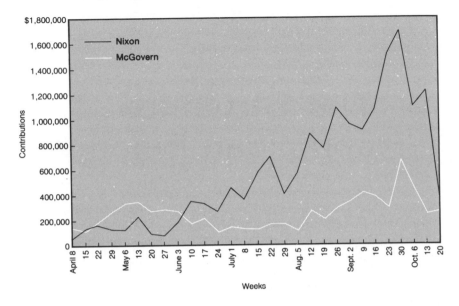

Figure 5

Total Disclosed Contributions of $100 or More to Nixon and McGovern by Week

finance, since these are more likely to be constant and repetitive givers, the party's backbone, and the source of continuing influence money.

After the 1972 election, the Ripon Society sponsored a very detailed study of these middle-range contributions that was conducted at the State University of New York at Albany. The General Accounting Office made available a complete list of all *individual* contributors who made contributions of $100 or more to every presidential campaign from the April 7 start of disclosure through the election. This information was put into a computer and subjected to an extensive analysis to see just where everyone's disclosed money came from, when it came, and who gave it. Some of our conclusions are presented in this chapter; more conclusions and the methods used are found in Appendix 1. The following observations about Nixon's money refer to contributions in this category unless otherwise specified.

Overview

The Nixon fund-raising campaign (after April 7) got off to a slow start. In part this was the result of the law itself — many people gave before the deadline to avoid disclosure — but it was probably also the result of a

244

Figure 6

Number of People Making Disclosed Contributions of $100 or More to Nixon and McGovern by Week

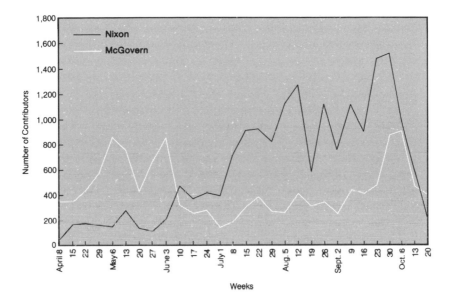

massive lack of enthusiasm for the President's candidacy that the nation-wide surveys also indicated during the same period. During April and May contributions to the President's various receptacles averaged around $150,000 per week, while George McGovern was averaging between $200,000 and $300,000 and his combined Democratic opposition was fluctuating somewhere between the two. Of course the Democrats were raising money to spend in primaries and the President had no one to contest, but it must have still appeared disquieting to the Nixon managers that the Democrats were running so far ahead of them in total receipts.

As the McGovern candidacy became more certain, Nixon's financial fortune changed. After the California primary there was a decided jump in Republican money, which surpassed McGovern for the first time during the second week in June. From then on, week by week, the Nixon totals rose, somewhat erratically but nevertheless decisively, until the end of September when they hit the rate of more than $1.5 million per week. (These figures are portrayed in Figures 5 and 6.)

During these seven months, the President raised approximately $17 million from these individual contributions of over $100. Before Labor Day, he received contributions from 8,940 people averaging about $900 apiece and after Labor Day, when the official campaigns began, he received contributions from another 5,961 people averaging $1,456 apiece. (McGovern's 5,669 pre–Labor Day contributions in this category by contrast averaged only $782, and his 3,659 post–Labor Day gifts only $850.)*

Table 7 shows where this $17 million came from by size of contribution

Dollar Contribution	SPRING-SUMMER		FALL	
	Number	Amount	Number	Amount
100–199	1,946	228,200	748	90,598
200–299	2,852	642,729	1,002	220,121
300–399	343	106,119	221	68,049
400–499	238	101,454	97	40,157
500–599	1,151	577,310	748	374,594
600–699	63	38,157	27	16,480
700–799	61	44,056	34	25,088
800–899	27	21,848	17	13,782
900–999	26	23,931	22	20,910
1,000–1,999	1,441	1,513,083	2,001	2,059,536
2,000–2,999	351	755,875	532	1,110,824
3,000–3,999	142	433,219	176	534,931
4,000–4,999	45	186,821	46	190,480
5,000–5,999	98	495,339	88	442,393
6,000–6,999	33	198,678	39	237,416
7,000–7,999	17	122,100	40	293,580
8,000–8,999	6	48,200	9	73,813
9,000–9,999	11	99,000	16	149,119
10,000 and over	89	2,513,624	98	2,719,171

TABLE 7.
Contributions to Nixon by Amount

and provides a fascinating panorama of the financial structure of a modern political campaign. Keeping in mind that the Republicans raised only $10 million in contributions smaller than these and that they raised around $20 million in large clandestine contributions, it is easy to see that the big contributor plays a very important role in presidential fund-raising. Still, the backbone of this disclosed money was the $1,000 contribution — Nixon received almost 3,500 of them. These are no longer considered "big," but their total impact is clearly large; more money was raised in this category than in any other. These figures should not surprise anyone, but they are interesting. Where the money came from geographically is even more interesting.

* When the same person gave more than once within each time period, these contributions were added together and counted as one contribution.

Concentration

The source of presidential campaign money is not only concentrated in the large contribution, it is also concentrated in the large financial center. Table 8 shows the distribution of contributions by state for both Nixon and McGovern. It is easy to see how New York, California, and Illinois play such a commanding role in Republican and Democratic finance, with Texas and Pennsylvania holding their own. The Midwest (outside the financial center of Chicago) was *not* a big contributor to the Nixon campaign, and the rest of the country was a very poor contributor even when its efforts are calculated on a per capita or a per income basis. The Deep South, which has money, was remarkably negligent in its contributions to President Nixon, despite his efforts to woo the region throughout his first administration.

Furthermore, the larger the contribution, the more likely it is to come from New York or California. We examined those contributors who made more than one contribution to the President and to McGovern. These multiple donors were either people who gave on different occasions or who split up their money on one occasion and gave it to different committees (a form of legal laundering easily uncovered in the computer era). The average contribution among these people was $3,400 before Labor Day and $6,400 after. This money was even more highly concentrated in the large states.

Despite the fact that the Heartland of America is supposed to be the bastion of Republican strength, it is emphatically not the bastion of Republican financial strength. New York still leads in this category, and the Northeast on a per capita basis does very well indeed. This is not, we repeat, simply a case of more money being there than elsewhere; on the basis of money available, more comes from the megastates.

There are many reasons for this. First, big money is usually *solicited* money and is much more easily raised on an organized basis where it can be gathered together. Second, and more important, large donations are usually *imitation* money, more easily raised where a lot of donors in one financial or business community are induced to get on a bandwagon. Third, money in financial centers is usually *habitual* money cultivated over the years by party fund-raisers who have not really combed the outback, so to speak, and whose lasting connections are concentrated in these centers.

Occupation

What kind of people contribute significant donations to the Republican party? Businessmen. Our occupational analysis of contributions to the presidential campaigns of 1972 (based on a random sample of contribu-

| | SPRING-SUMMER | | | | FALL | | | |
STATE	No. of Contr.	Total Dollars	Pct. Natl. Total	Mean Contribution	No. of Contr.	Total Dollars	Pct. Natl. Total	Mean Contribution
Alabama	77	41,668	.51	541.14	74	56,999	.66	770.26
Alaska	46	22,696	.28	493.39	21	15,800	.18	752.38
Arizona	62	41,891	.51	675.66	61	86,617	1.00	1,419.95
Arkansas	27	26,764	.33	991.26	66	29,565	.34	447.95
California	1,457	1,046,734	12.84	718.42	589	1,213,771	13.98	2,060.73
Colorado	91	139,334	1.71	1,531.14	35	39,973	.46	1,142.09
Connecticut	220	162,239	1.99	737.45	133	293,615	3.38	2,207.63
Delaware	54	88,273	1.08	1,634.69	42	82,532	.95	1,965.05
D.C.	278	236,086	2.90	849.23	123	162,834	1.88	1,323.85
Florida	385	465,599	5.71	1,209.35	229	260,852	3.00	1,139.09
Georgia	136	69,374	.85	510.10	117	119,189	1.37	1,018.71
Hawaii	51	51,850	.64	1,016.67	71	85,152	.98	1,199.32
Idaho	17	9,410	.12	553.54	9	6,750	.08	750.01
Illinois	533	776,020	9.52	1,455.95	249	457,821	5.27	1,838.64
Indiana	148	83,122	1.02	561.64	92	80,410	.93	874.02
Iowa	79	27,621	.34	349.63	31	97,124	1.12	3,133.03
Kansas	60	29,498	.36	491.63	96	86,692	1.00	903.04
Kentucky	46	31,561	.39	686.11	14	38,585	.44	2,756.07
Louisiana	83	59,874	.73	721.37	39	48,505	.56	1,243.72
Maine	45	24,593	.30	546.51	15	7,800	.09	520.00
Maryland	449	354,078	4.34	788.59	206	175,843	2.03	853.61
Massachusetts	162	115,216	1.41	711.21	169	154,334	1.78	913.22
Michigan	257	192,048	2.36	747.27	341	335,895	3.87	985.03
Minnesota	167	196,119	2.41	1,174.37	136	254,340	2.93	1,870.15

State							
Mississippi	37	10,079	.12	272.42	15	7,725	.09	515.01
Missouri	182	84,940	1.04	466.70	180	209,542	2.41	1,164.12
Montana	10	3,022	.04	302.21	9	18,050	.21	2,005.56
Nebraska	60	38,865	.48	647.75	36	29,000	.33	805.56
Nevada	35	20,860	.26	596.00	2	2,000	.02	1,000.00
New Hampshire	26	9,073	.11	348.97	6	6,627	.08	1,104.50
New Jersey	232	189,981	2.33	818.88	259	348,522	4.01	1,345.64
New Mexico	50	31,297	.38	625.94	40	35,600	.41	890.00
New York	864	1,204,613	14.78	1,394.23	789	1,569,449	18.08	1,989.16
North Carolina	121	45,164	.55	373.26	36	26,953	.31	748.69
North Dakota	9	5,895	.07	655.01	4	1,450	.02	362.50
Ohio	354	205,125	2.52	579.45	287	257,808	2.97	898.29
Oklahoma	163	80,462	.99	493.63	129	159,070	1.83	1,233.10
Oregon	181	90,776	1.11	501.52	35	47,013	.54	1,343.23
Pennsylvania	327	327,596	4.02	1,001.82	333	496,636	5.72	1,491.40
Rhode Island	33	30,005	.37	909.24	15	13,956	.16	930.40
South Carolina	83	47,406	.58	571.16	35	23,265	.27	664.71
South Dakota	18	6,235	.08	346.39	1	1,000	.01	1,000.00
Tennessee	112	132,604	1.63	1,183.96	172	189,936	2.19	1,104.28
Texas	358	599,820	7.36	1,675.47	209	459,349	5.29	2,197.84
Utah	27	16,247	.20	601.74	11	9,286	.11	844.18
Vermont	16	4,214	.05	263.37	6	2,950	.03	491.67
Virginia	256	263,159	3.23	1,027.96	126	146,000	1.68	1,158.73
Washington	145	70,531	.98	548.49	43	40,100	.46	932.56
West Virginia	31	8,518	.10	274.77	7	1,750	.02	250.00
Wisconsin	160	240,616	2.95	1,503.85	130	222,901	2.57	1,714.62
Wyoming	18	6,475	.08	359.72	8	31,462	.36	3,932.75

TABLE 8A.
Contribution Distribution by State to Nixon

	SPRING-SUMMER				FALL			
STATE	No. of Contr.	Total Dollars	Pct. Natl. Total	Mean Contribution	No. of Contr.	Total Dollars	Pct. Natl. Total	Mean Contribution
Alabama	15	5,250	.12	350	9	2,621	.08	291
Alaska	4	840	.02	210	6	712	.02	118
Arizona	33	12,220	.28	370	31	8,165	.26	263
Arkansas	6	2,482	.06	413	16	4,743	.15	413
California	1,039	725,202	16.34	697	432	687,727	22.11	1,591
Colorado	46	36,234	.82	787	53	20,802	.67	392
Connecticut	227	160,045	3.61	705	204	190,552	6.12	934
Delaware	7	12,789	.29	1,827	24	3,472	.11	144
D.C.	228	104,109	2.35	456	126	106,098	3.41	842
Florida	118	92,075	2.07	780	55	61,681	1.98	1,121
Georgia	17	6,019	.14	354	29	11,212	.36	386
Hawaii	8	4,000	.09	500	10	3,620	.12	362
Idaho	7	1,529	.03	218	3	543	.02	181
Illinois	202	285,700	6.44	1,414	367	216,529	6.96	590
Indiana	18	9,153	.21	508	31	55,896	1.80	1,803
Iowa	13	4,895	.11	376	17	4,000	.13	235
Kansas	17	20,148	.45	1,185	34	33,157	1.07	975
Kentucky	44	20,021	.45	455	15	7,597	.24	506
Louisiana	15	10,782	.24	718	20	7,187	.23	359
Maine	8	4,288	.10	536	11	3,537	.11	321
Maryland	156	159,478	3.59	1,022	113	77,114	2.48	682
Massachusetts	355	212,116	4.78	597	182	164,879	5.30	905
Michigan	245	78,845	1.78	321	65	38,734	1.25	595
Minnesota	74	20,817	.47	281	51	17,694	.57	346

State									
Mississippi	9	10,560	.24	1,173	7	5,890	.19	841
Missouri	61	19,881	.45	325	41	10,292	.33	251
Montana	5	610	.01	122	6	5,900	.19	983
Nebraska	28	15,670	.35	559	35	27,311	.88	780
Nevada	3	31,105	.70	10,368	6	1,973	.06	328
New Hampshire	42	21,302	.48	507	47	19,117	.61	406
New Jersey	248	216,293	4.87	872	126	88,324	2.84	700
New Mexico	31	24,235	.55	781	32	13,534	.44	422
New York	1,354	1,518,218	34.20	1,121	545	691,165	22.22	1,268
North Carolina	60	94,857	2.14	1,580	23	9,148	.29	397
North Dakota	12	1,806	.04	150	5	532	.02	106
Ohio	138	103,594	2.33	750	179	124,716	4.01	696
Oklahoma	21	6,619	.15	315	15	3,505	.11	233
Oregon	38	44,130	.99	1,161	30	31,013	1.00	1,033
Pennsylvania	205	81,371	1.83	396	92	44,751	1.44	486
Rhode Island	40	11,045	.25	276	18	10,795	.35	599
South Carolina	4	1,216	.03	304	4	801	.03	200
South Dakota	16	6,751	.15	421	21	4,194	.13	199
Tennessee	18	6,662	.15	370	10	2,832	.09	283
Texas	72	58,800	1.32	816	158	63,681	2.05	403
Utah	18	6,251	.14	347	14	89,125	2.86	6,366
Vermont	29	16,075	.36	554	19	13,964	.45	734
Virginia	55	33,461	.75	608	64	24,058	.77	375
Washington	63	20,823	.47	330	54	14,276	.46	264
West Virginia	7	4,200	.09	600	14	2,512	.08	179
Wisconsin	63	18,286	.41	290	127	48,925	1.57	385
Wyoming	1	100	.00	100	3	439	.01	146

TABLE 8B.
Contribution Distribution by State to McGovern

tors, as explained in Appendix 1) revealed some startling results. About 60 percent of those contributors who gave more than $100 to Richard Nixon during 1972 were businessmen, and they gave 70 percent of his money. Considering that these figures do not include the clandestine contributions of the Howard Hugheses of this world (which would push the dollar category much higher) these figures are astounding. (George McGovern, incidentally, who raised two-thirds as much money as Nixon did in this dollar range, received only 25 percent of it from businessmen, so it cannot be said that only businessmen have the resources to contribute to presidential campaigns; see Figure 7.)

Breaking the President's contributions down by *types* of businessmen, we found that over 23 percent of his grand total were owners, chairmen of the board, chief executive officers, and presidents of businesses and corporations (including small businesses as well). These contributors also gave the most money of any occupational category and made the largest per capita contribution. Middle- and lower-range business executives constituted another 19 to 20 percent of Nixon's contributors. The size of their contributions was also relatively large. Bankers, insurance men, brokers, and other financial people comprised another 10 percent of his contributors, while real estate developers, salesmen, builders, and miscellaneous businessmen made up another 7 percent.

Concurrent with these extraordinarily high figures for business are a set of extremely low figures for professionals. Lawyers, CPAs, and similar professionals constituted only 7 percent of Nixon's total contributors; doctors and other medical professionals, 5 percent; engineers about 2 percent; self-employed professionals about 1 percent; and academicians less than 1 percent. The numbers are so small that some of these actual percentages are not statistically significant, but the total professional category added up to about 15 percent of his contributors — and that figure is both statistically significant and very low. The size of contributions by professionals was also much lower than among businessmen. While this is not surprising, it is a further indication of the lack of prominence professionals enjoy in Republican party circles and the lack of support, relatively speaking, by professionals for the Nixon campaign. The average contribution in the business categories was over $1,000. The average contributions in the professional categories were approximately $530 for lawyers, $230 for doctors, $700 for engineers, $230 for academicians, and just over $100 for self-employed professionals. Retirees and housewives made up the bulk of Nixon's other contributors, although there were some farmers and ranchers in the totals.

McGovern, on the other hand, had a dramatically different contribution pattern. Fifteen percent of his contributors were owners and chief officers of businesses, a good performance for him. But only 8 percent were from the lower management levels in business, only 2 percent from the financial community, and less than 2 percent were connected with

Figure 7

Occupational Distribution of Contributors

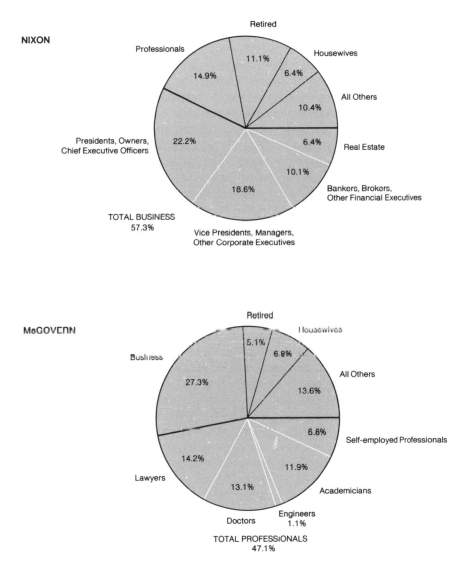

NIXON

Retired 11.1%
Professionals 14.9%
Housewives 6.4%
All Others 10.4%
Presidents, Owners, Chief Executive Officers 22.2%
Real Estate 6.4%
Bankers, Brokers, Other Financial Executives 10.1%
Vice Presidents, Managers, Other Corporate Executives 18.6%
TOTAL BUSINESS 57.3%

McGOVERN

Retired 5.1%
Housewives 6.8%
Business 27.3%
All Others 13.6%
Self-employed Professionals 6.8%
Lawyers 14.2%
Academicians 11.9%
Doctors 13.1%
Engineers 1.1%
TOTAL PROFESSIONALS 47.1%

real estate — altogether about a quarter of his contributors. On the other hand, professionals, who constituted only 15 percent of Nixon's total, made up almost 50 percent of McGovern's. Lawyers made up 14 percent; doctors, 13 percent; academicians, 12 percent; and self-employed professionals (including a sizable number of entertainers), 7 percent; engineers and clergymen each were 1 percent of his total. The size of the contributions is not dissimilar to the Nixon patterns — professionals are smaller than business — but in money received from all sources, professionals naturally hold a significantly higher equity. One point should be noted: McGovern was notoriously negligent in recording the occupation of his donors. This practice reduces somewhat the significance of his figures.

The rest of McGovern's money came principally from housewives, government employees, and retirees — and he received a significantly lower percentage in this last category than Nixon did. Hardly any workingmen or women are recorded as giving an individual contribution of $100 or more to either Nixon or McGovern. The labor unions, of course, raise large sums through small donations, but it is remarkable that the middle-class blue- and white-collar workers made almost no direct contributions to presidential candidates in 1972 that exceeded $100.

McGovern's success in attracting the money of the professional class stands in stark contrast to Nixon's poor performance among this group. In absolute numbers, substantially more professionals gave $100 or more to McGovern than contributed a like sum to Nixon. In fact, the professionals as a group contributed more money to the McGovern campaign this year than labor did, and in total political contributions for 1972 campaigns, there is evidence that the professionals made a bid to replace labor as the second largest source of political money (after business).

With the professionals becoming more influential in politics, the Republican party is neglecting this important source of revenue and support, the natural constituency of the moderate and progressive wing of the party. The rightward trend that the administration took no doubt dried up a lot of money in this area. If the party is not careful, the professionals will nurture their relationship with the Democratic party and supply it with the kind of resources that it has received only from labor in the past. Republicans may well ponder this fact: more lawyers made contributions to McGovern than to Nixon.

Professionals are the fastest-growing segment of our society and could constitute an important counterinfluence to business within the elite of the Republican party. There is no inherent reason why professionals could not be attracted to the party and there is no bar to their becoming influential within it. They are the wave of the future. As one prominent Republican lobbyist for a large midwestern concern observed, the new professionals, the experts, the engineers, and the "knowledge" sector of the society is where the national power may lie in a couple of decades.

Regional Breakdowns

The regional breakdowns of financial contributions are very interesting and present a portrait of Republican centers of influence across the country (see Figures 8 and 9.)

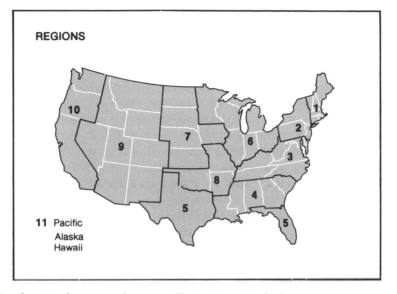

REGIONS

11 Pacific
Alaska
Hawaii

In the Northeast, and especially in New York, businessmen constitute an even higher percentage of President Nixon's contributors than they do nationally. The New York figures are not surprising. Owners and chief executives constitute 33 percent of his total; managers and lower executives, 13 percent, financial figures, 21 percent; and real estate men, about 6 percent. There is no other major category of contributor in New York. Its financial sector is understandably the highest in the country and the management level is *considerably below* the national average.

In California, by contrast, owners and chief executives make up less than 20 percent of the contributors; management, on the other hand, constitutes 20 percent; while finance is only 5 percent; and real estate is comfortably above the national average at 9 percent. California is the only large state where professionals make up 20 percent of Nixon's contributors, and a comfortable percentage of these are lawyers. (His native state seems to be the only place where lawyers give significant contributions to him in large numbers.) With respect to the size of contributions, California businessmen in all four categories give smaller ones than New York businessmen. In the management and real estate categories, these contributions are considerably smaller.

California's contributions to national campaigns are a relatively new phenomenon. Richard McAdoo, grandson of Woodrow Wilson, son of William G. McAdoo, and a Nixon campaign official, told us that California businessmen have become politically aware in the modern sense only recently, long after eastern and midwestern businessmen did. California has a tradition of small contributions and the pattern persisted in 1972. As Table 9 shows, Nixon's contributors in the $100 and $200 range exceeded his New York contributors in the same categories by 1,085 to

Figure 8
Regional Distribution of Contributions

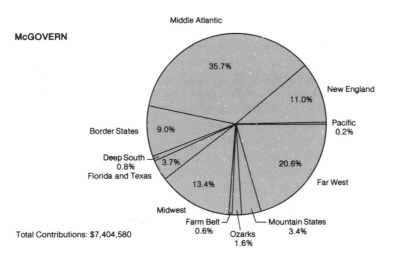

NIXON

Middle Atlantic 25.0%

Border States 12.0%

Deep South 2.9%

Florida and Texas 10.8%

New England 5.0%

Pacific 1.0%

14.8%

Far West

19.9%

Total Contributions: $16,551,631

Midwest

Mountain States 3.0%

Ozarks 1.9%

Farm Belt 3.6%

McGOVERN

Middle Atlantic 35.7%

New England 11.0%

Border States 9.0%

Pacific 0.2%

Deep South 0.8%
Florida and Texas
3.7%

20.6%

Far West

13.4%

Midwest

Farm Belt 0.6%

Ozarks 1.6%

Mountain States 3.4%

Total Contributions: $7,404,580

488. Aside from the large number of California small contributors, the contribution patterns before Labor Day are remarkably similar in the two states. In the fall, however, the organized fund-raising of more traditional New York money created a very different pattern. The large number of $1,000 contributors (who made up 21 percent of Nixon's New York fall money) contrasts dramatically with his California $1,000 contributors. Nixon lost ground in California during the campaign and this was re-

Figure 9
Regional Distribution of Contributors

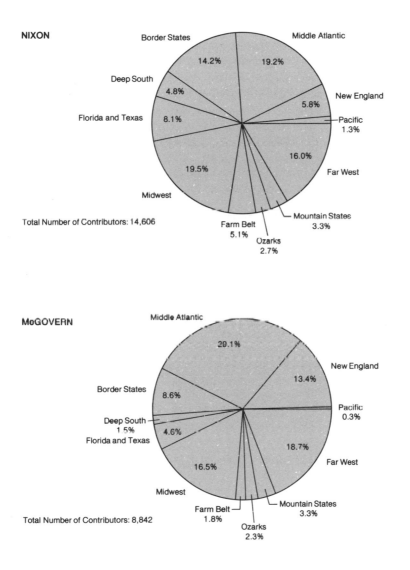

NIXON

Total Number of Contributors: 14,606

MoGOVERN

Total Number of Contributors: 8,842

flected in his contributions. The much more erratic pattern of California giving reflects the financial realities of a state whose fund-raising practices are much more wide open and free-wheeling than they are in the East.

In the Midwest the contribution pattern among businessmen is different than either in the East or in California. Financial money is more prevalent than in California, less prevalent than in the East. Ownership

DOLLAR CONTRIBUTION	CALIFORNIA		NEW YORK		ILLINOIS		MICHIGAN		OHIO	
	Summer	Fall	Summer	Fall	Summer	Fall	Summer	Fall	Summer	Fall
100–199	410	200	111	42	96	58	61	30	84	36
200–299	402	73	196	79	168	66	77	56	148	57
300–399	37	20	24	19	23	6	7	15	14	11
400–499	18	4	33	21	22	7	10	2	9	9
500–599	202	53	135	77	78	38	34	25	36	30
600–699	6	1	6	6	8	3	0	2	1	0
700–799	11	0	1	6	0	1	2	4	1	3
800–899	2	4	1	0	2	3	0	0	1	1
900–999	1	2	3	3	5	1	1	2	0	1
1,000–1,999	246	89	97	315	76	39	45	184	34	110
2,000–2,999	57	64	66	121	18	10	12	8	8	24
3,000–3,999	25	22	31	32	15	6	6	6	6	6
4,000–4,999	6	8	6	11	6	2	0	1	3	0
5,000–5,999	11	11	21	17	4	3	2	1	6	2
6,000–6,999	5	1	7	11	2	0	2	0	2	0
7,000–7,999	5	21	3	7	1	2	0	2	0	0
8,000–8,999	0	1	3	2	0	0	0	0	0	1
9,000–9,999	1	4	1	2	1	0	0	1	1	1
10,000 and over	13	14	19	20	8	6	1	2	0	1

DOLLAR CONTRIBUTION	ALABAMA		FLORIDA		TEXAS		ARIZONA	
	Summer	Fall	Summer	Fall	Summer	Fall	Summer	Fall
100–199	37	4	130	24	81	23	9	7
200–299	17	12	82	50	109	36	24	7
300–399	3	2	13	4	15	8	2	0
400–499	2	0	6	5	8	7	1	0
500–599	7	13	49	22	53	25	9	7
600–699	0	1	0	1	4	1	1	0
700–799	0	0	0	2	3	0	2	0
800–899	0	0	1	0	2	0	0	0
900–999	0	1	3	0	0	2	0	0
1,000–1,999	8	40	66	74	56	55	10	35
2,000–2,999	0	0	20	36	10	22	0	2
3,000–3,999	1	0	4	3	3	8	2	0
4,000–4,999	0	1	3	2	2	1	0	0
5,000–5,999	1	0	4	3	5	6	1	2
6,000–6,999	0	0	2	1	3	6	1	1
7,000–7,999	0	0	0	1	0	1	0	0
8,000–8,999	0	0	0	0	0	0	0	0
9,000–9,999	0	0	1	0	0	1	0	0
10,000 and over	1	0	5	2	4	8	0	2

TABLE 9.
Contributions to Nixon per Category

contributions are much more significant than in California, not as significant as in the East, and the middle-range management contributions are much higher than in either of the other regions. A lot of the financial money in the Midwest comes from Chicago, and the management money is quite evenly spread throughout. Midwestern industry and politics are such that these figures should not be surprising. Business is more industrial in the region and the patterns of giving reflect this condition. Interestingly, Ohio was not a major source of direct contributions to the Nixon campaign. The state party fund-raising efforts were very significant in 1972 and Ohio was one of the handful of states in the country where local fund-raising cut into White House fund-raising more than the other way around. Table 9 portrays the contribution patterns of Ohio, Illinois, and Michigan for the summer and fall of 1972.

In the South, most of the Republican money came from the New South or Outer South areas. The Deep South, as we have said, made a very poor effort. The number of business contributors in this area was somewhat lower proportionally than in the rest of the country, and the pattern within the business community was quite different. Owners were a clear first, with 25 percent of the donations; lesser executives and financial figures constituted 13 percent and 9 percent, respectively. Real estate money was stronger than in the country overall, and there were more retirees in the region than in the nation as a whole thanks to Florida — 25 percent of Nixon's contributors there were retired.

The average contribution in the South was far below the national average except in Florida, Texas, and Virginia, the most nonsouthern of the southern states. The contribution patterns in the area show that most of the disclosed contributions came in $100 and $200 amounts, with only a scattering of larger contributions. The region — except for the three largest contributing states — had very few disclosed contributions of $1,000 or more. Table 9 gives the contribution patterns for Alabama, Florida, and Texas.

Southern businessmen, while generally conservative by national standards, are generally very progressive by local standards. They are the agents of change throughout the region and they enjoy a kind of political and social influence that businessmen enjoy in almost no other region of the country. The new entrepreneur and manager in the South has the same status that businessmen had in the Midwest during the early part of the century. In this generally nonunionized region he is the center of affairs and potentially an influence of vast proportions. Southern businessmen traditionally were Democrats. Yet the growth of new industry in the South, the new currents in southern politics, and the increasing need for businessmen to acquire a national perspective have led many southern businessmen to look favorably on the Republican party. The southern textile industry has many Republican owners and managers, such as in the Piedmont region of North and South Carolina. Texas is a great exception to this rule. There the conservative business community remains Democratic — and runs the state. Federal money and new business executives moving into the area have created a more fluid situation, but the strength of the party organization and its national connections have made it more expedient for businessmen to remain in their traditional political pattern. A lot of money, however, can be raised in Texas for national Republicans, and the bargaining power that these Democrats exercise in the Republican party is great indeed.

The contribution patterns of the Plains and Mountain states are also unique. Owners of businesses, presidents, and bankers contribute the bulk of the business money. Middle management contributes very little. This region, with some exceptions, is a very dry one for fund-raisers. Per capita and per income, it is only slightly above the South in political contributions. The agribusiness industry is a very important source of political influence and executives of this sector are among the largest contributors to the Republican party. But money is not as important to local politics or as available to national fund-raising as elsewhere.

In Arizona, for instance, there is very little "big" money. Nixon received only two disclosed contributions of $10,000 or more during the campaign and only eleven of $2,000 or more. He received a modest number of $1,000 contributions (45) and not very much money from smaller donations. Arizona money itself is often California money coming in for investments, and the retirees, Arizona's fastest-growing population segment, often have their money held in trust for them in Chicago. There is very little union money in Arizona, hence there is little stimulus for business to make a large effort to raise contributions. There is no philanthropic class, although there are some philanthropists. There is also little new money from the first-generation wealthy. This is not to say that Arizona is incapable of raising money for its own politics or for a favorite son, for example. And on a per capita basis it did quite well by Richard Nixon. It is to say that the resources for sustained, organized, and large giving are not there — or anywhere else in this area.

We could present a much more detailed analysis of the structure of Republican finance, but for the purposes of our argument it is not necessary here. The important point is the concentration of financial influence: concentration in large donations, in a very few regions, and in one occupational category. This concentration does not reflect anything inherent in the nature of things political or financial, it simply reflects the fact that business feels that it has a stake in the future of the Republican party and its candidates. If professionals felt they had a similar stake their influence would grow, along with their money. This would be true for other groups as well.

The point is that whenever there is such a concentration, it is possible to bring about wide-scale changes in influence by broadening the base, so to speak. There is no inherent reason why more money couldn't be raised in Kansas or Arizona, aside from the traditions of those states. It would have to be raised in smaller amounts and with different techniques than those employed in Manhattan and it would probably be less efficient to use those techniques. Nevertheless, the geographic base of financial support could be broadened dramatically. On the whole, such an expansion would probably help the conservative wing of the party since the areas of least financial effort are politically conservative regions.

But the base of party finance could also be expanded vocationally. We have shown that the professionals are a group that might be tapped extensively for support that in turn would create a base for influence within the party. White-collar workers are another possibility. They would probably aid the moderate wing of the party if they were brought into an influential position.

The finance strategists of the party no doubt will examine the contribution patterns of 1972 and plan to tap the obviously vast regions of unexplored potential, both geographic and sociological. If they succeed, their efforts will serve to shift and change the nature of influence within the party. But for now, business is where the action is, and the business community is a complex proposition.

13

Business: The
Influence of Influence

While the contribution patterns of 1972 show that the business community plays a dominant role in Republican finance, these raw statistics
say very little about the nature of business influence. With so many
businessmen contributing so much money to the party, it seems quite fair
to call the Republicans the party of business, but just what does that
mean? Are these contributions the result of personal preference or of
professional interest? Are they thrust upon the party by a business
community seeking favors, or are they solicited by politicians from
reluctant contributors? How does money "buy" influence? Is it the size of
the contribution, the source of the contribution, or the relationship it
creates that is decisive? How does the nature of influence vary with
different kinds of elected officials? Does business differentiate between
influencing officials already elected and influencing the electoral process
itself? What role do businessmen play in internal party conflicts? What
kind of businessmen support one faction of the Republican party and
what kind underwrite other factions? How often do the general attitudes
and life styles of businessmen and women take precedence over their
narrow interests when they define their relationship to the party? Is there
a relationship between business and Republican politicians that tran-
scends the purely financial one?

Furthermore, how is the influence of business changing in the strategic
age? Will business, like labor, find that new methods of political practice
make it more difficult to exercise a traditional role in party affairs? Most
important, how do the changing political requirements of business affect
its political attitudes? How does its increased need for dealing with the

government at all levels change its attitude toward government, toward politics, and toward the Republican party?

The picture is very complicated. The business community is far from monolithic. The financial community, while more cohesive, is still fragmented in many ways. Factors of geography and corporate status play their roles. Certain industries behave in certain ways, others in other ways. Industry-government relationships vary from cozy to hostile. And there is always the question of personality.

There are three major categories of business contributions: old money, new money, and corporate money. Each has its own characteristics and its own special kind of influence.

Old Money

Old money — the contributions of the wealthy and established first families of the Republican party — is concentrated in the East and especially in New York City, although a significant amount comes from other parts of the country. Generally speaking, this group is motivated by idealistic impulses and the cause of better and more responsible government. They usually give modestly, but regularly, to the party and view the erratic but often large gifts of the new rich to be inappropriate. Proud of their ability to influence politics through their support of actors who emulate their ideals, they shy away from the more questionable quids pro quo that dominate so much of modern political financing. They are not at all indifferent to government policies, but they approach them more from the standpoint of governmental philosophy than from the standpoint of narrow interests.

Within the Republican party there is progressive old money and conservative old money. The former includes such men as Gardner Cowles, John Swift, Walter Thayer, John Hay Whitney, William Burden, the Houghtons, and of course the Rockefellers. These men were active in the Eisenhower and Dewey campaigns, but they supported Richard Nixon with much less enthusiasm because he seemed to them to be more a politician and less a statesman. Conservative old money supported Richard Nixon enthusiastically. It includes such people as Helen Clay Frick, Elmer Bobst, and Don Kendall. Although their positions on men and issues may differ, the progressive and conservative contributors of old money are quite similar in their patterns of contribution and in the nature of the influence they exercise.

First of all, they are consistent givers. Miss Frick, for example, a lady in her mid-eighties, an authentic legend in the history of American finance and the daughter of a partner of Andrew Carnegie, has been giving for years. According to Herbert Alexander, she gave $20,000 to the party in

1952, $26,300 in 1956, $18,570 in 1964, and $19,500 in 1968. In 1972 she and her brother together contributed more than $20,000. It is reported that President Nixon has called her on a number of occasions and asked her to send money to a number of campaign committees, and the checks went out immediately. She is not alone. Several other old families have underwritten Republican efforts for years.

Consistent giving, however, has its drawbacks. It soon comes to be taken for granted by the recipients, and in the case of old money, it is often regarded as donated with little effort. The favors returned for the favors bestowed are usually less significant than the favors returned to the unusual, first-time, or unexpected donations. Should a Mellon not contribute or contribute substantially less, it would be taken as a sign of extreme displeasure. But should a Mellon simply continue to contribute it would be regarded almost as an act of duty, not as an act of choice. To overcome this problem, old money can occasionally make exceptional contributions and then receive exceptional consideration in return, but this is not usual.

One reason that old money tends to be very stable is that it is largely managed money, and the managers are usually interested in a wide range of projects, politics being only one. The political contribution is often regarded by the manager as a means of keeping a hand in the game and of maintaining access to the political leadership in case some emergency arises, but it is generally not regarded as influence money. It is not the kind of money that would go into secret funds or would try to arrange shady deals in the Justice Department. Both liberal and conservative old money is usually given for larger principles of governmental stability and performance.

This is not to say that old money is indifferent to the actions of government. Quite the contrary. It represents most of the major business groups in the United States. For instance, the Mellons have major interests in oil (Gulf), mining (Koppers), aluminum (Alcoa), and insurance (General Insurance). The Pews own a controlling interest in Sun Oil; the du Ponts are in U.S. Rubber and Phillips Petroleum as well as in their own chemical business. The Rockefellers are in almost everything.

In other words, any governmental decision affecting a major industry is likely to affect one of America's most wealthy and powerful families. However, these families and especially their money managers have found that corporate lobbying techniques are a considerably more effective means of protecting their interests in the long run than are contributions by prominent stockholders to political campaigns. There are exceptions to this practice, but by and large old money is not given to protect the vast holdings of wealthy families or the specific interests of a given corporation. Old money is given much more in pursuit of a philosophy of government or from a sense of responsibility. These aims may not be unrelated

265

to basic interests, but the distinction is important. Not to understand it would be to misjudge seriously the nature of the contribution and the form of influence it buys.

Old money, however, has not always played such a passive role. In 1940 these establishmentarians assembled the forces that captured the national Republican party from its congressional, conservative, isolationist, and traditional wings. They were inspired to make a massive effort for two reasons. First, they wanted to combat the New Deal more effectively than the traditional party could. Roosevelt was perceived as a direct threat to their interests, and they had no confidence in the party leaders who had run the campaign of 1936. The second reason was Hitler. The old money interests of New York were strongly pro-British and they didn't want an isolationist Republican candidate to make a political issue out of aid to England. By nominating Wendell Willkie, a progressive, nontraditional candidate who took a pro-Allied stand, they attempted to solve both these problems.

Throughout the 1940s and the early 1950s opposition to the New Deal and commitment to an international role provided strong incentives for the eastern establishment to nominate progressive candidates (who might win) and confirmed internationalists (who would maintain America's world role). But with the triumph of Eisenhower and a growing consensus among the parties on both domestic and international policies, the direct interests of old money became less and less threatened by either party. With their interests no longer on the line, the eastern establishment became less directly concerned with the inter- and intraparty rivalries and began to relax its control over the party.

Concurrent with the decline of political necessity was a lessening of interest by Wall Street *as a community* in Republican politics and a simultaneous increase of scattered individual concerns that led to large but much less effective attempts to play a role in party affairs. The divisions between progressive and conservative old money became more pronounced. The efforts of the progressive establishmentarians in 1964 and 1968 were really commendable exercises in civics, whereas their efforts between 1940 and 1952 had been regarded as acts of semisurvival. In the first of these two periods Wall Street was able not only to raise money but to assemble talent and use influence in a coordinated fashion — which they did not do in subsequent years because the situation did not seem at all apocalyptic. Between 1940 and 1952, for example, New York used its financial, legal, commercial, and public relations communities extensively to nominate Willkie, Dewey, and Eisenhower. It used its many resources in a coordinated way, and put some of its brightest middle-level personnel into the fight.

In 1964 and 1968, however, Wall Street used money and some talent, but certainly not in a coordinated fashion. Lots of money was spent, and a number of enthusiastic people were enlisted, but other resources — in the legal and public relations professions — were not employed as they had been in the forties and the fifties. Had Wall Street acted with a major effort in a unified way, it would have nominated Nelson Rockefeller in 1968. The point is that Wall Street is increasingly fragmented and what is left of the eastern establishment cannot really act coherently under present conditions. To put together the kind of real influence that it exerted in the past would be a major task. Money alone is not sufficient, nor is talent. What is needed is a *reason* for men and women of strong potential influence to get involved politically. Without a direct threat to their other interests it is unlikely that they will. Of course, a major economic or constitutional catastrophe might supply the reason — but that is something else altogether.

The 1968 Rockefeller candidacy illustrates this fragmentation. Rockefeller was able to get the support of most of the liberal old money — the Whitneys, the Thayers, and the Mellons, to name a few. But Wall Street and the financial community did not give him unified support, and more important, it did not give him the kind of wider influence and enthusiastic backing that would have been necessary to win. The Rockefellers are certainly respected in New York, but they are not universally loved. The governor's independent attitudes and pro-labor rulings have alienated a lot of business support in the past. In the final analysis, all that Wall Street will do for Rockefeller is raise money — a major contribution to most candidates, but a less fundamental requirement in his case.

Furthermore, the kind of influence that Wall Street and the establishmentarians exercised in the past has not only decreased in potential because the Street cannot be sufficiently motivated to exercise it, it has decreased because the kind of influence they can exercise is becoming less and less relevant to the nomination of a President. Twenty years ago, Wall Street could exercise a lot of influence on the delegate selection process because vast numbers of delegates were selected in traditional ways through the influence of a small number of politicians who usually had close associations with the business community, which in turn was influenced to some extent by Wall Street. These connections with correspondent banks, regional law firms, and with influential businessmen around the country are still there, but they are less binding now than in the past. More important, the nature of the nominating process is changing so swiftly that these relationships would not be decisive even if they were stronger. With the nomination increasingly decided in primaries and packed caucuses, the kind of direct influence that used to be exercised is no longer possible. That influence depended on personal associations and professional connections much more than on money. Ironic though it may seem, the new politics, with its emphasis on hard cash, has undercut Wall Street tremendously. Influence is now exercised either by the ideologically committed (which Wall Street cannot control) or by the indirect means of contributing money to candidates in the hope that it can be used effectively by the new professionals. Wall Street can raise a lot of money for this purpose, but so can others. Money is of decreasing utility in politics after a certain plateau is reached and sources of support other than old money can easily be found to reach that plateau. As the basis of power shifted from connections to money, Wall Street lost its major source of influence. It now must compete on equal terms with new money and corporate money. And in this game it is more reluctant to use the less than genteel methods of the new strategists.

New Money

New money — the contributions of the first-generation wealthy and the first-generation political donor — is quickly replacing old money as the principal source of large contributions to the Republican party. Although there is new money in New York, it is usually associated with the Midwest and California. It is given from different motives than old money is and the nature of its influence is also quite different.

Unlike old money, new money is generally given with a specific quid pro quo in mind, but the variety of these quids is enormous and the motives for giving form a broad spectrum, as some examples from 1972 will illustrate.

Sympathetic Hearing. There are many examples of campaign donations given with the expectation of favorable government action. One such 1972 donation was made by Ray Kroc of McDonald's hamburger chain, who gave more than a quarter of a million dollars to the Nixon campaign. Kroc has been lobbying to have the minimum wage paid to young people lowered — a potential benefit of major proportion to his hamburger stands. Although no actual "deal" was made, it was expected that he would get a sympathetic hearing.

Ego Massaging. Another form of quid pro quo is the social and psychological boost given to a donor in return for a contribution. A colorful example is provided by John Rollins, a self-made millionaire from Delaware. He has been a large contributor to Richard Nixon and in return he gets invitations to White House functions and frantic calls from White House fund-raisers to perform "special jobs" for the President. One such "job" took place during the 1969 Cahill campaign for governor of New Jersey. During the final weeks a film was made of President Nixon endorsing Cahill. The campaign staff notified the White House that they wanted to show the tape, but they lacked the TV-time cost of $25,000. Within two and a half hours from the time the White House received the call, a helicopter landed in front of the governor's headquarters and out stepped a messenger, with the requisite amount of cash in a briefcase. Having one's ego massaged is a definite component of campaign giving, and the ultimate ego trip is being told by the White House that you are a friend in need.

Positive Mental Attitude. Although it has been suggested that Clement Stone would like to have been offered the ambassadorship to the Court of St. James, it is more likely that his reputed $2 million contribution to the President's reelection campaign was made because he likes Richard Nixon, supports his policies, and sees in him the kind of person who has successfully employed the "positive mental attitude" that Stone regards as the reason for his own success. Stone knew Nixon personally — he met him in connection with the Boys Club, which both were active in — and he has always admired Nixon's "guts." Stone is openly contemptuous of the management kind of businessman who in his view lacks nerve, and he is more than willing to support those politicians who exhibit it. A close associate of his suggested that "Clem gives to keep Nixon and to assure good government" — and he probably does. His quid is seeing a man with whom he identifies in the White House.

Dislike of McGovern. McGovern's economic policies, and the so-called radicalism associated with his early rhetoric, were exploited well by CREEP. One example of a convert was Norman Levine, a top sales executive with Aetna Insurance. A long-time liberal Democrat, Levine worked on many Democratic campaigns and was approached to run for Congress. But with the rise of student activism and the threat to "traditional American values," Levine found that what he had always considered liberal values were conservative. With the nomination of George McGovern, Levine went to work for Nixon. He contributed and formed a speakers bureau to assist the President's reelection campaign. As one of the new rich who have worked long and hard to accumulate a substantial fortune, Levine could not abide McGovern's candidacy. He said that he could not stand to see the system that allowed him to rise to his present successful position be threatened by an upsetting force.

Under the Table. This listing would be more pleasant but less complete if it failed to include some of the more specific quids pro quo that were arranged through federal agencies in return for campaign contributions. Although many of them involved corporations, others included deals with new money. The Vesco case is history. There were many more. As one seasoned Washington observer put it, "All these evils existed before, but Nixon extended them in quantum leaps. The impression was that the government was for sale."

Although new money is given for a variety of reasons, it has certain characteristics that tend to make it more influential than old money. First of all, new money is not managed money, but money directly under the control of its owner. The new rich are highly individualistic people, speculators by temperament, and ready to jump into such a risky business as backing a candidate. The money seems more theirs, less their family's, and hence they have less compunction about spending it. Few people will act as restraints on them because their success in accumulating the money seems to vindicate their overall judgment.

Second, the erratic nature of new money works to the advantage of the contributor. It cannot be taken for granted; it is unexpected money and therefore money with a higher bargaining position. Since it is not given as the result of a stylized pattern or from a sense of responsibility, expectations of results are higher and the donor works to realize these expectations.

Third, the erratic style of the new contributors enables them to keep up with the rapid inflation of the campaign dollar. Campaign contributions don't count for what they used to, and old money has not kept pace the way new money has. A striking example of the galloping inflation that has hit the political market is the decline and fall of the $1,000 contribution over the last few years. Nick Kotz traced this in the *Washington Post:*

> In 1967, a $1,000 contribution to President Johnson's campaign gave the contributor a membership in the "President's Club" and an invitation to several parties where he could meet the President and cabinet members. In 1969, a $1,000 contribution gave the donor membership in President Nixon's "RN Associates," and a party where a member might meet a cabinet officer at best. By 1971, a $1,000 contribution gave the donor a gold-plated "RN" pin and a form letter from the President.

Finally, new money is contributed by people who feel that they have more at stake in the immediate political process than the managers of old money. The newcomers on the financial scene are becoming interested in politics now more than ever before. The role of government is more pervasive, they are affected by it more, there is a heightened interest in politics across the board, and their ability to influence politics has been increased by the new reliance on contributions. This enthusiasm and the relationships between donor and recipient are the crucial variables. Old money is relaxed money; new money is vital and intense. It also happens to be more conservative. There are exceptions to this, of course, but businessmen who have made their own fortunes tend to support an individualistic and "boot-strap" approach to social questions.

These categories of old and new are stereotypes, of course. There are many contributors who fall somewhere in between, both in patterns and motives of contribution. But they do define the starting point of Republican finances, with old money committed slightly more to progressive and moderate candidates and new money overwhelmingly committed to the more conservative philosophy.

There is, however, a third major category of business influence: the whole range of corporate giving. On the surface it appears much more sophisticated than the polite practices of old money or the erratic patterns of new money. It is not the managed money of the old families or the unmanaged money of the new entrepreneur. It is the managed money of management. It is sometimes the best investment a corporation can make and it is a rapidly expanding facet of our politics.

Corporate Money

The most extensive, sophisticated, and organized form of influence in America is exercised by the corporate lobbyist, whose job is to establish a working relationship between the business and the political communities. In recent years the government has come to play an increasingly important role in the calculations of major corporations — especially established corporations — and the Washington representative of these firms has become a major figure in the modern economy. In many ways the nature of American capitalism is changing from the free enterprise system to the government-dominated franchise system of corporate dependence on governmental favors. With such changes in vast sectors of the economy, the relationship between corporations and politicians has become very close. Traditionally, most corporations just wished to be left alone. Today they wish to be given much governmental attention.

To acquire positive attention a vast system of corporate lobbying has been instituted. In many ways this system is a finely polished machine and it clearly wields tremendous influence. But what is the nature of its influence and what is its potential? How well is this instrument of persuasion adapted to partisan influence? What impact on Republican politics does it and might it exert?

To understand the precise nature of this influence — its potentials and its limits — it is necessary to examine its methods of contributions, the nature of influence the contributions bring, and the relationship of this influence to the power structure of the party.

METHODS OF CONTRIBUTION

Most corporate money is given directly by officers of corporations to the campaign funds of a candidate. It is usually quite clear to the recipient that this money is corporation money, not personal money, and this practice has become an eminently acceptable one in the mores of politics (despite legal restrictions on direct use of corporation funds for campaign donations). Such contributions are seldom spontaneous, however. First, there is the pressure exerted by companies on their high-level executives to give to a certain candidate because it is corporate policy to do so. Salaries often have a built-in increment for this purpose and team spirit, corporate interest, and, most important, reputation with higher-ups are sufficient to extract a given tithe.

Second, pressure is exerted by other businessmen or by the fund-raisers of politicians through many means. One observer told us, "You can raise lots of money by mail from most people, but that is not the way to get money from businessmen. You gather them together." And that is precisely the best technique. Bring fifteen wealthy businessmen together who know each other only by reputation. Have one give a strong presentation for the candidate in question and have another exclaim afterward that the speaker "made a hell of a lot of sense" and that he will put up $10,000. If you can arrange for two people to do so, even better. The rest of the men in the room are almost obligated to contribute at least $10,000 or suffer a loss of reputation. The sense that "everyone else" is doing it is a very strong incentive in business and can be used even if people are not physically present.

Aggressive fund-raising is the starting point of modern politics. An excellent example of sophisticated fund-raising is the 1972 Percy campaign in Chicago. Using the vehicle of fund-raising dinners and direct solicitations, the Percy campaign was able not only to raise adequate funds but to cut seriously into CREEP's fund-raising efforts in Chicago — one of the few places in the country where that happened. It would not be true to say that Percy shut Nixon out of Chicago money, but Illinois did not produce nearly what it should have for the President during the height of Percy's efforts. What Percy did was to have several leaders of the business and financial community aggressively solicit money from among their fellows and make the kind of contributions they never would have made without aggressive solicitation. More and more it is the politician, not the businessman, who is the initiator of the contact. The "influence" of business over the politician is increasingly sought by the politician himself. This has profound implications for the nature of that influence.

In recent years two new methods of indirect corporate giving have become increasingly important: "Good Government" funds and BIPAC, business's answer to COPE.

"GOOD GOVERNMENT" FUNDS

Many companies have started funds to channel contributions from employees to political candidates. More often than not they are designed to encourage lower-level employees to make small contributions, but they are occasionally used to convey sizable amounts from executives.

Ford Effective Citizenship Program. Ford began bipartisan fund-raising campaigns among its employees in 1956 and the program became annual in 1960. Sets of double envelopes and contribution cards are distributed down the chain of command, with each executive contacting the management employee reporting to him. The employee places his check and contribution card with name, address, and phone number in the inner envelope and seals it. He checks the party for which the contribution is intended on the outside and places it inside the plain outer envelope, which is returned to his immediate supervisor. It then goes through superiors to a central collection point, where the outer envelope is opened and the inner one sent to the designated party.

General Electric Company "Dollars for Citizenship." GE programs differ across the nation, but are conducted biennially using several techniques. Most important is an in-plant solicitation, where the employee is provided with a contribution card that he completes privately and returns to the solicitor in a sealed envelope. Unopened envelopes are returned to representatives of designated local banks that make the distribution to the candidate or the party of the employee's choice.

The second method is the same as the first, except that employees mail the contribution directly to the bank. The third method involves a direct mail to the campaign.

GE allows political promotions such as in-plant rallies, candidate visits, and candidate literature in company publications. Candidates are also allowed to stuff vending machines with political messages that drop out with the candy.

Hughes Aircraft Active Citizenship Campaign. Hughes Aircraft began a program in 1964 that was oriented toward developing employee interest and participation in four areas: voter registration, information on issues and candidates, fund-raising, and voting. Employees can contribute voluntarily either by payroll deduction or by check and money order. Hughes promises absolute secrecy.

The company asserts that since the program started more than 17,000 employees have been registered to vote in-plant, that more than 300 candidates have had plant site rallies, that more than $421,000 has been donated by nearly 30,000 workers to parties and candidates, and that more than 95 percent of eligible employee voters have turned out.

There are many more examples and variations of these patterns of giving. Eastman Chemical, a subsidiary of Eastman Kodak Company, uses a payroll deduction plan for employees that is distributed by two company executives and a lawyer. U. S. Steel conducts companywide nonpartisan solicitations of its executives. Chrysler Corporation collected money in 1972 by appealing to 3,000 executives of the company to send their contributions in before the April 7 filing deadline. (Lynn Townsend, chairman of the board of Chrysler, was a regional chairman of the Business and Industry Committee to Re-elect the President.)

This kind of organized giving is not yet a major influence in shaping the political structure of the country. This role still remains with the individual giver, who operates on a personal basis with the candidate. In

1972 business groups dispensed only a half million dollars, the bulk of which went to congressional races. Compared to total giving that year, this effort was minuscule.

But these committees do have an effect and they are useful in extending the practice of campaign giving. By channeling funds to certain key races, the committees can achieve an impact beyond their relatively modest means. The new campaign disclosure law requires the committees to open their books, but individuals who donate to the committees are not required to report, at least not explicitly, and these groups may be used to disguise contributions.

Most important, these funds can be used by companies as part of a policy of bipartisan contributions so that they can hedge against every eventuality. No matter who wins, the chances are that some of the corporation's employees made a contribution to him. The bipartisan nature of corporate giving is an increasingly important dimension of its political influence.

BIPAC

The Business and Political Action Committee has been in existence for ten years. It was started by its present executive director, Robert Humphreys, "to create a better balance in Congress." And to maintain a "voice for business" on Capitol Hill.

Because business covers such a broad spectrum of interests, BIPAC feels it does not represent any special interest. It is bipartisan, but because more businessmen belong to the Republican party, the majority of its membership outside the South is Republican.

BIPAC is active in both primaries and general elections, moving in to support an aspirant only when there is a clear difference between candidates in terms of their support for business generally. Funds are sent to BIPAC in the form of dues and are placed in a special account administered by a six-member committee of three Republicans and three Democrats. There are sixty board members throughout the country who monitor races and provide feedback on the political climate in each state.

BIPAC publishes a quarterly newsletter and a bimonthly digest of political trends and developments. It does not lobby, according to Humphreys; its only interests are to promote business influence in government and to provide political education in the business sector; "there used to be a strong resentment of politics by business, but we have helped a lot to close this information gap."

In addition to these direct and indirect methods of contributing money legally to campaigns, there are many other ingenious methods of "laundering" funds that eventually go to candidates. For example, there are:

274

- Skimming (where employees are paid on the assumption that a specified percent of their salaries will be turned over to a specified party).
- The payment of inflated fees to outside counsel, with the understanding that some of this will be forwarded to a campaign.
- Poker games between the candidate and the corporate executives, where the candidate is allowed to win.
- The use of illegible names on the contribution records.
- Inflated bonuses; expense accounts for trips not taken.
- Payment in kind, such as the use of typewriters, company cars, clipping services, and telephones (even if the candidate reimburses the corporation for telephone usage, he escapes having to pay the usual very heavy deposit required of many temporary political offices).
- Extended leaves of absence by company employees to work on a campaign.
- Block purchases of books written by the candidate (thus putting the book on the best-seller list and enabling the chairman of the board to ingratiate himself with those to whom he gives such a popular item).
- Staging a "happening," complete with professional entertainment, to coincide with a candidate's visit to the district.
- A sympathetic interview with the candidate in the company newspaper, which is free publicity and the equivalent of a campaign contribution.

One ingenious method was described to us by a lobbyist who characterized it as relatively common. The XYZ corporation, wanting to see that Representative Q gets reelected, commits itself to providing $1,000 for the campaign. It writes to ten of its officers, informing them of the commitment and telling them how many letters were sent out. To the addressee this message is completely clear. XYZ's political officer then telephones Representative Q, informing him that if he sends fund-raising literature to Messers Alpha, Beta, Gamma, etc. (the lucky ten), he will receive XYZ's commitment.

It is clear from these few examples that there are many ways in which a corporation can transfer resources to a political candidate. It is also clear that the financial requirements of the new politics have created ready-made devices for influence peddling. In traditional, "nonexpensive" politics it was somewhat easier to distinguish between a bribe and a gift since favors had to be bestowed more directly. The new practices, by establishing new receptacles, have blurred this distinction.

275

The Nature of Corporate Influence

Corporate giving is extensive, but how extensive is corporate influence? More important, how much influence do corporations exercise within the councils of the Republican party? Strange though it may seem, their influence is very spotty and far less than that exercised by labor in the traditional Democratic party. One reason is that business is much more disorganized than labor. Far more important is that the vast machines created by corporations for political activities are designed to influence the legislative and administrative processes much more than the political processes. Of course there are corporations that exercise a preponderant influence on party affairs in various localities (Republican politics in Idaho, for example, is dominated by a couple of major corporations); many corporate executives interest themselves in party affairs, and some major firms release their executives for political activity. But the major corporations' ability to influence the changing power positions within the party as a whole is very limited at present even though its future potential is vast.

Just what is the nature and focus of corporate influence? The organized and professional influence of a modern corporation is quite different than the individualistic efforts of either old or new money. It would be a serious and cynical oversimplification to assume that corporate political giving and political favoritism is handled on a strictly quid pro quo basis. Notwithstanding the spectacular excesses of 1972, most of which were forced on corporations by Republican fund-raisers, most sophisticated observers would agree that the little black bag stuffed with greenbacks belongs to another era. It has become massively counterproductive, as those in the executive branch who recently used it have found out. In its place are much more civilized forms of reciprocity.

One reason for the demise of the black bag is the context in which modern influence is peddled. With an ever-expanding political system and the increasing influence of youth, women, minority groups, and other special interests, the impact and influence of money has become less pronounced. No longer is the large contributor, usually a businessman with a favor to ask, necessarily the man with first access to a congressman's inner sanctum. The big donor is still an important part of the matrix that makes up the system, but as the system has expanded and the power structure has become more complex, neither the astute politician nor the wise businessman is willing to pocket or to be pocketed. The politician has too diverse a constituency to allow himself to be bought by any one group, and no group can afford to practice the kind of politics that will result in "owning" a congressman. It creates a bad image and it's becoming too expensive. Not that it isn't sometimes tried, but as more people become interested in the performance of their national leaders, it just isn't smart.

276

The key to good lobbying is access, a very subtle concept. Corporations want a hearing for their views — a favorable hearing optimally, a fair hearing when possible, but at least a hearing. Hearings themselves, however, often involve a series of subtle relationships between the man of influence and the person he is trying to influence. The merits of the case presented are not everything. The personal relationship between the two is often a crucial variable and a very important determinant of the outcome. Access to a hearing can be the product of many things, and a campaign contribution is one of the most frequent.

More often than not, the size of the contribution is not the most important factor in obtaining access. A contribution of $500 well placed might easily gain more access than a much larger contribution clumsily placed. Few congressmen or officials wish to appear to be taking a bribe, and a large donation awkwardly given begins to look like one. The ability to get a hearing with a crucial staff member is often all that is needed to make a case for a certain position, and small money can buy that opportunity, especially if it is small money from a big concern. As one seasoned lobbyist told our interviewer, it isn't who you are but what you represent. Of course, big money can buy access too. As another Washington lobbyist put it, referring to the ITT affair, "Hal Geneen was able to see the most powerful people in antitrust in a couple of days. Now *that* is access."

But it is usually not simply the money, it is the relationship that the money can facilitate. A personal relationship with a high official or a congressman is the most desirable commodity in this formal-informal world. Money, of course, can be used to create that relationship, but not blatantly. As one congressman on a key committee told us, "I'm sick and tired of lobbyists running around with $100 bills in their hands trying to strike up a personal relationship." The personal dimension is extremely important in any political configuration of "in" politics and contributions can be a means of "buying in."

The modest political contribution is similar to an insurance policy that the company may never have to use but that just might be valuable at some time. Sustained giving, even on a moderate scale, is part of a relationship that can be constantly reinforced by visits from the Washington representative, by lunches with a staff member, by the routine provision of information, or by a host of other methods through which this relationship grows and access is secured. Techniques are usually quite straightforward, but often different.

For instance, a freshman congressman was interviewed several days after he moved into his new Capitol Hill office. The formalities of orientation and swearing in were hardly over before the Washington representatives from several of the major industries in his district stopped by to introduce themselves, to invite him to lunch, and to explain their positions on upcoming decisions that he faced. During the inaugural reception, several businessmen from the district were observed in friendly discussion with him. (These businessmen and other contributors had received invitations from the congressman. The total campaign contributions amounted to about $114,000 collected from 2,000 contributors, with every contribution over $10 being reported.) The largest employer in his district had contributed $700, or $50 from each of fourteen executives of the company. He said he did not feel this company's contribution was out of line or he would have returned it. Clearly these businessmen were well on their way to obtaining access to the congressman and his key staffers. The fact that they had been invited is crucial. In the two-way street of campaign funding it can never be forgotten that the candidate is soliciting support as much as the contributor is soliciting influence.

While Congress is in session, the members generally expect and actually receive a variety of attention. Entertainment is a must, and plush wining and dining is by far the most popular type. Lately, the winning ways of the Washington Redskins have made football tickets an attractive alternative. Should things at the Capitol get cold, or the weather turn more dismal than usual, there is always the opportunity for the congressman to fly to Miami or some such spot to address a business convention with all expenses paid and a suitable honorarium provided.

A respected Washington lobbyist for one of the larger companies occasionally takes a different tack in his efforts. When possible, he projects coming national trends as they begin to develop and tries to become involved before the subject becomes a full-fledged issue. He brings the problem to the attention of those who might be affected so they can act on it. His efforts at "influence" include giving symposiums at which he attempts to create a favorable political climate to deal with these problems.

WHERE IS ACCESS DIRECTED?

The astute lobbyist will know the correct congressmen on both sides of the aisle. Business is very bipartisan when it comes to lobbying, and it has found that it can deal very well with a vast range of officials. This ability has led business to be less and less interested in supporting "its own" candidates. Interference at that level of the political process is more clumsy and less manageable. The implications for intraparty contests are therefore self-evident. The more business can deal with both sides, the less important it is who wins, and the more risky it is to support one candidate in a close race — the only kind of race where support makes any difference. Certainly some races are singled out, such as Senator Sparkman's 1972 contest in Alabama (had he lost, liberal William

278

Proxmire would have succeeded to his chairmanship of the Banking and Currency Committee). Such cases, however, are more the exception than the rule.

Congressmen are certainly not the only recipients of attention, and a close examination of current lobbying practices reveals subtle shifts in federal power these days. While many still ask who runs the Congress, it seems more appropriate to ask what does the Congress run. The answer is, increasingly less. Executive preemption in foreign affairs is extensive (and the interests of Big Business in foreign policy is by no means inconsiderable). Also, the growing amount of federal domestic economic regulation is clearly no longer within the province of either the Senate or the House. There is, of course, a touch of irony in all this since it is Congress who creates and appropriates for the various regulatory agencies. But it is the President who is able to establish the tenor of regulatory action by appointments and other means. That the regulators have an unbroken record in favor of the regulated is not even an open question for the serious student of administrative agencies.

More and more of the decisions, then, that have a vital impact on the nation's business community are being made less and less in Congress. While certain key legislators can still command interest and attention because of their committee status, the large majority are of no real consequence, and are often pursued more as a result of habit than of necessity.

How does one get access to *appointed* officials? There are all the obvious methods, but a new dimension to this game is the presidential campaign contribution. Whereas lobbyists a decade ago could focus largely on Congress, now they must look to the White House. The political war chests of the Executive are the means of doing so, and CREEP encouraged this tendency, to say the least.

One problem with this shift is that there is a difference between legislative lobbying and executive or administrative lobbying. The legislative official is one among many and the object of lobbying is usually a general posture or a long-run voting pattern. The executive has direct responsibilities for decisions and the object of lobbying with him is usually to influence a very specific decision or ruling. The specificity of the desire makes the nature of the transaction look much more like an immediate quid pro quo. Legislatures are *supposed* to be the recipients of influence — by voters, by factions, and by interest groups. Lobbying with legislators is certainly a legitimate part of the democratic process. But administrators are employed to carry out the will of the legislature. Influencing them is somehow a less legitimate exercise. The inability of legislatures to act in a decisive way, however, has made it necessary for the large corporation to take its influence elsewhere, and this has led to a dramatic increase in the possibilities for a conflict of interests.

279

The pro-business milieu that characterizes much government and most Republican politics at all levels in this country is not simply the result of a conscious effort by business interests, but it is the natural outgrowth of a fundamental American ideology that identifies national interests with corporate prosperity. Until recently, the thesis has gone unchallenged that business values are to be afforded deference over other interests, be they sociological, cultural, or ecological. Even labor, with its concern for employment, is increasingly protective of business. We no longer hear the phrase "the business of America is business," but corporate wealth is still granted preferential status.

Furthermore, Republican politicians and businessmen have always enjoyed a special relationship. They often come from the same educational and social background. They adopt the same life style. They are at ease with each other. They both have a great deal of interest in preserving the status quo. To Republicans, businessmen are one of their own. There is certainly nothing wrong with this, but it is often necessary to understand how important it is in obtaining access. After all, access in the final analysis is not just a hearing, it is a communication, and the most successful communications occur in a language of mutual sympathy. Furthermore, the career patterns of many individuals take them back and forth between the public and private sector. It would be naïve to think that their basic ideological perspective alternates accordingly.

LIMITS

Corporate lobbying, despite its extensiveness, is a very specialized form of influence. It is designed for specific purposes and it has created a series of relationships that are tailored to meet the requirements of its immediate objectives. It is not flexible, and the more it tries to extend the *nature* of its influence (rather than simply the *territory* of its influence), the less sophisticated it becomes. Not surprisingly, the requirements of business define the nature of its influence. Legislation, rulings, regulations, appointments, and interpretations affecting both the immediate conduct and the long-range development of the firm are of special importance. The nature of the political process and even the personnel involved are of secondary concern. The whole lobbying machine is designed to influence the decisions of people in key positions and much less to influence the process by which they get to key positions.

Major corporations have two principal instruments of influence, money and the network of contacts and personal relationships that their representatives have built up both in Washington and in the various states. Both of these are designed to influence people, not politics or its processes. As long as politics remains in the realm of the personal — in the cloakroom and the conference room — business can exercise a large amount of power because its instruments of influence are designed for that purpose. The more the political process is a public, open, and pluralistic enterprise, the more at a loss business is. In such a situation it cannot rely on the forms of direct influence that it is so adept at. It must rely instead on the indirect influence of contributing money to candidates, which in turn can be used to affect the political process. This is a less efficient form of influence, and a much less successful one.

There is also one major self-imposed limitation on the political influence of the corporation, a limitation dictated by the realities of modern business-government relationships. First of all, as every corporate executive knows, government touches business in so many ways — "with such mysterious motives and intentions," as one lobbyist put it — that businessmen have to be constantly on guard. Second, they have to deal with so many agencies and branches of government that there are many effective veto powers over large areas of corporate concern. As a result, a large business simply cannot afford to be too partisan and cannot interfere too extensively in any contest whose outcome is in doubt — if either contestant could seriously hurt that business. It is simply much *safer* either to stay out or to support both sides. (Supporting both sides, however, is an abdication, not an exercise, of influence in most cases.) Business, therefore, is likely to intervene in partisan contests or other difficult situations only rarely and then with a great deal of selectivity. Smaller businesses and individual businessmen, of course, can afford to depart from this pattern, but major corporations cannot.

The officers of major corporations are somewhat less under this constraint, but here another limitation intervenes. If executives want to become engaged in an effective political effort, they can do it in two ways, either by participation or by contribution. The former would be unusual. As one official of the Business and Industry Division of CREEP put it bluntly, "Businessmen don't want to participate. All they want to do is give some money and then go back to the country club and crab about how the government is running things." The latter is more effective — in situations where money is decisive.

The problem is that political activity by corporations has become a way of life in a situation where the government passes laws, purchases goods and services, issues licenses, dispenses subsidies and franchises, approves pay and price increases, protects and nurtures certain industries, supplies services essential to the conduct of business, and regulates public resources. Edwin Epstein described this setting as generating a "political imperative" for corporations whose existence may depend upon chance twists of governmental policy (in *Business and Society Review*). For virtually every business, the possession of governmental largesse (the permitted price increase, the large contract, the certificate of compliance, the license to operate) is a life-and-death matter. But because it is a life-and-death matter it is simply very risky to intervene incautiously in areas where control cannot be exercised very well and where outcomes are doubtful. Therefore corporations are very reluctant to intervene in intraparty disputes even at the highest level.

The Future of Business Influence

As the nature of American politics changes from the more "political" to the more "strategic" form of interaction, the old forms of influence become less relevant to modern practice. The establishment and old money relied upon their business, legal, and political connections to dominate the party nationally. The business community traditionally has exercised its influence in a personal medium, focusing on personal contacts and personal access to politicians and party officials. Also, corporations are best equipped to deal with politicians on the personal level.

Yet, as we have seen in Chapter 11, the power of the politician and the traditional party worker is on the wane. The new strategists seem to be more important than the old politicians. The highly cultivated ability to influence the politician, then, will become less relevant to national party control. For if these party officials and elected representatives become less influential in a presidential nominating process, then the ability to deal with them, however effective it might be in the immediate sense, will be less and less effective in the larger sense. Just as labor lost influence in the Democratic party when the nominating power shifted away from the politicians and party officials, so business will lose power in the Republican party as a similar shift occurs.

Business, like labor, can make adjustments. The new managers replacing the old politicians are very congenial to business practices, mores, and life styles — more so in many ways than the old politicians. Furthermore, as we have seen, money is the lifeblood of the new managers and business is the principal source of money in the Republican party. On the surface it might seem that the shifts in power discussed in Chapter 11 might increase, not decrease, the influence of business in the party. But this is not the case at all.

What the new strategists have done is to open the process up dramatically by placing the primary voter and the caucus attender at the center of the system. In many ways this is commendable, but what has happened is almost revolutionary. The managers have simply created a situation of great instability where it is almost impossible for anyone to exercise a predictable amount of influence over the nominating process. Money can be raised to subsidize given intraparty contests, but this is a much less effective means of influence than the old political relationships.

If business is to keep a hand in this newly created and fluid situation it must go public, so to speak, because all of its private influences are becoming increasingly irrelevant. But going politically public is the last thing it wants to do. It is little wonder that there is a tendency in business now more than ever to be bipartisan and to focus on the elected official, not the candidate.

If business did go public, it could work toward creating an acceptable method of campaign contributions and it could then contribute to its favorites in the hope that the new strategists and public relations experts would do the rest — and it might be successful. Alternatively it might find a candidate it wanted and organize its executives into a political machine to support such a presidential hopeful — again it might be successful. But each of these methods is risky; they expose the participants to retaliation should they lose. The incentives to mount a major effort on a national scale in support of a candidate would have to be very strong.

Throughout this chapter we have referred repeatedly to the dramatic increase in government-business contacts. The relationship between business and government is becoming increasingly important — and it is in a state of flux and change at the present moment. Should government interfere with business as little as possible? Should government serve primarily as the regulator of industry, curbing its excesses? Or should government and industry enjoy a symbiotic relationship, a condition of coziness and mutual support? Different industries and politicians have different answers to these questions, and the ensuing debate is extraordinarily important within the Republican party. Business's political interest, now as always, is primarily to define the relationship between itself and government. Yet today the business community is deeply divided on this question. Some businessmen want a much more intense and cultivated relationship, while others want to see the relationship reduced as much as possible.

This is not a trivial debate, for it reflects a much larger debate over the nature of government itself that is beginning to take place in America. With respect to business, it is a debate over what business expects from government. With respect to the wider audience, it is a debate over what all of us expect from government.

This debate also has an important impact on the nature of power within the Republican party, since it gives business the opportunity to be a meaningful participant in an ideological controversy. As we shall see presently, ideological power is an important counterbalance to organizational power, and business's loss of influence in the latter might be compensated for by the former.

To understand both the extent of this debate and its implications for business, we must examine the nature of Republican conservatism, since it is among the conservatives that this debate has become articulate and it is through the conservative movement that business might regain some of the power within the party that it is beginning to lose.

14

Conservatives:
The New Right
Challenge and the
"Secure Society"

"The only real Republicans are conservatives; the rest are Democrats disguised as Republicans." In the power configurations of the party this assertion is an extraordinary weapon. By making a claim to be the high priests of Republican orthodoxy, the conservatives have put the rest of the party on the defensive. They have subtly redefined the rules of the game and outflanked the centrists and moderates in the process.

On the surface this proposition is patently absurd — which is why its appeal is so interesting. For example, there is no reason why there should be any such thing as a "real" Republican, Democrat, or whatever in American politics. Such appellations are more appropriate for medieval theologians, Marxist metaphysicians, and Platonic idealists than for modern American politicians. Even if there were such a category, there is no reason why "realness" should be a product of doctrinal belief any more than service to the party or loyalty to its institutions and traditions. But even if doctrine is the determining factor of the realness of a Republican, why should the real Republican be the one that adheres to a set of doctrines that very few Republicans believed in a decade ago, that no Republican President has embraced extensively, that are diametrically opposed to the historical principles of the party, and that have been recently pirated from both wings of the Democratic party? Indeed, it is very interesting. Before we proceed to a discussion of these sublime essences, however, it is important to see how this condition came about.

Business and Reform

The Republican party has never been homogeneous — although it usually has been more homogeneous than the Democratic party. It has always had divisions, and some of these divisions have been doctrinal. Lincoln himself was tormented by party squabbles, and after his death the "radical" and "nonradical" wings of the party feuded over such policies as Reconstruction and the social role of business. The moderates won that particular contest by bringing the party into the orbit of the Gilded Age's expanding business community, thereby outflanking the doctrinaire radicals whose appeals were blunted by the weariness of a country tired of crusades. These pragmatists, however, did not have clear sailing for long since the relationship between party and business soon became so cozy that the issue of scandal was raised. The crusade against the South was replaced by the crusade against the "rascals," and the mugwump movement of the 1880s split the party once more, electing Grover Cleveland as a reform Democrat. However, with the administration of William McKinley a major synthesis was achieved. The party abandoned its crusades for social causes, and it cleaned house enough so that the charge of blatant corruption, so prevalent in earlier administrations, was finally removed.

Furthermore, McKinley solved some of the economic difficulties that had beset the country since the 1870s, and he earned for his party the reputation of prosperity. Those who charged him with "stand-patism" in many ways were paying him a compliment, for his administration brought stability after the turbulent economic swings of the last quarter of the nineteenth century. His election was the true "aligning" election of the period. Before him the elections were very close; after him (with the exception of the Wilson episode) they were very similar in outcome until 1932.

Yet the economic question persisted and itself became a crusade, succeeding the crusades against slavery and corruption. The populist movement, the silver movement, and the monopoly question became the crucial political problems of the period, replacing the "social questions" of the 1860s and 1870s. As the economic question became paramount, another division arose within the party: the Progressive vs. the "standpatter." After McKinley, the Roosevelt "trustbusters" seemed to symbolize the triumphs of the progressive wing. Yet this was a vast illusion. The pragmatists and the centrists with their business associations always have succeeded in controlling the party in the long run. The Progressives, like the mugwumps and "radicals" before them, represented the nonbusiness factors in the party — the clergy, the professionals, and the intellectuals — all of whom exercised authority within the party for a brief period of time (and provided healthy debate), but whose long-run power position in each case was undercut by a shift in sentiment. (People got sick of racial reform; a housecleaning removed the issue of corruption; Wilson's reforms extracted the teeth of the Progressives.) The business base of the party kept moving along — occasionally set back, but based on a much more lasting foundation — while the reformers rose and fell with the issues. Into the twenties this was the situation, and into the disasters of the thirties. Harding, Coolidge, Hoover — each in his very different way was the President of the business community. And many of the intellectuals and reformers gave up and joined the Democrats.

The Eisenhower-Taft Consensus

The 1940 coup of "Wall Street over Main Street," as it has often been styled, was different from previous reform movements since it was the triumph of one part of the business community over another. The Wall Street that asserted itself in the 1940s, however, was a very different community than the Wall Street of pre-Depression and pre-Wilsonian America. It was more mature, less aggressive, and more stable. Furthermore, maturity had brought with it a degree of enlightenment and social responsibility. It was a Wall Street willing to move to the left of Main Street in its policies, a community both shrewdly and sincerely committed to global responsibilities and enterprises. To some extent it provided replacements for the intellectuals who had left the party a generation earlier — its lawyers, its economists, and its media associates — hardly reformists, yet certainly more open-minded in many ways than the Main Street culture it defeated. These establishmentarians were not the descendants in any way of the earlier reform movements of the party, but they did for a while provide a focal point for those who wanted to move ahead. Eisenhower was a magnificent symbol of the Republican moderates: forward-looking, yet cautious; honest, yet shrewd; responsible, yet not stodgy or narrow-minded.

In many ways, however, it was Taft, not Eisenhower, who articulated and defined the traditional Republican philosophies — although Eisenhower embraced these philosophies far more extensively than many of his orthodox critics have acknowledged. Although extolled by Main Street, Taft's philosophy was very sophisticated and it relied as much on legal principles as on economic verities. It was based on a sense of limited, responsible, honest, and efficient constitutional government. A balanced budget, a capitalistic economy, a limited bureaucracy, a legal tradition, a separation of powers, a separation of the military from the political, a respect for the Constitution, a respect for the law, a respect for the rights of the opposition, and a larger sense of fair play were the basic domestic positions eloquently articulated by Taft, but carried out rather well by Eisenhower. To be sure, Eisenhower's economic policies were less ortho-

287

dox than Taft's and his background in Europe gave him a much broader international perspective than Taft ever had. Furthermore, the necessities of office led him to innovate to an extent that Taft never envisioned. But the two men were not as far apart on issues as many have suggested, and when it came to respect for the Constitution, the laws, and the spirit of representative democracy, these two men symbolized the finest impulses of the modern Republican party.

The Eisenhower-Taft brand of Republicanism, however, was not as vigorous on the state and local levels as it was successful on the national level. The New Deal still defined American politics in the 1950s and the Republicans were the local minority in many areas of the country. In 1958 their status was made painfully clear by defeats throughout the country. The Eisenhower magic did not descend to the local level, and at that level in so many regions of the country the traditional brand of Republicanism did not seem to have a winning appeal.

To overcome this problem, many Republican candidates in the 1960s became strategic politicians and began to imitate the Democratic party in those regions of the country where Republicans were not in the majority. The northern Republicans began to embrace the New Deal and became "liberals" while the southern Republicans began to embrace the principles of the southern Democrats and became "conservatives." In so doing, both departed from the orthodox Republicanism of the Taft-Eisenhower variety. (In areas where Republican orthodoxy could win, Republican orthodoxy persisted.) This aping of the Democrats had one very significant result: it bequeathed to the *Republican party* the divisions of the Democratic party, and destroyed the old unity of the party that had existed throughout the Eisenhower period. The Democrats had been described by John Hay at the turn of the century as a "fortuitous concurrence of unrelated prejudices." More charitably, they were a coalition. The Republicans, first by copying the Democrats in South and North, later by pirating groups of them away, inherited this fortuitous situation. By the end of the 1960s, then, the party had three major elements: the conservatives, the traditionalists, and the liberals, or "moderates." Clear distinctions are usually impossible in politics and each of these groups merged to some extent into the others, but the overall picture is a useful one. The traditionalists have evolved into what may be called the Old Right. The conservatives, largely from the South, are staking out a claim to be called the New Right, and the moderates, largely centrists, are to some degree associated with doctrines of the Old Left, but principally embrace an updated version of the Eisenhower-Taft consensus.

The Old Right and the New Right

To some, the conservatives who came to party power in the 1960s appear to be a monolithic force, while to others they appear to be an aggregation of fragmented, often quarreling, factions. Both images have some validity, since the name "conservative" still has some ideological appeal and the minority status of the movement tends to unite its many factions against the liberal opposition. We shall detail the various factions within the movement on the grounds of their *political* relevance, but first we must make one fundamental conceptual distinction between the Old Right and the New Right. At present this division remains blurred, but it will grow increasingly sharp in the near future since their fundamental assumptions are so antagonistic to each other that the conservative movement will soon polarize along these conceptual lines.

The Old Right is the most authentic representative of the Enlightenment's "liberal tradition" founded by the American revolutionaries of the eighteenth century. Embracing both the Jeffersonian and Hamiltonian traditions in American politics, the Old Right believes in individual freedoms, equality of opportunity, limited government, constitutionalism, property rights, capitalism, and many other principles articulated by John Locke, reiterated by Thomas Jefferson, and in this century given historical interpretation and content by the works of Louis Hartz.

The economic doctrines of the Old Right start with the principles of property rights and free markets. Laissez-faire capitalism, embodied in the entrepreneurial firm, with competition, risk, profit, and efficiency as the criteria for survival, constitutes the classic image of economic orthodoxy. The role of government should be limited (in the economic sphere) to the minimum activity necessary to make the system operate. Balanced budgets, monetary (not fiscal) policies to compensate for cyclical swings, and perhaps some antitrust activity to preserve a free market are generally all that is required aside from a functioning legal structure. Although the Old Right has never totally adhered to a doctrine of free trade internationally, it is emphatically not protectionist at home and has strong theoretical affinities for international trade expansion. Unions have always been suspect. The right-to-work law is not universally embraced by the Old Right, but the idea of a corporation as a contractual, not a social, aggregation is deeply felt. If unions are to exist, collective bargaining and the adversary process are the logical requirements of this open image of society.

The political doctrines of the Old Right are related to the economic doctrines. Karl Marx and Charles Beard notwithstanding, there is much evidence that the political doctrines preceded the economic. Constitutionalism, the supremacy of law, strict construction (in the old sense), a government of limited powers, a Bill of Rights, individual freedom of choice, individual responsibility under the law, political equality, and above all, nonpaternalism are the basic propositions of political orthodoxy. A sense of equality makes it very difficult for members of the Old Right to be racists, although their governmental and proprietary philosophies make it equally difficult for them to accept governmental action on behalf of minorities.

The Old Right looks at America as the promise (fast disappearing. perhaps) of a set of universal principles of democracy and republicanism whose validity sanctions America's role in the world. Patriotism is the product not of nationalistic but of universal impulses. The military is as separate from the political as the religious is, and the standing army or church militant is regarded as a basic threat to the political and intellectual freedom of the society. Communism has always been perceived as a major threat to the nation, but crusading international ventures have been usually greeted with suspicion. "Live and let live" is a fundamental principle of the Old Rightists, and to them the isolationism of the American Heartland has often made a lot of sense.

Above all, the Old Right is committed to freedom as the unifying principle of its philosophy—personal, political, intellectual, and economic freedom. These beliefs form a coherent and consistent approach to politics. Formerly they were called "liberal" views, but because they are an authentic inheritance from our past, those who adhere to them may reasonably call themselves conservatives because they wish to conserve and preserve our traditional values.

The New Right, however, is something very different although it also has an authentic claim to the conservative label. Its unifying principle is not freedom but security — personal, proprietary, economic, political, and national security. Although many of its doctrines have been passionately embraced by Nixon's New Majoritarians, they are largely inherited from both wings of the Democratic party, which is why they can be used to some extent to entice the Southerner and the northern working-class Catholic away from their traditional political habitat. In many ways John Connally is the symbol both of this doctrine and of its questionable parentage.

The economic doctrines of the New Right are very important. First of all, its communicants do not believe in laissez-faire capitalism. To them the free market, the balanced budget, and the unmanaged economy are rapidly becoming "obsolete" doctrines. The entrepreneurial firm with risks, competitition, and reliance on efficiency is now being replaced with the modern equivalent of a guild, the corporation whose success depends not upon economic proficiency but on political privilege, the firm whose survival is dictated not by the harsh laws of the market but by the soft coziness of political accommodation.

Subtle shifts in the nature of American capitalism are having profound impacts on the nature of political doctrine. As we saw in Chapter 13, the government has become the most important single factor in many firms' calculations, and the relationship between government and business over the years has moved from benign indifference to regulatory hostility to close accommodation. The result is increasingly business-by-franchise in vast sectors of the economy. Political bargaining and manipulation, not market considerations, are increasingly dictating the nature, the policies, and the survival of modern corporations and conglomerates. The businessman who formerly wished to keep the government at arm's length now finds himself in a passionate embrace. This new morality is depriving the businessman of his independence, his freedom, and above all his ability to innovate. In return, however, he is acquiring security, protection against the implications of his own mistakes — the very opposite arrangement to nonmonopoly capitalism, which, despite all its abuses, at least provided rewards for innovation and efficiency.

The New Right is beginning to formulate a new kind of socialism, a socialism for the middle and upper classes based not on the assertions of rights but on the exercise of privilege. This doctrine of governmental redistribution is creating a vast network of subsidized organizations, both public and private, whose lifeblood comes not from the marketplace but from the federal treasury, which in turn must tax the more independent sectors to sustain this ever-increasing flow of money. As with so many things governmental, these subsidized, franchised, and protected corporations and institutions are becoming less and less efficient and are serving as a drag upon the entire productivity of the country.

This new socialism — corporate socialism or corporatism — is slowly becoming a very powerful doctrine in this society, which is why the New Right is such an important and growing force. (Ideologies go beyond the stage of short-run fads only when there are powerful interests to sustain them.)

But the subsidized corporation is not the only economic interest that is a potential beneficiary of the New Right philosophy. Labor is also a force in search of security. The protected job, the return to tariffs and quotas, the governmental subsidy of inefficient corporations and threatened industries, the governmental guarantee against business failure, the management of the economy with its never-ending phases, the substitution of governmental regulation for collective bargaining procedures — in short, the replacement of a capitalistic economy by a corporatist economy, if well handled, also benefits labor and tends to mitigate the differences between it and business. Big Labor and Big Business are becoming increasingly cozy in modern America. Big Government might well join in. Protection and paternalism go very well together and the New Right's concern for the security of jobs, the security of profits, and the security of status stands in stark contrast to the Old Right's concern for economic freedom and personal mobility.

Since this socialism-corporatism-paternalism is diametrically opposed to the economic doctrines of the Old Right, it is not surprising that there are many other differences between these two groups who call themselves conservatives. First, and very important, the New Right rejects the insistence of the Old Right that the military be kept as separate as possible from politics and the political process. The famous military-industrial complex is a symbol of New Right power, and the repeated justification of Big Government in terms of national security is one of its principal arguments. The subsidized nature of the major weapons systems industry fits very well into this pattern of inefficient coziness, and the Lockheed loan is a great symbol of the new feudal order. Many legislators voted for and against this loan for many reasons, but conservatives split down the middle. The Old Right voted against the loan, the New Right for it. Those who voted for it justified their votes in the terminology of New Right philosophy: guaranteed employment, national security, corporate subsidies, and, in effect, the franchise system. Those who voted against it did so in the name of Old Right economic orthodoxy.

Second, these cozy relationships between business and government have led to a much less sensitive notion of what constitutes a conflict of interest. Since intense lobbying and reciprocal pressures and accommodations by government and business are considered normal by the practitioners of this philosophy, the traditional ethical practices of the Old Right no longer seem applicable. If government and business exist for the security of each other, then what is wrong with mutual back-scratching? The Watergate scandal and its attendant funding disclosures may have horrified the Old Right, but the New Right, interested in security and mutuality, seemed more disturbed by the reaction to Watergate and the counterproductivity of the caper than by the caper itself.

Third, the paternalism of the New Right, like the paternalism of the Old Left, believes in a greater governmental role in social questions. The New Right consistently embraces the efforts of federal agencies to limit the application of the Bill of Rights to individuals in the name of a new social security, that is, security for the society. Furthermore, the corporatism and the feudalism of the New Right, these great justifications of status and the security of status, make it much easier for their adherents to acquiesce in racist policies that the egalitarians of the Old Right could never tolerate.

Fourth, there is a regional distinction of importance between the Old and the New Right. The New Right started in the South — in the *Democratic* party — and spread to the Republican party. The paternalism, feudalism, and even socialism present in this philosophy have a distinct southern flavor to them although their appeal now goes much further. Texas is the home of this philosophy. Democrats Lyndon Johnson and John Connally have collectively done more to spread it about than anyone. This is the region that has become intensely dependent upon federal economic subsidies for its oil, construction, and defense industries. Its textile industry — which *is* efficient — is still dependent on tariffs and quotas. It is a very different economic climate than the Midwest, for example, where industry is largely unsubsidized and the doctrines of the Old Right still prevail among business leaders.

But the appeals of the New Right extend far beyond the South. Its doctrines provide the logical philosophy to unify the New Majority coalition of Southerner, northern working-class Catholic, and Republican businessman, thereby bringing into the "Republican" party the two largest elements of Franklin Roosevelt's *Democratic* coalition. We have seen how the doctrine of economic security might unify business and labor; it is also easy to demonstrate how the doctrine of status security can unify the southern Anglo-Saxon conservative Protestant and the northern ethnic conservative Catholic.

Both these groups feel threatened and both are insecure. They feel threatened most of all by blacks, but also by hippies, by youth, by intellectuals and liberals, by almost any force that might change their social status. Drugs, the new morality, abortions, the fragmentation of the family, the decline of religion, and the weakening of the institutional church are undercutting the social and philosophical points of reference of both groups. It is little wonder that each embraces the doctrines of Americanism to regain the security that liberal pluralism seems to be destroying. Instead of meeting these legitimate problems head on, instead of competing, as it were, both these groups are seeking a refuge in the secure protection of a conservative doctrine that seems to justify their status in the corporate image of society.

Finally, the international politics of the New Right provides a number of departures from the traditions of the Old Right. The New Right is quite willing to engage in foreign adventures. Oil is one of its principal fiefdoms, although not all oil is controlled by it. In such adventurous industries political and economic influence go hand-in-glove. John Connally's trips to the Middle East, ITT's escapades, and Robert Vesco's enterprises are only some publicized examples of the international dealings of the New Right and the coziness of governmental-corporate relationships. The rapid rise of foreign investment by many industries has lent support to its principles. The New Right is internationalist, the Old Right very hesitant in international affairs.

Furthermore, unlike the Old Right, whose patriotism was tied to a defense of our individual rights and freedoms, the New Right focuses on our collective privilege, that is, our privilege as a nation and as a culture. It is not our freedom as Americans but our power as America that is important. The New Right is asserting a nationalistic, not a universal, principle, and this is a total repudiation of two hundred years of our history. Ever since the American Revolution our foreign policy has been largely tied to the assertion and defense of a set of consistent universal principles such as freedom of the seas, making the world safe for democracy, and preventing aggression. Even our isolationism traditionally was justified in terms of preserving our universal principles from the corruptions of foreign influences. But the New Right disagrees. To them the American Revolution is a symbol of our national independence from Great Britain, not a symbol of our individual independence from tyrannical government. To them our international history has been a catalogue of episodes that increased our power, not a series of encounters that preserved our principles. To them our mission is ourselves.

The Old Right disagrees in principle with these New Right philosophies, but the symbolic power of the word "patriotism" is as strong as the symbolic power of the word "conservatism." National security superficially unites the Old and the New Rights, but it cannot for long because it will soon be clear to the Old that the New Right is undercutting, not augmenting, our security.

The Old Right has always argued that the welfarism and social security of the New Deal were dangerous to America because they sapped the strength of the Republic and created a softer society. To some extent this has been true. Welfarism and the decline of the work ethic have taken a toll, but it can be argued that in human terms the benefits have been worth the cost since abject poverty and total human misery have been alleviated to some extent. The relief of the lower classes of society may have created some "softness," but that damage is minuscule compared to what would happen if the most productive and creative parts of the society were allowed to "go soft," so to speak. The Old Right may well argue that if the top two-thirds of America is allowed to participate in an increasingly welfarist ethos, the damage to the society will be fantastic. The paternalism of the New Right will soften – to use the old phrase – the leadership, the potential innovators, the managers, and other key figures in the society.

The Old Right will soon perceive that nothing will hurt this country more than embracing the doctrines of the New Right. Despite what so many people say, the true power of a country lies in the strength of its society, not in the number of weapons it has at any given moment. Is that country a going concern? Is it efficient and economical? Is it united? Can it deal with change? Can it produce? Can it innovate? How fast is it growing? Are its leaders responsible and patriotic? Does it have a resilient moral fiber at its core that gives its citizens the courage and will to defend it? Or is it a country living on its reputation and its past, a stumbling and faltering giant grasping at every opportunity to assert its position and protect its failing industries. Is it inefficient and stagnating, internally divided, having to legislate its patriotism and buy off its dissidents? Is it corrupt, are its intellectuals disillusioned and its moral fibers weakened? The Old Right may well argue that if the policies of the New Right are adopted we shall be in even more serious trouble than we are now. The new corporatism provides the greatest social and economic rewards to status and size, not to efficiency and creativity. It is based on philosophies that will seriously disillusion our brightest citizens and transfer power to the blindly loyal, who are not necessarily our shrewdest people. The insistence on security rather than freedom will ironically reduce security very quickly as our industrial plant becomes less and less competitive, as our unions cease putting the kind of pressure on management that leads to increased efficiencies, as our inventors and innovators are bought off by those with government-backed vested interests in the status quo, as we safely drift off to sleep behind the protectionist tariffs that prevent foreign competition from making our industry more competitive.

This is not to say that the practitioners of the New Right lack personal drive. It is to say that the net effect of their efforts is to lower the efficiency of the situation. The focus of their energies is not on maintaining a competitive situation and an autonomously going concern. Rather, it is on making things easy for themselves, and this is what disturbs the Old Right.

The Old Right may also perceive that we will lose our sense of purpose and vision both at home and abroad. The goal of security is not the source of inspiration that the goals of freedom and change are. Those who choose the soft route, the lazy alternative, and the secure situation not only are forgotten, but never really contribute to the strength, the growth, or indeed the genuine security of a nation. America has always been the one country that was never afraid of the future — and the Old Right will argue that it will be a sad day when we become so.

How much longer can the meaningless word "conservative" paper over these fundamental distinctions between the image of a free society and of a "secure" society, as the New Right rhetoricians no doubt will style it? How long will it be before the Old Right recognizes that protection, privilege, and paternalism are not consistent with its true doctrines? The Old Right may at times lack compassion, but it does not lack energy, innovation, and the enterprise born of freedom and competition. It can never ally itself for long with those philosophies that will guarantee that we become that famous second-rate power before many more decades elapse.

But the New Right has its strengths. Powerful interests are moving to support it as the nature of the American economy changes from a largely capitalistic order to a corporatist one. The Old Right was largely relevant for a laissez-faire capitalistic society and a society of individuals exercising individual responsibility. Its doctrines of personal freedom and property rights were supported by powerful economic interests that coincided well with individuals' interests in freedom and limited government. But the independent economic interest is fast disappearing and, like so many reform movements in the Republican past, the Old Right must rely now more and more upon intellectuals and noneconomic concerns for its support. This is not yet the case totally, since there are still many businessmen who believe in a laissez-faire capitalistic economy and who confuse the two rights. But the trends in capitalism are clear. The New Right may well have the interests on its side while the Old Right is left with simply its doctrinal appeals. These appeals will still be strong since they embrace the great traditions of the Republic, but they will be weakened by the loss of one of their principal benefactors. The New Right will be more and more "where it is at" in the conservative movement and the Old Right will become increasingly aware of its limits.

The relationship between business and government that we examined in the previous chapter, then, will have a dramatic impact on the future of the Republican party as a party. Old money, new money, and corporate money may well split down the middle along Old Right–New Right lines and future contests within the Republican party may well reflect this new division more than the old divisions discussed above. A nomination contest between Charles Percy and John Connally, for example, would be a dramatic symbolic confrontation between champions of the entrepreneurial and of the corporatist economic philosophies.

The point is that business and economic interests can find in the philosophies of the Old and New Right a vehicle for exercising influence within the party that the old organizational structures do not provide. Instead of trying to influence the politician or the new manager or the organization in the traditional sense, some businesses can lavish their resources within the context of an ideological movement and can realize a much larger payoff. But business as a whole will not be united in this enterprise; it will be deeply divided.

Conservatives, then, provide a very interesting spectacle, and it is clear that the assertion that conservatives and Republicans are one and the same is false. The conservatism of the New Right, with its brands of socialism and paternalism, is a direct inheritance from both wings of the Democratic party — and is an amalgam of that party's philosophies. This is one of the great ironies of our modern politics.

The Conservative Coalition

The conservative coalition in America consists of a number of overlapping constituencies, some of which adhere largely to the principles of the Old Right, others of which adhere principally to the doctrines of the New Right, while yet others are internally divided along Old-New lines. In his excellent book, *The Goldwater Coalition*, John Kessel identified four basic sources of support that the Arizona senator enjoyed in 1964: the Republican organizational loyalist, the ideologue of the conservative "movement," the foreign policy hard-liner, and the Southerner. Today it would be accurate to add two more conservative groups that Goldwater did not attract, the business conservatives and the ethnic working-class conservative.

It is easy to see where these various groups stand on the question of Old and New Right philosophies. (1) The Republican organizational loyalists are still committed to Old Right policies, although the New Right has made some significant gains among them. The New Majoritarian philosophies, which draw heavily on New Right principles, have made many traditional Republicans uneasy because the Eisenhower-Taft philosophy of government still has strong appeals to most traditional Republican loyalists. (2) The foreign policy hard-liners, with their concern for national security, support virtually all of the domestic positions of the New Right regarding security measures, but they are very skeptical of the New Right's willingness to wheel and deal with Russian and Chinese "businessmen." The foreign policy hard-liners consist of two groups, the conservative defense intellectuals and those citizens whose ancient homelands have been overrun by communist powers (Cubans, East Europeans, and the China lobby). The first of these groups is very small, but influential in "security" affairs and totally in accord with the New Right. The second group, in its strong anticommunism, is more skeptical of New Right domestic policies unless they can be shown to support national security objectives. (3) The southern conservatives are divided, but seem to be moving definitely in the New Right direction. Texas and Florida are bastions of New Right practices, and those sections of the New South that are identified with the military-industrial complex and the aerospace industries provide the greatest concentrations of New Right adherents outside of southern California. Out-country South — the home of the George Wallace enthusiast — is very susceptible to the New Right philosophy. The textile South remains largely Old Right in orientation and many southern business leaders remain committed to the principles of laissez-faire, but the overall picture among southern conservatives shows a strong New Right trend. (4) The ethnic conservative is almost totally New Right in orientation and the sources of his convictions have been described above. (5) The business conservatives are, as we have said, split between the entrepreneurs of the Old Right and the corporatists of the New Right.

The conservative coalition contains one other very important element: the members of the conservative movement, an aggregation of intellectuals and activists who form the nucleus of conservative political power in the Republican party. These are the men and women who engineered the nomination of Barry Goldwater in 1964 and who have exercised a great deal of influence in Republican politics ever since. It is they who motivate and counsel conservative politicians, who spend conservative money, who create conservative organizations, and who know how to use their connections with the other elements of the conservative coalition in order to keep it together. Above all, it is they who know how to combine strategy with ideology in order to create political power. And they, too, are divided along the lines of Old and New Right philosophies.

The members of this movement can be divided into intellectual activists and political activists, and can be further divided into three general clusters: the New York *National Review* cluster, the Washington, D.C., cluster, and the Heartland cluster of middle America. As one moves from the New York to the Washington cluster, and finally to the Heartland cluster, there is a decrease in emphasis on the intellectual, the philosophical, the literary, and the religious, and an increase in emphasis on the anti-intellectual, the practical, and the political. Thus Heartland members of the movement are quite uneasy about *National Review* editor William Buckley's willingness to associate socially with those people they consider to be such obvious radicals as Norman Mailer and John Kenneth Galbraith. They are also uneasy about such editorial positions as the *National Review*'s advocacy of the legalization of marijuana on civil libertarian grounds.

Table 10 lists a number of conservative movement organizations, including most of the important ones.

There is so much overlapping between these groups in terms of membership and associations that they can truly be said to form a movement. For example, the Young Americans for Freedom, an historical outgrowth of the 1960 Youth for Goldwater Movement and a major force in his 1964 nominating campaign, was midwifed by William F. Buckley, Jr., of the *National Review*. Also, the Intercollegiate Society of Individualists (now known as the Intercollegiate Studies Institute, or ISI), an institution that distributes literature to college students, operated as a mailing-list organization out of the *Human Events* offices during its first years. The national field director of the ISI, Dan Lipsett, founded the Philadelphia Society in 1965. F. Clifton White, prime engineer of the 1964 Draft Goldwater movement and one of the originators of the Syndicate, the right-wing clique which for years ran the national Young Republicans, was also the national presidential campaign manager for Ronald Reagan in 1972. That campaign was staffed mainly by members of YAF and the YRs.

This intertwining of the various groups can also be seen by examining the officers and directors of the American Conservative Union. Its current chairman is M. Stanton Evans, editor of the *Indianapolis News,* author of a number of conservative movement books, and an author of the Sharon Statement, which marked the founding of the Young Americans for Freedom. Also holding offices at the ACU are Tom Winter, the current editor of *Human Events;* Representative John Ashbrook, former YR Syndicate leader and the conservative movement congressman who opposed President Nixon in three primaries during the 1972 campaign; David Jones, a former aide to Senator James Buckley, former political director of YAF, and reportedly the current power behind the throne

MOVEMENT DIVISIONS	NEW YORK CLUSTER	WASHINGTON CLUSTER	HEARTLAND CLUSTER
Intellectual Organizations	1. *The National Review* 2. *The Conservative Book Club* 3. Arlington House Publishers	1. *Human Events* 2. The Philadelphia Society	1. Intercollegiate Studies Institute (ISI) 2. *The Intercollegiate Review* 3. Harding College 4. Center for Rational Alternatives 5. Institute for Public Affairs Research
Political Action Groups	1. The Conservative Party of New York	1. American Conservative Union (ACU) 2. Americans for Constitutional Action (ACA)	1. National Federation of Young Republicans (YRs) 2. Young Americans for Freedom (YAF)

TABLE 10.
Conservative Movement Groups

among right-wing conservatives in the Young Republicans; Neil Mc-
Caffrey, president of the Conservative Book Club and head of Arlington
House Publishers; J. Daniel Mahoney, chairman of the New York State
Conservative party; Stefan T. Possony, a leading conservative intellectual
who is currently at the Hoover Institute of War and Peace; William
Rusher, publisher of the *National Review* and one of the movement's
principal theoreticians; Tom VanSickle, F. Clifton White's executive
assistant in the Draft Goldwater movement and chairman of the National
Federation of Young Republicans in 1965; and Robert Bauman, one of
the leaders of the YAF, major actor in the Syndicate, Maryland congressman, and one of the leaders in the Ashbrook campaign.

Despite this intertwining of personnel and organizations, the divisions
between the Old and New Right are beginning to be felt within the
movement. Generally speaking, the intellectual organizations are still
committed to the civil libertarian views of the Old Right, while the
activist organizations, with the exception of the ACA, are moving decisively in the direction of the security-conscious New Right. There are
many reasons why this is not surprising. But the major reason for this
shift in values and emphasis is that the New Right has interests to sustain it while the Old Right seems to depend almost entirely on its
ideology for support. An ideological movement, basing its appeal simply
on its ideology, can succeed in the short run and can accomplish a number
of political objectives. But for it to persist in the long run it must align
itself with interests. It is this, more than any other factor, that is enabling
the New Right to phase out the Old in so many activist movement
organizations.

The Power of the Conservatives

It is very difficult to gauge the power of the conservatives in the Republican party since the nature of power is continually shifting and being
redefined. There can be no doubt, however, that the conservatives are
strong and that the New Right conservatives are potentially the strongest
faction within the movement.

In 1964 the conservatives not only nominated their candidate in the
teeth of rank-and-file and organizational opposition, they nominated him
by a wide margin; it was only the spectacular nature of his defeat that
prevented them from totally dominating the party in the years afterward. In 1968 they held the balance of power in the convention and gave
the nomination to Richard Nixon in a very close contest. In 1972 they
attempted to run a protest candidate against the President and failed
miserably. This campaign, however, was very instructive since it illustrated some of the strengths and weaknesses of the conservative movement.

Relations between the Nixon administration and the various groups of the conservative movement had begun to deteriorate almost from the start of the Nixon presidency. The difficulty resulted from the gap between Nixon's conservative rhetoric and his "pragmatic" policies that we examined in Chapter 2. In the area of domestic politics the conservatives argued that candidate Nixon

> said that we have to put an end to the huge federal deficits which fuel inflation and pick the pockets of every American. He warned against the dangers of an increasingly regimented economy. He pledged to oppose any scheme for a guaranteed annual income. . . .
> He spoke out for more individual initiative in the old American style.
> — REPRESENTATIVE JOHN ASHBROOK
> December 29, 1971

Yet President Nixon during his first three years in office had produced $60 billion worth of budget deficits. In the Moynihan-sponsored Family Assistance Plan the administration backed a program that called for a guaranteed annual income and that would have, according to movement estimates, doubled the number of people on welfare (although this is a matter of definition, since FAP would have replaced welfare with a guaranteed income).

Candidate Nixon had run on the traditional conservative Republican position that price controls would not work and were an attack on the free enterprise system. But President Nixon put forward

> his program of peacetime wage and price controls — a scapegoating tactic historically employed by inflationist governments to blame their own malfeasance on private citizens.
> — REPRESENTATIVE JOHN ASHBROOK
> December 15, 1971

In the area of foreign policy candidate Nixon had taken the traditional conservative position that the United States had to be the most powerful nation in the world. But President Nixon abandoned

> any mention of "superiority" or strategic "edge." Instead, the talk is of "sufficiency" — a Johnsonian concept of parity attacked [by Nixon] in 1968. Little if anything has been done to upgrade the condition of our arsenal which, as pointed out in a special study compiled by Dr. William Schneider for the American Conservative Union, represents in its dilapidation a clear and present danger to American security.
> — REPRESENTATIVE JOHN ASHBROOK
> December 29, 1971

For the first two years of the administration, movement members had tried to work from within to achieve their aims, but their strategy failed. In October 1970, YAF's national office proposed to the leaders of the *National Review, Human Events,* and the American Conservative Union that they get together periodically to coordinate policy positions on major issues. In January 1971, the first "Conservative Summit Meeting" was held. Those attending expressed concern over the administration's policies in a number of areas, but no unified position was taken on how the movement should go about turning the policies around.

Between January and July 1971, the administration carried out its policy of normalizing relations between the United States and China. This reversal and the refusal of the administration to call for an increase in American preparedness brought matters to a head. On July 26 an expanded summit meeting was held with representatives present from other groups within the movement.

The Manhattan Twelve, as they were labeled, included editor William F. Buckley, Jr., and publisher William Rusher of *National Review;* editor Thomas Winter of *Human Events;* Randal C. Teague, the executive director of YAF, and J. Daniel Mahoney, the chairman of the New York State Conservative party.

At this meeting, the participants agreed on a declaration that terminated their support for President Nixon. Their reasons were:

1. His failure to respond to the rapid advance of the Soviet Union into the Mediterranean Basin.
2. His failure to warn against the implications of the current policies of the West German government (Willy Brandt's *ostpolitik*).
3. His overtures to Red China, done in the absence of any public concessions to Red China to American and Western causes.
4. And, above all, his failure to call public attention to the deteriorated American military position in conventional and strategic arms, which deterioration, in the absence of immediate and heroic countermeasures, can lead to the loss of our capability, the satellization of friendly governments near and far, and all that it implies.

— Human Events
August 7, 1971

If the movement leaders expected some conciliatory move by the administration they were disappointed. On October 12, 1971, the Manhattan Twelve hired Jerry Harkins, who had run Goldwater's Missouri campaign in 1964, to explore the feasibility of running someone against the President in the primaries. On November 30 Harkins reported that his sounding in New Hampshire led him to believe that there was the possibility that a significant success might be gained in the primary there.

The next step was to find someone willing to carry the conservative banner. The prime candidate was California Governor Ronald Reagan, but he balked at the offer. Bill Rusher, who was integrally involved in the Draft Goldwater movement, Tom Winter, and YAF President Ron Docksai then approached Ohio Congressman John Ashbrook.

John Ashbrook was and is very much a member of the movement. He was one of the founders and a past chairman of the American Conservative Union. He has had a long association with the Young Americans for Freedom and was one of the organizing leaders of the Syndicate faction of the YRs. He is on the steering committee of the Committee of One Million Against the Admission of Red China. Since 1960 he had served in the House of Representatives, earning a reputation as one of its most conservative members. In 1972, the Americans for Constitutional Action's Index gave him a rating of 97 out of 100. As soon as it became clear that a man of these credentials would make the challenge, Spiro Agnew and John Mitchell both tried to placate the insurgents, but without success.

As the Ashbrook campaign got underway it was evident that the movement considered itself the largest and most impressive element within the conservative Republican coalition. They felt that the other parts of the coalition — what they called the Old Guard of conservatism and what we largely call the Old Right — no longer had the numbers and power to determine events. For example, editor Jerry Norton wrote in the *New Guard,*

> Evidently both the President and a number of Old Guard conservative political leaders are laboring under some false impressions. The President believes the Old Guard represents the bulk of the conservative movement, the movement that provided most of the grass roots workers in 1968. The Old Guard believes that because they buy the Nixon rhetoric, the rest of the movement should too.
>
> What many in the movement believe is that unless the President and the Old Guard correct those impressions, the former will find himself out of a job and the latter will find themselves with no followers.

Unfortunately for the movement, it was not the President's impressions that needed correcting. CREEP responded vigorously to the Ashbrook challenge. First it shut off the congressman's political support. Great pressure was applied not only on Goldwater, Reagan, Tower, and their supporters, but also to young movement congressmen. People close to the Ashbrook campaign claim that before he decided to run he had received promises of support from many fellow conservative legislators. But as the campaign unfolded, none of these supporters came forward, leaving Ashbrook and his activists alone.

More important, the Nixon managers shut off Ashbrook's financial support. It is a traditional assumption — and in many cases a true one — that the groups that make up the movement are backed by several large financial contributors. Liberal critics are continually pointing to such organizations as the Alfred P. Sloan Foundation, the William Volker Fund, the Pew Foundation, the Donner Foundation, and the Relm Foundation as sources of a large percentage of movement funds. They did not, however, fund Ashbrook's campaign, and nobody else did.

Things got so bad during the Florida primary that the campaign could not afford an advance man and Ashbrook had to share a hotel room with a member of his staff. Although the campaign spent between $10,000 and $15,000 producing TV spots, there was not enough money to purchase the air time to show them.

Given these circumstances it is not surprising that the campaign failed. It had been Ashbrook's hope that "if we could get 10 to 15 percent in New Hampshire . . . we could broaden that to 25 in Florida, and that would give us enough momentum to put us in the running in a number of other primaries." But the results did not follow this plan. In the New Hampshire primary, where Barry Goldwater had received around 20,000 votes in 1964, Ashbrook got about 11,000 (9.6 percent) in 1972, even though he had the strong public support of William Loeb, powerful publisher of the *Manchester Union Leader*. In Florida, while George Wallace was destroying several liberal candidacies on the Democratic side, Ashbrook accumulated 36,617 votes, or 8.8 percent of the total. Finally, in California — the state that had appeared to be Ashbrook's brightest hope because of its reputation as the home of the conservative legions that had backed Goldwater — he obtained only 224,922 votes, or 9.8 percent of the total. Thus, in a series of primaries, the conservative movement failed to get 10 percent of the vote, even in low turnouts. By contrast, the only serious challenge from the Left of the party, Congressman McCloskey's New Hampshire primary effort, netted an impressive 20 percent of the vote in that presumably conservative state.

It would be foolish to conclude that Ashbrook's failure was the result simply of CREEP efficiency or, alternately, of a decline in conservative power within the party. His failure was the result of an inability to assess the real sources of conservative strength within the party. These lie not so much with ideological purity, organizational skills, or movement loyalties, but rather with the concurrence of solid interests *with* ideological proficiency. It might have been possible to have gone much further on the basis of ideological appeal alone had conservative interests remained neutral, but the powers of a sitting President were employed to marshal the conservative interests against Ashbrook. Ideology on its own did not go very far.

SOURCES OF CONSERVATIVE POWER

In the broadest sense of the word, however, the source of conservative power is ideology. After all, ideology is what a movement is all about.

But how is ideological power exercised? We have examined both organizational and financial power; their relevance to the political picture is self-evident. The relevance of ideological power, however, is much more subtle. There are three components to it.

First, ideology can motivate activists. This is its most common use and is a very important one. The ability to stimulate volunteers and quasi-volunteers gives the ideological movement an important resource that more normal political operations often lack. Enthusiasm is a good substitute for cash in any campaign. Furthermore, strong ideological commitments can be easily manipulated by movement leaders. With larger ends justifying a vast range of means, a great deal of strategic flexibility is created by ideological commitment. This too is a valuable resource. Workers can be commanded to perform their duties, not simply cajoled, and a paramilitary atmosphere can bring discipline to the cadres.

Beyond the immediate organization, ideology can be very helpful in stimulating sympathizers to vote in primaries and to attend caucuses in much greater numbers than the less ideologically motivated. It is well known that Republican "activists" are more conservative than Republican voters, and that in low-turnout primaries a decided edge is given to the highly committed. These tendencies were exploited extensively in 1964 and again in 1968 and it is not necessary to dwell upon them.

This first use of ideology to achieve party power is best effected in open situations, in primaries, caucuses, and in other events that are usually assaults upon the traditional party organization. But there is a second use of ideology, far more subtle than the first, that is most effective within a party organization: ideology can redefine the nature of internal political debates. It can help redefine what a party is. Here again the conservatives have been very effective.

As we noted, the 1960s saw a sharp rise in the incidence of strategic politics within the Republican party. Candidates began to ape the Democrats in many regions of the country and the new managers began to phase out the party figures in Republican campaigns. These twin tendencies began to raise doubts in the minds of party officials about their roles in the party and about its role in the electoral process. Was the party simply supposed to service candidates and to help win elections or did it have a broader policy function? Was a party meant to stand for something? Since the moderates and the pragmatists in the party had been the chief "offenders" in the employment of the new strategic politics, the conservatives exploited this situation and began to assert the plausible argument that a party should be founded on principles. This argument had a persuasive ring to it and was attractive to those party faithful who were not "with" the new politics, but who could find some satisfaction in being told that they were "better" Republicans because they were more doctrinaire and more interested in preserving Republican orthodoxy than in imitating the Democrats. Ignored by the pragmatists and humiliated by the new managers, many party officials found solace in the conservative argument that in one area at any rate they were superior to those who were replacing them. Party officials have historically been more conservative than the party rank and file anyway, and they were a fertile field for exploitation.

But how did the conservatives establish the presumption that theirs was the true Republican orthodoxy? How did they create the widely held impression that "the only real Republicans are conservatives"? Although this argument took many forms, its basic logic was relatively simple: a Republican is not a Democrat; Democrats are liberals; a Republican is therefore not a liberal; those who are the farthest away from being liberals are conservatives; those who are the farthest away from being Democrats are conservatives; the most genuine Republican is he who is farthest away from being a Democrat; the most genuine Republican is a conservative. Quod erat demonstrandum. Add to this that a choice is not an echo and the argument is complete — or so it seems.

To the extent that the conservatives have convinced people that Republican means non-Democrat and nonliberal, they have created a powerful ideological instrument. First, this definition tends to obscure the divisions within the conservative movement since both Old Right and New Right can accurately be termed nonliberal, if not non-Democrat. Also, this presumption of orthodoxy potentially gives the conservatives vast power within the party organization. If they can define to their own satisfaction who is a "real" Republican, they have a virtual power of excommunication. They put the rest of the party on the defensive with respect to its party patriotism and acquire an impressive instrument for placing their personnel in key party posts. The argument that party officials, at any rate, ought to be "real" Republicans is a powerful one, and the conservatives have used it with a great deal of proficiency.

The third use of ideology is potentially the most important: ideology can align and justify interests. The normal image of an ideological movement suggests that the basis of ideology is a set of higher principles, moral commitments, and eternal verities. There is also the presumption of justice. "Narrow interests" seem to be what ideological movements are trying to overcome. Old Right and New Left intellectuals share this characteristic (and little else). But what happens if ideology and interests can be brought together so that the ideology serves as a moral justification for the pursuit of the interest? Then the result is awesome.

It is this use of ideology that the New Right conservatives threaten to employ with devastating effect. The policies of national security, corporate security, job security, and personal security can be welded together into a powerful conservative ideology that already has shown its ability to motivate the faithful in such organizations as those we mentioned above. Furthermore, this ideology directly supports the powerful interests of the new corporatists who can be mobilized to supply the money, the enthusiasm, and the personnel for political activities. The doctrines can align the supporters and the supporters can reinforce the doctrines. With these powerful interests working with them, and with an ideology to supply the moral justification for their activities, the strategists of the New Right can view their position with some satisfaction.

It is now easy to see why Ashbrook fared so badly. His candidacy did attract some ideological support from the first of these three categories; he was able to get the purists of the movement behind him. But he was unable to employ ideology in the second two ways. He could never make a case that he was the "real" Republican while Richard Nixon somehow was not, and he could not align these powerful interests behind his ideology because the President had already aligned them behind himself in a more traditional political fashion. Left with pure ideological considerations, he was in a difficult position. In such a context, the technical and political power of the White House could operate unhindered and the Ohio congressman was crushed.

THE FUTURE OF CONSERVATIVE POWER

It would be a mistake to assume that the conservatives are all-powerful in the Republican party. The division between Old Right and New Right is real and becoming more evident as time goes on. The conservatives in the administration have suffered many setbacks as a result of Watergate, which has undercut their power since the doctrines of the New Right in many ways seem responsible for the attitudes that led up to it. The wheeler-dealers and new corporatists have temporarily run for cover.

Furthermore, it seems possible that many of the conservatives' assets could be neutralized. They have no monopoly on Republican money. They are building a power base within the organization, but it is far from complete. They cannot count on the power of the White House with certainty. Their tacticians and strategists are presumably no more proficient than the tacticians and strategists that others could employ. And they have no sterling figure around whom they can rally. Certainly everyone would agree that 1973 saw a sharp diminution in their position and serious suggestions that others might replace them in the corridors of party power.

Yet there are limits to these illusions. The conservatives of the New Right have one thing that no other major faction within the Republican party has — a secure power base. They are the authentic representatives of a powerful interest and their record of performance is such that the interest knows they will deliver. They have been temporarily eclipsed by a temporary phenomenon, but their party power position will survive these setbacks because it is based on long-range propositions. No matter how many candidates are destroyed and careers ruined by the Watergate scandal, the continued existence of a long-range interest reinforced by a strong ideology will give the New Right a resiliency and staying power of the first magnitude. Its influence in the party does not depend on the charisma of one man or on the proficiency of a set of tacticians. It is based on the solid foundation of constituency interest, and this is a fact that the rest of the party must face head on.

It is probably not surprising that modern politicians pay less and less attention to the problem of establishing a lasting power base since they are seduced by the logic of strategic politics, which counsels them to keep their options open, and by the advice of the new technicians, who inform them that public relations and electoral tactics are all that are necessary to win elections. But in the long term, a power base is a handy thing to have, as so many politicians have found out too late. Public opinion is a volatile affair and dexterity alone cannot guarantee a politician success unless he has something more solid to fall back on. George Romney found this out in 1967; Edmund Muskie and John Lindsay found it out in early 1972. Spiro Agnew discovered it in 1973. The opponents of the New Right may well benefit from their example.

15

Control of the Republican Party

The Limits of Tactics and Strategy

Probably no Republican beyond the New Right embrace has a solid power base outside his home state, and many presidential hopefuls lack even that. Our thinking has been so caught up in the language and spirit of the new strategic politics, however, that these rootless hopefuls don't seem to be disturbed by their condition. It is a common feeling that good political managers employing sound campaign tactics can create the kind of public image for their client that will win him the nomination — with a bit of luck. This assumption is wrong. The lack of a strong and committed power base imposes a strategic difficulty on any presidential hopeful that the vague category of "public support" cannot easily overcome in a situation so complicated as a modern presidential nomination. The candidate with a power base — even if it is small but enthusiastic — enjoys a tremendous strategic edge over the candidate without one. Of course, if no one has a power base and someone is nominated, it will be said that the nomination was secured in the absence of a power base. But this will not happen in the Republican party in 1976; the New Right candidates have a power base and no doubt will use it most effectively.

But the argument can be extended beyond candidates. Whole factions of the Republican party find themselves increasingly without a solid party constituency. The Old Right, for example, suddenly sees itself representing less and less as the New Right usurps the mantle of conservative orthodoxy, as the nature of American capitalism shifts in the direction of corporatism, and as the traditional party organization loses its influence in the presidential nominating process. The moderate and progressive wings of the party are in even worse shape. Their strength lies in their centrist position within the country, not within the party. Their constituency is the increasing number of independents who control elections but who do not count for much in party affairs. This is why Republican moderates have a better record in statewide general elections than any other group of politicians in either party — and why they are simultaneously the least influential major political force within either party. In most areas of the country they simply lack a party constituency.

Faced with this problem nationally, the progressive wing of the party in recent years has relied on sheer strategy to secure the nomination of one of its candidates, and it has always attributed its defeat to a failure in tactics: "If we had only been more organized . . . If we only had had the right candidate . . . If we had only started sooner . . . If we had only entered a different set of primaries . . . If we had only let the new pros run the campaign . . . If we had only taken someone else's advice . . . How many times have we heard these tactical explanations for failure?

The whole thesis of this book is that strategic politics has its limits and there is no better illustration of these limits than in intraparty contests. It is quite true that Barry Goldwater and George McGovern were nominated as a result of excellent tactics. But their success was made possible by the existence of a solid constituency that provided the basis upon which tactics could operate. Nixon's 1968 triumph also employed sound tactics — but he too had a constituency. Rockefeller's effort in 1968 went as far as it did, not because he employed good tactics, but because he assembled a power base among elected officials — and this was not solid by any means.

These examples seem to indicate that a power base comes first and tactical proficiency second. Why is this logically the case? It is quite clear that the road to a national nomination is a very hazardous course. There are always opponents and potential opponents who lie in wait for the slightest opportunity to hurt the candidate. There are always unknown crises and national events that erupt without a moment's warning and create vast difficulties for the candidate and his managers. There are always reporters drooling in anticipation of some slip that can be used to damage the image of the candidate. There are always the "accidents of fate" that create some strange configuration of opponents in a crucial primary, that change the rules of the game at the last minute, or that remove someone from the scene. And there are the more controllable hazards that nevertheless are not entirely predictable — the incompetence of a manager, the occasionally unavoidable failure of an advertising theme, or the unexpected defection of a crucial supporter. To the extent that the nominating process approaches a pure game between players, these hazards must multiply since it becomes increasingly in the interests of strategists to create such difficulties for the opposition.

If a candidate does not have a strong power base within the party, it is very difficult for him to deal with these hazards and pitfalls effectively. Without a solid constituency, the sources of his strength are two: the dexterity of his strategists and the expectations of his future possibilities. The first can never guarantee success. No candidate can ever assume that he has a monopoly of talent, and even if he has a good edge in this respect, sheer calculation and good political instinct will not always work. Even the best political strategists make mistakes. And even if a candidate is lucky in this respect, the odds in favor of his surmounting every pitfall by dexterity alone are very slim; there are just too many situations where the best strategists are utterly unable to predict the long-term results of their actions. Since this is the case, mistakes are highly probable.

But if mistakes are highly probable, then the second resource — expectation of future possibilities — becomes very shallow. If the strength of this baseless and rootless candidate depends on predictions that he will win, then slight reverses resulting from these inevitable mistakes become very serious. The political strategist, like the stock market speculator, tends to have an extrapolative view of reality, and movement in one direction is usually extrapolated way out of proportion. An initial surge may bring a flood of opportunity money and bandwagon support. But a slight reverse will make people conclude that the candidacy is finished. A minor drop in a popularity poll, a slightly poorer performance than expected in a primary, or even the defection of one or two supporters can set the whole extrapolative evaluation into a dramatic downward spiral. With nothing to hold it up, as the speculators say, the market will crash.

In a deeper sense this applies not only to the expectations of other strategists and opportunistic supporters but to the wider public as well. Popular support is very fluid in this age of nonalignment, and it is sensitive to short-term revision. Much public support can be based on the impression that a candidate is a going concern, that he looks like a winner, and as a winner, that he looks like a credible leader. But this image is obviously very fragile in the face of short-term reverses. It is not that the public is fickle, it is more that it needs a sound reason for staying with someone — and it cannot simply be that he is expected to win. Should his chances begin to appear slightly doubtful, the doubts will snowball and his candidacy will collapse. It should not be at all surprising that Romney's brainwash and Muskie's lachrymation brought about an immediate collapse of their candidacies; there was no base of support beyond the opportunistic extrapolations of the political speculator and the shallow public appeal of a "good image." Nixon's fall in 1973 had similar characteristics (even though his base of support was somewhat stronger); he simply had failed to establish a solid constituency.

For a presidential candidate to survive the inevitable reverses of the nominating process he needs a stronger source of support than tactical dexterity and a good image with the public. He needs people who will put up money and volunteers who will make an extra effort in his behalf, even when the going gets rough. And most of all he needs a substantial base of support that is so interested in his candidacy and his future prospects that it will sustain and animate him when he suffers reverses, rather than requiring him to animate it in times of difficulty. Hubert Humphrey, for example, in his long political career, has said and done as many dumb things as Nixon, Romney, and Muskie combined. But he has always bounced back because organized labor was there to sustain him. This is the true value of a constituency and it gives a candidate or a party faction tremendous advantages. It is like the strategic reserve that can be brought into action when the enemy has broken through the line or threatens a certain position. Without it the simple dynamics of the nominating process dictate tremendous odds against the success of any hopeful.

There are, then, two tasks that a prospective candidate or a hopeful party faction must perform if either wants to be successful in capturing control of the party. First, he must establish a secure power base. Second, he must make the support of that power base relevant to the nominating process; the support must be effectively mobilized. These are two very different tasks. The first is a political or an ideological task. The second is a strategic or a tactical problem, depending on the party situation at the moment. In the contemporary Republican party the conservatives of the New Right have met the first of these requirements and can happily focus on the second. The rest of the party has to pay attention to both if it wants to exercise effective control in the future.

Constituencies and Power Bases

While strategy requires a power base, it is politics that creates one. A solid constituency cannot be established overnight and it cannot exist for long in an atmosphere of high strategy. For a politician (or a party faction) to create a solid power base, he must convince his constituency that it has a significant stake in his political future. He must have the reputation of delivering to that constituency and he must create the expectation that its future and his are bound together. Such expectations are not the product of momentary arrangements of expediency but of long-range cultivations of relationships. Trust, mutuality, and reciprocity are the ideal components of these relationships, but expectations based on past performance will suffice. Establishing such relationships is a political task in the old sense of the word and the wise politician will spend a lot of time and effort at it because it is the key to party power.

Although few politicians who remain in office for long neglect their constituencies totally, there is an increasing trend in statewide and national politics to take supporters for granted and search for the fluid. In the politics of general elections this tactic has its drawbacks, as we saw in Chapter 9, but in party politics the drawbacks are increased even more. Furthermore, very few politicians outside of the New Right have addressed themselves to the problem of creating a lasting *national* constituency that could serve them. How many politicians in today's Republican party — to the left of Howard Baker — could genuinely say that large numbers of people across the country feel that they have a stake in the future prospects of that politician? How many people across the country feel that they have a stake in the success of a moderate Republican candidate in general? In 1968 a large number of party officials across the country felt (erroneously, as it turned out) that they, as party officials, had a stake in the future of Richard Nixon. For years union members and officials across the country have felt that they had an interest in the future of Hubert Humphrey. In 1972 thousands of Democrats felt that they had a stake in the future of George McGovern's candidacy, and today countless more feel that way about Teddy Kennedy. Although each of these constituencies was founded on a different basis — party interest, economic interest, ideological interest, and a combination of all of these — each was nevertheless solid and lasting. It is on such constituencies that successful candidacies are based, and the creation of such constituencies is the first requirement of a serious and winning campaign for a presidential nomination. Where do such power bases get created? In the party organization, in various interest groups such as the business community, and in segments of the electorate at large.

THE PARTY ORGANIZATION

As we have said, the party organization was Nixon's principal constituency in 1968 and he parlayed this power base into a nomination. What is the situation today? As noted in Chapter 11, the party organizations across the country are in such disarray that many might ask if their support is at all relevant to a successful nominating campaign; do the organizations count for anything in an age of primaries and packed caucuses? Perhaps the organization can be made to count for something if it supports a candidate strongly and if he has the tactical proficiency to make that support relevant to the nominating process. The organizations, though weak, cannot be ignored. How can a constituency be established among them?

The New Right, as we saw in Chapter 14, has made a bid to establish a power base within the regular organizations across the country. It has used its ideological persuasiveness to suggest that only "real" Republicans be appointed to party posts, and that the organizations have an interest in the future of the New Right because only it will reward them on the basis of loyalty to "true" principles. But the New Right is not the only faction that can create a constituency within the organization. The moderate wing of the party has always suggested with a great deal of plausibility that the party organization has a stake in the moderates' success because the moderates are more likely to *win* a general election. The moderates and progressives in many states, however, have tended to ignore the party machinery as they played strategic politics, and therefore the conservatives have shot back with the plausible rejoinder, "Winning for what?" What benefit does a party official receive if his winning candidate ignores him during and after the election? In so many states the moderate wing has simply let the conservative wing take control by default; moderates have failed to demonstrate to party officials that these officials have a stake in a moderate party. The Bliss model of party organization provides a natural constituency for the moderates, for such a party in the North, Midwest, and West would, in its organizational wisdom, also perceive an organizational stake in the nomination of middle-of-the-road candidates with good prospects of winning. If such candidates had the wisdom, after winning, to reciprocate and aid in the process of party-building and maintenance, they could establish a strong base of support within the party organization. But the moderates, if they wish to do so, must work toward a political situation in which the organization has as much of a stake in winning as it has in maintaining its alleged ideological chastity. The organization is in such bad shape that some small efforts at party-building will go a long way toward establishing a lasting constituency.

But the moderates and other opponents of New Right conservatism would also do well to combat the ideological edge that their antagonists have established. There is no reason why they cannot make a case that they are just as good Republicans as the conservative imports from the Democratic party.

Elected officials are also a possible area for constituency-building. The New Right conservatives have some base of support here, but they are at a serious disadvantage because they are concentrated in a region of the country where there are not too many Republican elected officials. To create a power base among such officials is difficult unless a candidate or a segment of the party can create a stake for these officials in that candidate's or faction's success. The traditional methods here have been patronage, cabinet posts, and the promise to those not interested in such rewards that a strong performance at the polls will have a beneficial coattail effect in the state. These instruments of constituency-building, however, have a decidedly short-term flavor about them and really are not sources of lasting support in themselves except in special circumstances. Within reason, all candidates can offer cabinet posts, patronage, and to some extent coattails. Such offers do not create constituencies, just temporary allies.

The one way, however, in which a candidate or a party faction could create a lasting and strong constituency among elected officials — especially executive elected officials — is by convincing them that if that candidate or faction came to power it could help them solve some of their administrative problems within their constituency. Rockefeller used this argument in 1968 with some degree of success. If elected officials — governors, mayors, and so forth — could be convinced that the policies and the performance potential of certain candidates would help them solve their problems and thereby strengthen their own political positions, then they might have an interest and a stake in the future of those policies and the politicians who would be most likely to carry them out.

With respect to these two groups, then, current power configurations give an edge to the New Right conservatives, but it is hardly a decisive edge, and other elements in the party could redress the imbalance by doing a little homework — and by continuing to do homework in the long run.

THE INTERESTED INTERESTS

There are many interests that take more than a passing glance at Republican politics. Business is certainly the largest of these, but professionals, women, youth, agriculture, and even labor have some stake in the future of the party. What stake do they have in the future of certain candidates or in the future of certain wings of the party? Who has an interest in seeing the Republicans become a New Right party or an Old Right party or a moderate-progressive party? In which factions or candidates will these interests perceive the basis of a lasting mutual relationship?

We have looked at business to some extent; let us look briefly at some of the others. It has not been possible here to examine the attitudes and potentials of these various interests but we can sketch some of their dimensions. The professionals are an interesting case in point. In Chapter 12 we saw that the Nixon fund-raisers did remarkably poorly among professionals and we suggested that here was a large untapped constituency for the Republican party. It is also the natural constituency of the moderate wing of the party. Professionals are generally well educated; they tend to be liberal on human questions and conservative on financial questions. They do not depend on the government for their support in most cases, and they are sufficiently independent that the new corporatist philosophies have little appeal to them. By and large they are not racists. They have an interest in limited, moderate, and efficient government. Furthermore, they are not without assets. They are one of the most rapidly growing sectors of the society, they are affluent, they are concerned and politically aware. But they do not perceive that they have a stake in the future of the moderate and progressive wings of the Republican party. They are a vast untapped resource that the moderates could easily employ to counter the resources engaged by the New Right. But to make this resource relevant to the requirements of the moderate wing, the professionals of suburban America who vote for moderate Republicans in general elections must be convinced that their future is tied to the future of a progressive Republican party. This is not a strategic task or a public relations task, it is a political problem that would involve the creation of a long-term set of relationships, mutual expectations, and increased participation in Republican politics by this potentially very powerful group.

Women are also an interest group, and the specter of thousands of organized women storming the citadels of party power is plausible enough to give any politician pause for thought. It is interesting to note that the women at Miami Beach in 1972 were the only group who forced the White House to change a plank in the platform or to adopt a rule that it didn't want. If a candidate or party faction could convince a large number of activist women that they had a stake in his or her future, a strong center of power might be created. Women have been active in Republican affairs for years. But they have not been a force to be reckoned with by the party leadership, nor have they played a decisive role in the nomination of a national candidate.

The major reason why this vast potential remains inactive is that the Republican woman is largely a person content to let men assume a leadership role in politics. Few politicians have sought to build a power base among them. They are, to be sure, many women activists in the party, but they are still a small, if growing, minority. Republican women focus largely on traditional women's political activities and, with some significant exceptions, do not, as women, engage in battles to affect the course of party affairs.

In most regions of the country, all of the great political upheavals of the last decade have left the traditional Republican woman largely unchanged. She is ready to fight, bleed, and die for a cause affecting her family, such as busing, but is usually appalled by minority-group activism and the drug scene. She is completely at a loss to understand the problems of the ghetto, not because she is without compassion, but because her background has never included anything even faintly comparable. Because she follows the work ethic, she feels this is the solution for most of the problems of those on welfare.

She is slow to run for office and slow in assuming the mantle of leadership; although she believes women could do as well as men, she just is not militant or demanding. Her husband is the head of the household and she is accustomed to directing her activities to accommodate him, the children, and the comfort of her home. In this way, short-term projects or

316

"fellowship" fulfills her needs for projecting outside the home. She views the National Women's Political Caucus with disdain, much as her forebears once regarded the League of Women Voters or the NAACP. She is happy in her socioeconomic superiority and she is not especially interested in change. She is not terribly thrilled by the appointment of a woman to a top position, and the chances are that she will be the first to vote against a woman candidate in a man-woman contest.

No one should consider this picture completely derogatory. These women are the backbone of the suburban and small towns in America. They keep the churches and the local charities going and provide a great deal of stability to the entire social fabric of the Republic. Many of them are well informed on the issues of the day, but most rely upon the six o'clock news and an occasional newspaper for their political information. They are not likely to get too involved with great questions of the day and they are inclined to move more with the pleasant aspects of politics than with the unpleasant. To say that these women are inactive would be wrong, but to say that they are activists would be equally false.

Yet times are changing. It may soon be possible to create a genuine constituency among women as an interest group. Although there are wide differences among women — as among men — on most issues, there are still a set of issues involving women's rights and privileges that might provide the basis for a solid constituency. The chances are that the moderate wing of the party would have an advantage over the more conservative or traditional wings in this respect.

Youth is also a potential constituency of an aspiring candidate. There was some speculation that Senator Brock — a New Right conservative — would exploit his position as the head of the youth movement in CREEP and, together with his long-time assistant, Ken Reitz, establish a constituency among this group on a nationwide basis. Unfortunately for him, Reitz became involved in the Watergate fiasco and the effort collapsed. It probably would have anyway because it was a tactical effort, not a political one. Of course youth can be easily attracted to causes, and in the Republican party these causes in the past have tended to be conservative. The Youth Division of CREEP was in many ways more pragmatic than ideological, however, and there is obviously a vast untapped potential for moderates who have no place to go but up. The youth vote has never been engaged in a serious Republican presidential nominating contest, with the possible exception of the 1972 New Hampshire primary, where the results were not discouraging for moderates. Youth is indeed a possible constituency, but not one to be attracted on the basis of short-term considerations.

Agriculture is another example of an interest that could form the basis of a meaningful constituency. The farmers of America are dwindling in numbers, but they are important in Republican politics in a number of states. Their natural constituency has been — and remains — the Old

317

Right. In fact, outside of the organization, they are the most solid constituency the Old Right has retained.

These few examples will suffice to make the point that Republican politicians of the Old Right and of the moderate wings are simply not making the effort to create solid constituencies, and hence solid bases of power. They are not giving Republicans or potential Republicans the conviction that they have a stake in their future. The constituencies are there for the asking, and the potential power that they would convey is vast. But the efforts are not being made. By continually focusing on last-minute tactics, the opponents to New Right control of the Republican party are loading the dice against themselves. It is not that they wait too long, it is that they focus on the wrong approach to nomination politics. Hence the conservatives have become so powerful.

ALIGNMENT AND REALIGNMENT

The New Right conservatives are a powerful force in the Republican party, not only because they have a solid constituency, but also because they have been able to exercise a major influence over the conservatives of the Old Right. The word "conservative," as we have seen, is a powerful ideological instrument, and it alone has been sufficient to disguise vast differences among doctrines and to preserve strong alliances among people that have very little logic to them at all. As people become aware of these differences and divergences, however, new possibilities present themselves to the opponents of the New Right. Constituency-building can be more than the exercises described earlier; it can also be the larger exercise of realigning interests and perceptions among members of a party so that the more traditional exercises in constituency-building can proceed effectively.

An excellent opportunity now presents itself to the moderate wing of the party — and to the traditionalists of the Old Right — namely, to explore the possibility of forming an alliance to check the excesses and dangerous policies of the New Right. Such an alliance could be based on firmer foundations than the current alliance between the two Rights and would restore the party to more authentic *Republican* principles. If anyone doubts the possibility of such an alliance or feels that the conservative movement is truly monolithic, let him simply ponder the question of whether Old Right champion Howard Baker is closer in his fundamental outlook to Jesse Helms or to Charles Percy.

What would be the basis of such a political realignment within the Republican party? The first constituency would be the entrepreneurial businessman, that beleaguered individual who tries to stand on his own two feet without the support of government subsidies and who is frankly annoyed at being taxed to support the inefficiencies of government

318

bureaucracies and corporatist industries. He is the natural constituency of both the Old Right and the progressives. The second constituency is the professional, who is equally fed up with the Democratic party's insistence on bureaucratic solutions to all our problems but who is reluctant to embrace the Republican party wholeheartedly because the corporatist policies of the New Right are an anathema to him. The entrepreneurial businessmen and the professionals are some of the most dynamic and energetic forces in our society. As a united constituency they would form a superb power base within the Republican party.

What policies would tend to unite the Old Right with the moderates? There are many. Both can agree on sound economic doctrines. Responsible fiscal policies, intelligent and sober monetary policies, stern measures to fight inflation, and a restoration of confidence in the dollar are closer to the hearts of both groups than to the hearts of the New Right, whose thinking is primarily responsible for the "Nixonomics." The restoration of the marketplace as the regulator of the economy and the restoration of a system that provides economic benefits to efficiency and productivity, not to size and political privilege, unites both these wings of the party against the New Right.

Another area is the field of human rights. Both the Old Right and the moderates are appalled at the use of the doctrine of national security to enable the federal executive to trample on the rights of American citizens and to justify retrospectively almost any activity it sees fit to employ in furthering its own political ends. Both the Old Right and the moderates are committed to the Bill of Rights and to the principle of equality of opportunity for every citizen. And their political support does not depend on doctrines of thinly disguised racism that the New Right activists have found so handy.

In questions of national security and foreign policy there are also many common grounds between the two wings of the party. Their joint approach to these questions can best be described as one of prudence: refrain from adventurism; recognize the necessity of dealing with everyone because there are no rational alternatives; but when dealing with everyone, remember that our allies are more important to us than our potential adversaries. With respect to national security both groups have a strong common interest in a massive examination of the true efficiencies and inefficiencies of our defense situation. Blind spending to support the economic position of certain corporations is counterproductive to national security, and the sober views of Old Right and moderate Republicans may well join in concluding that the efficiency of an industrial plant is as important as its size when it comes to questions of international competition in weapons systems and military preparedness.

In short, it would be possible for the moderate wing to meet the Old Right on grounds of economics, for the Old Right to meet the moderates on grounds of human rights, and for both to converge on an internationalism of prudence and restraint. In all of these questions today each is closer to the other than to the New Right. Such an alliance, then, would provide the basis for creating a solid constituency within the Republican party on which candidates could build. It could be given ideological coherence and could neutralize the kind of ideological nonsense that the New Right is pouring forth. But such arrangements do not just happen; such constituencies do not just appear. They are the work of traditional politicians exercising their historical and legitimate function of mutual accommodation and party-building. They are also the result of moving away from strategic thinking. It is about time that Old Right and moderate politicians stop asking how they can get the vote of a constituency and start asking how they can give that constituency a stable and lasting stake in their future.

The Relevant Power Base

The creation of a constituency is only the first step toward nomination and party control. The support of that constituency must be made relevant to the nominating process; of what use is even the strongest support if it cannot be effectively mobilized?

Recent years have seen a revolution in party affairs. The events of 1972 in the Democratic party took everyone by surprise because a very small power base was used in such an efficient way that it proved decisive. What made this possible was both an opening up of the party and a massive disorganization on the part of the opposition. The Republican party is almost as open. On the statute books in state after state are inscribed the possibilities for party revolution — no matter what happens to the party's own reform efforts. If present trends continue, over two-thirds of the delegates to the 1976 convention will be elected in primaries, and it is safe to presume that these will be contested primaries. California, New York, Pennsylvania, Illinois, Ohio, Michigan, New Jersey, Florida, Massachusetts, Indiana, North Carolina, Tennessee, and Wisconsin all have primary laws on their books and winning candidates will be forced to enter and succeed in many of these. The whole process of winning will take massive, well-organized, and presumably well-funded political machines if any one candidate wishes to have a solid chance of winning the nomination without depending on the accidents of fortune. Although many of these big states had primaries in 1968, most went uncontested because there were favorite son candidates (California, New York, Ohio, Pennsylvania, New Jersey, and in a sense Massachusetts, where the uncontested favorite son lost). It is unlikely that this will be the case in 1976. Too much pressure will be exacted for governors and senators to hold out. An aware public will not want to play the favorite son game, and the decline of party organizational strength will seriously undercut the power of these potential favorites. The whole nominating process faces the vast uncertainties of a completely new game played in a new stadium.

In such a situation the political campaign in its modern sense will come into its own in a way Republican politics has never experienced before. No longer will the candidates be able to campaign largely among the party "kingmakers" because they will count for very little — unless efforts are made to restore their princely power. Men like Thurston Morton, Douglas Dillon, Lucius Clay, and Len Hall will be joined in honorable obscurity by Strom Thurmond, Clarke Reed, and perhaps even Clifton White. No longer will elected officials have their former eminence — unless efforts are made to make that eminence once more relevant to the nominating process. No longer will party officials count for much in the nominating process — unless steps are taken to augment their position. Campaigning among them as Richard Nixon did in 1968 will be far less relevant than it was then.

Where will the power lie? Increasingly with those Republicans and *Independents* who want to exercise it on primary day and caucus night, this broad and currently amorphous "constituency" that can make and break candidacies with alarming rapidity but whose actions are so difficult to predict or to control. Faced with this situation, how can candidates proceed?

Some might move to restore the power of the organization — if that was their constituency. Hopefuls could certainly do this in their own states and encourage it in others. A strong Bliss-model party could effectively return politics to the favorite son option, and encouraging party officials to fill delegate slots in a number of states could meet with success. There are various stratagems that could be devised to strengthen the party organization and augment its role in the nominating process. Such a strengthening would simultaneously underwrite elected officials and business interests who have strong and lasting ties to both elected officials and party organization leaders.

But if the organization is not restored, the counterorganization will have its day. Massive nationwide efforts will have to be instituted that will require much money and many workers. It is easy to see how the New Right, with its strong constituency and coherent ideology, can work very well in such a situation. There are several ways of matching it, however. The entrepreneurial businessman can provide both money and managerial skills given sufficient incentives, but his effort would have to be more than perfunctory. An association of businessmen with all their skills and resources would constitute a powerful influence within the party if it could be organized. And the professionals, whose Democratic cousins provided the manpower and especially the money for the Mc-Govern effort (as we saw in Chapter 12), could be similarly mobilized to provide these same two resources. These groups are large untapped sources of political power in the Republican party and they are ready to support a candidate who will give them a reason to support him. Their manpower, organizational skills, and money can be brought to bear on the situation in an immediate and effective manner. The open party is where they can be most effective, and they will tend to support progressive Republicans.

The point is that the possibilities for innovation and imagination are vast. Once the constituency is established the proficient tactician can find ways to mobilize it effectively and imaginatively into convention delegates as long as he is aware of the shifting dimensions of party power. But the key remains the constituency. How can these groups — these larger groups — be mobilized around a set of principles that will give them a stake both in the future of those principles and in the future of those politicians who might be expected to carry them out? That is the most important problem facing moderate and progressive Republicans today.

III

UP FROM
WATERGATE

16

The Progressive Republicans and the Energetic Class

Strategic politics has brought with it a period of fleeting coalitions, aggregations of voters and interests that form and reform as the concerns of one moment are replaced by the issues of another. In such a situation, neither an ideological approach to politics nor a coalition approach in its traditional sense can form the basis of a stable power position. The first of these will rise and fall as the nation is attracted to, then bored by, then finally repelled by the specific doctrines of a given ideology. The second of these can be broken open by a clever strategist in the opposition camp. What the Republican party needs to do, if it is to enhance its long-run political position, is to create a national constituency based on some enduring principles that will not rise and fall with every whim and twist of the increasingly fluid electorate. If it has a series of policies and positions that appeal across the board to Americans as Americans — not simply as isolated interest groups — then it will achieve a strong long-range position that will enable it to deal with the short-range issues as they rise and fall. If it can establish a record of performance and a reputation for reliability in a number of key areas, then it will be able to meet the momentary challenges of fleeting issues more effectively.

The point is that the party must establish a solid base from which to build its majorities, but that base can no longer be an aggregation or loose coalition of varying interest groups such as the New Right coalition of the South, northern working men, and Republican businessmen, or the Old Right coalition of business, agriculture, and traditional Republicans. To be sure, a majority must consist of such groups, but any *given* coalition can be broken open in modern American politics by a careful selection of issues and discontents. The only way in which either party can achieve a degree of political stability in the long run is to create a national constituency, a broad appeal on national questions of lasting concern that will enable that party to have a starting point from which to build its coalition of the moment. With such a national base — if it can be secured — the Republican party will have some appeal to almost everyone, so that it can depend on attracting almost anyone at some point in the ups and downs of our modern strategic era. The only way to achieve such a power base is to perform consistently with a number of lasting principles that are both Republican and effective. For the Republican party to survive as a party it must do three things: It must stand for something Americans want. It must stand for something it can actually deliver to Americans, and it must in fact deliver. Otherwise it will be caught up in increasingly strategic situations where it can never expect better than a flip-of-the-coin chance at success and probably will not survive for long as an institution. In short, what we as Republicans need is a politics of "can do" that will appeal to a broad range of Americans so that at any time or moment we will be in a better position to put together a winning coalition than we would be if we simply aggregate interest groups around one issue at one time. This is both responsible policy and sound political strategy.

Let us be more specific. In the new strategic age coalitions rise and fall on the basis of an issue. Unemployment aligns the national electorate one way. Race aligns it another way. Foreign policy aligns it a third way. Watergate has aligned it yet another way. Other issues will align it as they rise and fall. Some of these same issues may create different alignments at different times. As we have seen, our whole politics is rapidly becoming like a contest for mayor in a large city. Faced with this situation, the first impulse of the politician is to be dexterous — to shift back and forth, to straddle fences, to patch together ad hoc constituencies. This is a possible but a dangerous strategy. Things are moving so fast these days even in national politics that such dexterity has serious limits. A winning coalition assembled around one issue can be broken apart when some other issue becomes salient. Because the parties no longer have their historical role of internal log rolling — buying people off on one issue by satisfying them on another — it is very difficult to be politically dexterous in the full public glare. The second impulse is to tie together a coalition around an issue that the politician himself creates in the tradition of a demagogue. This can work for a while, but not for long. The opposition can neutralize the issue by adopting it, or it too can find another issue and do the same thing.

The soundest political strategy in these circumstances is to find a set of issues that appeals across the board to a wide range of constituencies and establish a reputation for delivering on them. If this can be done, then the party that succeeds in doing so has achieved a strong strategic position with respect to the opposition. With appreciation from a wide range of people it is very easy to deal with specific challenges from the Left or Right or anyplace else. Nothing can guarantee success in politics, but a widely based power position is the most secure thing that a modern politician can hope for. With such a base he is simply in a better position to resist any challenge that the opposing strategists might make. But the key is performance. Without it there can be no lasting constituencies of any sort.

The Potential of Progressive Republicans

Progressive Republicans have embraced the doctrines of strategic politics as much as others have and we have paid a price for it. To be sure, the progressives have won elections and written good records of accomplishment, but we have not done so in a party context. Our problem has been that we lack a coherent philosophy and therefore have never been able — as progressive Republicans — to establish either a narrow base of enthusiastic supporters or a broad base of grateful constituents. To be sure, individual progressive Republicans have done so in state after state, but more on the basis of personal qualities and pragmatic performances than on the basis of a set of policies that would be applicable on a national basis. We have produced a galaxy of stars who lack a coherent constituency.

Why has this situation occurred? First, the rank and file of the party tend to be more "conservative" (by the language of the recent past) than progressive Republicans are. The hierarchy is even more so. Therefore the progressive Republican usually has to play ball with the conservatives to win nominations — he cannot appear to be a threat to them. But this precludes his attempting to attract other progressives into the party. He has to move to the Right to get the nomination, then back to the Left to win the election. Amazingly, many have succeeded, but when they do they tend to build themselves a constituency within the larger electorate that is a personal, not a Republican, constituency. Should a progressive Republican politician commit himself strongly both to the party and to a progressive policy, he would risk alienating Independents and Democrats on the first count and party conservatives on the second. Faced with these choices, progressives in the past have often ignored the party — which is why we are left with no major base within it.

It is time for us, however, to abandon strategic politics and return to party politics. The confusions of Watergate have given us this opportunity and the growth of the New Right should give us the incentive. There are several concrete steps that we must take if we want to play an effective role within the Republican party.

First, we must reach out our hands to the Old Right and establish some

327

working relationships with it — and there are many principles on which we can both agree. Freedom, capitalism, entrepreneurship, and programmatic accomplishment are sound doctrines that unite us both. The growth of government power at the expense of civil liberties is a concern of each group. The paternalism, socialism, and corporatism of the New Right should be regarded by progressives and Old Rightists alike as a threat to our basic values. To be sure, there are areas of disagreement between us — we have historically favored more government intervention in the economy and on behalf of minorities — but we should be willing and anxious to listen to them on economic questions if they are willing to listen to us on questions of civil liberties. This alliance in defense of historic Republican principles could be a very strong one.

Second, we must work to create for ourselves a larger constituency within the Republican party. It is simply poor strategy and poor politics to sit around waiting for some progressive candidate to win the nomination through tactical proficiency. If we can create a constituency, then we will have a power base with which to operate. If we do not, then we are loading the political dice against ourselves to an enormous degree.

Third, the natural constituency of the progressive Republican is the professional, and we must bring many more professionals into the positions of power within our party. We have seen how business can be influential, and what the limits of that influence are. We have also seen how the New Right threatens to take a certain segment of the business community and use it as a major power base that might operate in conjunction with a strong ideology. We must counter this threat to our party by bringing the professionals and the entrepreneurial businessmen together into an alliance based on a set of coherent principles that will enable us to serve their interests — and that will enable them to regard our future as important to them. The farmer, too, would be a strong possibility since he is not enamored of the New Right doctrines.

The professionals at present are largely not Republicans (witness the contribution patterns we saw in Chapter 12). They are independents, and they are among the most rapidly growing sector of our society. They can be attracted to the Republican party, but not on appeals to racism or the new corporatism. They are a class that does not look with favor on the new socialism, although they do accept certain parts of the New Deal as givens in a modern society. Their issues are honest and effective government, responsible finance, civil liberties, quality of life and the environment, efficiency in the economy, and freedom to pursue their professional life without government interference. These are the issues that the Old Right and the progressives alike support — and professionals will vote for and support this kind of Republicans. Our job is to bring these professionals into the Republican party and thereby give them a stake in our future so that they will become our active and enthusiastic constituency.

But to do so we need an approach to society and government that is coherent, credible, and attractive. We need some principles around which we as Republicans can unite, principles that will persist throughout the ups and downs of fleeting coalitions, principles that can form the basis of a national constituency, and principles that we can make effective because we can deliver to a constituency on the basis of them.

Five Principles for Republicans

It has been repeated for quite some time that the country is in trouble, and it certainly is. We are in the middle of a massive and chronic economic crisis. We have pressing and persistent racial problems. There is the energy crisis. Our armed forces are pathetic shadows of their former selves. Our urban crises are still there. Crime abounds. Our schools in city after city are becoming either detention centers or glorified playpens, neither of which seems to have the capacity to produce students with a commitment to academic excellence or self-improvement. Our transportation system, despite recent stopgap measures, is in vast disarray. Much of our major industry is stagnant. Our standard of living is effectively static. Our environment is not being improved to the extent that it might. And there is always Watergate — eternally. We have no lack of problems.

What we seem to lack is the ability to deal with them head on, and that is because we have lost confidence in ourselves and in our national purpose. We have lost the sense of fun in problem-solving. We tend to blame our problems on others rather than solving them ourselves. We rely too much on the government. We think too much in terms of our relative positions: we fear that if someone else gets ahead it is at our expense. If we can regain our sense of confidence, if we can regain a *genuine* sense of pride in our country, not the false vanity that calls for repeated public display and thereby underscores its insecurity, then at least we will have made some headway. It seems that what we must do is focus on the things we *can* accomplish and thereby re-create a sense of accomplishment and excitement so that a national spirit of problem-solving can be restored. If we can accomplish a set of useful and positive goals as a nation, then people will begin to focus on these accomplishments as much as upon the narrow considerations that lead us all to regard society as a zero-sum situation, where one person's gain is purchased at the expense of another person's loss. We offer five principles that we think the Republican party should follow that will lead to concrete accomplishments and that will enable us to get out of the doldrums in which we are now floundering. These are not expediencies of the moment; they are the kind of long-range propositions on which lasting constituencies are built. They are not revolutionary, rather, they are sound and solid. They are not panaceas for all our difficulties; they are frameworks within which to approach true difficulties. But we believe they are principles that the Republican party as a party can be moved to embrace in a long-range future.

Foreign policy is the one area where the Nixon administration has written a record of lasting significance. It finally ended American involvement in Vietnam. It opened the door to China. It opened the door a bit wider to Russia. It took some dramatic steps to resolve the Middle East crisis. It brought about an end to ideological politics in the international arena and replaced it with the more solid basis of calculated interest. These were not unilateral accomplishments — world conditions made them possible — but the Nixon administration took advantage of conditions to realize these objectives. The Republican party would do well to continue this tradition and to become associated with it in the minds of the American public. What are its basic components? First, there is the willingness to deal with all nations in the world on a business-like basis, to trade with them, to talk with them, and to recognize their intrinsic existence. Second, and just as important, there is a commitment to give preferential treatment to our historical allies. This is very important. All nations are not the same in this world. Some are coldly calculating; others are motivated by impulses other than sheer expediency. Some nations, such as those of western Europe and perhaps Japan, approach America on the basis of transnational cultural ties. With such nations it is important to cultivate more lasting relationships than short-term expediencies might dictate. In international as well as in domestic politics a solid constituency provides an excellent starting point for strategic calculations. It is only prudent that we create relationships with other countries that give them a stake in our future and in our prosperity. The Nixon-Kissinger model of international relations is emphatically not based on a sheer "balance of power" doctrine. Rather, it is based on a preponderance of power doctrine where the United States and its western allies, bound together by cultural, social, and economic interests, hold a preponderance of power of sufficient strength that no combination of forces can be assembled against them. Maintaining these solid relationships is more important to future world stability than dexterous maneuvers between Russia and China ever will be. It has been necessary to employ dexterity in the creation of this world order, but there are limits to dexterity imposed by domestic considerations and the ability of statesmen.

Therefore, as Republicans, we should adhere to prudent internationalism, dealing with the communists, but never forgetting that they are communists, dealing with our allies, but never forgetting they they are our allies.

At home we should reassert our historical commitment to freedom that has been eroded by the forces of paternalism and security on the one hand and bureaucracy on the other. It is in the most fundamental sense our greatest strength. Measure it any way you want, America is still the freest nation in the world. Our press is the least regulated, our government is one of the least centralized of any major power. Our legal institutions are the most independent of political control. Our Bill of Rights gives the greatest latitude to the citizen of any modern society. And these are facts to be proud of, not ashamed of. But our freedom goes far beyond them. We can innovate more extensively than most other nations. Our individuals have a wider degree of personal choices in terms of their vocations, their purchases, and their life styles. Our society is more free-wheeling than any other and our economy is still less regulated, formally or informally, than that of any other industrial state. These conditions must be preserved at all costs, but the trend is against them. Too many institutions have a stake in reducing individual freedoms. Big government tends to regulate for the sake of regulation, and to stifle our freedoms in the name of some objective that more often than not is never achieved, but that serves as a justification for continued regulation. Big Business is increasingly resistant to innovation and individual enterprise. Big Labor follows suit. Freedom is always limited in the name of some short-term goal, and that goal may be legitimate. What happens, however, is that long-run purposes cannot be well defined by regimented persons, only by free individuals. Many of our best minds are rejecting a regimented order and are proceeding to vocations, especially the professions, where they can exercise a greater degree of freedom. It must never be forgotten that freedom built this country and has made it strong, viable, and decent. Departures from its principles have led occasionally to short-term advantages but never to long-range gains. It would be triple folly to extend any further the new corporatism and paternalism that so many find to be comforting alternatives to the exhilarative dangers, responsibilities, and rewards of a free society.

But what does a commitment to freedom mean in terms of policy realization? It means a greater emphasis on capitalism and the free market economy, less emphasis on the franchised corporation, the cost-plus contract, and the phased regulation of prices and wages. It means an end to agricultural supports and restrictions. It means a commitment to expanded trade internationally and a reduction in protectionist tariffs and quotas. It means realistic antitrust policies to preserve the market. It means the removal of many regulations in many industries (like rail-roads, for example) that have grown up over the last decades or half century. It means no more Lockheed loans.

But freedom goes far beyond these principles. It involves the principle that government should encourage others to do many things that government now does itself. Reprivatization should replace bureaucratization. Semipublic corporations, private businesses, universities, foundations, and voluntary associations should be encouraged to work in the public sector instead of the government taking over so much and doing so little. From the encouragement of self-help operations in the ghetto to the principle of urban homesteading (which encourages occupants of build-ings to acquire title to them), to the principle of black capitalism, to the sale of the Post Office to genuine private enterprise, there are thousands of ways in which the government could get out of activities that it doesn't do well and that private individuals could do much better. Expanded ownership policies and increased proprietary opportunities for the poor are approaches most consistent with extending individual freedom. De-centralized decisionmaking and policies of greater local autonomy are highly consistent with these views.

But there is more to freedom than just economic and social policies. This country needs a rededication to the Bill of Rights: a right to privacy from government snooping, a right to be secure in papers and posses-sions, a right to speak out without fear of intimidation. This list is familiar and we can add the other clauses that we have come to cherish. But these rights are in danger. As the doctrines of security supplant the principles of freedom in so many minds, we stand in danger of doing to ourselves those things we have fought so hard to prevent others from doing to us. When the question of liberty is presented in terms of concrete policies — pornography, dossiers, dissent, disruption, defendants' rights, freedom of information, freedom of speech and expression of unwelcome opinions, freedom of the press to be abusive, rights of citizens to be left alone — all these put the doctrine to a severe test, and Republicans more and more have sided with government and security than with freedom. Even though it is hard for us to do so emotionally in many cases, we must remember that our commitment to freedom and equity must extend beyond our own interests. As Watergate showed us so dramatically, government cannot always be trusted to be the final judge of what is and is not permissible. We have seen the doctrines of security abused exten-sively for mean purposes. It seems prudent for us all to remember that the price of liberty is eternal vigilance and that an attack on one man's freedom is an attack on the freedom of us all. If one doubts the authen-ticity of this view, let him reflect upon how men of the stature of Robert

Taft and Dwight Eisenhower would have reacted to the illegalities of Watergate.

A third sound Republican principle should be the doctrine of efficiency. It is a principle that is consistent with the principles of freedom and openness and inconsistent with bureacratization and paternalism. While the slogan "the efficient society" would have a cold and harsh ring to it, there is one major point about efficiency that should be remembered, namely, that it is the basis of our standard of living and without it there would certainly be a dramatic increase in material deprivation throughout. What is wrong with our economy, and much of our society, is that we are experiencing a crisis of efficiency. No matter how you look at it or disguise it, there is only one way in which a society can make lasting material progress: when the same number of people can produce more goods and services. That is the meaning of increasing efficiency. Our economy is stagnating today because some policies of government, bureaucracy, and labor are interacting to prevent increased economic efficiency. Our whole international position is declining because productivity is not rising as fast as wages. Our whole domestic situation is getting increasingly worse for the same reasons. The Democrats have no real solution to the problem; their policies, if anything, encourage inefficiencies. It is our job through positive and negative incentives to focus the attention of both business and labor on the necessity of increasing productivity.

There is one dimension to the efficiency crisis that everyone should reflect on extensively: it is undercutting our security position dramatically. We are pricing ourselves out of the security market just as fast as we are pricing ourselves out of almost every other market. Those who are so concerned with security should take heed. Our military is allocating its resources more to salaries than to hardware and research. The ratio of support troops to combat troops is astronomically high. Our procurement policies and our cost overruns are creating situations where we are purchasing equipment under the most disadvantageous conditions possible. Even our military tactics are neglecting the doctrine of efficiency. The North Vietnamese were so successful (considering their resources) because they were able to tie down vast American resources for little expenditure of their own. Efficiency ratios are at the heart of human conflict as well as at the center of human progress. On both counts we are losing and the Republican party might be expected to do something about it.

In addition to becoming the party of prudent internationalism, freedom, and efficiency, the Republican party must earn — re-earn — a reputation for responsibility. This is a wide field. There are obviously some immediate problems of honesty and integrity that must be met. There can be no question that the Watergate business has created severe problems for the party. And there can be no question that the way to appear honest is to be honest. There should be no further business with juvenile delinquents, petty crooks, fabricators, large-scale swindlers, and the other shady characters that have moved so freely of late in the corridors of Washington. This goes without saying in normal times, but occasionally needs repeating. This tradition of Grant, Harding, and Nixon is not one that Republicans need continue.

But responsibility goes far beyond honesty and integrity. It involves a sense of limit and restraint, a sense of quiet and effective performance. It involves a respect for institutions and procedures. It involves a reputation for moderation and reciprocity, not extremism and an unchecked drive for success at the expense of principle. Above all, responsibility envisions a doctrine of *service* to the public, not mastery of the populace. It carries with it a feeling of compassion, understanding, and respect for others. Under Eisenhower the Republican party enjoyed this reputation because it earned it. It must earn it once more.

KNOWLEDGE

If freedom has been the principal source of our historical strength, the expansion of knowledge and the growth of our technology have been freedom's most important by-products. How many great minds have fled to this country to escape the tyranny of closed societies? It has not always been the fear of personal liquidation that brought so many great men to our shores — although there has been that, too. The opportunity to seek knowledge unencumbered by governmental regulation has served as a magnet for great minds and as a source of our tremendous industrial and technological plants.

Knowledge and technology are our most important products, and the only industries with the possible exception of basic agriculture where we are competitive on a lasting basis. It is to these we must turn if our world leadership is to continue; despite many suggestions to the contrary, these expanding treasures really do depend on freedom, innovation, and the energetic application of individual talent. These are the areas in which the world looks to America for leadership, and they are areas that the government is beginning to neglect and that industry is beginning to downgrade. This neglect is a serious, short-sighted mistake. The expansion of knowledge, the development of new processes, the augmentation of efficiencies, and the releasing of creative energies have made this country strong and respected. The expansion of knowledge and technology are the keys to the future and if this nation is to deal with the future, it must live in the future and master it.

Consider the space program — that much-maligned enterprise — which is the symbol, really, of what is right with America, not what is wrong. The space program works. The equipment functions relatively well. The personnel are trained to accomplish their tasks with a high degree of proficiency. The object of expanding our knowledge of the universe is the most fundamentally sound purpose of any the federal government pursues. There is a spirit of "can do" about the whole program, and although training breeds a degree of regimentation, the problems and the crises encountered have led to repeated expressions of creativity, individualism, and the affirmation of human capacities. It has brought to America more prestige than any other single program since the Marshall Plan, and the reason for this prestige is that our space research is an affirmation of positive, not negative, values. Who can seriously doubt for a moment that the future of the human race lies in the expanded knowledge and exploration of the universe without and the universe within? Who can doubt that the nation that leads the world into these universes will receive more respect and genuine gratitude from the rest of the world than any amount of military hardware could ever purchase? The world is changing. New forms of power and prestige are replacing the older forms. If we cling to the structures of the past we shall certainly lose the future. The point is that such things as the space program are positive endeavors that open the way to an expanded future. They are with the trends of human aspirations, not against them.

And there are so many other things we could be doing that fit into this category. If there is any area where the "public sector" needs expanding, it is in the area of scientific research. If there is any long-range national or human purpose, it must be to find out more about ourselves and the universe in which we live.

The Energetic Class

The Republican party would do well to embrace these five principles and begin to build a series of positive programs around them. The point we should emphasize is that there are a lot of things we *can do* in this society; there are a lot of specific tasks we can accomplish that will give us back some of our old self-confidence and that will enable us to regain our sense of mission and pride. Consider the following, all of which should be perfectly possible to accomplish in the near future — if we make commitments to them. We could:

- Overhaul our ground transportation system and build a network of completely automated railways, privately run, that are in effect giant conveyor belts for industry. Such a program would do wonders for the overall efficiency of the economy by providing vastly cheaper transportation than is currently available.
- Find a chemical or medical cure for heroin addiction. Consider the impact of this on both organized and street crime.
- Tax the polluter and forget about legal proceedings. Let the polluter find an economical means of dealing with the problem himself.
- Initiate a full-fledged expansion of the modular housing concept and the manufactured dwelling by removing the restrictions imposed by archaic codes and artificial union interference.
- Let private industry take over the delivery of mail in the United States.
- Give the power industry appropriate incentives to convert from fossil fuels to nuclear energy and thereby achieve self-sufficiency in energy production.
- Expand agricultural research to develop new plant strains that will double the productive capacity of the earth's acreage over the next decade and a half.

Suppose America began to accomplish these tasks, and many others like them. What would such accomplishments do for us? We would begin to have a sense of positive movement. We would begin to regain that confidence in ourselves that we have recently lost because we would be moving with the direction of human aspirations freely expressed in a free society. And if any political party can give to this country the sense that once more we have become a going concern, that party need not worry too much about the next election.

With a program that emphasizes what we *can do,* the Republican party could make a very broad-based appeal to the vast segment of the society that wants to be creative and is committed to accomplishment. This energetic class should be the focus of our appeals not simply because it is the most dynamic part of the society and potentially the most powerful, but because it is a group of people that cuts across traditional classes and creates a base of support that can be delivered to, unlike so many other aggregations that have been propounded for the party's consideration.

Who belongs to the energetic class? The nonsubsidized businessman who runs his plant with a high degree of efficiency, who stands on his own two feet, who is not afraid of some competition, who is as happy to innovate and change as he is to rest on his laurels, who is not so taken up with sheer profits that he is afraid to reinvest his capital. The corporation manager who spends more time at the plant than at the country club. The scientist who does not regard his job as a nine-to-five routine. The surgeon. The ghetto organizer who institutes programs to feed those who are starving and undernourished and who works to release the creative

336

energies of his constituents. The workingman who doesn't mind putting something extra into his efforts, who takes pride in his work, and who shows his boss how to improve plant productivity. The craftsman who doesn't make shoddy goods. The army officer who takes sufficient pride in his unit to see that it really performs — and not just on paper. The honest police investigator who has respect for the law. The dairy farmer who reinvests his none-too-large earnings to improve his herd and build up his capital plant. The office manager who is interested in running a tight ship. The office worker who is as interested in performance as his boss. The innovative engineer. The lawyer who has to build up a practice or work to retain one. And so many others.

What do all these people have in common? They don't need the government to hold their trousers up. They are committed to accomplishment and excellence. They like to see society performing in an honest and efficient manner. Most important, they are the kind of people who innovate, improve, and exercise their freedoms in a constructive way. These are the workers, managers, capitalists, and professionals in the best sense of these words.

But what about the poor, the blacks, and the discriminated against? For too long and too often, the doctrines of self-reliance have been used as excuses to keep these people in a genuine status of subservience — and at an incredible cost in terms of human values and national resources. There are people who are genuinely unable to contribute to society and the humane thing to do is to care for them. Yet a large number of people genuinely want to be productive and useful but are kept from being so by the practices of others. This is a national scandal and the creative energies of these people must be released. All this has been said a thousand times before, but very little has been done about it. Those who need help should be helped, but those who don't should sink or swim on their own, whether they be the welfare chiselers in New York City or the welfare chiselers who are running the cost-plus corporation.

It is the energetic class that can save our party from the principles of the New Right, and it is the energetic class that can save America from the stagnation and decay that threaten us. This is the class that favors prudent internationalism, freedom, efficiency, responsibility, and knowledge, while opposing paternalism, socialism, corporatism, and big government. These are the people that will be running America in the near future unless the government makes it impossible for them to do so. We need them in the Republican party. With them, the Republican party can once more look to the future. The progressives and the Old Right can establish a strong constituency among the traditional Republicans, the professionals, the entrepreneurial businessmen, the independent farmers, and so many other members of the energetic class who are without genuine representation today. And both can appeal beyond their immediate constituencies to a larger national constituency whose interest is the future of America. With such a vision — and only with such a vision — can we overcome the narrowness of short-term game playing and perceive the future with a genuine perspective.

There is, however, one other problem that confronts us as Republicans and as Americans. The Constitution of the United States is in danger, and no assessment of our future can ignore this basic imponderable and awesome fact.

17

The Future
of the Constitution

The strategic practices of modern politics are here with us to stay. No matter how much legislation is passed to curb the activities of politicians and no matter how many sermons are preached against them, they will continue to be strategists and manipulators. The decisionmaking approach to life has become so deeply imbedded in our consciousness that there is no way to expel it from our behavior. Nor should we. Intelligent and responsible decisionmaking in its proper role has made possible most of the advantages of modern civilization. It is based on an accurate, if limited, perception of reality, and it can liberate us from the superstitions and fictions of other approaches to human relationships. All we are saying is that strategic thinking must remain the servant of human beings, not become their master.

As we have seen, however, strategic thinking does have a dynamism of its own that can compel people to behave against their will and against their better judgment. Its requirements are rigorous, its logic is demanding, and its laws are constraining. It is not always beneficial, and actions based on it are not always constitutional. There are some serious questions that can be asked about the proper role of strategic thinking in a constitutional democracy.

What is the meaning of *representation* in our age of increased deterrence and game playing between politicians and electorates? How can the use of strategy, with its emphasis on logic and expertise, be made compatible with democracy and its emphasis on the popular will? How can the increasing tendency to seek a pure power position be made compatible with the obvious requirement that a government perform and deliver to its constituencies? How can a system based on law be made compatible with an attitude of unrestrained game playing? How can restraint — the necessary starting point of any constitutional order — be made compatible with the strategic imperative of accumulating power to preserve options? How can the adversary process — that noble expression of productive conflict — be sufficiently restrained so that it remains productive? Above all, how can we keep strategic thinking under control so that it reinforces rather than subverts democratic principles? These important questions must be placed in a proper perspective.

The Constitution
and the Strategic Perspective

The basis of any constitution is the way men and women think about politics. Their values, their perceptions, their sense of justice, their sense of purpose, their attitudes toward each other, and their overall perception of reality must be the framework within which they define their politics and write their rules for political conduct. In the broadest sense of the word, a constitution is an expression of these values. It is not only a set of rules that prescribes the conduct of politics, it is also a codification of values dominant in a society at a given point in time. One problem with America today is that our values are rapidly changing — and with them our perception of the Constitution.

For the first century and a half of our national existence the Constitution was genuinely regarded as an object of veneration. It was a form of higher law, a unique document, a contract whose clauses were approached with reverence and whose interpretations more resembled biblical scholarship than any other secular enterprise. Deeply imbedded in the national psyche, it was a force unto itself. Although it may surprise modern politicians, most presidents of the last century and the first part of this one genuinely wrestled with their consciences to determine if a proposed action violated or did not violate the letter and the spirit of our higher law. Some people still do. But a "government of laws, not of men," as the saying went, is not very compatible with the new strategic attitudes toward politics. As our politics becomes more manipulative, as winning replaces equity in our political pantheon, as the game plan mentality replaces the service mentality, our society becomes so changed in its basic attitudes that it is hardly capable of understanding what a constitutional Republic is in the traditional sense. To many groups in the society the Constitution is rapidly becoming a political football to be maneuvered and manipulated in the service of some short-range objective. The Old Left started the process and now repents its indiscretion; the New Left has accelerated it. The pragmatists found that a manipulative attitude toward the Constitution suited them very well indeed, and the New Right has embraced the game with abandon. Mainly, the Old Right, much to its credit, has preserved in its attitudes the kind of respect the Constitution traditionally enjoyed, a respect that maintained the balance of government very well. But to an increasing number of politicians today, constitutional authority is simply that which can be gotten away with before someone else interferes.

It was not always so. When the Constitution was written in the eighteenth century, the political perceptions of America were dominated by two great intellectual traditions, the Calvinism of the Puritans with its strong Judaic underpinning and the rationalism of the Enlightenment with its logical and strategic requirements. These two traditions were woven together by such men as John Locke and Thomas Jefferson, and their synthesis dominated our perceptions of political reality until very recently. Right, obligation, authority, trust, covenant, representation, will, duty, transgression, punishment, and responsibility were concepts that formed the basis of politics in this system of thought. Humans were regarded as moral entities, not as biological realities, and justice, not cleverness, was the means of evaluating human performance. These Calvinist perceptions, however, were quite compatible with strategic thinking and the two formed a powerful union. Success was not frowned upon — within certain rules of procedure — and strategy in the service of justice was regarded as a highly desirable expedient. The point, however, is that the two were paired together. Even those founding fathers who flirted with atheism inherited from their surroundings the moral categories of the Calvinist-Enlightenment synthesis. Their secular state was still based in part on a set of moral principles inherited from a strong religious tradition. It is little wonder that these men thought in terms of a higher law obligating people to certain forms of political behavior, and it is not surprising that they created a Constitution in their image of obligation.

Today the political perceptions of many Americans — especially those in the elite positions of our society — are becoming truly secularized. The old synthesis is breaking down. Political frames of reference are changing. We hear much less about *will* these days and much more about *choice* and *decision*. A law is not perceived as an *obligation* as much as a *deterrent*. *Authority* in its traditional sense is being replaced by a concept of *power*. *Right* (which is closely related to authority and obligation) is also becoming thought of as *power*. (There is no more striking evidence of this latter tendency than the way in which modern insurgent demands for rights rapidly change to demands for power.) Covenants become contracts. Trust becomes a simple matter of expectation and prediction.

We are not passing judgment on this tendency — although we do pass judgment on some of its side effects. We are simply asserting that when people begin to perceive politics in terms of power, decision, strategy, deterrence, and calculation, they behave differently than when they perceived it in terms of authority, will, judgment, obligation, and right.

It is therefore not surprising that political behavior is changing, since the nature of political activity depends on the nature of political perception. And, as our attitudes toward politics change, it is little wonder that our attitudes toward the Constitution and constitutional government change as well. This raises a disturbing question. If our Constitution was written by and for people with one sense of political reality, how can it be relevant to people with another sense of political reality? How is our traditional sense of constitutionalism compatible with our new practices of decisionmaking and high strategy? Will not the new logic, devoid of its moral components, subvert the Constitution? These are not trivial questions and they are not asked lightly.

There are many elements to our constitutional structure, but let us examine three important ones and describe the impact of the new strategic logic on each. The first principle is democracy, the assertion that the government exists at the behest of the people for the purpose of carrying out their will. There are many ways in which their will can be exercised, but under the Constitution the principle of representation is the most important one and forms an integral part of our concept of democracy. The second principle is republicanism, the embodiment of a long-range perspective that serves as a restraint on democracy and gives validity and legitimacy to institutions and other guided restrictions on the popular will. The third principle is the adversary process, the effective foundation of our doctrines of freedom and openness in the society at large, a principle that defines the relationship between the various parts of our constitutional structure. Each of these three elements, in turn, is threatened by the hyperstrategic practices of modern politics.

DEMOCRACY, DECISIONMAKING, AND PERFORMANCE

In our traditional form of political perceptions, the democratic element of our constitutional scheme rested upon the principle of will. The government existed at the behest of the people; it was ordained by them, and their duly chosen representatives were supposed to carry out their mandated will. (Since the Constitution was not wholly "democratic" there were other concepts at work here, but will served as the basis of the democratic principle.)

Today, however, this principle is no longer applicable in many circles because its meaning has changed dramatically. Our elites, trained in the virtues of the new linear perspective, do not think in terms of will but in terms of options and choices; the human activity, formerly called a will and based on a judgmental view of reality, is now called a decision and is based on a linear, causal (domino) view of reality. This is not a universally accepted view, but it is the basis of the new decisionmaking approach to life. Will, in the meantime, has become a pejorative concept and is equated with arbitrariness — willfulness — and is taken as a sign of inferiority that is to be overcome by good rational psychological prescriptions.

A decision, however, is not an arbitrary exercise, nor need it be a judgmental one in the moral sense. It can be subjected to rules of procedure and it can be evaluated much more operationally than a will can. Therefore, since it can be evaluated more easily and since it can be subject to rules, a decision can best be made by an expert who can be so designated by the continual success of his decisions. People can be trained to make decisions, and it is possible to suggest with some degree of certainty that some people are better decisionmakers than others or that they are specialists in certain areas of decisionmaking. It therefore makes good sense for decisions to be made by professional decisionmakers and it makes equally good sense for these decisionmakers to be evaluated on grounds of their performance.

What does this do to our political categories? First, the will of the people ceases to be a very relevant political concept; if anything it becomes a negative category since it is equated with arbitrariness, the least desirable behavior pattern from the standpoint of a decisionmaker. It is replaced by the *decision* of the people, a more rational category and hence subject to evaluation on a more rigorous basis. The decision of an electorate or a people is not to be taken lightly, but how much less authoritative it sounds than the *will* of the people. And it is easy to question. The case can be made that the people are not as capable of making decisions as expert decisionmakers are. There is a plausible ring to this — and throughout our history there have been strong checks to the expression of the popular will — but it is much easier for a *decisionmaker* to conclude that he, not the public, is best equipped to deal with reality than it was for a more traditional elite to assert that its *will* was superior to that of the public.

Representation and the decisionmaker

Although this problem is new in its current formulation, it has many antecedents and in one form or another it has always been with us. Consider representation. We have always had two competing views of what a representative should be. The first is that he should stand in the place of his constituency and should articulate its desires and act as it would if it were there. In this view, the agent of the people exists to carry out their will — or their decisions, in the modern formulation. The second view of representation suggests that the representative should act in the interests of his constituency as he, not they, may perceive them. He is still their representative since he is presumably acting on their behalf although not necessarily at their behest. He asserts that they should return

343

him to office because they respect his competence and character, not because they necessarily agree with his specific short-range positions.

In practice most good representatives try to combine these two principles in some reasonable fashion. The growth of decisionmaking as the central function in our society, however, lends support to the second image of representation and has a tendency to carry the argument one step further — that the expert should make most of the important decisions on the grounds of his expertise, that he can perform better in the decisionmaking role than anyone else can. There is a very persuasive ring to this argument, but it is easy to see how it undercuts the democratic principle and ultimately subverts the representative principle as well. Generally speaking, the image is that politics sets goals and experts devise means to attain them, but with the distinction between means and ends becoming increasingly blurred in our open-ended world, there is no logical reason why a decisionmaking expert cannot claim to be able to set goals as well. After all, in an open-ended situation, there is no logical distinction between decisionmaking to devise means and decisionmaking to define ends.

If this argument is taken to its logical conclusion — certainly a big if — it is clear that a great deal of distance can occur between the governors and the governed. The governors can assert that their decisions should prevail because they are based on sounder foundations: better decisionmaking procedures, better information, a greater ability to predict expected outcome, more experience, and so forth. The governors might even feel that if they are really sure of themselves, their commitments might justify a degree of coercion or deception with respect to the public — for the public's own good. After all, the purpose of good decisionmaking is success and the ability to carry out the requirements of the decisions. On the road to success, short-term obstacles can be overcome in the pursuit of longer-term objectives. Hence a degree of coercion and deception appears plausible and beneficial — for the public's own good.

The process, however, tends to bring the public and the government into a conflict relationship. Under the old scheme of representation there was a form of mutuality: the public supported the representative and the representative delivered to the public. This was never perfect, but the notions of will and consent were clearly operating within it. If a representative disagreed with his constituency his duty was to exercise leadership and to convince the electorate to change its mind — or to go his own route in the hope that the electorate would eventually see the wisdom of his ways. There was, at any rate, no *inherent* justification for coercion or deception. To be sure, the traditional machine knocked heads together, but even this exercise was above board — and not universally acclaimed. But now the underlying logic of our perceptions seems to be moving in a direction antagonistic to representation and democracy.

One result is a tendency by the electorate to fight back and to coerce the government. Not only have minority groups rebelled against the government and tried to coerce it (rather unsuccessfully), but silent majorities have asserted their rebellions against expertise in many ways. This is not a Left-Right phenomenon but a universal one. The Left resents the activities of "faceless bureaucrats" and the Right deplores the practices of the "do-gooders." The former objects when the bureaucracy rams a new road through the bird sanctuary and the latter protests when the school buses roll along it. This protest has taken many different forms, but quite often it is expressed by some mode of attack upon the government. The danger is that both the electorate and the government will begin to view each other in increasingly hostile and contemptuous terms. We are a long way from this, but the assertions by the expert that the people *cannot* perform and by the people that the government *does not* perform are not made in a spirit of mutuality.

Only a fool would assert that a complex modern industrial state could be run without a large number of competent decisionmakers, and no one would suggest that the government could operate without them either. But if the decisionmaking mentality becomes paramount in politics, it is reasonable to ask what the proper role and function of popular decisionmaking are. What kinds of decisions are best made by the people? What kind of decisions are best made in a decentralized way? Above all, how is it possible to preserve a democratic principle in a milieu of specialized expertise?

Expertise and power struggles

These are clearly constitutional questions of the first order and must be examined more closely. First, however, it is instructive to see how the new decision theories and attitudes toward expertise are changing the relationships between our principal organs of government.

The basic assertion of the decisionmaker is that he can perform, that he can behave successfully in the jungle of increasing complexities. This is a fundamental assertion because performance is a major source of power. Americans have always admired those who perform and have rewarded them handsomely. If an expert is truly an expert — if he can perform — he can expect power to gravitate in his direction. This phenomenon has underlaid the dramatic constitutional shifts of recent years as the executive department as a whole asserted its superiority over Congress, as the White House then asserted its superiority over the executive department, and then, in the face of Watergate (a massive lapse in performance), the federal bureaucracy asserted its authority over the White House, creating a final repository of power in its logical place — with the permanent expert. This process was both tragic and amusing.

The takeover of congressional functions by the federal executive has a long history and it is not necessary to detail it. The crucial factor at each

345

stage of the game, however, has been the concept of performance. The executive over the years has asserted that it can perform better than the Congress — that it can draw up legislation better, that it can budget better, that it can conduct foreign affairs better, and even that it can handle public relations better. The ability to perform has attracted the authority to perform, and power has gravitated toward the executive. This whole process has had the consent and often enthusiastic blessing of Congress.

Occasionally, however, Congress tries to reassert its prerogatives but it seldom succeeds. Since it asserts these powers categorically, not functionally, all the arguments about performance remain, and power either stays where it was or quietly returns there. In fact, the executive has Congress in a position where everything it does on its own terms seems to be negative, dysfunctional, or counterproductive; every move it makes in defiance of executive privilege seems to obstruct, not augment, the performance of government. This is a bad position to be in when the criterion for power is the ability to perform.

Within the executive branch there has also been a gravitation away from the White House per se in the direction of the permanent bureaucracy, which also asserted its ability to perform. When the Nixon administration came to power it tried to reverse this trend, as previous presidents had to some extent. This attempt was most visible in foreign affairs (where there were some strong precedents), but it occurred at home as well. The cabinet was reduced in authority, the power to hire and fire was used extensively to ensure compliance, funds were withheld selectively, and there were attempts to dismantle agencies without the consent of Congress. The Office of Management and Budget became the central power of this activity and the whole White House staff asserted massive prerogatives. These procedures were detailed in Chapter 2.

The White House, however, made a fatal mistake. It accumulated power from the federal bureaucracy in the name of performance — but it failed to perform! With the exception of foreign affairs, where the contrasts are striking, the White House accumulated power as part of a game plan that envisioned the accrual, but not the exercise of power for the purpose of governmental performance. As soon as Watergate exploded, the federal bureaucracies struck back and used the same criterion of performance to justify their declaration of independence from political supervision. The FBI and the CIA forced the appointment of careerists as their directors; the Justice Department took formal moves to dissociate itself from political pressure. The Pentagon, always quite independent, strengthened its distance. And so forth throughout the government.

These tendencies are all disquieting since the democratic component of our constitutional structure seems to be rapidly disappearing. The elected official (especially at the highest levels) is increasingly playing the public relations game and avoiding the responsibilities of his office. As game

346

playing comes to dominate the behavior of politicians, the Washington scene becomes a giant, but sterile, power struggle between political institutions. While all this is happening, however, the forces of order are taking over gradually — especially the bureaucracy — while the politicians play their games and shun their responsibilities. Certainly not all politicians behave this way — although more are being forced to. The point is that unless they begin to perform again and serve a useful function they will continue to lose power. Congress can pass legislation asserting its prerogatives in a never-ending stream, but unless Congress starts to *perform* again, it will never regain its power. The same is true for the White House. Those who wish to see an effective balance of national power should look less to abstract definitions of legal relationships and more to actual activities. Those who wish to see an effective system of representative democracy must require the elected official to start doing his job once again — to make the relevant decisions that our complex society requires. He should be provided with the expertise to make this role possible, but the decisions should remain his and of those he represents. But this can only be a partial solution to a more fundamental problem.

REPUBLICANISM, RESTRAINT, AND THE LONG-RANGE PERSPECTIVE

The democratic principle is not the only element of our constitutional structure that is circumscribed by the new perception of political reality. The republican principle fares little better. Republicanism is a concept as diffuse as democracy, but in our scheme of government it is almost synonymous with the idea of restraint. The separation of powers, the creation of institutions to perform long-term functions and to check each other's excesses, the creation of institutions to restrain the people's excesses, and the limitation of authority in general — these are republican principles. It is not too much to suggest that the restraints imposed on government by the Bill of Rights are fundamental manifestations of republicanism at work.

We need not dwell at length on the incompatibility of the republican principle with unvarnished strategic thinking. Many of the arguments discussed in the previous section are relevant here, and it should be obvious that a principle based on a respect for laws, institutions, and procedures is incompatible with an attitude of game playing that is restrained only by the counterproductivity of its postulated actions. But a few points should be made.

First, republican principles embrace a sense of limit: limited government, limited powers on institutions, and limited practices by politicians. The Constitution is intended to impose restraints on the whole political scene, and a sense of constitutionalism among the politicians and the citizenry implies that certain activities are proscribed per se — there are things that just aren't done, not because they are counterproductive, but because they are unconstitutional and wrong. The tendency to aggrandize, to try to win at all costs, and to use every noncounterproductive weapon against the opposition is simply not reconcilable with our traditional republican sense of limit.

Second, a sense of limit is closely related to our historical principle of the rule of law. Americans have always maintained that our constitutional form of government was based on a set of higher laws that took precedence over the narrow legislation and short-range practices of the politician. The commitment to the rule of law itself is a form of restraint and limit, a civilizing force that was intended to regulate the conduct of government and institute rules of procedure by which political actions could be regulated. But the hyperstrategist cannot admit to the rule of law that appears to him to be a massive fiction. From his viewpoint, the only laws are laws of strategy and feasibility. Custom and tradition are not barriers to action. Precedents are made to be broken and exploited. Above all, law to the strategic mentality is not an *obligation,* it is merely a *deterrent,* and there is no intrinsic regulation to a deterrent. Deterrents are simply part of the larger calculations of payoffs to be acknowledged or defied as the exigencies of the moment prescribe. To a person who perceives reality exclusively in terms of causal chains, material relations, and anticipated payoffs, there can be no higher law.

Third, there can be no sense of right. How can a person's *rights* be logically defined if the relationship between people is defined largely in terms of decisions, expectations, and incentives? *Powers* are very much a part of the strategic mentality, but *rights* come from those higher laws and moral perceptions of reality that hyperstrategists ignore in their practices.

Fourth, republican principles are based on a respect for institutions and institutional restraints. True republicans recognize the long-term value of institutions in a free society. Even if they disagree with the current policies and practices of a given institution, they do not try to subvert it as an institution. They may proceed by constitutional means to try to change those policies or practices. but they do not attack the institution itself. They don't try to augment the power of the executive when "their" man is President and the power of the Congress when "their" man isn't President. They don't try to augment judicial authority when the court is favorable and circumscribe it when the court is not. They recognize the need for balance and the value of lasting institutions. To the game planner, however, institutions are just part of the game. To subvert them in the pursuit of a short-range objective may be difficult, but it is certainly an important option. They are there to be manipulated and there is nothing sacred about their powers — or their continued effective existence.

The republican principle, then, is based on a commitment to *procedure:* due process is the supreme republican virtue. It underlies our doctrine of separate powers, of institutional integrity, of the supremacy of law, and of the rights of citizens, which may not be denied without it. But these commitments to the restraints of procedure are made from a long-term perspective. They transcend the narrowness of momentary expediency. The strategic mentality finds them so annoying because it is committed to a short-range perspective.

There is, however, no inherent advantage to the short-range perspective. A decisionmaker can always take the longer view, and as he does he achieves a degree of maturity that the game plan mentality does not admit. The mature decisionmaker appreciates the value of honesty, trust, and moderation. He knows the importance of a good reputation and the worth of sticking to solid principles and procedures. He begins to see that his actions are setting precedents for others to follow and that he will have to live with the implications of these precedents in the long run. Also, he begins to deal with most people in terms of mutuality, not deterrence, because he recognizes that deterrence, in the absence of authority, is a short-run expedient and long-run disaster because it creates in the correspondent an overwhelming desire to strike back when the moment is opportune. He appreciates the value of institutions. He recognizes the basic reciprocity of most situations and he is sufficiently confident in the solidity of his position that he can resist the temptations of short run expediencies. He is more cautious but generally much more resolute when he has committed himself to a course of action. And he knows the fine art of giving the short-term game player sufficient rope to hang himself.

THE ADVERSARY PROCESS, STRATEGY, AND FREEDOM

The most fundamental constitutional procedure employed in the American system is the adversary process. It lies at the center of our legal structure; it justifies our doctrine of checks and balances; it is embodied in the electoral process and the party system; it informs our theories of countervailing forces; it is the essence of debate and political dispute; it is present in our system of hearings and investigations; and it provides one of the soundest rationales for freedom of speech and press. It goes further. Competition, free markets, and in many ways the incentive structure of the society are based on notions of conflict and adversity.

But the adversary process, this great structural reality that distinguishes our society from a corporatist one, is based to a large extent on the free exercise of strategy. Competition and conflict are fundamental virtues, not vices, and they stimulate the vitality while inspiring the freedom of the Republic. We certainly would not want to do without

349

them; however, there are several problems inherent in the adversary process.

First, it needs a judge. In our legal system, there are both judges and courts of last resort. In our electoral system, the voter is the judge. In our market system, the consumer serves this function. In a legislature, it is the majority. But what about the basic structure of the government — Congress, the executive, the courts, and the bureaucracy? Here there is no judge, nor can there really be one in an institutional sense. With the parties themselves being the judge, there is a great potential for conflict unless they are restrained by some external force or by a basic respect for the system itself.

The adversary process is a great guarantor of our freedoms — and its preservation is vital — but it has another fundamental drawback: one adversary might achieve such a dominant position that it could always win. A monopoly in the market, a cabal in the legislature, or a condition of hegemony by one branch of government is always possible, and from the standpoint of the hyperstrategist this condition is his logical objective and his ultimate standard of success.

Also, the adversary process was never intended to be an end in itself; it was always regarded as instrumental to some further end. In court it was felt to be the best route to justice; in the marketplace, to quality; in elections, to leadership; in debates, to truth; and in government, to freedom. In each of these employments strategy was vital, but secondary, in the logic of the process. When, however, the adversaries begin to approach a pure strategic relationship — a condition of total commitment to winning at all costs and by all procedures — the original objects of the adversary process are subverted. When attorneys in court use "every trick in the book," justice does not necessarily result. When the manufacturer uses every trick in the book with respect to the consumer and competitor, quality does not necessarily result. When the debater uses every trick in the book, truth does not necessarily result. When the electioneer uses every trick in the book, leadership does not necessarily result; and when the presidency uses every trick in the book, freedom and good government do not necessarily result.

The reverse phenomenon is equally bad. The adversary process can be subverted by collusion even more decisively than by the excessive employment of high strategy. Price-fixing in commerce and coziness in government are as dangerous to our system of democracy as hyperstrategy and war-gaming. It would be triple folly to suggest that the excesses of the adversary process be eliminated by circumscribing the process itself, since the obvious alternative to a constitution based on the adversary system is one based on the corporatist image of society. And that is not what we need because it would rapidly eliminate our freedoms and replace them with that fatuous gift of paternalistic security discussed in Chapter 14. The adversary process is indeed the foundation of our freedoms, our vitality, and our energy. If we are to remain an energetic society, it must be strengthened, not reduced.

Strengthening the Institutions

The adversary process, then, should clearly remain the basic premise of our constitutional order — a premise that distinguishes our democracy from the paternalistic "democracies" so popular in the rest of the world, and a premise that lays the foundation for republicanism by justifying a governmental system of checks and balances, separation of powers, and a vast private sector in the largest sense of the word "private." It should continue to define the structure of our government, our economy, our jurisprudence, and our intellectual enterprises.

But how can we deal with the excesses of strategic thinking that are nourished so well by the adversary process? Let us look at the problem where it is most important, in the relationship between the various elements of our federal system. As we have seen, there are two great tensions in Washington: between Congress and the White House and between these two elected organs and the permanent bureaucracy. We have also seen how these tensions are resolving themselves. The decision-making ethos and the crisis of performance in Congress have shifted power in the direction of the executive as the result of both a long-range process and a quick power grab by the Nixon administration. The Watergate scandal and its attendant game playing excesses, however, have resulted in a shift of power *within* the executive branch to the permanent bureaucracy. And we have seen how these shifts have undercut the democratic principle by removing the decisionmaking process from the people, the republican principle by upsetting the checks and balances, and the adversary process by locating power in the bureaucracy — the one institution of government that is most susceptible to corporatist and paternalistic impulses.

If this pattern of events continues, our whole constitutional structure will gravitate in a most unpleasant direction. The solution to our problems is conceptually rather simple — and certainly obtainable in practice. We must restore the ability to perform to the elected institutions. What would this mean?

First, it is obvious that Congress needs to be strengthened. But as we have already said, it cannot be strengthened by the mere assertion of power, only by the effective exercise of it. There are many measures it could take to enable it to begin functioning again positively. Internal reorganization, increased staff, updated operating procedures, and many other suggestions have been made and should be carried out. The problem is that so many legislators wish to give the appearance of performance, but heaven forbid that they should have to govern! But govern they must if power they want.

Second, the presidency needs strengthening. In light of Watergate and other noxious events that have followed, it may not seem logical to advocate strengthening the presidency in the context of restoring a system of checks and balances, but close examination will show why this must happen. (It is, incidentally, quite consistent with our own principle of taking a long-range view of institutions. We see no reason to attack an institution just because the wrong man happens to be occupying it at a given moment, just as we reject the merely strategic use of the argument that "the office must be protected" to keep that man in power.) There are certainly a number of aspects of the modern presidency that should be eliminated — especially all the nonsensical monarchial mystiques that have grown up around it — but its essential powers must not only be preserved, but augmented *within the context of a performing Congress.* The game plan mentality and the activities of the hyperstrategists *reduced* the ability of the presidency to perform its policymaking and legislative functions as we saw in Chapter 2. Watergate reduced it even further. If the power of the presidency to perform these functions is not restored, then even in the context of an increasingly strong Congress, the leadership of the government will continue to drift in the direction of the bureaucracies, the courts, and other agencies of a less democratic nature.

What we are suggesting is that both Congress and the White House have to increase their ability to run the government. We also suggest that a close look be taken at the separation of powers principle. As many have said, the document drafted in the 1780s envisioned a separation of powers that has evolved in this century into a *sharing* of powers. It might be good to take a step backward. If Congress could put its house in order, it might again be able to budget and legislate and the executive might turn a bit more of its attention to the problem of administering the federal bureaucracy and conducting the country's foreign policy. We are certainly not advocating a neat division here, but the more each backs away from the shared powers situation, the less a zero-sum relationship will exist between the branches of government. There is simply no reason why, under our constitutional structure, we cannot have in an institutional sense the strongest executive, the strongest legislature, and the strongest Court of any country in the world. This arrangement is possible because the strength of each can be measured on an absolute scale of performance rather than on a relative scale of institutional comparison. Separation makes this possible and it is a very healthy part of the Constitution.

We would also like to see some performance at the state and local levels. There is much talk about decentralization these days, but setting forth schemes and drawing up plans will remain an exclusively intellectual exercise unless something is done to make state and local government work. We are emphatically in favor of decentralization, but we know it cannot work effectively unless the local institutions are themselves workable. Power cannot be lastingly conveyed in a dynamic and open system, it can only be earned.

It is easy to see why we consider an ethos of performance to be the logical antidote to the hyperstrategic game plan mentality and why we want our elected institutions to perform once more, making decisions and running the various governments. First, the adversary process would be preserved. A revitalized Congress, actually doing its job, would not have to worry about executive takeovers. A revitalized executive would not have to worry about bureaucratic erosions of its power. The dynamic relationship between the branches would be preserved. The point is that those who want to see the system preserved should not focus on the system but on the elements of the system. It is not the relationship between the elements that should be dwelt upon, but the intrinsic capacities of those elements. If the capacities in an absolute sense can be augmented, then the adversary process itself will take care of the relationships.

Institutional strengthening will remove two dangers that we examined above: the danger of hegemony and the danger of a lapse into corporatist practices. The focus on performance and intrinsic capacities will also reduce the third threat to the adversary process, its tendency to degenerate into hyperstrategic contests. The sterile game playing between the branches (that we have seen so much of lately) will be recognized for what it is, an exercise in mutual futility that can never lead to a lasting rearrangement of the true power configurations.

It goes without saying that a strengthened role for elected institutions will augment the democratic principle and enable the electorate to participate more extensively in the decisionmaking process. The strengthening of local governments will do the same. There is certainly no evidence that the people are failing to perform. There is no evidence that they cannot play a vital role in the decisionmaking process of a complex society. As we saw in the first part of this book, they remain responsible, sober, balanced, and intelligent across the board.

There is also much evidence that they see beyond the narrow strategies of the game players. They have always been the best judges of whether the society is moving in the right direction or not. They are less indifferent now than ever. And they remain the best judges of their own interests. There is much validity to Justice Holmes's plea that the Lord save us from those who would save us from ourselves. People recognize their stake in the society, and they are probably better judges than the experts of how that society performs because they are on the cutting edge of that performance and not insulated from reality by bureaucratic superstructures.

Also, it is becoming widely acknowledged that decentralized decision-making is more efficient in many ways than centralized decisionmaking. The whole process of bringing the decisionmaking power in government back to the local levels holds much promise — if appropriate guarantees are made that all the people have the opportunity to participate.

Finally, these simple suggestions would strengthen the republican principle. Performance demands a long-term perspective (which is why the hyperstrategists avoid it). It is irrevocably tied to a doctrine of accountability and responsibility. The strengthened institutions would preserve the separation of powers, and the potential for decentralization would be vastly augmented. The mitigation of naked power plays between the branches and agencies would tend to induce a sense of restraint. Although these practices would not themselves restore the sense of constitutionalism and higher law, they would go a long way toward making such a restoration possible.

Restoring the Parties

There is one other major remedy for the excesses of strategic thinking, and that is a revitalized political party. The first part of the book described how parties are being ignored. In Chapter 11 we saw how strategic thinking of a certain variety tended to make them obsolete. The problem is how to restore them.

Ideally, parties are quite consistent with the three constitutional principles that we just examined. First, they obviously can be a vehicle for representative democracy. They certainly can be a means of conveying the will or decision of a constituency to the organs of government. Furthermore, by their very nature, they should be constituency-oriented and based on principles of mutual loyalties. In this sense, the hyperstrategic impulse that leads to a condition of mutual game playing can be curbed. Second, parties are part and parcel of the adversary process and they tend to mitigate some of its excesses because of their long-range perspective. Unlike a given candidate at a given moment, they have an interest in procedure and reciprocity. They must live with precedent and they resist departures from practice. Third, as institutions of our constitutional system, the great parties of the country are quite consistent with republican principles, not simply because they enjoy a long-term perspective, but because they are decentralized and are part of a larger system of checks and balances.

Parties, however, have been severely weakened in recent years for all the reasons we have seen, and their future is cloudy. To reconstruct them will not be a trivial enterprise. But it may be a necessary one if strategic excesses are to be curbed. The game players and the hyperstrategists may

354

have to be ensnared and enmeshed in a party context to curb the undesirable parts of their activities.

There are three images of a party that bear examination: the managerial party, the ideological party, and the political party in the traditional sense.

1. *The managerial party* — exemplified by CREEP and the new machine envisioned in the end-run game plan of Chapter 11 — is an organization that would depend on public relations for its loyalties and that would exist primarily to service candidates with expertise and money. It would be hyperpragmatic and hyperstrategic. Basing its policies on the results of survey research, it would try to be flexible and move with the current directions of public opinion. It would be a party run by professionals who would increasingly depend on nonvolunteer help to perform its chores. It would, in its highest form, raise the art of political persuasion to new levels of technical competence.

The problem is that the managerial party would lack a soul — which is not a minor drawback. Its chief advantage, flexibility, is only a short-run asset. Very soon its maneuvers would undercut its own base of support. Even the most flexible managers cannot juggle constituencies forever, and the more flexible the party becomes, the less loyal are its adherents. Furthermore, this kind of party would move the political process in the strategic direction very quickly. Although it would be very much a part of the adversary process, it would tend to abuse that process and render it less productive. As methods of political persuasion and coercion become more sophisticated, the democratic principle would be endangered. Finally, such parties would not enjoy either the sense of restraint or the long-term perspective because they would be focusing more on short-term objectives by the very nature of their enterprise.

2. *The ideological party.* The McGovern movement is a prototype of the ideological party. Some conservative suggestions for the future of the Republican party are further examples. The ideological party would be committed to a specific viewpoint and would differ from the managerial party because it would presumably be less flexible; it would stand for a principle and compromise that principle tactically but not politically. It too would be susceptible to hyperstrategic practices in pursuit of its objectives and would generally share with the managerial party an affection for the new political techniques.

Its major difficulty is that it would have to be small to be pure. It would tend to last longer than the managerial party because it would have a more secure power base, but it would find it very difficult to extend its constituency while holding its ideology. There is simply no nationwide ideology at this moment that could sustain such a party for long. It is highly susceptible to a phaseout of the relevance of its ideology as the great issues of the day shift back and forth.

355

Such a party would make an excellent contribution to the adversary process, and it would be somewhat less susceptible to the strategic excesses of that process than the managerial party is because it would be less doctrinally flexible. It would also be a more valid institution from the viewpoint of representative democracy; it would at any rate have a constituency and it presumably would represent that constituency to the degree permitted by its own strategic requirements. With respect to a republican impulse, the ideological party has difficulties, however. It may have a long-range view, but this view tends to be apocalyptic, not restrained. It has little respect for institutions and procedures. Winning to implement a doctrine is its principal reason for existence and all adversaries are regarded with a greater degree of hostility than they are by a managerial party.

3. *The old political party.* The traditional political party also has advantages and disadvantages. It is logically a part of the adversary process, but much less so than either of the first two images because it retards advancement, it tends to reach excessive accommodations with its adversaries, and it lacks the combative energy exhibited by both the new manager and the ideologue. On the positive side, however, it is very much a democratic institution. It has a constituency, and delivering to it is one of its major objectives. It deals in personal much more than in strategic relationships. It is more flexible in a political sense than the ideological party and less so than the managerial. It is also an institution well versed in the need for restraint and accommodation both internally and externally. It is an obvious antidote to high strategic politics; how many times have we heard that "if professional politicians had been running the campaign, Watergate would not have happened"?

None of these images of a party is satisfactory by itself. What we need is a balance between them. We need a party that enjoys technical competence — that goes without saying in modern American politics. But we also need a party that stands for something, and, in standing for something, that restrains the excesses of strategic flexibility that the purveyors of technical competence tend to promote. Meeting these two requirements, however, will not by itself restore the political party. They are only the first step toward constituency-building. This function served by the old party must also be restored. Politicians must begin once more to deliver to their constituencies, not merely with personal favors and financial largesse, but on the basis of concrete programs and political initiatives.

As we said in Chapter 9, you cannot align the country around temporary expediencies, around slogans, around personalities, or around short-range ideological distinctions. The country can only become aligned around the principle of lasting constituencies. And the relationship between a constituency and a party is a political one. It is the restoration of

356

this form of political relationship that will put manipulative strategy back into its proper place, and make the adversary process once more a productive, not dysfunctional, element in our society. The restoration of such a relationship is possible because it is in the long-term interests of both party and politician.

These suggestions for strengthening institutions are not revolutionary, but the result of their implementation would be a solid first step in the direction of restoring our system. The fact that these recommendations are so modest indicates that we feel our current problems are not the result of a structural breakdown in the government.

What is vastly more important — what is required above all else — is a basic shift in attitude, a return to the spirit of constitutionalism and law. As the progressives of the early twentieth century led the country out of the strategic politics of the gilded age, so now it is time for a new set of progressives to do likewise.

APPENDICES

Finance 1972

The realm of campaign financing is an extraordinarily complex one, in part because the contributors and recipients want to make it so. After the 1972 election, the Ripon Society conducted a massive study of the financing of the 1972 presidential election campaigns. We did not take an "investigatory" approach; our purpose was not muckraking, but political analysis. Our sympathies lie strongly with those who are trying to get to the bottom of the many notorious scandals, but so many are doing so much that we will leave that part of campaign finance analysis in their able and eager hands. Basically, all we wanted to know was who gave money to the presidential candidates: what kind of people, by occupation, by region, by political persuasion; when did they give it; in what amounts did they contribute? The new campaign finance law enabled us to look closely at such questions for the first time.

We obtained from the General Accounting Office their massive listing of presidential contributors shortly after the election — and added some supplementary material to their original printouts — so that our data base was the complete, but *preliminary*, report of all contributions made between the April 7 filing deadline and the "Five-Day Report" that was published five days before the election. We then put onto computer cards the amount, the date, the recipient, and the state of origin of each contribution made to a presidential committee. When more than one contribution was made by the same person, each was given an identical code number so that they could be aggregated for that person, and, if desired, counted as one contribution. Since the GAO had alphabetized its listing, this was not too difficult. In honor of Stewart Mott, who made an enormous number of contributions, we called this process motting. The GAO had two data bases; in effect, before and after Labor Day. We therefore motted the data within these two time periods, but did not mott it between the time periods. Therefore aggregated data is presented in two different time periods whenever it appears.

We created several categories of recipients: (1) "Nixon," which included contributions to his various national committees, his state and local finance committees, the Republican National Committee, and to Agnew; (2) "McGovern," which included contributions made to his numerous national, state, and local committees, plus contributions made to the Democratic National Committee *after* his nomination (which seemed a reasonable distinction); we also added the very few contributions declared for Eagleton and Shriver; (3) "Wallace," which included the various Wallace committees; and (4) "Assorted Democrats," which aggregated Humphrey, Jackson, Muskie, Lindsay, Mills, Chisholm, Bayh, Harris, Hughes, Hartke, Sanford, and several other declared presidential candidates.

This data was then cleaned. We removed all contributions under $100. (McGovern had declared a fair number of these; Nixon hardly any.) We removed all contributions whose dates were not identifiable. (Here McGovern had *considerably* more than Nixon.) We removed all contributions that were not directly made by *individuals*. We removed all contributions made before the April 7 deadline, but still reported. We did not count loans, repaid loans, or other conveyances that were not contributions.

The reporting procedures and our "cleaning" introduced some biases to the data. The Nixon fund-raisers clearly had encouraged people who wanted to make a $100 contribution to make it in two or more parts to escape reporting requirements. Their contributions in the $100 range were smaller in numbers than those in the $200 range — a strong violation of the overall contribution patterns. Hence the Nixon $100 category is probably not a very accurate one. Those reporting McGovern's contributions, on the other hand, were very negligent in reporting the date and especially the occupation of the contributor. This latter tendency, combined with our cleaning the data of nonidentifiable dates, reduced the McGovern totals by about 5 percent — a point to keep in mind when comparing them to the Nixon data. These nondated contributions tended to be small, however.

The significance of our data lies in its observations on the middle-range contribution. The large contributions have been publicized extensively in the press and have been analyzed by many sources. The small contribution still remains a mystery in terms of who gave it and where it came from, although an analysis of the contributor lists of both parties might shed light on this subject. The middle-range contribution, however, is probably the most significant of these as far as the future is concerned,

since large contributions are often one-shot affairs and face an uncertain future in terms of restrictive legislation. Remember that at all times these are the contributions of *individuals* and do not include the gifts of labor or other groups.

We put our data to three basic uses. First, we examined *where* the contributions came from and in what amounts. *In all cases* the locations described were the declared addresses of the contributor, not the address of the committee receiving the contribution. An enormous amount of cash was shuttled from one state to another in each campaign. Tables 8A and 8B, on pages 248–251, portray the results of this study. Again, the reader should focus on the middle-range contributions, since most of the large ones were reported early, late, or not at all. The information in Tables 11 and 12 also comes from this analysis. These are motted or aggregated figures; that is, if one contributor made two contributions during the summer, these are numbered and counted as one.

The second variable we examined was *when* the money was given. Here we did not mott the material, but broke it open according to date. We then compiled this data into a series of time-flows that showed *when* the contributions were made nationwide, by region, and by state. We also broke the data down by size of contribution, by region, and by time, so that we could compare the time-flow of small and middle-range contributions with that of contributions overall. This data is presented in Figures 1, 2, 5, and 6. Appearing later in this appendix are the time-flows of the small contributions ($100–$499) and the $1,000 contributions broken down by region. An accompanying map indicates the regions.

The third variable was occupation. The published GAO material did not include the occupation of the contributor, so we drew a random sample 1/15 of the entire population after it had been aggregated by contributor (so that there would be no bias in favor of multiple contributors). This sample was drawn on the basis of a random numbers chart to remove the possibility of cyclical bias in the alphabetical list. This sample was then taken to the GAO office in Washington and the occupations of the contributors were sought in the original reports filed with the GAO by the various committees. The Nixon sample size was 590 and of these, occupations were identifiable on 388. The McGovern sample size was 480 of which only 178 were identifiable. (The contributions were identified, but the space for occupation was blank on an enormous proportion of them.) Therefore the significance of the smaller breakdowns within the McGovern data is not great, but the overall breakdown between business and professional is valid. The missing occupational categories did not vary drastically in their overall breakdowns from those with data present. This data was presented in Chapter 12 in Figure 7. This random sample was drawn from the contributions made during the summer months. The larger contributions of the fall probably indicate that the percentage of money coming from businessmen increased near the end of

the campaign. Also, the large contributions made before and after this filing period were chiefly from businessmen and therefore would significantly increase this percentage.

We also analyzed the multiple contributors, although we do not have space here to present extensive findings. In brief, multiple contributors were more concentrated in the big states and gave substantially more money. We would be happy to supply further details or results upon request.

In this appendix we have provided some additional data to supplement the material presented in Chapter 12 and other places in the book. First, Tables 11 and 12 provide a state-by-state breakdown of the Wallace and assorted Democrats contributions. Since the data is based on post–April 7 material, the totals are small: Wallace's represents the five weeks before the assassination attempt (although some money came in later). The assorted Democrats were only two months away from the certainty of a McGovern nomination. Still, there are some interesting conclusions from this data. First, Wallace was certainly the "poor man's candidate." His money came largely from the South, and many states during this five-week period had no reported contributions. The mean Wallace contribution was well below the national average. Second, the assorted Democrats received the overwhelming bulk of their money from just a handful of states — and much of it came from large contributions. Finally, it should be recalled that during the same period McGovern was financing his campaign out of a large number of small contributions, and out of loans. (The Nixon and McGovern tables appear in Chapter 12).

In Tables 13, 14, 15, and 16 we present the breakdowns by dollar category for each candidate by state. Again, recall that the $10,000+ category, while substantial, is not representative of the whole campaign because of reporting procedures. These figures aggregate the contributions within the summer and fall periods, and then combine the two aggregations. This means that two contributions by the same person within the summer are counted as one, but two contributions, one given in summer and one in fall, are counted as two. These figures speak for themselves, but the most important point to notice is the large numbers of $1,000 contributions made to each candidate. This size contribution was very significant in campaign financing this year and will probably be more so in the future as the large contribution is restricted.

Figure 10 shows the flow of the $100 to $499 contribution and the flow of the $1,000 contribution in eleven regions of the country. It is interesting to observe that McGovern did quite well during the primary campaigns, fell off sharply during the summer, and picked up again only in September. These charts show that Nixon's contribution patterns in these categories were a bit more erratic. He did not do well in spring or early

STATE	NO. OF CONTR.	TOTAL DOLLARS	% OF NATL. TOTAL	MEAN CONTRIBUTION
Alabama	127	56,789	18.6	447.2
Alaska	0	0	0.0	0.0
Arizona	6	1,030	0.3	171.7
Arkansas	7	1,300	0.4	185.7
California	23	4,812	1.6	209.2
Colorado	1	1,000	0.3	1,000.0
Connecticut	2	720	0.2	360.0
Delaware	1	500	0.2	500.0
D.C.	2	1,002	0.3	501.0
Florida	97	35,856	11.8	369.6
Georgia	45	12,242	4.0	272.0
Hawaii	2	1,000	0.3	500.0
Idaho	2	450	0.2	225.0
Illinois	13	2,713	0.9	208.7
Indiana	24	9,307	3.1	387.8
Iowa	2	210	0.1	105.0
Kansas	3	820	0.3	273.3
Kentucky	2	800	0.3	400.0
Louisiana	40	37,650	12.4	941.3
Maine	0	0	0.0	0.0
Maryland	11	2,108	0.7	191.7
Massachusetts	6	14,940	4.9	2,490.0
Michigan	42	20,188	6.6	480.7
Minnesota	0	0	0.0	0.0
Mississippi	13	2,310	0.7	177.7
Missouri	8	6,400	2.1	800.0
Montana	1	148	0.1	148.0
Nebraska	1	100	0.0	100.0
Nevada	1	300	0.1	300.0
New Hampshire	0	0	0.0	0.0
New Jersey	7	1,400	0.5	200.0
New Mexico	1	200	0.1	200.0
New York	12	4,700	1.5	391.7
North Carolina	23	4,920	1.6	213.9
North Dakota	0	0	0.0	0.0
Ohio	17	14,450	4.7	850.0
Oklahoma	5	1,700	0.6	340.0
Oregon	2	200	0.1	100.0
Pennsylvania	14	6,677	2.2	476.9
Rhode Island	0	0	0.0	0.0
South Carolina	5	925	0.3	185.0
South Dakota	0	0	0.0	0.0
Tennessee	37	15,007	4.9	405.6
Texas	74	32,890	10.8	444.5
Utah	1	300	0.1	300.0
Vermont	1	100	0.0	100.0
Virginia	12	4,165	1.4	347.1
Washington	2	200	0.1	100.0
West Virginia	0	0	0.0	0.0
Wisconsin	7	1,400	0.5	200.0
Wyoming	0	0	0.0	0.0

TABLE 11.
Contributions to Wallace by State

STATE	NO. OF CONTR.	TOTAL DOLLARS	% OF NATL. TOTAL	MEAN CONTRIBUTION
Alabama	6	6,050	0.3	1,008.3
Alaska	0	0	0.0	0.0
Arizona	4	3,300	0.1	825.0
Arkansas	11	26,800	1.1	2,436.4
California	321	503,331	20.9	1,568.0
Colorado	7	5,650	0.2	807.1
Connecticut	12	3,935	0.2	327.9
Delaware	3	2,320	0.1	773.3
D.C.	108	98,629	4.1	913.2
Florida	81	58,665	2.4	724.3
Georgia	9	13,523	0.6	1,502.6
Hawaii	3	800	0.0	266.7
Idaho	0	0	0.0	0.0
Illinois	26	46,500	1.9	1,788.5
Indiana	9	7,817	0.3	868.6
Iowa	2	400	0.0	200.0
Kansas	0	0	0.0	0.0
Kentucky	2	800	0.0	400.0
Louisiana	3	2,700	0.1	900.0
Maine	41	28,865	1.2	704.0
Maryland	57	45,819	1.9	803.8
Massachusetts	81	43,236	1.8	533.8
Michigan	29	14,636	0.6	504.7
Minnesota	152	232,440	9.6	1,529.2
Mississippi	0	0	0.0	0.0
Missouri	11	43,400	1.8	3,945.5
Montana	2	600	0.0	300.0
Nebraska	9	6,511	0.3	723.4
Nevada	3	3,500	0.2	1,166.7
New Hampshire	6	2,605	0.1	434.2
New Jersey	13	10,675	0.4	821.2
New Mexico	7	1,650	0.1	235.7
New York	197	594,496	24.7	3,017.8
North Carolina	50	15,675	0.7	313.5
North Dakota	0	0	0.0	0.0
Ohio	112	69,351	2.9	619.2
Oklahoma	4	2,600	0.1	650.0
Oregon	6	2,074	0.1	345.7
Pennsylvania	185	135,340	5.6	731.6
Rhode Island	9	4,600	0.2	511.1
South Carolina	3	3,000	0.1	1,000.0
South Dakota	0	0	0.0	0.0
Tennessee	2	1,750	0.1	875.0
Texas	5	301,519	12.5	60,303.8
Utah	1	1,000	0.0	1,000.0
Vermont	0	0	0.0	0.0
Virginia	23	14,330	0.6	623.0
Washington	25	7,433	0.3	297.3
West Virginia	1	500	0.0	500.0
Wisconsin	7	7,900	0.3	1,128.6
Wyoming	0	0	0.0	0.0

TABLE 12.
Contributions to Assorted Democrats by States

STATE	$100–$499	$500–$999	$1,000–$4,999	$5,000–$9,999	$10,000+
Alabama	77	22	49	2	1
Alaska	43	12	10	2	0
Arizona	48	19	49	5	2
Arkansas	62	26	4	0	0
California	1,160	282	515	50	27
Colorado	69	25	26	4	2
Connecticut	175	65	102	5	6
Delaware	31	17	39	6	3
D.C.	181	50	151	16	3
Florida	313	75	206	12	7
Georgia	136	29	83	4	1
Hawaii	45	30	43	3	1
Idaho	13	4	9	0	0
Illinois	443	139	172	13	14
Indiana	143	24	69	2	2
Iowa	77	17	13	0	3
Kansas	69	26	58	3	0
Kentucky	38	11	8	1	2
Louisiana	55	20	43	3	1
Maine	36	14	10	0	0
Maryland	294	105	211	11	1
Massachusetts	153	56	113	11	0
Michigan	255	68	262	8	3
Minnesota	119	40	122	10	6
Mississippi	39	0	7	0	0
Missouri	190	43	121	4	4
Montana	11	2	3	3	0
Nebraska	53	16	24	2	1
Nevada	19	5	13	0	0
New Hampshire	23	3	6	0	0
New Jersey	218	72	182	13	6
New Mexico	46	9	34	1	0
New York	523	238	339	77	39
North Carolina	111	21	24	1	0
North Dakota	7	3	3	0	0
Ohio	364	74	89	13	1
Oklahoma	136	36	115	2	2
Oregon	164	18	32	0	2
Pennsylvania	314	98	224	12	10
Rhode Island	24	10	13	0	1
South Carolina	87	14	13	2	2
South Dakota	12	5	2	0	0
Tennessee	107	25	146	5	1
Texas	286	90	157	22	12
Utah	28	6	2	2	0
Vermont	17	4	1	0	0
Virginia	207	59	94	6	6
Washington	113	42	31	1	1
West Virginia	30	7	1	0	0
Wisconsin	154	56	63	8	9
Wyoming	15	4	5	1	1

TABLE 13.
Number of Contributions to Nixon by Amount

STATE	$100–$499	$500–$999	$1,000–$4,999	$5,000–$9,999	$10,000+
Alabama	18	4	2	0	0
Alaska	10	0	0	0	0
Arizona	51	8	5	0	0
Arkansas	16	3	3	0	0
California	1,139	154	153	16	10
Colorado	84	11	2	0	2
Connecticut	288	68	63	8	3
Delaware	27	2	1	0	1
D.C.	242	50	54	5	3
Florida	105	36	19	3	2
Georgia	31	8	7	0	0
Hawaii	13	3	2	0	0
Idaho	9	1	0	0	0
Illinois	422	86	56	5	10
Indiana	39	6	1	2	1
Iowa	25	4	1	0	0
Kansas	39	4	4	2	2
Kentucky	41	10	7	1	0
Louisiana	27	3	4	1	0
Maine	11	5	3	0	0
Maryland	190	29	40	6	3
Massachusetts	341	95	93	3	3
Michigan	251	32	26	0	1
Minnesota	96	18	11	0	0
Mississippi	6	4	5	1	0
Missouri	82	12	8	0	0
Montana	10	0	0	1	0
Nebraska	47	5	10	0	1
Nevada	5	1	2	0	1
New Hampshire	65	13	10	1	0
New Jersey	250	45	65	7	4
New Mexico	38	11	11	0	1
New York	1,363	197	267	45	27
North Carolina	63	5	11	0	4
North Dakota	17	0	0	0	0
Ohio	259	55	44	3	6
Oklahoma	29	3	4	0	0
Oregon	58	2	5	0	2
Pennsylvania	217	40	37	3	0
Rhode Island	45	7	5	1	0
South Carolina	6	1	0	0	0
South Dakota	30	4	3	0	0
Tennessee	22	3	3	0	0
Texas	185	21	28	5	1
Utah	24	3	4	0	1
Vermont	25	12	10	1	0
Virginia	86	19	12	1	0
Washington	104	8	4	1	0
West Virginia	16	4	1	0	0
Wisconsin	169	13	6	1	1
Wyoming	4	0	0	0	0

TABLE 14.
Number of Contributions to McGovern by Amount

STATE	$100–$499	$500–$999	$1,000–$4,999	$5,000–$9,999	$10,000+
Alabama	86	19	21	1	0
Alaska	0	0	0	0	0
Arizona	6	0	0	0	0
Arkansas	7	0	0	0	0
California	21	1	1	0	0
Colorado	0	0	1	0	0
Connecticut	1	1	0	0	0
Delaware	0	1	0	0	0
D.C.	0	2	0	0	0
Florida	67	15	13	0	0
Georgia	41	1	3	0	0
Hawaii	0	2	0	0	0
Idaho	2	0	0	0	0
Illinois	12	0	1	0	0
Indiana	20	1	3	0	0
Iowa	2	0	0	0	0
Kansas	2	1	0	0	0
Kentucky	1	1	0	0	0
Louisiana	31	4	4	1	0
Maine	0	0	0	0	0
Maryland	11	0	0	0	0
Massachusetts	3	1	1	1	0
Michigan	37	1	4	0	0
Minnesota	0	0	0	0	0
Mississippi	12	1	0	0	0
Missouri	3	4	1	0	0
Montana	1	0	0	0	0
Nebraska	1	0	0	0	0
Nevada	1	0	0	0	0
New Hampshire	0	0	0	0	0
New Jersey	7	0	0	0	0
New Mexico	1	0	0	0	0
New York	10	2	0	0	0
North Carolina	22	1	0	0	0
North Dakota	0	0	0	0	0
Ohio	13	3	0	1	0
Oklahoma	4	1	0	0	0
Oregon	2	0	0	0	0
Pennsylvania	13	0	1	0	0
Rhode Island	0	0	0	0	0
South Carolina	5	0	0	0	0
South Dakota	0	0	0	0	0
Tennessee	30	6	1	0	0
Texas	60	11	3	0	0
Utah	1	0	0	0	0
Vermont	1	0	0	0	0
Virginia	11	1	0	0	0
Washington	2	0	0	0	0
West Virginia	0	0	0	0	0
Wisconsin	7	0	0	0	0
Wyoming	0	0	0	0	0

TABLE 15.
Number of Contributions to Wallace by Amount

STATE	$100–$499	$500–$999	$1,000–$4,999	$5,000–$9,999	$10,000+
Alabama	5	0	0	1	0
Alaska	0	0	0	0	0
Arizona	2	0	2	0	0
Arkansas	2	3	2	4	0
California	193	46	62	11	9
Colorado	4	1	2	0	0
Connecticut	8	4	0	0	0
Delaware	2	0	1	0	0
D.C.	57	24	25	3	1
Florida	56	4	19	2	0
Georgia	4	2	1	2	0
Hawaii	2	1	0	0	0
Idaho	0	0	0	0	0
Illinois	9	7	8	1	1
Indiana	6	1	1	1	0
Iowa	2	0	0	0	0
Kansas	0	0	0	0	0
Kentucky	1	1	0	0	0
Louisiana	2	0	1	0	0
Maine	13	16	12	0	0
Maryland	36	8	11	1	1
Massachusetts	54	15	10	2	0
Michigan	14	11	4	0	0
Minnesota	113	16	18	2	3
Mississippi	0	0	0	0	0
Missouri	5	3	1	1	1
Montana	1	1	0	0	0
Nebraska	3	4	2	0	0
Nevada	0	1	2	0	0
New Hampshire	4	0	2	0	0
New Jersey	3	5	5	0	0
New Mexico	6	1	0	0	0
New York	88	25	53	20	11
North Carolina	38	8	4	0	0
North Dakota	0	0	0	0	0
Ohio	73	13	24	2	0
Oklahoma	1	1	2	0	0
Oregon	5	0	1	0	0
Pennsylvania	111	31	36	5	2
Rhode Island	5	1	3	0	0
South Carolina	0	0	3	0	0
South Dakota	0	0	0	0	0
Tennessee	1	0	1	0	0
Texas	3	0	1	0	1
Utah	0	0	1	0	0
Vermont	0	0	0	0	0
Virginia	12	3	8	0	0
Washington	20	4	1	0	0
West Virginia	0	1	0	0	0
Wisconsin	2	1	4	0	0
Wyoming	0	0	0	0	0

TABLE 16.
Number of Contributions to Assorted Democrats by Amount

Figure 10

Contributions to Nixon and McGovern by Representative Categories and Region

Region 1   New England

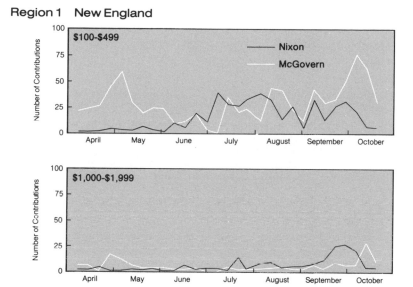

Region 2   Middle Atlantic

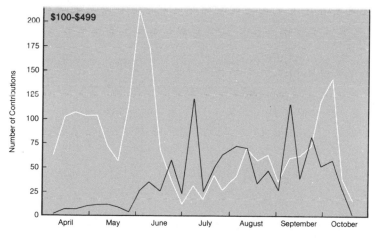

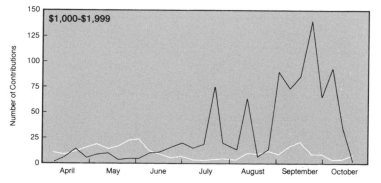

Region 3   Border States

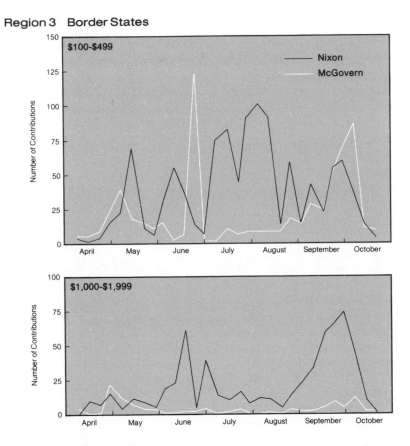

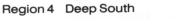

Region 4   Deep South

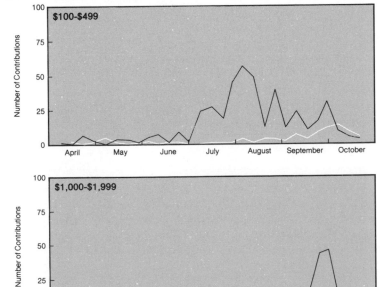

Region 5 Florida and Texas

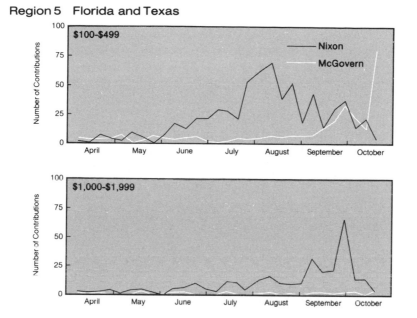

$100-$499

Number of Contributions

Nixon
McGovern

April May June July August September October

$1,000-$1,999

Number of Contributions

April May June July August September October

Region 6 Midwest

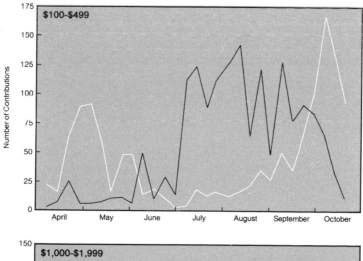

$100-$499

Number of Contributions

April May June July August September October

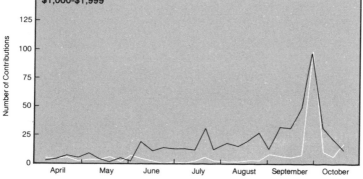

$1,000-$1,999

Number of Contributions

April May June July August September October

Region 7   Farm Belt

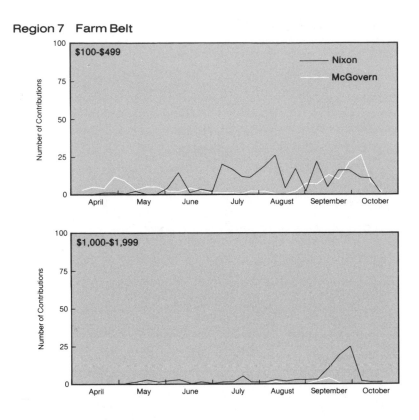

Region 8   Ozarks

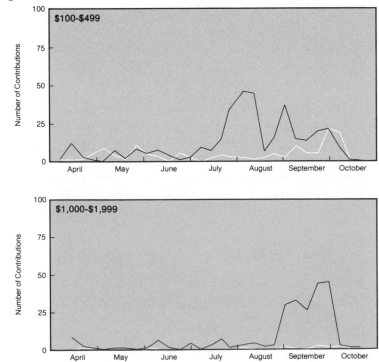

Region 9   Mountain States

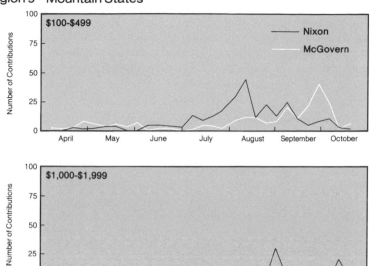

$100-$499

Nixon
McGovern

Number of Contributions

100
75
50
25
0

April   May   June   July   August   September   October

$1,000-$1,999

Number of Contributions

100
75
50
25
0

April   May   June   July   August   September   October

Region 10   Far West

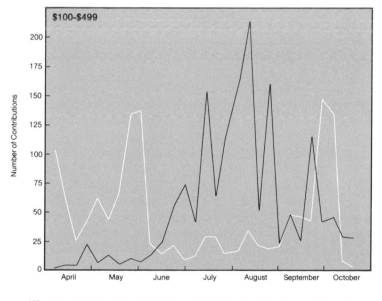

$100-$499

Number of Contributions

200
175
150
125
100
75
50
25
0

April   May   June   July   August   September   October

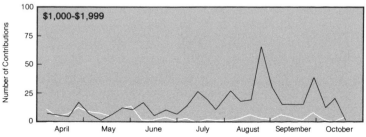

$1,000-$1,999

Number of Contributions

100
75
50
25
0

April   May   June   July   August   September   October

Region 11　Pacific

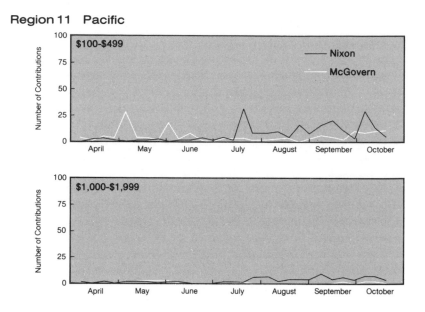

DOLLAR CONTRIBUTION	SPRING-SUMMER		FALL	
	Number	*Amount*	*Number*	*Amount*
100–199	2,198	247,333	1,681	204,554
200–299	1,350	292,808	838	183,720
300–399	316	98,538	196	61,765
400–499	164	68,199	70	29,019
500–599	576	289,174	311	156,600
600–699	69	42,255	42	25,672
700–799	64	46,135	25	18,239
800–899	31	25,887	17	14,029
900–999	23	20,904	6	5,556
1,000–1,999	537	595,093	304	334,578
2,000–2,999	134	300,464	50	108,964
3,000–3,999	53	167,533	30	93,216
4,000–4,999	20	86,284	4	16,241
5,000–5,999	50	253,845	31	157,012
6,000–6,999	12	75,274	10	61,582
7,000–7,999	12	89,042	1	7,500
8,000–8,999	3	25,350	2	16,000
9,000–9,999	5	45,508	0	
10,000　and　over	52	1,669,144	41	1,616,809

TABLE 17.
Contributions to McGovern by Amount

summer anywhere. With the McGovern candidacy and the Eagleton affair, Nixon's money began to rise dramatically, especially among small and middle-range contributors, throughout most of the country. By and large, however, this summer surge spent itself, and contributions in this range began to taper off and eventually drop near the end of the campaign. The major exception to his pattern was the Northeast, which saw Nixon increases in small dollar contributions in September and October. We assume that most of this money is commitment money, contributed by people who supported the President, disliked McGovern, and therefore contributed early. Big money, however, and especially the $1,000 contribution did not flow in until much later than small money in most regions of the country. In almost every area big money followed small after a time lapse of a few weeks. We assume that the surge of $1,000 contributions during the fall included a lot of opportunity money and heavily solicited money. A glance at these charts will show some fascinating fluctuations and variations in Presidential contribution patterns.

Finally, Table 17 shows the overall breakdown of the McGovern money that corresponds to Nixon's breakdowns that appear in Table 7.

Bibliography

For reasons of style we have not used footnotes in this book, although we have often cited our sources in the text. These sources were many and varied, with books, newspapers, and personal interviews being the most important. The following is a partial list of the many publications we consulted.

BOOKS

Alexander, Herbert E. *Financing the 1968 Election*. Lexington, Mass., D. C. Heath, 1971.
———. *Money in Politics*. Washington, D.C., Public Affairs Press, 1972.
Barber, James D. *The Presidential Character*. Englewood Cliffs, N.J., Prentice-Hall, 1972.
Barone, Michael, Grant Ujifusa, and Douglas Matthews. *The Almanac of American Politics*. Boston, Gambit, 1972.
Broder, David. *The Party's Over*. New York, Harper & Row, 1972.
Bruno, Jerry, and Jeff Greenfield. *The Advance Man*. New York, Bantam, 1971.
Campbell, Angus, P. E. Converse, W. E. Miller, and D. E. Stokes. *The American Voter*. New York, John Wiley, 1960.
Chester, Lewis, Godfrey Hodgson, and Bruce Page. *An American Melodrama*. New York, Dell, 1969.
Evans, Rowland, and Robert D. Novak. *Nixon in the White House: The Frustration of Power*. New York, Random House, 1971.
Hess, Stephen, and David Broder. *The Republican Establishment*. New York, Harper & Row, 1967.
Hymen, Sidney. *Youth in Politics*. New York, Basic Books, 1972.
Kessel, John Howard. *The Goldwater Coalition*. Indianapolis, Bobbs-Merrill, 1968.
Key, V. O. *The Responsible Electorate*. New York, Vintage, 1966.

378

Levy, Mark R., and Michael S. Kramer. *The Ethnic Factor*. New York, Simon & Schuster, 1972.

Lubell, Samuel. *The Hidden Crisis in American Politics*. New York, Norton, 1970.

————.*The Future While It Happened*. New York, Norton, 1973.

Machiavelli, N. *The Prince*. New York, Modern Library, 1950.

May, E. R., and Janet Fraser. *The Managers Speak*. Cambridge, Harvard University Press, 1973.

Neustadt, Richard. *Presidential Power*. New York, Wiley, 1960.

Phillips, Kevin P. *The Emerging Republican Majority*. New York, Doubleday Anchor, 1969.

Pierce, Neal. *The Megastates of America*. New York, Norton, 1972.

Polsby, Nelson W., and Aaron Wildavsky. *Presidential Elections: Strategies of American Electoral Politics*. New York, Scribner's, 1972.

Saloma, John S., and Frederick H. Sontag. *Parties*. New York, Knopf, 1972.

Scammon, Richard, ed. *America Votes*, 8 vols. Washington, Public Affairs Press, 1955–1971.

Scammon, Richard, and Ben J. Wattenberg. *The Real Majority*. New York, Coward, McCann, and Geoghegan, 1970.

Schlesinger, A. M., ed. *History of U.S. Political Parties*. New York, Chelsea House, 1972. Especially Vol. 4, with Lee Heubner, "Republican Party 1952–1972."

Tarrance, V. Lance, and Walter DeVries. *The Ticket-Splitter*. Grand Rapids, Eerdmans, 1972.

White, Theodore S. *The Making of the President*, 4 vols.: 1960, 1964, 1968, 1972. New York, Atheneum, 1960–1972.

PERIODICALS

Congressional Quarterly
Human Events
Monday (alas, now defunct)
National Journal
National Review

New Republic
Newsweek
Time
U.S. News and World Report
Washington Monthly

NEWSPAPERS

We relied heavily on the *New York Times*, the *Christian Science Monitor*, and the *Washington Post* for broad national coverage. We also read and clipped the following newspapers around the country:

Atlanta Constitution
Baltimore Sun
Birmingham News
Boston Globe
Charlestown (W. Va.) *Daily Mail*
Chicago Tribune
Cleveland Plain Dealer
Denver Post
Des Moines Register
Detroit News
Hartford Times
Houston Chronicle
Idaho Statesman
Indianapolis Star
Jackson (Miss.) *Clarion-Ledger*
Los Angeles Times
Louisville Courier-Journal
Miami Herald

Milwaukee Journal
Minneapolis Tribune
Nashville Tennessean
New Orleans Times-Picayune
Newark Star-Ledger
Omaha World-Herald
Portland Oregonian
Portland (Me.) *Press Herald*
Philadelphia Bulletin
Pittsburgh Press
Providence Journal
Raleigh News and Observer
Richmond Times-Dispatch
St. Louis Post-Dispatch
Seattle Post-Intelligencer
Sioux Falls (S.D.) *Argus Leader*
Wichita Eagle
Wilmington (Del.) *Journal-News*

Nationwide Surveys

In this study we made use of information from the following nationwide surveys; much of this material was published in newspapers or released by the polling firm; some was made available to us directly by the company involved as indicated by an asterisk (*).

Cambridge Research Institute*
The Gallup Opinion Index
Harris Survey
Samuel Lubell
Oliver Quayle
Sindlinger & Company*
Daniel Yankelovich, Inc.*
CBS Postelection Voter Survey
NBC Indicator Precinct Study*
Washington Post Survey conducted by Peter Hart Research Associates

Statewide surveys appearing in newspapers (alphabetically by state)

Los Angeles Times Poll (Dorothy D. Corey Research Co.)
Denver Post Poll (Research Services, Inc.)
Connecticut Poll (Decision Research Corp.)
WSB-TV Poll (Atlanta) (Research Division of the Cox Broadcasting Co.)
Chicago Sun Times Poll
The Tribune Poll (Chicago)
The Iowa Poll (Conducted by the *Des Moines Register*)
Topeka Capitol Journal Poll (Human Resources Corp.)
Boston Globe Poll (Becker Research)
Detroit News Poll (Market Opinion Research Co.)
Minnesota Poll (*Minneapolis Tribune*)
New York Daily News Poll
Columbus Dispatch Voting Machine Poll
Oregonian Poll (Bardsley and Haslacher, Inc.)
The Rhode Island Poll (Providence Journal)
The Texas Poll (Belden Associates)

The 1972 survey conducted by the Survey Research Center at the University of Michigan was not available in time to use in this book, although we did make use of earlier SRC material as noted in the text.

OTHER SOURCES

We used many other sources of information in this book. The personal experience of the authors was one. Interviews were another. We conducted dozens of these with former campaign officials, labor officials, businessmen, lobbyists, conservative and establishment figures, congressmen, party officials, and so forth. Many of these people wished to remain anonymous; we have cited them in the text when they had no objections to being quoted.

The financial disclosure material described in Appendix I came from the GAO's *Alphabetical Listing of Campaign Contributions,* together with the various supplements to this report, the summary sheets of all financial committee reports, and many of the original filing sheets themselves.

Official voting returns for both primary and general elections were carefully processed to achieve the results described in Chapter 9. The Joint Center for Political Studies was a valuable source of information about black voters.

Any further questions about the data used in this book should be sent to the Ripon Society and we shall be glad to answer them.

Index

Colson, Charles, 20, 65, 95, 107, 178, 181, 182; and Attack Group, 66
Committee: on Racial Equality, 28; of One Million Against the Admission of Red China, 303; on Political Education, *see* COPE; to Re-elect the President, *see* CREEP
Common Cause, 243
Communications Workers of America, 173, 184
communism as issue, 30, 91, 106, 171, 182–183, 297
compartmentalization of appeals, 58–62, 77
Congress, U.S., 113; and Nixon administration, 9, 10, 65, 107; Democrats in, 39, 71–72; Republicans in, 39, 66, 72; and impeachment process, 114; and takeover of power from, 219, 279, 345–347, 351, 353; need for strengthening, 351–353
Connally, John, 221, 223; vs. McGovern, 56–57, 148; and Democrats for Nixon, 68; and New Right, 290, 292, 293, 296
"Consciousness Alpha," 11
Conservative Book Club, 299, 300
Conservative Party of New York, 299, 300, 302
conservatives, 222, 223, 224; Nixon and, 31, 35, 42, 43–45, 301, 303; Goldwater and, 37, 296–297; and American Conservative Union, 43, 44, 298, 299, 301, 302, 303; and Republican party, 71, 206, 220, 285, 288, 296, 305–307, 327; on West Coast, 212; and Old vs. New Right, 288–300, 306–307, 312, 314, 318–319; coalition of, 296–300; in South, 297; three clusters of, 298–300; power of, 300–308, 318; "Summit Meeting" of, 302; and Old Guard, 303; and use of ideology, 304–307, 318; and Watergate, 307
constituencies: and traditional politicians, 17, 18, 320, 356; McGovern and, 19, 132–134, 159, 313; creation of, 19, 141–142, 312–313, 315–322, 327, 328, 356–357; effect of strategy on, 23–25, 48, 187–193, 196, 213; of labor, 168; need for, 224–225, 311–312, 326–327; diversity of, 276; of Old and New Right, 296–298, 300, 309, 314, 318–320, 321, 337; and national interest, 337. *See also* fluidity
Constitution, U.S., 4, 217, 339; and Nixon strategists, 10–11; endangered, 338, 340; change of attitudes toward, 340, 341–342; creation of, 341; three principles of — (democracy) 342, 346, 347, 353, 355, (republicanism) 342, 347–349, 354, (adversary process) 342, 349–351; and separation of powers, 352
Construction Industry Stabilization Committee (CISC), 180
Cook County Central Committee, 144, 145
Coolidge, Calvin, 287
COPE (Committee on Political Education): origin and techniques of, 80–81, 162–163, 168; and Humphrey cam-

paign, 163–164, 169; and McGovern, 169, 170, 172, 174
CORE (Congress of Racial Equality), 28
corporate influence. *See* influence, business and corporate
corporate money. *See* money, corporate
corporations. *See* business community
corporatism. *See* socialism
Cort, Stewart S., 82
cost-benefit analysis, use of, 15, 16
Council: for Urban Affairs, 27, 29; on Environmental Quality, 28; on Domestic Affairs, 36; on Executive Organization, Advisory, 42
Cowles, Gardner, 264
Cox, Archibald, 113
credibility: Nixon administration and, 6–7, 10; importance of, 7, 153; and Watergate, 111–113; and McGovern, 112, 152, 153–155, 156
CREEP (Committee to Re-elect the President), 46, 53, 56, 73, 355; creation of, 7, 51, 59, 62–63, 231; Jewish Division, 60; Business and Industry Division, 61, 74, 79–84, 281; and fund-raising, 63 (*see also* fund-raising); organization and staff, 64–70; Speakers Bureau, 67, 86, 269; Political Division, 68–69; Special Voter Group Division, 68, 69; Physicians Committee, 69; Nationalities Division, 69; Spanish-speaking Americans Division, 69, 75–79; Transient Voter or Special Ballots Division, 70; and YVP, 70, 84–88, 317; and party loyalty, 71, 189; and support for Democrats, 71–72; vs. Democratic coalition, 74; Finance Committee, 81; juvenile delinquency in, 99; and Watergate, 103, 109; National Maritime Division, 181–182; and labor, 182; and Nixon's successor, 223, 236–239; and Ashbrook challenge, 303–304
Crippling Strikes Prevention Act, 181
Cronkite, Walter, 105
Cuban voters, 75, 297. *See also* Hispanic-American voters
Cuellar, Mike, 78
Cunningham, George V., quoted, 120
cynicism, growth of, 24–25

Dailey, Peter, 67
Daley, Richard J., 20; and McGovern, 144–145, 174
Davis, True, 140
Davis-Bacon wage protections, 175, 179
Dean, John, 111; quoted, 95
decisionmaking: and strategic thinking, 12–14, 70–71, 342–343; in traditional politics, 51, 70–71; and domino theory, 91–92, 97, 342; and long-range view, 99, 349; and the public, 343, 344–345, 353. *See also* strategy and strategic thinking
DeLury, Bernard, 69, 182, 183
DeLury, John, 69, 182
democracy and democratic principles, 342, 346, 347, 353, 355; representation under, 17, 18, 343–345
Democratic National Committee, 76, 362

384

Democratic National Convention: (1968) 169; (1972) 135, 136–137, 138; union delegates at, 166–167, 170; voting population at, 169–170

Democratic party, 320; and votes for Nixon, 7, 20, 57, 67, 68, 136, 193–194; and McGovern, 19, 56–57, 126, 129, 133–134, 136–138, 142, 144–145, 154–155, 219; and labor, 28, 137, 159–163, 168, 169, 174–175, 178, 184–185, 194, 203, 276, 282; coalition and Nixon strategy against, 35, 37, 53, 57, 74, 146, 154–155, 185, 190, 191, 194–196, 199, 200; in Congress, 39, 71–72; superior organization of, 51; loyalty to, 56–57, 63, 190, 196, 199; CREEP's support of, 71–72; and Hispanic-American voters, 74–77, 79; and young voters, 84, 86, 88; government agencies and, 102; and Farmer-Labor party, 120; Meany quoted on, 161, 188; in 1970 campaigns, 192; and traditional vote, 193–196, 203, 224, 290, 293; and social welfare, 199–201; and race issue, 201–203; regional voting, 204–212, 260–261; power within, 218, 219; and 1972 fund-raising, 245, 362, 364, 366, 370 (see also fund-raising); and professional class, 254, 287, 319, 321; "disguised as Republicans," 285; aped by Republicans, 288, 296, 305; and New Right, 290, 292–293; and efficiency crisis, 333. See also Democratic National Committee

demonstrations and protests, 6, 48, 102, 104, 345

Dent, Harry, 33, 34, 38

Depression of 1930s, 119–120

desegregation, 33–35, 38, 42, 44

DeVries, Walter, his The Ticket-Splitter (co-author), 23–24, 191, 192

Dewey, Thomas E., 264, 266

Dillon, C. Douglas, 321

Docksai, Ron, 303

Dockworkers' unions, 164, 177, 181

Dodds, Bill, 167, 179, 185

Dole, Robert, 16, 230, 231

domestic policy: and symbolism, 6, 45; of Nixon administration, 26–29, 31, 41–42, 46, 65, 178, 301; of New Right, 297

domino theory, 91–93, 97, 100, 342

Dougherty, Bill, 128

Drucker, Peter, 42; his The Age of Discontinuity, quoted, 27

du Pont family, 265

Dutton, Fred, 77

Eagleton, Thomas F., and Eagleton affair, 107, 108, 142, 145, 147, 362; and McGovern and effect on, 20, 125, 135, 137–138, 141, 150, 153, 156, 192, 376; Nixon administration and, 46, 54; quoted, on history of illness, 139–140

Eagleton, Mrs. Thomas F. (Barbara), 139

Eastland, James O., 72

Eastman Chemical, 273

efficiency, doctrine of, 333

Ehrlichman, John, 3, 36, 46, 65, 89

Eisenhower, Dwight D., 39, 100, 266, 333, 334; and vice-presidential problem, 21; and South, 32, 207; and Adlai Stevenson, 106; Republican National Committee under, 228–229; old money and, 264; -Taft philosophy of government, 287–288, 297

electoral college: strategy, 20, 147, 148–149; "reform," 213

electoral process, 10, 217

electorate. See constituencies

Electrical Workers, International Brotherhood of, 164, 173

Elfin, Mel, 139

Ellsberg (Daniel) case, 106, 113

energetic class, the, 335–338

Enlightenment, the, 289

Environmental Protection Agency (EPA), 6, 61

Epstein, Edward, 281

establishment, the: Republican, 87, 169, 219, 266; Democratic, 129, 133–134, 166–167

Evans, M. Stanton, 298

Evans, Rowland, 33

Evans, Tom, 231

executive branch. See presidency, the

Failor, Ed, 66

Family Assistance Plan (FAP), 5, 44, 45, 60, 61, 301

Farenthold, Frances ("Sissy"), 145

Farmer, James, 29

farmers, 120, 204–205, 317–318, 328

"Farmers for the President," 61

Faubast, Michael, 127

FBI, 102, 104, 106, 109, 113, 346

Federal Election Campaign Act (1971), 82

Federation of Women's Clubs (Republican), 227

Field poll, 129

Finance Committee to Re-elect the President, 81

Finch, Robert, 34

Fischer, Max, 60, 69

Fitzsimmons, Frank, 176, 180–181

"Five-Day Report," 361

Flemming, Arthur, 64

Flemming, Harry, 64–65

Florida: primary elections in, 21, 304, 320; McGovern in, 122, 123–124, 125, 134; voting cycle in, 207, 209, 210; campaign contributions in, 259, 260; and New Right, 297

fluidity: importance of (to candidate) 20–21, (to voter) 23; creation and increase of, 21, 47, 191–193, 196, 313; of minority groups, 23, 77, 192–193; and South, 32–33, 194, 203, 206–211, 247, 260–261; of business community, 79–80; of young voters, 87, 156–157; during summer of 1972, 156–157; and decline of parties, 188–193; regional, 204–206, 211, 212; of power, 221–222. See also constituencies; ticket-splitting

Ford, Gerald, 222

Ford Effective Citizenship Program, 272–273

foreign policy: of Nixon administration, 6, 29–31, 45, 46, 101, 301, 302, 330, 346; old money and, 266; Big Business and, 279; New Right and, 293–294, 297; Old Right and moderate approach to, 319
Fortas, Abe, 35
freedom, commitment to, 290, 331–333
Frelinghuysen, Peter, 178
Frick, Helen Clay, 264–265
fund-raising: by Nixon strategists, CREEP and, 7, 63, 81, 101, 110–111, 237–238, 239, 241, 243–262, 270, 276, 303–304, 362–364, 367, 377; in business community, 81, 247, 252–254, 255, 261, 263–275, 276; McGovern and, 101, 116, 130, 147, 245–247, 250–251, 252–254, 321, 362, 363, 364, 368, 376, 377; use of power in, 110–111; unions and, 163; state organizations and, 233; professionalism and, 235; Ohio State party and, 239–240, 241; by assorted Democrats, 245, 362, 364, 366, 370, 376; and "laundering" funds, 247, 274–275; among professional class, 252–254, 255, 315; Wall Street and, 267–268; inflation and, 270; in Percy campaign, 272; in bipartisan efforts, 272–274; lobbyists and, 277–278; in Ashbrook campaign, 303–304; by Wallace, 362, 364, 365, 369. See also money, corporate; money, new; money, old

Galbraith, John Kenneth, 171, 298
Gallup poll(s): "government by," 21–22; (1968) 23, 193; (1970) 41; (1971) 42; (1972), 23, 100–101, 135–137, 152–157, 191, 193. See also polls and surveys
game plan mentality, 3–4, 16, 50, 348, 352; origin and language of, 11–12, 15; and voter contempt, 24–25, 48; and Watergate, 91–100, 103, 351, 352; and lack of tenacity, 98–99, 124; and failure of Nixon plan, 176; and avoidance of responsibility, 346–347; antidote to, 353–354
Geneen, Hal, 277
General Accounting Office (GAO), 130, 244, 361, 363
General Electric Company "Dollars for Citizenship," 273
Gilded Age, the, 286, 357
Goldberg, Arthur, 183
Goldberg, Larry, 69
Goldwater, Barry, 39, 80, 221, 224; and South, 32–33, 207; campaign, 37, 107, 300, 302, 304; and conservatives, 37, 296–297; compared to McGovern, 155, 157–158; and New Deal, 199–200; in Midwest and Mountain states, 204, 211–212; nomination of, 219, 310; and Republican National Committee, 228, 229; Draft movement, 298, 300, 303; and Ashbrook campaign, 303
Gompers, Samuel, 172; quoted, 160
Goodell, Charles, 40, 72; quoted, 43
"Good Government" funds, 272–274

Gordon, Kermit, 177
Gore, Albert, 206
Gorton, George, 85, 87
government-business relationships. See business community
Graham, Billy, 104
Graham, Katharine, quoted, 105
Grant, General U. S., 100, 334
Great Society, 9, 163
Green, William, 160
Green v. County School Board of New Kent County, Virginia, 34, 42
Grenier, John, 229

Haiphong Harbor, mining of, 45
Haldeman, H. R., 3, 64, 65, 67, 89, 90
Hall, Len, 321
Hall, Paul, 165, 182
Hanrahan, Edward V., 144, 145, 196, 197, 198
"Hard Hat March on Wall Street," 178
Harding, Warren G., 287, 334
Harding College, 299
Harkins, Jerry, 302
Harlow, Bryce, 40
Harrington, Milton, 83
Harris, Charles, 175
Harris, Fred, 362
Harris, Louis, and Harris poll, 40, 55, 137, 154, 155
Hart, Gary, 20, 77, 108, 125, 142, 143
Hartke, Vance, 362
Hartz, Louis, 289
Hawaii: 1972 voting in, 213; campaign contributions in, 248
Haynsworth, Clement, 35
Head Start program, 27
Health, Education and Welfare (HEW), Department of, 27, 29, 102; and desegregation issue, 33, 34, 44
Heartland of America, 247, 290, 298, 299. See also Midwest
Helms, Jesse, 318
Hesburgh, Theodore, 9
Hickel, Walter J., 36, 68
Hidalgo, Ed, 78
Hispanic-American voters, 60, 194; and CREEP strategy, 69, 75–79; and Democratic party, 74–77, 79
Hitler, Adolf, 12, 152, 266
Hodgson, James, 176
Hoffa, James, 160, 180
Hoffman, Abbie, 127
Holmes, Oliver Wendell, 353
Hoover, Herbert, 287
Hoover, J. Edgar, 102
Houghton family, 264
House Labor Committee, 175
House of Representatives, 17
Hudson County (New Jersey) machine, 145
Hudson Institute, 11
Huebner, Lee, 29
Hughes, Harold E., 141, 362
Hughes Aircraft Active Citizenship Campaign, 273
Human Events, 43–44, 298, 299; quoted, 302

386

Humphrey, Hubert H., 54, 57, 102, 108, 313; and South, 32, 193; 1968 campaign, 32, 51, 56, 101, 129, 160, 163, 193; 1970 campaign, 65; and Hispanic-American voters, 75, 76, 194; 1972 campaign, 122, 124–125, 126, 127, 128, 130–131, 136, 167, 169, 170, 212, 362; and McGovern, 128–129, 135, 136, 169, 174; and labor, 133, 160, 162, 163–164, 166, 167, 169, 170, 225, 312; refuses vice presidency, 141; and farm belt, 204; campaign contributions to, 362

Humphreys, Robert, 274

Hunt, E. Howard, 111

Hyman, Sidney, 88

hyperstrategist mentality: defined, 15; and domino theory, 92, 97, 100; and contingency thinking, 93–95, 348; political implications of, 96–97; insecurity and immaturity of, 97–100, 103; and McGovern, 98, 121. See also game plan mentality; strategy and strategic thinking

ideology: moralist trend toward, 18; and McGovern campaign, 19, 132, 355; as basis for alignment, 191, 213, 291, 300; as source of power, 221, 291, 304–307, 318, 325; and Wall Street, 267; business as fundamental American, 280, 283, 296; of New Right, 321; and ideological party, 355–356

Illinois: campaign contributions in, 247, 258; primary law in, 320

ILWU (International Longshoremen and Warehousemen Union), 177, 181. See also Dockworkers' unions

image-building, 13, 225; dangers of, 6–7; vs. power base, 309, 311

impeachment, 9, 114, 184

Independent voters, 136, 137, 213, 321, 327. See also American Independent party; third party

Indiana, 145; primaries in, 122, 126, 320

inflation and campaign contributions, 270

influence, business and corporate, 263; money and, 264–275; lobbying and, 265, 271, 275, 277–279, 280; future of, 267–268, 282–284, 296; and personal relationships, 277–278, 280–281, 282. See also business community; lobbying; money, corporate; Wall Street

Innis, Roy, 28

Institute for Public Affairs Research, 299

integration. See desegregation

Intercollegiate Review, The, 299

Intercollegiate Studies Institute (ISI), 298, 299

Interior, Department of, 68

internationalism. See foreign policy

IRS, 59, 61, 102, 105, 176

Italo-American voters, 193, 198–199

ITT affair, 110, 277, 293

Jackson, Andrew, 100

Jackson, Henry ("Scoop"), 57, 108, 362; vs. McGovern, 127, 128; and labor support, 133, 167

Jacoby, Neil, 177

Javits, Jacob, 16, 43

Jefferson, Thomas, 289

Jennings, Paul, 174

Jewish voters, 60, 194

Job Corps, 27

Johnson, Haynes, 161

Johnson, Hiram, 212

Johnson, Lyndon B., and Johnson administration, 54, 184, 192, 270; programs of, 27, 33, 199–200, 201, 301; 1964 landslide for, 39, 194, 202; and Hispanic-American voters, 75; and Vietnam war, 98–99; press and, 101; demonstrators and, 102; renomination blocked, 116; and labor, 172, 174; and New Right philosophy, 292

Johnson, Mike, 163

Johnson, Wallace, 66

Joint Center for Political Studies (JCPS), 193

Joint Chiefs of Staff, 30

Jones, David, 298

Jones, Jerry, 68

Jones, Paul, 69

Justice, Department of, 44, 59, 61, 346; and special favors, 34, 104, 181, 182, 186; resentment in, 102, 106

Kahn, Tom, 169

Kalmbach, Herbert, 96

Kayser, Paul, 69

Keenan, Joe, 173

Kefauver, Estes, 206

Kemp, Jack, 77

Kendall, Don, 69, 83, 264; quoted, 80, 81–82

Kennedy, Edward (Ted), 55, 101, 106, 108, 136, 148, 313

Kennedy, John F., 54, 107, 172, 174, 183, 224; and administration strategy, 12, 21, 92; 1960 campaign, 21, 51, 108, 167, 194; and Hispanic-American voters, 75; and voting on civil rights issues (1960), 201, 202. See also Kennedy clan

Kennedy, Robert F., 51, 115, 116, 167

Kennedy clan, 121, 140, 160

Kent State episode, 178

Kentucky, voting cycle in, 207, 209

Kessel, John, his The Goldwater Coalition, 296

Kilpatrick, James J., 152

King, Bruce, 145

Kirkland, Lane, 164, 165

Kissinger, Henry, 29, 60, 151, 330

Klein, Herb, 64

Kleindienst, Richard, 9, 72

knowledge, expansion of, 334–335

Kotz, Nick, quoted, 270

Kroc, Ray, 268

Labor, Department of, 27

labor and labor unions: and Democratic party, 28, 120, 137, 159–163, 168, 169, 174–175, 178, 184–185, 194, 203, 276, 282; and Nixon, 80–81, 101, 160, 163, 164, 165, 168, 171, 172, 174, 175–183; and McGovern, 132, 133, 136, 137, 159,

labor and labor unions (*Continued*)
165, 166–175, 194; and Humphrey, 133, 160, 162, 163–164, 166, 167, 169, 170, 225, 312; and Wallace, 133, 134, 162, 163, 166, 168; women and blacks in, 162, 165, 166, 185; fund-raising from, 163; fragmentation of, 164–166; and social issues, 165, 173–174, 182–183, 280; and Republican party, 165, 184–186; leadership of, 165–166, 167–168; "disenfranchisement" of power of, 166–168; and Big Business, 291. *See also* AFL–CIO; individual unions
Labor Committee for McGovern-Shriver, 173
Labor Committee to Re-elect the President, 182
"Labor party," 160, 163
La Follette, Robert, 120, 160
Landrum-Griffin Act, 179
La Raza Unida (Chicano organization), 77
Latin Americans. *See* Hispanic-American voters
"laundering" funds. *See* fund-raising
League of Women Voters, 317
Lee, General Robert E., 100
Left, New, 12, 87–88
Lenin, V. I., 12
Levine, Norman, 269
Lewis, John L., 160
liberals, 43, 45. *See also* Right, Old
Liddy, G. Gordon, 95
Life, 66, 170
Liggett and Myers, 83
Lincoln, Abraham, 43, 286
Lindsay, John, 43, 122, 123–124, 230, 308, 362
Lipsett, Dan, 298
Lithuanian-American voters, 198
lobbying: corporate, 265, 271, 275, 277–279, 280, 292; bipartisanship in, 278, 281–282, 283; legislative vs. administrative, 279
Locke, John, 289
Lockheed loan, 61, 292, 332
Lodge, Henry Cabot, 58, 222
Loeb, William, 122, 123, 304
Lofton, John, 230
loyalty, party: strategists and, 16, 19, 71; and politics of representation, 17, 23; destruction of, 21, 96–97, 98, 189, 213; in Democratic party, 56–57, 63, 190, 196, 199; and CREEP, 71, 189
Lukens, Donald ("Buz"), 77

McAdoo, Richard F., 70, 255
McAdoo, William G., 255
McCaffrey, Neil, 300
McCarthy, Eugene, 88, 115, 116, 121, 124, 167
McCarthy (Joseph) era, 172
McCloskey, Paul, 43, 45, 304
McCord, James, 111, 112
McCrossen, Eric, 145
McGinniss, Joe, his *The Selling of the President*, 67
McGovern, George S.: nomination of, 19, 108, 115–116, 121–134, 143, 166, 201, 219, 310; and constituency, 19, 132–134, 159, 313; campaign (as strategic exercise) 19, 21, 115–116, 131–134, 142–143; (postconvention) 63, 135–155; (antimilitarism of) 99, 119, 127, 132, 134, 136, 152, 225; and Democratic regulars, 19, 56–57, 126, 129, 133–134, 136–138, 142, 144–145, 154, 219; and Eagleton affair, 20, 125, 135, 137–138, 141, 150, 153, 156, 192, 376; and fluid voters, 20, 137, 156, 157; and Wallace vote, 20, 52, 122, 132, 133–134, 204; and blacks and minority groups, 20, 76–77, 132, 146, 193–194; organization and problems, 22, 51, 52–53, 62–63, 70, 142–147, 168; and welfare issue, 45, 199, 200, 201; as "radic-lib," 46; image of, 52, 53–57, 60, 61, 62, 147, 150, 153–155, 158; and Attack Group, 66; and polls, 67, 135–137, 152, 154, 155–157, 192; fear of, 71, 79, 269; and business, 79, 80, 83–84, 269; and young voters, 84, 86, 87, 88, 146, 156, 157; and hyperstrategic approach, 98, 121; campaign contributions to, 101, 116 (*see also* fund-raising); as unknown quantity, 103, 135–136; and the press, 103, 147–148, 149–150; attacks Watergate episode, 112; credibility of, 112, 152, 153–155, 156; 1968 and 1970 campaigns, 116; background and character, 116–121, 132, 142, 153, 158; quoted, 118–119, 120, 127, 128, 134, 172; and Vietnam issue, 119, 127, 132, 134, 136, 147, 152, 154; and Depression, 119–120; in 1972 primaries, 121–126, 132, 134, 135, 136; and positions on issues, 128, 135, 147, 157, 199, 200, 201; and Humphrey, 128–129, 135, 136, 169, 174; and labor, 132, 133, 136, 137, 159, 165, 166–175, 194; and political compromise, 132; and tax reform, 134, 147; "desperation" moves, 147–152; compared to Goldwater, 155, 157–158; and Meany, 169–170, 171–173; and regional electorates, 193, 204, 205–206, 212, 321; and Catholic vote, 195–196; major factor in defeat of, 199; and professional class, 205–206, 321
McGovern, Mrs. George S. (Eleanor), 117
McGovern, Joseph C., 117, 120
McGovern, Olive (Mrs. Phil Briles), 117
MacGregor, Clark, 66, 112; as director of CREEP, 62–63, 65, 67, 68
McGrory, Mary, 140
Machiavelli, Niccolò, 105
Machinists, International Association of, 163, 164, 184
McIntire, Michael, 119
McKinley, William, 286
McNamara, Robert, 98; quoted, 95
McNaughton, John T., 98
Magruder, Jeb S., 64, 67, 68, 95; quoted, 103, 111
Mahoney, J. Daniel, 300, 302
Mailer, Norman, 298
Malek, Frederic, 20, 68, 69, 92

388

Republican party (*Continued*)
sippi (Agnew on), 37; in Congress, 39, 66, 72; and 1970 campaigns, 40–41, 43, 192; 1972 platform of, 46, 178, 316; and traditional campaign approach, 51, 62, 321; progressives and Republicans for Progress, 66, 309, 310, 327–328, 337; and polls, 67 (*see also* polls and surveys); fear of McGovern, 71, 79, 269; conservatives and, 71, 206, 220, 284, 285, 288, 296, 305–307, 327; and business community, 79–80, 175, 261, 263, 274, 276, 280, 282, 283, 318–319, 321; and young voters, 84–88, 224, 317; attacked by McGovern, 151; George Meany on, 161; and labor and unions, 165, 184–186; 1968 platform of, 178–179, 301; and Catholic vote, 195–196; and regional electorate, 204–213, 260–261, 317–318; power within, 217–224, 226, 227–233, 236, 239, 241–242, 282, 283, 300, 307, 309–310, 321; and strategic politics, 219–220, 305, 309–310, 327; and Goldwater nomination, 219, 310; women in, 224, 316–317; organization of, 226–233 (*see also* Republican National Committee); and state organizations, 232–233, 234, 236, 239–240, 241; "phasing out" of, 239; and professional class, 254, 315–316, 319, 321–322, 328, 337; and Wall Street, 266–268; "Democrats disguised as," 285; divided, 286–288, 296, 305; Eisenhower-Taft philosophy and, 287–288, 297; imitation of Democrats, 288, 296, 305; Old and New Right within, 289–298, 300, 306, 312–314, 327–328; need for power, 309–310, 325–326, 328; principles of, 318, 326, 328–336; possibilities for, 336–338, 355
responsibility: need for, 334; avoidance of, 346–347
Reuther, Walter, 162
revenue-sharing, 6, 28, 46, 101
Richardson, Elliot, 15, 44, 113
Riegle, Donald, 43
Rietz, Ken, 70
Right, New, 288, 327; and conservatives, 288, 290, 306–307, 312, 314, 318; principles and origin of, 290–293, 319; socialism of, 291, 328; vs. Old Right, 291–298, 300, 307, 318; international politics of, 293–294, 297; strengths of, 295–296, 300; constituencies of, 296–298, 300, 309, 314, 318–320, 321; power base of, 307–308, 309, 313–315, 328
Right, Old, 288; principles of, 289–290; vs. New Right, 291–298, 300, 307, 318; appeal and limitations of, 295–296, 319; constituencies of, 296–298, 300, 309, 318–320, 337; and Old Guard, 303; and New Left, 306; and Bill of Rights, 319; and alliance with Republican party, 327–328
Ripon Society, 24, 43; and *Forum*, 27, 29; study of 1972 campaign contributions, 244, 361

"RN Associates," 270
Rockefeller, Nelson, 43, 192, 220; and labor, 165, 182, 183, 185; in 1968 campaign, 223, 310, 315; and business support, 267
Rockefeller family, 264, 265, 267
Rodgers, Don, 182, 183, 185
Rodriguez, Chichi, 78
Rohan, Alexander J., 173
Rollins, John, 268
Romero, Cesar, 78
Romney, George, 36, 54, 102, 192, 230, 308, 311, 312
Roosevelt, Franklin D., 53, 160, 176, 266, 293
Roosevelt, Theodore, 160, 287
Rostow, Walt, 98
Rubin, Jerry, 127
Rusher, William, 300, 302, 303
Rusk, Dean, 98
Russia, policy toward, 297, 302, 330

Safire, William, 40
Saloma, John, his *Parties* (co-author), 188
Samuel, Howard, 174
Sanchez, Phillip, 75, 78
Sanders, J. Barefoot, Jr., 145
Sanford, Terry, 362
Saxbe, William, 15
Scammon, Richard, his *The Real Majority* (co-author), 39
Scherf, Margaret, 148
Schmitz, John, 71
Schneider, William, 301
Scott, Hugh, 15, 34, 35
Scranton, William, 107
segregation. *See* desegregation
Segretti, Donald H., 108
Segura, Pancho, 78
senior citizens, 86
Shannon, William V., quoted, 129
Sharon Statement, 298
Shriver, R. Sargent, 141, 145, 146, 172, 174, 362
Shultz, George, 28, 176
Silberman, Laurence H., 181
Sindlinger surveys, 136, 137
Sirica, John, 112, 113
Smith, Floyd E., 173, 176
Smith, Ken, 85, 86
Smith, Ralph T., 199
socialism, 291, 328
Social Security, 61, 200
social welfare. *See* welfare system
Sontag, Frederick H., his *Parties* (co-author), 188
South, the, 21; Nixon and, 31–35, 38, 194, 202, 211; Humphrey and McGovern in, 32, 193; fluidity of, 32–33, 194, 203, 206–211, 247, 260–261; and Republican party, 32, 36, 203, 206–209; strategy in, 32, 37, 41, 43, 44, 211; symbolic issues in, 38, 211; and Democratic party, 203, 206–209, 210–211, 260–261; Outer, cycles in, 206–209; and third party, 209, 211; Deep, volatility of, 210–211; fund-raising in, 247, 260–261; New